PRIVACY AND IDENTITY PROTECTION

PRIVACY

SELECT ISSUES AND LAWS FOR THE 21ST CENTURY

PRIVACY AND IDENTITY PROTECTION

Additional books in this series can be found on Nova's website
under the Series tab.

Additional E-books in this series can be found on Nova's website
under the E-book tab.

LAWS AND LEGISLATION

Additional books in this series can be found on Nova's website
under the Series tab.

Additional E-books in this series can be found on Nova's website
under the E-book tab.

PRIVACY AND IDENTITY PROTECTION

PRIVACY

SELECT ISSUES AND LAWS FOR THE 21ST CENTURY

DORIS B. DELRIO
EDITOR

nova publishers
New York

For permission to use material from this book please contact us:
Telephone 631-231-7269; Fax 631-231-8175
Web Site: http://www.novapublishers.com

Library of Congress Cataloging-in-Publication Data

ISBN: 978-1-62618-429-9

Published by Nova Science Publishers, Inc. † New York

CONTENTS

PREFACE

This book is a study of select issues and laws relating to privacy in the 21st century. Topics examined include an overview of federal law governing wiretapping and electronic eavesdropping under the Electronic Communications Privacy Act (ECPA); background and issues related to the USA PATRIOT Act reauthorization on government collection of private information; the United States v. Jones court case involving GPS monitoring, property and privacy; Fourth Amendment implications and legislative responses to drones in domestic surveillance operations; and the privacy and security concerns surrounding smart meter technology.

Chapter 1 – Fueled by stimulus funding in the American Recovery and Reinvestment Act of 2009 (ARRA), electric utilities have accelerated their deployment of smart meters to millions of homes across the United States with help from the Department of Energy's Smart Grid Investment Grant program.

As the meters multiply, so do issues concerning the privacy and security of the data collected by the new technology. This Advanced Metering Infrastructure (AMI) promises to increase energy efficiency, bolster electric power grid reliability, and facilitate demand response, among other benefits. However, to fulfill these ends, smart meters must record near-real time data on consumer electricity usage and transmit the data to utilities over great distances via communications networks that serve the smart grid. Detailed electricity usage data offers a window into the lives of people inside of a home by revealing what individual appliances they are using, and the transmission of the data potentially subjects this information to interception or theft by unauthorized third parties or hackers.

Unforeseen consequences under federal law may result from the installation of smart meters and the communications technologies that accompany them. This report examines federal privacy and cybersecurity laws that may apply to consumer data collected by residential smart meters. It begins with an examination of the constitutional provisions in the Fourth Amendment that may apply to the data. As we progress into the 21st century, access to personal data, including information generated from smart meters, is a new frontier for police investigations. The Fourth Amendment generally requires police to have probable cause to search an area in which a person has a reasonable expectation of privacy.

However, courts have used the third-party doctrine to deny protection to information a customer gives to a business as part of their commercial relationship. This rule is used by police to access bank records, telephone records, and traditional utility records. Nevertheless, there are several core differences between smart meters and the general third-party cases that may cause concerns about its application. These include concerns expressed by the courts and Congress about the ability of technology to potentially erode individuals' privacy.

If smart meter data and transmissions fall outside of the protection of the Fourth Amendment, they may still be protected from unauthorized disclosure or access under the Stored Communications Act (SCA), the Computer Fraud and Abuse Act (CFAA), and the Electronic Communications Privacy Act (ECPA). These statutes, however, would appear to permit law enforcement to access smart meter data for investigative purposes under procedures provided in the SCA, ECPA, and the Foreign Intelligence Surveillance Act (FISA), subject to certain conditions. Additionally, an electric utility's privacy and security practices with regard to consumer data may be subject to Section 5 of the Federal Trade Commission Act (FTC Act). The Federal Trade Commission (FTC) has recently focused its consumer protection enforcement on entities that violate their privacy policies or fail to protect data from unauthorized access. This authority could apply to electric utilities in possession of smart meter data, provided that the FTC has statutory jurisdiction over them. General federal privacy safeguards provided under the Federal Privacy Act of 1974 (FPA) protect smart meter data maintained by federal agencies, including data held by federally owned electric utilities.

Chapter 2 – The prospect of drone use inside the United States raises far-reaching issues concerning the extent of government surveillance authority, the value of privacy in the digital age, and the role of Congress in reconciling these issues.

Drones, or unmanned aerial vehicles (UAVs), are aircraft that can fly without an onboard human operator. An unmanned aircraft system (UAS) is the entire system, including the aircraft, digital network, and personnel on the ground. Drones can fly either by remote control or on a predetermined flight path; can be as small as an insect and as large as a traditional jet; can be produced more cheaply than traditional aircraft; and can keep operators out of harm's way. These unmanned aircraft are most commonly known for their operations overseas in tracking down and killing suspected members of Al Qaeda and related organizations. In addition to these missions abroad, drones are being considered for use in domestic surveillance operations, which might include in furtherance of homeland security, crime fighting, disaster relief, immigration control, and environmental monitoring.

Although relatively few drones are currently flown over U.S. soil, the Federal Aviation Administration (FAA) predicts that 30,000 drones will fill the nation's skies in less than 20 years. Congress has played a large role in this expansion. In February 2012, Congress enacted the FAA Modernization and Reform Act (P.L. 112-95), which calls for the FAA to accelerate the integration of unmanned aircraft into the national airspace system by 2015. However, some Members of Congress and the public fear there are insufficient safeguards in place to ensure that drones are not used to spy on American citizens and unduly infringe upon their fundamental privacy. These observers caution that the FAA is primarily charged with ensuring air traffic safety, and is not adequately prepared to handle the issues of privacy and civil liberties raised by drone use.

This report assesses the use of drones under the Fourth Amendment right to be free from unreasonable searches and seizures. The touchstone of the Fourth Amendment is reasonableness. A reviewing court's determination of the reasonableness of drone surveillance would likely be informed by location of the search, the sophistication of the technology used, and society's conception of privacy in an age of rapid technological advancement. While individuals can expect substantial protections against warrantless government intrusions into their homes, the Fourth Amendment offers less robust restrictions upon government surveillance occurring in public places and perhaps even less in areas immediately outside the home, such as in driveways or backyards. Concomitantly, as technology advances, the contours of what is reasonable under the Fourth Amendment may adjust as people's expectations of privacy evolve.

In the 112th Congress, several measures have been introduced that would restrict the use of drones at home. Senator Rand Paul and Representative Austin Scott introduced the Preserving Freedom from Unwarranted Surveillance Act of 2012 (S. 3287, H.R. 5925), which would require law enforcement to obtain a warrant before using drones for domestic surveillance, subject to several exceptions. Similarly, Representative Ted Poe's Preserving American Privacy Act of 2012 (H.R. 6199) would permit law enforcement to conduct drone surveillance pursuant to a warrant, but only in investigation of a felony.

Chapter 3 – In *United States v. Jones*, 132 S. Ct. 945 (2012), all nine Supreme Court Justices agreed that Jones was *searched* when the police attached a Global Positioning System (GPS) device to the undercarriage of his car and tracked his movements for four weeks. The Court, however, splintered on what constituted the search: the attachment of the device or the long-term monitoring. The majority held that the *attachment* of the GPS device and an attempt to obtain information was the violation; Justice Alito, concurring, argued that the *monitoring* was a violation of Jones's reasonable expectation of privacy; and Justice Sotomayor, also concurring, agreed with them both, but would provide further Fourth Amendment protections. This report will examine these three decisions in an effort to find their place in the body of existing Fourth Amendment law pertaining to privacy, property, and technology.

In *Jones*, the police attached a GPS tracking device to the bottom of Jones's car and monitored his movements for 28 days. At trial, the prosecution relied on Jones's movements to a stash house to tie him to a drug conspiracy. Jones was convicted and given a life sentence. The United States Court of Appeals for the District of Columbia Circuit reversed, holding that the evidence was unlawfully obtained under the Fourth Amendment. The Supreme Court agreed. The majority, speaking through Justice Scalia, explained that a physical intrusion into a constitutionally protected area, coupled with an attempt to obtain information, can constitute a violation of the Fourth Amendment. Although the Court's landmark decision in *Katz v. United States*, 389 U.S. 347 (1967), supposedly altered the focus of the Fourth Amendment from property to privacy, the majority argued that it left untouched traditional spheres of Fourth Amendment protection—a person and his house, papers, and effects. Because the police had invaded Jones's property—his car, which is an *effect*—that was all the Court needed to hold that a constitutional search had occurred.

The majority's test, however, provides little guidance in instances where the government need not physically install a device to conduct surveillance, for instance, by using cell phones or preinstalled GPS devices in vehicles.

To understand how the Court may rule on these technologies, one must look to the two concurrences, which provide a more global interpretation of the Fourth Amendment. Justice Alito, writing for a four-member concurrence, would have applied the *Katz* privacy formulation, asserting that longer-term monitoring constitutes an invasion of privacy, whereas short-term monitoring does not. He left it to future courts to distinguish between the two.

Justice Sotomayor's concurrence appears to provide the most protection, finding that both the trespass approach and the privacy-based approach should be utilized. She also questioned the rule that any information provided to a third party, which occurs in many commercial transactions like banking or computing, should lose all privacy protections.

Although all three opinions concluded that the government's action in *Jones* was a search, none expressly required that police get a warrant in future GPS tracking cases. (The government forfeited the argument.) Further, there is no clear indication of the level of suspicion—probable cause, reasonable suspicion, or something less—that is required to attach a GPS unit and monitor the target's movements. Additionally, there have been several bills filed in the 112th Congress, including Senator Patrick J. Leahy's Electronic Communications Privacy Act Amendment Act of 2011 (S. 1011) and Senator Ron Wyden's and Representative Jason Chaffetz's identical legislation, S. 1212 and H.R. 2168, the Geolocational Privacy and Surveillance Act (GPS bill), that would require a warrant based upon probable cause to access geolocation information.

Chapter 4 – Congress enacted the USA PATRIOT Act soon after the 9/11 terrorist attacks. The most controversial sections of the act facilitate the federal government's collection of more information, from a greater number of sources, than had previously been authorized in criminal or foreign intelligence investigations. The Foreign Intelligence Surveillance Act (FISA), the Electronic Communications Privacy Act (ECPA), and the national security letter (NSL) statutes were all bolstered. With the changes came greater access to records showing an individual's spending and communication patterns as well as increased authority to intercept e-mail and telephone conversations and to search homes and businesses. In some cases, evidentiary standards required to obtain court approval for the collection of information were lowered. Other approaches included expanding the scope of information subject to search, adding flexibility to the methods by which information could be collected, and broadening the purposes for which information may be sought.

Some perceived the changes as necessary to unearth terrorist cells and update investigative authorities to respond to the new technologies and characteristics of ever-shifting threats. Others argued that authorities granted by the USA PATRIOT Act and subsequent measures could unnecessarily undermine constitutional rights over time. In response to such concerns, sunset provisions were established for many of the changes.

Subsequent legislation made most of these changes permanent. However, a number of authorities affecting the collection of foreign intelligence information are still temporary. Three such provisions (the lone wolf, roving wiretap, and business record sections of FISA) are set to expire on June 1, 2015. Additionally, provisions added by the FISA Amendments Act of 2008, relating to the use of foreign intelligence tools to target individuals while they are reasonably believed to be abroad, will expire on December 31, 2012.

Chapter 5 – This report provides an overview of federal law governing wiretapping and electronic eavesdropping under the Electronic Communications Privacy Act (ECPA). It also appends citations to state law in the area and the text of ECPA.

It is a federal crime to wiretap or to use a machine to capture the communications of others without court approval, unless one of the parties has given his prior consent. It is likewise a federal crime to use or disclose any information acquired by illegal wiretapping or electronic eavesdropping. Violations can result in imprisonment for not more than five years; fines up to $250,000 (up to $500,000 for organizations); civil liability for damages, attorneys' fees and possibly punitive damages; disciplinary action against any attorneys involved; and suppression of any derivative evidence. Congress has created separate, but comparable, protective schemes for electronic communications (e.g., email) and against the surreptitious use of telephone call monitoring practices such as pen registers and trap and trace devices.

Each of these protective schemes comes with a procedural mechanism to afford limited law enforcement access to private communications and communications records under conditions consistent with the dictates of the Fourth Amendment. The government has been given narrowly confined authority to engage in electronic surveillance, conduct physical searches, and install and use pen registers and trap and trace devices for law enforcement purposes under ECPA and for purposes of foreign intelligence gathering under the Foreign Intelligence Surveillance Act.

In: Privacy: Select Issues and Laws for the 21st Century
Editor: Doris B. Delrio
ISBN: 978-1-62618-429-9

Chapter 1

SMART METER DATA: PRIVACY AND CYBERSECURITY*

Brandon J. Murrill, Edward C. Liu and Richard M. Thompson

SUMMARY

Fueled by stimulus funding in the American Recovery and Reinvestment Act of 2009 (ARRA), electric utilities have accelerated their deployment of smart meters to millions of homes across the United States with help from the Department of Energy's Smart Grid Investment Grant program.

As the meters multiply, so do issues concerning the privacy and security of the data collected by the new technology. This Advanced Metering Infrastructure (AMI) promises to increase energy efficiency, bolster electric power grid reliability, and facilitate demand response, among other benefits. However, to fulfill these ends, smart meters must record near real time data on consumer electricity usage and transmit the data to utilities over great distances via communications networks that serve the smart grid. Detailed electricity usage data offers a window into the lives of people inside of a home by revealing what individual appliances they are using, and the transmission of the data potentially subjects this information to interception or theft by unauthorized third parties or hackers.

Unforeseen consequences under federal law may result from the installation of smart meters and the communications technologies that accompany them. This report examines federal privacy and cybersecurity laws that may apply to consumer data collected by residential smart meters. It begins with an examination of the constitutional provisions in the Fourth Amendment that may apply to the data. As we progress into the 21st century, access to personal data, including information generated from smart meters, is a new frontier for police investigations. The Fourth Amendment generally requires police to have probable cause to search an area in which a person has a reasonable expectation of privacy.

---

* This is an edited, reformatted and augmented version of a Congressional Research Service publication, CRS Report for Congress R42338, from www.crs.gov, prepared for Members and Committees of Congress, dated February 3, 2012.

However, courts have used the third-party doctrine to deny protection to information a customer gives to a business as part of their commercial relationship. This rule is used by police to access bank records, telephone records, and traditional utility records. Nevertheless, there are several core differences between smart meters and the general third-party cases that may cause concerns about its application. These include concerns expressed by the courts and Congress about the ability of technology to potentially erode individuals' privacy.

If smart meter data and transmissions fall outside of the protection of the Fourth Amendment, they may still be protected from unauthorized disclosure or access under the Stored Communications Act (SCA), the Computer Fraud and Abuse Act (CFAA), and the Electronic Communications Privacy Act (ECPA). These statutes, however, would appear to permit law enforcement to access smart meter data for investigative purposes under procedures provided in the SCA, ECPA, and the Foreign Intelligence Surveillance Act (FISA), subject to certain conditions. Additionally, an electric utility's privacy and security practices with regard to consumer data may be subject to Section 5 of the Federal Trade Commission Act (FTC Act). The Federal Trade Commission (FTC) has recently focused its consumer protection enforcement on entities that violate their privacy policies or fail to protect data from unauthorized access. This authority could apply to electric utilities in possession of smart meter data, provided that the FTC has statutory jurisdiction over them. General federal privacy safeguards provided under the Federal Privacy Act of 1974 (FPA) protect smart meter data maintained by federal agencies, including data held by federally owned electric utilities.

OVERVIEW

Smart meter technology is a key component of the Advanced Metering Infrastructure (AMI)[1] that will help the smart grid [2] link the "two-way flow of electricity with the two-way flow of information."[3] Privacy and security concerns surrounding smart meter technology arise from the meters' essential functions, which include (1) recording near-real time data on consumer electricity usage; (2) transmitting this data to the smart grid using a variety of communications technologies;[4] and (3) receiving communications from the smart grid, such as real-time energy prices or remote commands that can alter a consumer's electricity usage to facilitate demand response.[5]

Beneficial uses of AMI are developing rapidly, and like the early Internet, many applications remain unforeseen.[6] At a basic level, smart meters will permit utilities to "collect, measure, and analyze energy consumption data for grid management, outage notification, and billing purposes."[7] The meters may increase energy efficiency by giving consumers greater control over their use of electricity,[8] as well as permitting better integration of plug-in electric vehicles and renewable energy sources.[9] They may also aid in the development of a more reliable electricity grid that is better equipped to withstand cyber attacks and natural disasters, and help to decrease peak demand for electricity.[10] To be useful for these purposes, and many others, data recorded by smart meters must be highly detailed, and, consequently, it may show what individual appliances a consumer is using.[11] The data must also be transmitted to electric utilities—and possibly to third parties outside of the smart grid—subjecting it to potential interception or theft as it travels over communications networks and is stored in a variety of physical locations.[12]

These characteristics of smart meter data present privacy and security concerns that are likely to become more prevalent as government-backed initiatives expand deployment of the meters to millions of homes across the country. In the American Recovery and Reinvestment Act of 2009 (ARRA), Congress appropriated funds for the implementation of the Smart Grid Investment Grant (SGIG) program administered by the Department of Energy.[13] This program now permits the federal government to reimburse up to 50% of eligible smart grid investments, which include the cost to electric utilities of buying and installing smart meters.[14] In its annual report on smart meter deployment, the Federal Energy Regulatory Commission cited statistics showing that the SGIG program has helped fund the deployment of about 7.2 million meters as of September 2011.[15] At completion, the program will have partially funded the installation of 15.5 million meters.[16] By 2015, the Institute for Electric Efficiency expects that a total of 65 million smart meters will be in operation throughout the United States.[17]

Installation of smart meters and the communications technologies that accompany them may have unforeseen legal consequences for those who generate, seek, or use the data recorded by the meters. These consequences may arise under existing federal laws or constitutional provisions governing the privacy of electronic communications, data retention, computer misuse, foreign surveillance, and consumer protection. This report examines federal privacy and cybersecurity laws that may apply to consumer data collected by residential smart meters. It examines the legal implications of smart meter technology for consumers who generate the data, law enforcement officers who seek smart meter data from utilities, utilities that store the data, and hackers who access smart grid technology to steal consumer data or interfere with it. This report looks at federal laws that may pertain to the data when it is (1) stored in a utility-owned smart meter at a consumer's residence; (2) in transit between the meter and the smart grid by way of various communications technologies; and (3) stored on computers in the grid. This report does not address state or local laws, such as regulations by state Public Utilities Commissions, that may establish additional responsibilities for some electric utilities with regard to smart meter data. It also does not discuss the mandatory cybersecurity and reliability standards enforced by the North American Electric Reliability Corporation, which impose obligations on utilities that participate in the generation or transmission of electricity.[18]

General federal privacy safeguards provided under the Federal Privacy Act of 1974 (FPA) protect smart meter data maintained by federal agencies, including data held by federally owned electric utilities. Section 5 of the Federal Trade Commission Act (FTC Act) allows the Federal Trade Commission (FTC) to bring enforcement proceedings against electric utilities that violate their privacy policies or fail to protect meter data from unauthorized access, provided that the FTC has statutory jurisdiction over the utilities.

It is unclear how Fourth Amendment protection from unreasonable search and seizures would apply to smart meter data, due to the lack of cases on this issue. However, depending upon the manner in which smart meter services are presented to consumers, smart meter data may be protected from unauthorized disclosure or unauthorized access under the Stored Communications Act (SCA), the Computer Fraud and Abuse Act (CFAA), and the Electronic Communications Privacy Act (ECPA). If smart meter data is protected by these statutes, law enforcement would still appear to have the ability to access it for investigative purposes under procedures provided in the SCA, ECPA, and the Foreign Intelligence Surveillance Act (FISA).

SMART METER DATA: PRIVACY AND SECURITY CONCERNS

Residential smart meters present privacy and cybersecurity issues[19] that are likely to evolve with the technology.[20]

In 2010, the National Institute of Standards and Technology (NIST) published a report identifying some of these issues, which fall into two main categories: (1) privacy concerns that smart meters will reveal the activities of people inside of a home by measuring their electricity usage frequently over time;[21] and (2) fears that inadequate cybersecurity measures surrounding the digital transmission of smart meter data will expose it to misuse by authorized and unauthorized users of the data.[22]

Detailed Information on Household Activities

Smart meters offer a significantly more detailed illustration of a consumer's energy usage than regular meters.

Traditional meters display data on a consumer's *total* electricity usage and are typically read manually once per month.[23] In contrast, smart meters can provide *near real-time* usage data by measuring usage electronically at a much greater frequency, such as once every 15 minutes.[24] Current smart meter technology allows utilities to measure usage as frequently as once every minute.[25]

By examining smart meter data, it is possible to identify which appliances a consumer is using and at what times of the day, because each type of appliance generates a unique electric load "signature."[26]

NIST wrote in 2010 that "research shows that analyzing 15-minute interval aggregate household energy consumption data can by itself pinpoint the use of most major home appliances."[27]

A report for the Colorado Public Utilities Commission discussed an Italian study that used "artificial neural networks" to identify individual "heavy-load appliance uses" with 90% accuracy using 15-minute interval data from a smart meter.[28] Similarly, software-based algorithms would likely allow a person to extract the unique signatures of individual appliances from meter data that has been collected less frequently and is therefore less detailed.[29]

By combining appliance usage patterns, an observer could discern the behavior of occupants in a home over a period of time.[30] For example, the data could show whether a residence is occupied, how many people live in it, and whether it is "occupied by more people than usual."[31]

According to the Department of Energy, smart meters may be able to reveal occupants' "daily schedules (including times when they are at or away from home or asleep), whether their homes are equipped with alarm systems, whether they own expensive electronic equipment such as plasma TVs, and whether they use certain types of medical equipment."[32] *Figure 1*, which appears in NIST's report on smart grid cybersecurity, shows how smart meter data could be used to decipher the activities of a home's occupants by matching data on their electricity usage with known appliance load signatures.

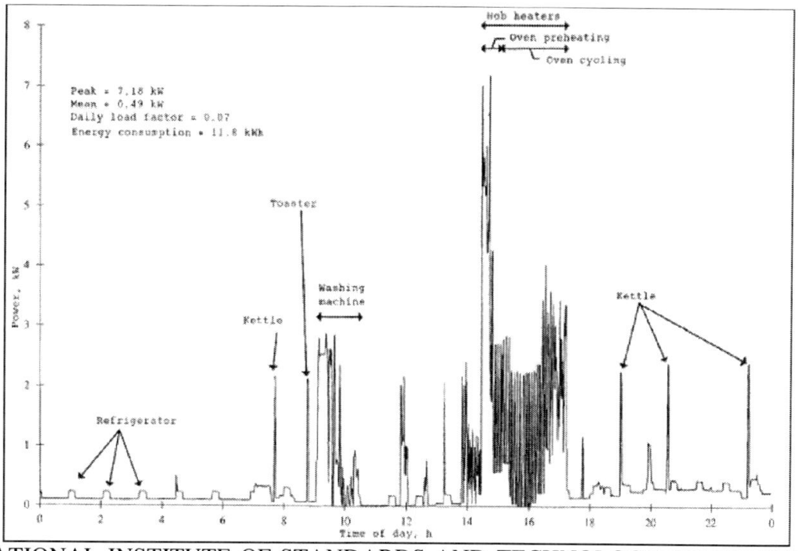

Source: NATIONAL INSTITUTE OF STANDARDS AND TECHNOLOGY (NIST), GUIDELINES FOR SMART GRID CYBER SECURITY: VOL. 2, PRIVACY AND THE SMART GRID 13 (2010), available at http://csrc.nist.gov/ publications /nistir /ir7628/ nistir-7628_vol2.pdf.

Note: Researchers constructed this picture from electricity usage data collected at one-minute intervals using a nonintrusive appliance load monitoring (NALM) device, which is similar to a smart meter in the way that it records usage data. For a comparison of the technologies, see COLORADO PRIVACY REPORT, supra note 6, at A-1 to A-9.

Figure 1. Identification of Household Activities from Electricity Usage Data. Unique Electric Load Signatures of Common Household Appliances.

Smart meter data that reveals which appliances a consumer is using has potential value for third parties, including the government. In the past, law enforcement agents have examined *monthly* electricity usage data from *traditional* meters in investigations of people they suspected of illegally growing marijuana.[33] For example, in *United States v. Kyllo*, a federal agent subpoenaed the suspect's electricity usage records from the utility and "compared the records to a spreadsheet for estimating average electrical use and concluded that Kyllo's electrical usage was abnormally high, indicating a possible indoor marijuana grow operation."[34] If law enforcement officers obtained near-real time data on a consumer's electricity usage from the utility company, their ability to monitor household activities would be amplified significantly.[35] For example, by observing when occupants use the most electricity, it may be possible to discern their daily schedules.[36]

As smart meter technology develops and usage data grows more detailed, it could also become more valuable to private third parties outside of the grid.[37] Data that reveals which appliances a person is using could permit health insurance companies to determine whether a household uses certain medical devices, and appliance manufacturers to establish whether a warranty has been violated.[38] Marketers could use it to make targeted advertisements.[39] Criminals could use it to time a burglary and figure out which appliances they would like to steal.[40] If a consumer owned a plug-in electric vehicle, data about where the vehicle has been charged could permit someone to identify a person's location and travel history.[41]

Even privacy safeguards, such as "anonymizing" data so that it does not reflect identity, are not foolproof.[42] By comparing anonymous data with information available in the public domain, it is sometimes possible to identify an individual—or, in the context of smart meter data, a particular household.[43] Moreover, a smart grid will collect more than just electricity usage data. It will also store data on the account holder's name, service address, billing information, networked appliances in the home, and meter IP address, among other information.[44] Many smart meters will also provide transactional records as they send data to the grid, which would show the time that the meter transmitted the data and the location or identity of the transmitter.[45]

Increased Potential for Theft or Breach of Data

Smart grid technology relies heavily on two-way communication to increase energy efficiency and reliability, including communication between smart meters and the utility (or other entity) that stores data for the grid.[46] Many different technologies will transmit data to the grid, including "traditional twisted-copper phone lines, cable lines, fiber optic cable, cellular, satellite, microwave, WiMAX, power line carrier, and broadband over power line."[47] Of these communications platforms, wireless technologies are likely to play a "prominent role" because they present fewer safety concerns and cost less to implement than wireline technologies.[48] According to the Department of Energy, a typical utility network has four "tiers" that collect and transmit data from the consumer to the utility.[49] These include "(1) the core backbone—the primary path to the utility data center; (2) backhaul distribution—the aggregation point for neighborhood data; (3) the access point—typically the smart meter; and, (4) the HAN—the home network."[50] Energy usage data moves from the smart meter,[51] and then to an "aggregation point" outside of the residence such as "a substation, a utility pole-mounted device, or a communications tower."[52] The aggregation points gather data from multiple meters and "backhaul" it to the utility using fiber, T1, microwave, or wireless technology.[53] Utilities typically rely on their own private networks to communicate with smart meters because they have found these networks to be more reliable and less expensive than commercial networks.[54]

As NIST explains, consumer data moving through a smart grid becomes stored in many locations both within the grid and within the physical world.[55] Thus, because it is widely dispersed, it becomes more vulnerable to interception by unauthorized parties[56] and to accidental breach.[57] The movement of data also increases the potential for it to be stolen by unauthorized third parties while it is in transit, particularly when it travels over a wireless network[58]—or through communications components that may be incompatible with one another or possess outdated security protections.[59]

SMART METERS AND THE FOURTH AMENDMENT

The use of smart meters presents the recurring conflict between law enforcement's need to effectively investigate and combat crime and our desire for privacy while in our homes. With smart meters, police will have access to data that might be used to track residents' daily lives and routines while in their homes, including their eating, sleeping, and showering habits, what appliances they use and when, and whether they prefer the television to the treadmill, among a host of other details.[60] Though a potential boon to police, access to this data is not limitless. The Fourth Amendment, which establishes the constitutional parameters for government investigations, may restrict access to smart meter data or establish rules by which it can be obtained.[61] The Fourth Amendment ensures that the "right of the people to be secure in their persons, houses, papers, and effects, against unreasonable searches and seizures, shall not be violated...."[62] This section discusses whether the collection and use of smart meter data may contravene this protection. Although there is no Fourth Amendment case on point, analogous cases may provide guidance.[63]

To assess whether there has been a Fourth Amendment violation, two primary questions must be asked: (1) whether there was state action; that is, was there sufficient government involvement in the alleged wrongdoing to trigger the Fourth Amendment; and (2) whether the person had an expectation of privacy that society is prepared to deem reasonable.[64] If the first question is answered in the affirmative, then the analysis moves to the second question. But if no state action is found, the analysis ends there and the Fourth Amendment does not apply. This subpart will first determine whether access to smart meter data by police, or by privately and publicly owned utilities, satisfies the state action doctrine, thereby warranting further Fourth Amendment review.

State Action: Privately versus Publicly Owned Utilities

Most of the safeguards for civil liberties and individual rights contained in the US Constitution apply only to actions by state and federal governments.[65] This rule, known as the state action doctrine, arises when a victim claims his constitutional rights have been violated, and therefore must prove the wrongdoer had sufficient connections with the government to warrant a remedy.[66]

Applying the state action test is intended to determine whether a utility's collection and dissemination of smart meter data is governed by the Fourth Amendment, and if so, to what extent. Although there are many variations in the governance and ownership of utilities—some are privately owned, others publicly owned, some federally operated, and still others nonprofit cooperatives—they generally fall into two broad categories: public and private.[67] This section will analyze the constitutional differences between privately and publicly owned utilities under the state action doctrine and a public records theory.

Privately Owned and Operated Utilities

It is broadly said that the Fourth Amendment applies only to acts by the government.[68] But there are at least two exceptions to this rule. First, if a utility performs a function traditionally exercised by the government, it may be considered a state actor under the public function exception. Second, the Fourth Amendment may apply when a private utility acts as an instrument or agent of the police.[69]

Under the public function exception, a nominally private entity is treated as a state actor when it assumes a role traditionally played by the government.[70] Determining when this exception applies has not proved easy,[71] but it is reasonably clear that private utilities do not, in most instances, satisfy it. In *Jackson v. Metropolitan Edison Co.*, a customer sued a privately owned utility under the Civil Rights Act of 1871 for improperly shutting off her service without providing her notice or a hearing.[72] The Supreme Court asked whether there was a close enough nexus between the state and the utility for the acts of the latter to be treated as those of the former.[73] Although the utility was heavily regulated by the state, it was held not to be a state actor.[74] The Court reasoned that the provision of utility service is not generally an "exclusive prerogative of the State."[75] Also absent was the symbiotic relationship between the utility and the state found in previous cases.[76] Though its holding was broad, the Court did not foreclose the possibility that a privately owned utility could be a state actor under different circumstances.[77] This possibility, however, appears narrow.

The Fourth Amendment may also apply to a private utility if its acts were directed by the government. Generally, searches performed by private actors without police participation or encouragement are not governed by the Fourth Amendment.[78] A search by a private insurance investigator, for instance, was not a "search" in the constitutional sense, though the evidence was ultimately used by the government at trial.[79] This result differs, however, if there is sufficient government involvement. If the search has been ordered or requested by the government, the private actor will become an "instrument or agent of the state" and must abide by Fourth Amendment strictures.[80] For example, the Fourth Amendment does not apply when a telephone company installs a pen register on its own initiative.[81] The same action constitutes a search, however, if requested by the government.[82]

This theory applies not only to direct instigation, but also on a broad, programmatic level. In the 1960s and 1970s the federal government required privately owned and operated airlines to institute new security measures to combat airline hijacking.[83] In *United States v. Davis*, the airline searched a passenger based on these requirements and found a loaded gun.[84] The Ninth Circuit held that it made no difference whether the search was conducted by a private or public official: "the search was part of the overall, nation-wide anti-hijacking effort, and constituted 'state action' for purposes of the Fourth Amendment."[85] Thus, if a private party is required to perform a search or collect data under federal or state laws or regulations, there will be sufficient state action for the Fourth Amendment to apply. Or, put another way, the government cannot circumvent the Fourth Amendment by requiring a private party to initiate a search or implement an investigative program.

This agency theory might apply to the collection of smart meter data. If the utility is accessing this information "independent of the government's intent to collect evidence for use in a criminal prosecution,"[86] the utility will not be considered an agent of the government for Fourth Amendment purposes. But there might be instances when government instigation will trigger further analysis. If, for example, the government requested the utility to record larger quantities of data than was customary (e.g., increasing the intervals from sub-15 minute intervals to sub-five minute or sub-one minute intervals), this would likely warrant Fourth Amendment scrutiny. Also, if the police requested the utility to hand over customer data, say, for spikes in energy commensurate with a marijuana growing operation, this would likely be a sufficient instigation to trigger further constitutional review. Other situations may arise where the government establishes a dragnet-type law enforcement scheme in which all smart meter data is filtered through police computers. This could also implicate the agency theory and warrant a finding of state action.

Publicly Owned and Operated Utilities

Although the Fourth Amendment (with its warrant and probable cause requirement) typically applies to public actors, in certain instances their collection of information may not fall under the Fourth Amendment or may prompt a lower evidentiary standard.

The Supreme Court has infrequently considered the scope of the Fourth Amendment "on the conduct of government officials in noncriminal investigations,"[87] and even less frequently as to "noncriminal *noninvestigatory* governmental conduct."[88] Nonetheless, there are two lines of cases that may apply to smart meters in which the Fourth Amendment may not apply at all (noncriminal noninvestigatory conduct) or may be reduced (noncriminal investigations). The key to this analysis is the government's purpose in collecting the data.

The Supreme Court has developed a line of cases dubbed the "special needs" doctrine that permits the government to perform suspicionless searches if the special needs supporting the program outweigh the intrusion on the individual's privacy.[89] It is premised on the notion that "'special needs,' beyond the normal need for law enforcement, make the warrant and probable-cause requirement impracticable."[90] If, on the one hand, the objective of the search is not for law enforcement purposes but for other reasons such as public safety[91] or ensuring the integrity of sensitive government positions,[92] then the doctrine will apply. If, however, the "primary purpose" or "immediate objective" was "to generate evidence *for law enforcement purposes*," then application of the special needs doctrine is not appropriate, and the government must adhere to general Fourth Amendment principles.[93] Again, the primary inquiry is the purpose of the search.

Some circuit courts of appeal have extended the special needs theory, holding that the Fourth Amendment does not apply (in contrast to a reduced standard of suspicion as with the special needs cases) unless the "conduct has as its purpose the intention to elicit a benefit for the government in either its investigative or administrative capacities."[94] In *United States v. Attson*, the Ninth Circuit held that the collection of blood by a government-employed physician, which was subsequently used by the police in a drunk driving prosecution, was not within the scope of Fourth Amendment protection.[95] The panel reasoned that the doctor drew the blood for medical purposes, not to further a governmental purpose in obtaining evidence against the defendant in its criminal investigation, so the Fourth Amendment did not apply.[96]

Applying these two theories to smart meters, a court would focus on the publicly owned utility's purpose in collecting the data. If it were for ordinary business purposes such as billing, informing the customer of its usage patterns, or aiding the utility in making the grid more energy-efficient, then it would not violate the Fourth Amendment. If, however, the public utility began aggregating data at the request of a law enforcement agency, with the purpose of aiding a criminal investigation or other administrative purpose, the Fourth Amendment would seemingly apply. As with private utilities, if the government requested that the public utility report any suspicious electricity usage, or created a program where certain data was regularly transmitted to the police, this might become investigatory and warrant Fourth Amendment protections. It appears law enforcement cannot evade Fourth Amendment restrictions by requesting a publicly owned utility to collect data for it.

Law enforcement might also request smart meter data under a public records theory. It is generally accepted that public records are not accorded Fourth Amendment protection.[97] Unless there is a state or federal statute prohibiting disclosure, "law enforcement access to state public records is unrestricted."[98] Thus the inquiry hinges on whether a document is a public record. Whether a person's utility records are public records differs from state to state.[99] Some states deem records of a municipally owned and operated electric utility as public records open for public inspection, while others have accorded these records statutory and constitutional protections.

In Florida, for example, records kept in connection with the operation of a city-operated utility are considered public records.[100] A similar policy applies in Georgia, where all records of a government agency, including utility records, must be open for inspection.[101] South Carolina, too, takes a similar approach.[102] It is not clear, however, from the reported cases whether these statutes permit access to personally identifiable information or simply operating records of the utility. Oklahoma is more explicit, permitting access to "records of the address, rate paid for services, charges, consumption rates, adjustments to the bill, reasons for adjustment, the name of the person that authorized the adjustment, and payment for each customer."[103] Oklahoma does protect some confidentiality, including "credit information, credit card numbers, telephone numbers, social security numbers, [and] bank account information for individual customers."[104] Other states, like Washington, specifically protect personally identifiable utility records. Washington does not require a showing of probable cause, but instead "a reasonable belief" that the record will help establish the customer committed a crime.[105] North Carolina likewise states that any "[b]illing information compiled and maintained by a city or county or other public entity providing utility services in connection with the ownership or operation of a public enterprise" is not a public record.[106]

Determining whether a utility is a state actor or whether smart meter data is a public record are merely threshold matters. A finding that an entity is a state actor or data is public does not foreclose law enforcement's ability to retrieve customer smart meter data, but instead activates the next step of Fourth Amendment analysis: whether the government invaded a reasonable expectation of privacy.

Reasonable Expectation of Privacy in Smart Meter Data

Under the modern conception of the Fourth Amendment, the government may not intrude into an area in which a person has an actual expectation of privacy that society would consider reasonable.[107] In the case of smart meter data, the government presumably seeks records in the custody of third-party utilities on the energy use at a specific home. However, a significant body of cases has refused to recognize constitutionally protected privacy interests in information provided by customers to businesses as part of their commercial relationships.[108]

This theory, the third-party doctrine, permits police access to the telephone numbers a person dials[109] and to a person's bank documents,[110] free from Fourth Amendment constraints.

There are two relevant differences, however, between smart meters and the traditional third-party cases that may warrant a shift in approach. First is the possible judicial unease with the notion that advancement of technology threatens to erode further the constitutional protection of privacy.[111] From that perspective, as technology progresses, society faces an ever-increasing risk that an individual's activities will be monitored by the government. This is coupled with the concern that the breadth and granularity of personal information that new technology affords provide a far more intimate picture of an individual than the more limited snapshots available through prior technologies. Do the richness and scope of new information technologies warrant increased constitutional scrutiny?

Second, smart meters can convey information about the activities that occur inside the home, an area singled out for specific textual protection in the Fourth Amendment and one deeply ingrained in Anglo-Saxon law.[112] Even when the Court declared that "the Fourth Amendment protects people, not places,"[113] ostensibly shifting away from a property-based conception of the Fourth Amendment, it has still carved out special protections for the home.[114] However, concomitant with the increased use of technology in our private lives is increased exposure of our private activities, including those conducted in the home. Commonly, we share more personal information, even as our concerns grow that more individuals, businesses, and others can glean more information about our personal lives as a matter of course. As with technology generally, does the fact that more of our lives are becoming "public" call for lesser or greater constitutional protection, and how does a "reasonable expectation"-based model continue to apply in a technologically intensive society?

This subpart will first look at the third-party doctrine as it is commonly conceived by the courts. Then it will discuss whether there are sufficient differences between the use of smart meters and traditional third-party cases to counsel against its application.

Third-Party Doctrine

Traditionally, there has been no Fourth Amendment protection for information a consumer gives to business as part of their business dealings.[115] This doctrine dates back to the secret agent cases, in which any words uttered to another person, including a government agent or informant, were not covered by the Fourth Amendment.[116] It was later extended to business records, giving police access to documents such as telephone records,[117] bank records,[118] motel registration records,[119] and cell phone records.[120] The Supreme Court has reasoned that the customers assume the risk that the information could be handed over to government authorities,[121] and also that they consent to such access.[122] Some lower courts have applied this theory to traditional analog utility meters.[123] This section discusses the possible application of the third-party doctrine to smart meters.

In *Miller v. United States*, agents of the Bureau of Alcohol, Tobacco, and Firearms (ATF) subpoenaed several banks for records pertaining to the defendant, including copies of the defendant's checks, deposit slips, and financial statements.[124] The defendant moved to suppress the records at trial, arguing that a warrantless retrieval of the bank records (his "private papers")[125] was an intrusion into an area protected by the Fourth Amendment. The Court disagreed, broadly declaring "the Fourth Amendment does not prohibit the obtaining of information revealed to a third-party and conveyed by him to Government authorities, even if it is revealed on the assumption that it will be used only for a limited purpose and the confidence placed in the third-party will not be betrayed."[126] The Court further noted that "the depositor takes the risk, in revealing his affairs to another, that the information will be conveyed by that person to the Government."[127]

Three years later, the Court extended the third-party doctrine to outgoing numbers dialed from a person's telephone.[128] In *Smith v. Maryland*, the defendant robbed a woman and began making obscene phone calls to her.[129] Suspecting Smith placed the calls, the police used a pen register to track the telephone numbers dialed from his phone.[130] The police failed to obtain a warrant or subpoena before installing the pen register.[131] The register revealed that Smith was in fact making the phone calls to the woman. In denying Smith's motion to suppress, the Court relied on the third-party doctrine, stating that "this Court consistently has held that a person has no legitimate expectation of privacy in information he voluntarily turns over to third parties."[132]

As applied to the telephone context, the Court found that "[w]hen he used his phone, [Smith] voluntarily conveyed numerical information to the telephone company and 'exposed' that information to its equipment in the ordinary course of business. In so doing, [Smith] assumed the risk that the company would reveal to police the numbers he dialed."[133]

Traditionally, utility records have been handled similarly to bank records and telephone records. Several lower federal courts have held that customers do not have a reasonable expectation of privacy in their utility records, thereby permitting warrantless access to these records. In *United States v. Starkweather*, the Ninth Circuit held that a person does not have a reasonable expectation of privacy in his utility records.[134] The panel reasoned that (1) these records were no different from phone records, and thus did not justify a different constitutional result; and (2) the public was aware that such records were regularly maintained, thereby negating any expectation of privacy.[135] The Eighth Circuit has also upheld warrantless police access to utility records in *United States v. McIntyre*.[136] The Eighth Circuit panel distinguished *Kyllo*, declaring that the means of obtaining the information in *Kyllo* (a thermal-imaging device) was significantly more intrusive than simply subpoenaing the records from the utility company.[137] The court held that "the means to obtaining the information is legally significant."[138] Likewise, the court in *United States v. Hamilton* held that the means of obtaining power records from a third-party by way of administrative subpoena as opposed to "intrusion on the home by 'sense enhancing technology'" is "legally significant," removing this type of situation from the *Kyllo*-home privacy line of cases into the *Miller*-third-party line.[139]

It is difficult to predict whether a court would extend this traditional third-party analysis to smart meters. The courts may seek to ensure the predictability and stability of the third-party doctrine generally and administration of utility services specifically, thus requiring a bright-line rule for all third-party circumstances.[140]

There is an advantage to a rule that is easy to apply, that allows utilities to better govern their affairs, and does not permit "savvy wrongdoers [to] use third-party services in a tactical way to enshroud the entirety of their crimes in zones of Fourth Amendment protection."[141]

However, there are three overarching considerations embodied in the use of smart meters that might weigh against the application of traditional third-party analysis.

These include (a) a person's expectation of privacy while at home; (b) the breadth and granularity of private information conveyed by smart meters; (c) the lack of a voluntary assumption of the risk or consent to release of this data.

Privacy in the Home

The location of the search mattered little in the traditional third-party cases, but it may take on constitutional significance with smart meters.[142] In the case of smart meters, the information is generated in the home, an area accorded specific textual protection in the Fourth Amendment, and one the Supreme Court has persistently safeguarded.[143] In no uncertain terms the Court has asserted that "[a]t the very core [of the Fourth Amendment] stands the right of a man to retreat into his own home and there be free from unreasonable government intrusion."[144] Even as technology advances—whether a tracking or thermal-imaging device or something new—the Court has maintained this bulwark. Because of the significance of the home, access to smart meter data may prompt a doctrinal shift away from the third-party doctrine. Several home privacy cases shed light on this possible approach.[145]

In *Kyllo v. United States*, the Court had to decide whether the use of a thermal-imaging device from the outside of a home that detected the amount of heat coming from inside the home was a violation of the Fourth Amendment.[146] In *Kyllo*, an agent of the Department of the Interior suspected Danny Kyllo was growing marijuana in his home with the use of high-intensity lamps.[147] The agent used a thermal imager to scan the outside of Kyllo's apartment to determine if he was using these "grow" lamps.[148] Thermal imagers can detect energy emitting from the outside surface of an object.[149] When scanning the home, the thermal imager produced an image with various shades of black, white, or gray—the shades darker or lighter depending on the warmth of the area being scanned.[150] From the passenger seat of his car, the agent scanned Kyllo's home for several minutes.[151] From his scan, he determined that the area over the garage and one side of his home were relatively hot compared to neighboring homes.[152] Based on utility bills, informant tips, and the results of thermal imaging, the agents obtained a warrant to search Kyllo's home.[153] As suspected, inside the home the agents found a marijuana growing operation, including over 100 plants.[154]

Justice Scalia first posited that "with very few exceptions, the question whether a warrantless search of the home is reasonable must be answered no."[155] Searches of the home were historically analyzed under the common law doctrine of trespass,[156] but during the mid-20th century the Court instead anchored the Fourth Amendment to a conception of privacy.[157]

While this test may be difficult to apply in the context of automobiles, telephone booths, or other public areas, it is made easier when concerning the home:

> In the case of the search of the interior of homes—the prototypical and hence most commonly litigated area of protected privacy—there is a ready criterion, with deep roots in the common law, of the minimal expectation of privacy that exists, and that is acknowledged to be reasonable. To withdraw protection of this minimum expectation would be to permit police technology to erode the privacy guaranteed by the Fourth Amendment.[158]

The Court ultimately held that "obtaining by sense-enhancing technology any information regarding the interior of the home that could not otherwise have been obtained without physical intrusion into a constitutionally protected area constitutes a search—at least where (as here) the technology in question is not in general public use."[159] *Kyllo* affirmed the notion that "an expectation of privacy in activities taking place inside the home is presumptively reasonable."[160]

The Court also protected home privacy by prohibiting the monitoring of the location of a beeper while inside a residence.[161] In *United States v. Karo*, with the consent of a government informant the police attached a beeper to the false bottom of a can of ether, which was sold to Karo.[162] The can of ether was transported between several residences and storage facilities.[163] The police used the beeper to monitor the location of the can several times while it was located inside of the residences.[164] The Court was asked to determine "whether the monitoring of a beeper in a private residence, a location not open to visual surveillance, violates Fourth Amendment rights of those who have a justifiable interest in the privacy of the residence."[165] The Court answered in the affirmative.

The Court reiterated the long-standing notion that "private residences are places in which the individual normally expects privacy free of governmental intrusion not authorized by a warrant, and that expectation is plainly one that society is prepared to recognize as justifiable."[166] Unless there are exigent circumstances, "searches and seizures inside a home without a warrant are presumptively unreasonable...."[167] The Court ultimately held that the warrantless monitoring of the beeper in the home was a Fourth Amendment violation.[168]

Kyllo and *Karo* demonstrate that the Supreme Court "has defended the home as a sacred site at the 'core of the Fourth Amendment.'"[169] Although neither the Supreme Court nor any lower federal court has ruled on the use of smart meters, a few propositions can be deduced from *Kyllo* and *Karo* bearing on this question.

Because smart meters allow law enforcement to access information regarding intimate details occurring inside the home, a highly invasive investigation that could not otherwise be performed without intrusion into the home, a court may require a warrant to access this data. In *Kyllo*, the police merely obtained the relative temperatures of a house,[170] and in *Karo* the police only generally located the beeper in the house.[171] Although this information was limited, the Court nonetheless prohibited such investigatory techniques. Smart meters have the potential to produce significantly more information than that derived in *Kyllo* and *Karo*, including what individual appliances we are using; whether our house is empty or occupied; and when we take our daily shower or bath.[172] Further, a look at *Figure 1, supra*, makes it clear that this level of information is much more intimate than prior technologies used by law enforcement. This depth of intrusion suggests that customers may have a reasonable expectation of privacy in smart meter data.

There is also a question whether smart meters are in "general public use." (The police must use technology not in general public use for *Kyllo* to apply.)[173] Unfortunately, the Court provided no criterion for making this determination.[174] Several courts applying this test have held that night vision goggles were in general public use.[175] One federal district court reasoned that the goggles were regularly used by the military and police and could be found on the Internet, so were considered in general public use.[176] In 2009, the Department of Energy estimated that 4.75% of all electric meters were smart meters.[177] The department projects that by 2012 approximately 52 million more meters will be installed.[178] With little guidance on this issue, it is uncertain whether this jump in numbers would elevate smart meters into the general public use category.

The means by which data is gathered also differentiates the thermal-imaging in *Kyllo* from smart meters. In *Kyllo*, the police independently gathered the information using the thermal imager; an agent went outside Kyllo's house and used the thermal imager himself.[179] With smart meters, the utility company compiles the information and the police subpoena the company for the data. This difference in means was material in one lower court analyzing access to traditional utility data.[180] It is not clear whether this difference advises against application of *Kyllo* here.

Mosaic and Dragnet Theories

The second factor guiding against the application of the third-party doctrine is composed of two interconnected theories: the mosaic and dragnet theories. The mosaic theory is grounded in the idea that surveillance of the whole of one's activities over a prolonged period is substantially more invasive than a look at each item in isolation.[181] In the case of smart meters, this is the difference between knowing a person's monthly energy usage, and being able to discern a person's daily activities with considerable accuracy. This theory intersects with dragnet-styled law enforcement techniques in which the police cast a wide surveillance net, taking in a wealth of personal information with the goal of finding criminal activity among the stream of data.

Although the Supreme Court has never formally adopted the mosaic theory, there seems to be a ready-made majority potentially willing to consider it.[182] In *United States v. Jones*, the police used a GPS tracking device to track Jones's movements for almost a month.[183] The majority, led by Justice Scalia, held that attaching a GPS device on a vehicle for the purpose of collecting information constituted a "search" under the Fourth Amendment.[184] The physical intrusion, rather than a *Katz*-type invasion of privacy, was the lynchpin of the decision.[185] Justices Alito and Sotomayor both agreed that this was a search, but on different grounds. Both discussed an adaptation of the mosaic theory as prohibiting police from tracking a person for an extended period of time. Justice Alito, joined by Justices Breyer, Ginsburg, and Kagan, assumed that a short-term search would not violate the Fourth Amendment, but that "the use of longer term GPS monitoring in investigations of most offenses impinges on expectations of privacy."[186] Likewise, Justice Sotomayor agreed with this "incisive" observation, noting that "GPS monitoring generates a precise, comprehensive record of a person's public movements that reflects a wealth of detail about familial, political, professional, religious, and sexual associations."[187] Both of these comments closely mirror those of the opinion below, which relied on the mosaic theory: "A person who knows all of another's travels can deduce whether he is a weekly church goer, a heavy drinker, a regular at the gym, an unfaithful husband, an outpatient receiving medical treatment, an associate of particular individuals or political groups—and not just one such fact about a person, but all such facts."[188]

Although the *Jones* majority did not embrace the mosaic theory, the concurrences demonstrate that five justices are flirting with the idea. These arguments resemble those made against the unfettered use of smart meter data. With smart meters, police would have a rich source of personal data that reveals far more about a person than traditional analog meters. Understanding a person's daily activities, including what appliances he is using, is a far leap from knowing his monthly energy usage. This is the difference between knowing about a single trip a person took and monitoring his movements over a month-long period. The breadth and granularity of the smart meter data may be seen as warranting application of the mosaic theory and may perhaps find receptive ears on the Court.

Additionally, the dragnet theory may apply to collection of energy usage data. This theory states that surveillance normally permitted under the Fourth Amendment—such as monitoring a person's movements on a public street—becomes an impermissible invasion of privacy when conducted on a prolonged, 24-hour basis.[189] "If such dragnet-type law enforcement practices as respondent envisions should eventually occur," Justice Rehnquist asserted earlier in *United States v. Knotts*, "there will be time enough then to determine whether different constitutional principles may be applicable."[190] Twenty-four hour access to our intimate daily activities, including what appliances we use, when we take our daily shower or bath, eat, and sleep, may push smart meters into the dragnet category.

Coinciding with the mosaic and dragnet theories is the difference in sophistication and the quantity of the data revealed between traditional third-party cases and smart meters. Comparing *Smith* with *Katz* provides insight into this distinction. Pen registers, as used in *Smith*, have "limited capabilities"—they can only record the numbers dialed from a phone.[191] In comparison, in *Katz* the police listened to the contents of Katz's phone call—the actual words spoken.[192] In noting this distinction, it seems the *Smith* Court, in permitting the use of pen registers, intentionally limited its holding to the discrete set of data conveyed—the telephone numbers dialed. Smart meters, to the contrary, have the potential to collect and aggregate precise detail about the activities inside the home. It is more than one packet of data, but reveals minute-byminute activity, something far more revealing, and arguably more like *Katz* than *Smith*.

Assumption of the Risk—Consent

The third difference between traditional third-party cases and smart meters is the nature of services involved and whether the customer actually assumes the risk or consents to this information being shared with others. Assumption of the risk and consent are the two leading theories supporting the third-party doctrine. In *United States v. Miller*, the customer "assumed the risk" that the bank would turn over the bank records to government authorities.[193] That was a risk he took in doing business with the bank. As to the consent theory, one commentator asked and answered the question as follows: "When does a person's choice to disclose information to a third-party constitute consent to a search? So long as a person knows that they are disclosing information to a third-party, their choice to do so is voluntary and the consent valid."[194]

With banking or telephone services, a customer has the option of transferring his business to another bank or another telephone carrier.[195] To the contrary, because electric utilities are essentially monopolies, the customer cannot simply switch services.

The only way to avoid the recordation of his electric usage is to terminate his utility service altogether, an impracticable option in modern society. As one state court has noted:

> Electricity, even more than telephone service, is a "necessary component" of modern life, pervading every aspect of an individual's business and personal life: it heats our homes, powers our appliances, and lights our nights. A requirement of receiving this service is the disclosure to the power company (and in this case an agent of the state) of one's identity and the amount of electricity being used. The nature of electrical service requires the disclosure of this information, but that disclosure is only for the limited business purpose of obtaining the service.[196]

It is not clear whether assumption of the risk or consent should apply to smart meters. It is reasonable to assume that customers understand utility companies must collect usage data to bill the customer for that usage. Customers receive their statement each month demonstrating this fact. However, most customers are probably not familiar with the sophistication of smart meters and the detailed data sets that can be derived from them. Even if customers are aware their utility usage can be recorded in sub-fifteen minute intervals, a reasonable customer would probably be surprised, if not shocked, to know that data from smart meters can potentially be used to pinpoint the usage of specific appliances. If knowledge of the sophistication of the data is a prerequisite to assumption of the risk or consent, it is difficult to say whether a reasonable customer would understand the privacy implications with this new technology.[197]

Because smart meters are an emerging technology not yet judicially tested, it is difficult to conclude with certainty how they would be handled under the Fourth Amendment. Further, beyond the possible constitutional implications of smart meters, federal communication and privacy statutes may also apply. As noted by Professor Kerr, "in recent decades, legislative privacy rules governing new technologies have proven roughly as privacy protective, and quite often more protective than, parallel Fourth Amendment rules."[198]

STATUTORY PROTECTION OF SMART METER DATA

This section discusses federal statutory protections that may be applicable to the contents of communications sent by a smart meter, independent of the Fourth Amendment, while they are either stored within the smart meter prior to transmission, during transmission, or after they have been delivered to the utility. Three federal laws, the Electronic Communications Privacy Act (ECPA),[199] the Stored Communications Act (SCA),[200] and the Computer Fraud and Abuse Act (CFAA)[201] may be applicable to these situations and are discussed in more detail below.

The Electronic Communications Privacy Act (ECPA)

ECPA, enacted in 1986, "addresses the interception of wire, oral and electronic communications."[202] The statute defines electronic communications as "any transfer of signs, signals, writing, images, sounds, data, or intelligence of any nature transmitted in whole or in part by a wire, radio, electromagnetic, photoelectronic or photooptical system that affects interstate or foreign commerce...."[203] Based on the description of the smart meter network provided above,[204] the envisioned transmission of customers' energy usage data by smart meters would seem to fall squarely within the definition of electronic communications under ECPA.

ECPA generally prohibits the interception of electronic communications, but also provides a mechanism for government entities to conduct such surveillance, and a number of other exceptions.[205] Additionally, the statute provides that interception under the procedures and exceptions set forth in ECPA, or pursuant to the Foreign Intelligence Surveillance Act, are the exclusive means for intercepting electronic communications.[206] The unlawful interception of electronic communications in violation of ECPA is generally punishable by imprisonment for not more than five years and/or a fine of not more than $250,000 for individuals and not more than $500,000 for organizations.[207]

Of particular relevance to the immediate discussion is the fact that ECPA permits interception of an electronic communication where a party to the communication has consented to such interception.[208] In the context of a smart meter network that is the subject of this report, it appears that the utility would be a party to all of the communication sent by the smart meters, since it is primarily receiving that information for its own billing purposes. Therefore, if the utility consents to law enforcement's interception of the traffic which is addressed to it, that surveillance would not appear to violate the prohibitions in ECPA.

ECPA also provides a procedural mechanism for law enforcement to conduct surveillance activities for investigative purposes without the consent of any party to the communication. The statute limits the types of criminal cases in which electronic surveillance may be used[209] and requires court orders authorizing electronic surveillance to be supported by probable cause to believe that the target is engaged in criminal activities, that normal investigative techniques are insufficient, and that the facilities that are the subject of surveillance will be used by the target.[210] It also limits the use and dissemination of information intercepted.[211] In addition, when an interception order expires, authorities must notify those whose communications have been intercepted.[212] Law enforcement may also conduct electronic surveillance when acting in an emergency situation pending issuance of a court order.[213]

The government may also conduct electronic surveillance under the authority of the Foreign Intelligence Surveillance Act (FISA). FISA governs the gathering of information about foreign powers, including international terrorist organizations, and agents of foreign powers.[214] Although it is often discussed in relation to the prevention of terrorism, it applies to the gathering of foreign intelligence information for other purposes.[215] Although some exceptions apply, such as for emergency situations,[216] the government typically must obtain a court order, supported by probable cause, from the Foreign Intelligence Surveillance Court (FISC), a neutral judicial decision maker, in order to conduct electronic surveillance pursuant to FISA.[217]

The Stored Communications Act (SCA)

The SCA was enacted in 1986 as Title II of the Electronic Communications Privacy Act (ECPA),[218] to "address[] access to stored wire and electronic communications and transactional records."[219] The SCA prohibits unauthorized persons from accessing a facility through which an *electronic communication service* (ECS) is provided; or obtaining, altering, or preventing access to an electronic communication while it is in *electronic storage* in an ECS.[220] The SCA also limits the circumstances in which providers of ECS or a *remote computing service* (RCS) may disclose information that they carry or maintain.[221] The SCA also provides a mechanism by which law enforcement may compel the disclosure of stored communications.[222]

The terms "electronic communication service," "remote computing services," and "electronic storage" are all specifically defined by the SCA. As described above, the SCA applies only to providers of either an ECS or an RCS; stored communications held by other types of entities are not protected by the SCA. Therefore, in order to determine whether the SCA would protect stored information collected by a smart meter, this report will first examine whether a utility's deployment of a smart meter network falls within the definition of an ECS or an RCS and then discuss the protections and disclosure restrictions that might apply to any smart meter network that qualifies as an ECS or RCS.

Electronic Communication Services

An ECS is defined by the SCA as any service which provides users "the ability to send or receive wire or electronic communications."[223] The statute also defines an "electronic communication" as "any transfer of signs, signals, writing, images, sounds, data, or intelligence of any nature transmitted in whole or in part by a wire, radio, electromagnetic, photoelectronic or photooptical system that affects interstate or foreign commerce."[224] As described above, one of the essential functions of a smart meter would appear to be the capability to transmit consumer electricity usage data to the smart grid using a variety of communications technologies.[225] These transmissions would seem to fall neatly within the

SCA's definition of an electronic communication. Therefore, whether a smart meter network would qualify as an ECS would likely depend on whether the deployed smart meters could be said to be providing this ability to users.

It is not clear whether it would be accurate to categorically describe smart meters as providing customers with "the ability to send or receive" communications. It could be argued that a utility customer would use the smart meter to transmit usage information to the utility, in the same way that the same customer uses a traditional meter to record household electricity usage over a billing period. However, the Ninth Circuit has suggested that an ECS should not include situations in which electronic communications are used only "as an incident to providing some other service, as is the case with a street-front shop that requires potential customers to speak into an intercom device before permitting entry, or a 'drive-thru' restaurant that allows customers to place orders via a two-way intercom located beside the drive-up lane."[226] On one hand, it may not be accurate to describe utility customers as users of smart meters at all, particularly if the deployment of such smart meters is intended principally for the benefit of the utility and does not change the experience of utility customers. On the other hand, some of the proposed uses of deployed smart meters may include using collected data for the benefit of the customers, for example by determining the energy efficiency of specific household appliances.[227] As a result, the ultimate classification of a particular smart meter network as an ECS may depend largely on the specific facts present, such as the manner in which it is marketed, or the ostensible purposes for which the transmissions are intended to be used.

If a smart meter network qualifies as an ECS, then transmissions containing smart meter data would be protected under the SCA only while such transmissions are in electronic storage, as that term is defined by the statute.[228] Therefore, one must first determine whether, and under what circumstances, the data collected by a smart meter network is in electronic storage in order to determine what protections apply.

For purposes of the SCA, a communication is in electronic storage at an ECS if it is in temporary, intermediate storage incidental to electronic transmission or in storage for backup protection.[229] As applied to the smart meter network, data residing on the smart meter itself prior to being sent to the utility would appear to be in electronic storage, as such storage is likely temporary and undertaken solely in anticipation of some eventual transmission to the utility. In contrast, once the data has arrived at the utility and resides on its servers, it may no longer be in temporary or intermediate storage. However, some form of the communications may still be being held for backup purposes, and in such a case might be considered in electronic storage under the statute. To the extent that the data would be considered in electronic storage, either while on the meter or on the utility's computers, the data would appear to be subject to the SCA's provisions applicable to providers of ECS.

The SCA prohibits intentionally accessing without authorization, a facility through which an ECS is provided and obtaining, altering, or preventing access to an electronic communication while it is in electronic storage.[230] Criminal penalties for violating the SCA's prohibitions on unauthorized access start at imprisonment for not more than one year (not more than five years for a subsequent conviction) and/or a fine of not more than $100,000.[231] However, violations committed for malicious, mercenary, tortious or criminal purposes are subject to higher penalties and may be punished by imprisonment for not more than five years (not more than 10 years for a subsequent conviction) and/or a fine of not more than $250,000 (not more than $500,000 for organizations).[232] Victims of a violation of the SCA also have a civil cause of action for equitable relief, reasonable attorneys' fees and costs, and damages equal to the loss and gain associated with the offense but not less than $1,000.[233]

The SCA generally restricts the ability of providers of ECS to disclose the contents of communications in electronic storage, if the ECS is offering those services to the public.[234] However, the statute also permits certain disclosures to law enforcement. Such permitted disclosures by a provider of electronic communication services to law enforcement can be either voluntary or compelled.

Normally, voluntary disclosure to law enforcement is authorized only if the contents of the communication were inadvertently obtained by the service provider and appear to pertain to the commission of a crime.[235] However, it should be noted that the utility in this case appears to be the intended recipient of all communications sent over the smart meter network, and the SCA's restrictions on disclosures of electronically stored information held by ECS or RCS providers may generally be overcome if an intended recipient of the communication consents to the disclosure.[236] Consequently, the utility may have more latitude to share communications in electronic storage with law enforcement than a traditional provider of ECS, such as a telephone company, would have.

For purposes of compelled disclosures to law enforcement, the SCA distinguishes between recent communications and those that have been in electronic storage for more than 180 days.

A search warrant is required to compel providers to disclose communications held in electronic storage for 180 days or less.[237] However, communications held for more than 180 days may be obtained by law enforcement through a warrant, subpoena, or a court order supported by specific and articulable facts sufficient to establish reasonable grounds to believe that the contents are relevant and material to an ongoing criminal investigation.[238] Customers whose communications have been disclosed are generally required to be given notice of such disclosure, but such disclosure may be delayed if notification might result in endangering the life or physical safety of an individual; flight from prosecution; destruction of or tampering with evidence; intimidation of potential witnesses; or otherwise seriously jeopardizing an investigation or unduly delaying a trial.[239]

Remote Computing Services

It is likely that the classification of a smart meter network as an RCS would similarly be fact-dependent. The SCA defines an RCS as a service in which computer storage or processing services by means of an ECS are provided to the public.[240] It is conceivable that the data collected by smart meters may in fact be stored or processed by the utility, but there is no indication that such storage or processing would be categorically provided as a service to the public, rather than solely for the utility's internal benefit.[241] If such service is not provided to the public, then it would likely be inaccurate to classify the smart meter network as an RCS. However, if one of the features of a particular smart meter deployment is to give customers the ability to store or process their usage data, then it would appear to qualify as an RCS.

For those smart meter networks which qualify as an RCS, the SCA generally protects the contents of electronically transmitted communications "carried or maintained on that service" for customers of the service. Disclosures of such information are generally prohibited,[242] but the SCA also provides a means for law enforcement to obtain access to the contents of such communications. The government may obtain a warrant supported by probable cause, or use a subpoena or a court order supported by specific and articulable facts sufficient to establish reasonable grounds to believe that the contents are relevant and material to an ongoing criminal investigation.[243]

However, use of a subpoena or court order supported by specific and articulable facts also requires the government to give prior notice to the customer whose information is sought, unless particular circumstances warrant delayed notice.[244]

RCS customers whose communications have been disclosed in violation of the SCA may pursue a civil cause of action for equitable relief, reasonable attorneys' fees and costs, and damages equal to the loss and gain associated with the offense but not less than $1,000.[245]

The Computer Fraud and Abuse Act (CFAA)

The Computer Fraud and Abuse Act (CFAA) prohibits intentionally accessing and obtaining information from a computer used in or affecting interstate commerce, without authorization or in excess of a granted authorization.[246] The definition of a computer for purposes of the CFAA is "an electronic, magnetic, optical, electrochemical, or other high speed data processing device performing logical, arithmetic, or storage functions, and includes any data storage facility or communications facility directly related to or operating in conjunction with such device" excluding "an automated typewriter or typesetter, a portable hand held calculator, or other similar device...."[247]

The servers on a utility's network would likely fall squarely within the definition of a computer under the CFAA.

Similarly, smart meters themselves also appear to meet the definition of a computer, insofar as they store customers' energy usage data and also perform logical operations by routing transmissions across the utility's network. Additionally, in light of the significant role that energy utilities play in the modern economy, the smart meter network would also likely be considered to have an effect on interstate commerce, even if they operate entirely within one state.

Therefore, intentionally gaining access to the utility's servers or smart meters to obtain customer data would likely constitute a violation of the CFAA if done without the utility's authorization or in excess of an authorization granted by the utility.

The criminal penalties for violating the unauthorized access provisions of the CFAA have a three tier sentencing structure. Simple violations are punished as misdemeanors, imprisonment for not more than one year and/or a fine of not more than $100,000 ($200,000 for organizations).[248]

At the next level, cases in which: "(i) the offense was committed for purposes of commercial advantage or private financial gain; (ii) the offense was committed in furtherance of any criminal or tortious act in violation of the Constitution or laws of the United States or of any State; or (iii) the value of the information obtained exceeds $5,000" may be punished by imprisonment for not more than five years and/or a fine of not more $250,000 ($500,000 for organizations).[249]

The third tier is for repeat offenders whose punishment is increased to imprisonment of not more than 10 years and/or a fine of not more than $250,000 ($500,000 for organizations) for a second or subsequent conviction.[250]

The Federal Trade Commission Act (FTC Act)

Section 5 of the FTC Act prohibits "unfair or deceptive acts or practices in or affecting commerce"[251] and gives the Federal Trade Commission (FTC) jurisdiction to bring enforcement actions against "persons, partnerships, or corporations" that engage in these practices.[252] In the past, the FTC has used its authority under Section 5 to take action against businesses that violate their own privacy policies or that fail to adequately safeguard a consumer's personal information.[253]

Although there do not appear to be any cases in which the FTC has taken action against an electric utility for failing to protect consumer smart meter data, the Commission would have authority to enforce Section 5 against a utility that fell within its statutory jurisdiction.

Covered Electric Utilities

This section considers whether the FTC would have Section 5 jurisdiction over each of the four types of electric utilities identified by the Energy Information Administration (EIA): investor-owned, publicly owned, federally owned, and cooperative.[254] It finds that the FTC clearly has jurisdiction over investor-owned utilities. It is unclear whether the Commission has jurisdiction over publicly owned utilities or federally owned utilities. The FTC could enforce Section 5 against for-profit electric cooperatives, and case law suggests that nonprofit electric cooperatives may also be subject to the act's requirements.

The FTC has jurisdiction to enforce Section 5 against "persons, partnerships, or corporations," with exceptions not applicable here.[255] Utilities that are "persons" or "partnerships" would be subject to the FTC's enforcement powers automatically,[256] as the statute does not provide any additional jurisdictional requirements for these entities. Most electric utilities, however, are organized as legal entities that would potentially fit within the definition of "corporation." The FTC Act states that, for the purposes of Section 5, the term "corporation":

> shall be deemed to include any company, trust, so-called Massachusetts trust, or association, incorporated or unincorporated, which is organized to carry on business for its own profit or that of its members, and has shares of capital or capital stock or certificates of interest, and any company, trust, so-called Massachusetts trust, or association, incorporated or unincorporated, without shares of capital or capital stock or certificates of interest, except partnerships, which is organized to carry on business for its own profit or that of its members.[257]

This definition, particularly in its use of the words "shall be deemed to include," suggests that a wide variety of legal entities could potentially constitute "corporations." Moreover, in *California Dental Ass'n v. FTC*, the Supreme Court remarked that the "FTC Act directs the Commission to prevent the *broad set of entities* under its jurisdiction" from violating Section 5.[258] In that case, the Court found that the term "corporation" also included *nonprofit* entities, so long as they imparted significant economic benefit to their members.[259] Thus, as the Court's opinion demonstrates, the key question when determining whether an entity is a "corporation" for the purposes of Section 5 jurisdiction is not what legal form the entity takes, but rather whether the entity is "organized to carry on business for its own profit or that of its members."

Investor-Owned Utilities

Investor-owned utilities are clearly subject to the FTC's Section 5 jurisdiction as "corporations." The EIA defines investor-owned electric utilities as those that "have the fundamental objective of producing a profit for their investors" and distributing these profits as dividends or reinvesting them in the business.[260] These utilities satisfy the definition of "corporation" under the statute because they are companies organized to carry on business for the profit of their investors.[261]

Publicly Owned Utilities

It is unclear whether the FTC has Section 5 jurisdiction over publicly owned utilities. The agency probably lacks jurisdiction over these utilities if it characterizes them as "corporations," but it is possible that it may have jurisdiction over them if it characterizes them as "persons." Publicly owned utilities include "municipals, public utility districts and public power districts, State authorities, irrigation districts, and joint municipal action agencies."[262] The EIA describes these as "nonprofit government entities that are organized at either the local or State level," are exempt from state and federal income taxes, and "provide service to their communities and nearby consumers at cost."[263] In contrast to investor-owned utilities or cooperatively owned utilities, publicly owned utilities obtain capital by issuing debt rather than selling an ownership interest in the utility to investors or members.[264]

As "Corporations"

Publicly owned utilities probably do not fall within the FTC's Section 5 jurisdiction over "corporations" because they are not organized to carry on business for profit. Rather, governments form these utilities for the sole purpose of distributing electricity to consumers at cost.265 Significantly, when publicly owned utilities realize net income—that is, revenues they earn in excess of their expenses—they either (1) use it to finance their operations in lieu of issuing more debt,266 or (2) transfer it to the general fund of the political subdivision that they serve.267 These utilities typically lack investors or members to which they could distribute net income as dividends.268 Thus, publicly owned utilities are probably not "organized to carry on business" for profit and are probably exempt from the FTC's Section 5 jurisdiction if characterized as "corporations."

As "Persons"

It is unclear whether a court would find that the FTC has Section 5 jurisdiction over publicly owned utilities as "persons," as a court could employ several different canons of statutory interpretation when deciding whether "persons" includes state or local government entities.[269] In the 1980s, the FTC attempted to assert Section 5 jurisdiction over two state-chartered municipal corporations—the cities of New Orleans and Minneapolis—as "persons," alleging that the cities engaged in unfair methods of competition by assisting taxicab companies in maintaining high prices and stifling competition.[270] The Commission later withdrew both complaints, and thus no court considered whether jurisdiction was proper.

More recently, the Commission has asserted jurisdiction over state government agencies that regulate certain professions such as dentistry,[271] optometry,[272] and funeral services.[273]

There appears to be only one court case that engages in a full discussion and interpretation of the meaning of "persons" under Section 5. In *California State Board of Optometry v. FTC*, the D.C. Circuit Court of Appeals considered "whether a State acting in its sovereign capacity is a 'person' within the FTC's enforcement jurisdiction."[274] The FTC had issued a rule declaring "certain state laws restricting the practice of optometry to be unfair acts or practices."[275] Petitioners, which were state boards of optometry and professional associations, argued that the court should strike down the rule because it went beyond the FTC's statutory authority.[276] In vacating the rule, the court found nothing in the relevant provisions of the FTC Act "to indicate that Congress intended to authorize the FTC to reach the 'acts or practices' of States acting in their sovereign capacities."[277]

A court approaching the question of whether "persons" includes publicly owned utilities would start with the language of the statute. Courts traditionally give broad deference to an agency when the agency interprets the extent of its own jurisdiction unless the reach of its jurisdiction is clear from reading the statute "under ordinary principles of construction."[278] Attempting to discern the Commission's jurisdiction under Section 5 of the FTC Act is difficult, as the statute does not define the term "persons" for the purposes of that provision. Title 1, Section 1 of the United States Code (the Dictionary Act) provides: "In determining the meaning of any Act of Congress, *unless the context indicates otherwise* ... the words 'person' and 'whoever' include corporations, companies, associations, firms, partnerships, societies, and joint stock companies, as well as individuals."[279]

However, the context in which "persons" appears in Section 5 probably forecloses the use of the default definition of "person" in the Dictionary Act. In Section 5, Congress listed the terms "persons," "partnerships," and "corporations" separately, which indicates that it intended to give each term independent significance. The terms "corporations" and "partnerships" would not have independent meaning in Section 5 if the term "persons" in Section 5 included the entities listed in the Dictionary Act. Furthermore, the FTC Act requires that "corporations" be organized for their own profit or the profit of their members in order for the FTC to exercise jurisdiction over them—a requirement it does not impose on the other entities.[280] By reading the term "persons" to include the entities listed in the Dictionary Act, the FTC could evade this additional requirement simply by bringing its complaint against an entity as a "person" rather than a "corporation"—a result that Congress probably did not intend. Thus, a court that ended its analysis here could find that the meaning of "persons" remains ambiguous. The court could then choose to defer to the FTC's broad interpretation of its own jurisdiction under the Supreme Court's decision in *Chevron USA., Inc. v. NRDC, Inc.*[281]

The *California Optometry* court, however, declined to defer to the FTC's interpretation of its own jurisdiction because it found that principles of federalism outweighed *Chevron* deference.[282] Quoting the Supreme Court's decision in *Will v. Michigan Department of State Police*,[283] the *California Optometry* court stated that "in common usage, the term person does not include the sovereign, and statutes employing the word are ordinarily construed to exclude it."[284] In the *Will* case, the Court considered whether the term "person" as it appeared in 42 USC. §1983 included a state.[285] The Court held that it did not, invoking the principles of federalism when it wrote that "[t]his approach is particularly applicable where it is claimed that Congress has subjected the States to liability to which they had not been subject before."[286] The Court found that the statute's language fell "far short of satisfying the ordinary rule of statutory construction that if Congress intends to alter the 'usual constitutional balance between the States and Federal Government,' it must make its intention to do so 'unmistakably clear in the language of the statute.'"[287]

The Court's decision in *Will*, as interpreted by the D.C. Circuit in *California Optometry*, suggests that Congress must clearly indicate in a particular statute when it wishes to subject states to a new form of liability, particularly when this would change the balance between state and federal authority by intruding on the actions a state takes in its sovereign capacity. There does not appear to be a clear indication that Congress intended the word "persons" in the FTC Act to subject publicly owned utilities to FTC enforcement actions.[288] Thus, if the FTC's enforcement of Section 5 against a publicly owned utility would alter the balance between the state and federal governments, a court might read "persons" to exclude these utilities. As the *California Optometry* court indicated, whether the balance is altered may depend on whether the operation of the utility amounts to the state acting in its sovereign capacity (balance altered) or merely engaging in a proprietary function (balance not altered).[289] The *California Optometry* court suggested that whether a state is acting in its sovereign capacity or engaging in a proprietary function may vary according to the antitrust laws' state action doctrine, a multi-pronged analysis that is beyond the scope of this report.[290] If a court found that the state was acting in its sovereign capacity when the state (or one of its subdivisions) operated an electric utility, the court could hold that the FTC does not have Section 5 jurisdiction because of the federalism principles and clear statement rule that guided the interpretation of the statute in *Will* and were adopted by the court in *California Optometry*.[291]

A third possible choice for a court would be to adopt the reasoning of the FTC and find that Congress clearly intended "persons" to include government entities, because under the other antitrust laws, the term "persons" includes state and local government entities, and the antitrust laws, including the FTC Act,[292] should be read together.[293] The *California Optometry* court acknowledged this argument, writing that "several Supreme Court decisions hold that a State *is* a person for purposes of the antitrust laws."[294] The court ultimately rejected the argument, however, because it found that "when a State acts in a sovereign rather than a proprietary capacity, it is exempt from the antitrust laws even though those actions may restrain trade," and that this state action doctrine may "limit the reach of the FTC's enforcement jurisdiction."[295] Thus, if a court found that a state acted in its *proprietary* capacity when the state (or one of its subdivisions) operated a public utility, then the state action doctrine would not apply, and it would be possible for a court to find jurisdiction even under the *California Optometry* case. The FTC has advanced this reasoning, arguing that the state boards over which it asserts jurisdiction do not amount to the states acting in their sovereign capacities.[296] Whether the operation of a particular publicly owned utility consists of the state acting in its sovereign capacity or engaging in a proprietary function may vary according to the antitrust laws' state action doctrine, a multi-pronged analysis that is beyond the scope of this report.[297]

Thus, whether a court would find that the word "persons" in Section 5 includes certain government entities such as publicly owned utilities is unclear because it may depend on which, if any, of several principles of statutory construction the court adopts. A court could, among other options: (1) find that the meaning of "persons" in Section 5 is ambiguous, and thus defer to the FTC's broad interpretation of its own jurisdiction because of the *Chevron* doctrine; (2) find that the statute is ambiguous, but that principles of federalism outweigh the court's usual *Chevron* deference to the Commission's interpretation of its own jurisdiction—a determination that may require a court to find that the state is acting in its sovereign capacity when the state (or one of its subdivisions) operates an electric utility; or (3) find that Congress clearly intended "persons" to include government entities because Section 5 should be read together with the other antitrust laws, under which the term "person" includes state and local government entities—a determination that may require a court to find that the state is performing a proprietary function when the state (or one of its subdivisions) operates a utility.

Federally Owned Utilities

It is unclear whether the FTC could enforce Section 5 against a federally owned utility. Indeed, there does not appear to be any case in which the FTC has sought to enforce Section 5 against a federal agency.[298] The FTC probably lacks Section 5 jurisdiction over the nine federally owned utilities operating in the United States[299] if it characterizes them as "corporations." Like publicly owned utilities, federally owned utilities are not organized for profit. As the EIA notes, "federal power is not sold for profit, but to recover the costs of operations and repay the Treasury for funds borrowed to construct generation and transmission facilities."[300] If the Commission characterizes these utilities as "persons," it is unclear whether a court would find that this term includes government entities.[301]

As a practical matter, FTC enforcement of Section 5 against federally owned utilities is probably unnecessary in the context of smart meter data because of other federal laws, such as the Privacy Act,[302] that would likely protect this data when it is stored in records systems maintained by federal agencies, including federally owned utilities.[303]

Cooperatively Owned Utilities

For-profit electric cooperatives would clearly fall within the Commission's Section 5 jurisdiction over "corporations" operated for their own profit or that of their members.[304] Indeed, the FTC has maintained jurisdiction over for-profit cooperatives as "corporations" in the past, including a rural healthcare cooperative[305] and a wine maker.[306] However, it appears that most electric cooperatives—and particularly the cooperatives that will receive funds under the Department of Energy's Smart Grid Investment Grant program—are nonprofits.[307]

It is possible that the FTC would have Section 5 jurisdiction over these nonprofit electric cooperatives as "corporations" organized for profit. These distribution utilities are owned by the "consumers they serve," and those that are tax-exempt must "provide electric service to their members at cost, as that term is defined by the Internal Revenue Service."[308] However, when the activities of a cooperative result in revenues that exceed the cooperative's costs, these "net margins ... are considered a contribution of equity by the members that are required to be returned to the members consistent with the organization's bylaws and lender limitations imposed as a condition of loans."[309] Thus, in contrast to publicly owned utilities, which typically transfer any net income to the general fund of the government that they serve, electric cooperatives return net margins to their members as equity, and when that equity is retired by the board of directors, members receive cash payments.[310] Although it does not appear that a court has considered whether the FTC has Section 5 jurisdiction over a nonprofit electric cooperative that returns its net margins to its consumer-members in addition to providing them with electricity service, the Supreme Court, as well as lower federal courts, have issued guidance on factors that a court may consider in answering this question.

Applicable Law

Under Section 5, the FTC Act requires that a "corporation" be "organized to carry on business for its own profit *or that of its members*."[311] In *California Dental Ass'n v. FTC*, the Court considered whether the FTC could enforce Section 5 against a "voluntary nonprofit association of local dental societies" that was exempt from paying federal income tax and furnished its members with "advantageous insurance and preferential financing arrangements" in addition to lobbying, litigating, and advertising on their behalf.[312] The Court found that the FTC had jurisdiction over the California Dental Association as a "corporation," stating that

> the FTC Act is at pains to include not only an entity "organized to carry on business for its own profit," but also one that carries on business for the profit "of its members." While such a supportive organization may be devoted to helping its members in ways beyond immediate enhancement of profit, no one here has claimed that such an entity must devote itself single-mindedly to the profit of others. It could, indeed, hardly be supposed that Congress intended such a restricted notion of covered supporting organizations, with the opportunity this would bring with it for avoiding jurisdiction where the purposes of the FTC Act would obviously call for asserting it.[313]

The Court declined to specify the percentage of a nonprofit entity's activities that must be "aimed at its members' pecuniary benefit" to subject it to FTC jurisdiction.[314] However, the Court wrote that a "proximate relation" must exist between the activities of the entity and the profits of its members, and implied that the activities must confer "more than *de minimis* or merely presumed economic benefits" on the members.[315] The Court's justification for this result was that "nonprofit entities organized on behalf of for-profit members have the same capacity and derivatively, at least, the same incentives as for-profit organizations to engage in unfair methods of competition or unfair and deceptive acts."[316]

It is clear that the FTC may still have Section 5 jurisdiction even when the benefits that a nonprofit provides to its members are secondary to its charitable functions. In *American Medical Ass'n v. FTC*, the Second Circuit considered whether the FTC could enforce Section 5 against three medical professional associations, including the American Medical Association (AMA), a nonprofit corporation composed of "physicians, osteopaths, and medical students."[317] The court, acknowledging that the associations served "both the business and non-business interests of their member physicians," found jurisdiction because the "business aspects" of their activities, including lobbying for members and offering business advice to them, subjected them to the FTC's jurisdiction despite the fact that the business aspects "were considered secondary to the charitable and social aspects of their work."[318]

When determining whether jurisdiction exists, a court may consider other factors in addition to the benefits that the nonprofit provides to its members. In *Community Blood Bank v. FTC*, the Eighth Circuit considered whether a "corporation" included all nonprofit corporations.[319] The appeals court held that the FTC lacked Section 5 jurisdiction over nonprofit blood banks because the banks' activities did not result in "profit" in the sense of "gain from business or investment over and above expenditures."[320] The blood banks, the court observed, lacked shares of capital, capital stock, or certificates, and were "organized for and actually engaged in business for only charitable purposes."[321] One bank's articles of incorporation touted the entity's charitable purposes, and all of the banks were exempt from paying federal income taxes.[322] Upon dissolution, the corporations would transfer their assets to other charitable or nonprofit organizations.[323] In addition, none of the funds collected by the blood banks had "ever been distributed or inured to the benefit of any of their members, directors or officers."[324] The court found that these factors made the blood banks "charitable organizations" both "in law and in fact," exempting them from the FTC's Section 5 jurisdiction.[325]

Analysis

The case law suggests several factors that a court may weigh when determining whether a private, nonprofit entity composed of members, such as an electric cooperative, is subject to the FTC's Section 5 jurisdiction as a "corporation."[326] The most significant factor is whether the nonprofit provides an economic benefit to its members that is more than *de minimis* and that is proximately related to the nonprofit's activities. This benefit need not be the sole—or even primary—function of the nonprofit. Additional factors that the case law suggests weigh in favor of a finding of jurisdiction include that the nonprofit: (1) has gain from its business or investments that exceeds its expenditures; (2) has shares of capital or capital stock or certificates; (3) is not organized solely for charitable purposes or does not engage only in charitable work; (4) has articles of incorporation that list profit-seeking objectives; (5) is subject to federal income tax liability; (6) would distribute its assets to profit-seeking entities upon dissolution; and (7) distributes any of the funds it collects to its members, directors, or officers.

It is possible that the FTC has Section 5 jurisdiction over nonprofit electric cooperatives, although the outcome in any particular case may depend on the characteristics of the individual utility. A court could find that the typical nonprofit electric cooperative provides "economic benefit" to its members in at least two ways: (a) by providing electricity service to members;[327] and (b) by returning net margins to members in the form of patronage capital, which is an ownership interest in the cooperative that is later converted to cash payments to members when that capital is retired.[328] With regard to (a), it is likely that a court would find that electricity service is an "economic benefit" as defined in the case law. In *California Dental Ass'n*, the nonprofit professional association provided "advantageous insurance and preferential financing arrangements," as well as lobbying, litigation, and advertising services to its members.[329] In *American Medical Ass'n*, the nonprofit lobbied on behalf of its members and offered business advice to members.[330] These benefits, it is assumed, enabled the members to more easily conduct business profitably. Electricity service allows people to conduct activities at all times of the day, and thus provides a similar and clearly significant economic benefit to those who use it, whether for business or recreational purposes. As the primary objective of an electric cooperative is to provide electricity service to members, the necessary proximate relation between the activities of the nonprofit and the benefit to its members clearly exists.

Despite its pecuniary nature, there are a few problems with considering benefit (b), patronage capital, to be an "economic benefit" as defined by the Court. First, it is not clear that patronage capital actually is a benefit. A court could view patronage capital as a no-interest *loan* from the consumer-member to the utility,[331] or, because it is typically allocated to member accounts in a manner proportional to members' spending on electricity, simply a *refund* of money collected from the members that reflects the actual cost of providing service in a particular year.[332] If adopted by a court, neither of these characterizations would appear to be consistent with the "profit" that the statute describes[333] or the "economic benefit" that the Supreme Court requires for a nonprofit to be a "corporation."

Second, even if a court found patronage capital to be an economic benefit, it is not clear that it is more than *de minimis*. Patronage capital must be "retired" before members receive cash payments for it.[334] Retirements are made at the discretion of the cooperative's board of directors because the capital is needed to finance the cooperative's ongoing expenses, and thus retirement of a class of capital typically occurs after a long rotation period, such as 20 years.[335] Although the Supreme Court did not hold that an "economic benefit" must produce *immediate* advantage to the members of a nonprofit, a court could potentially view the decades-long delay in cash payments as significantly decreasing the degree of economic benefit that the capital provides. In addition, patronage capital would probably be considered *de minimis* if the cooperative's net margins were small, as this would mean that little capital would be issued to members. It is thus difficult to discern whether a court would find that an economic benefit accrues to members as a result of their receipt of patronage capital, which nevertheless probably bears the requisite "proximate relation" to the activities of the cooperative that produce any net margins distributed as capital.

With regard to the additional factors, those favoring jurisdiction include (2) cooperatives typically have shares of capital stock, including patronage capital;[336] (3) cooperatives do not operate solely for the benefit of the people outside of the organization like the nonprofits in *Community Blood Bank* did because cooperatives provide electricity service and patronage capital to their members;[337] and (7) an electric cooperative typically returns any net margins to members in the form of patronage capital, an ownership interest refunded to consumer-members as cash when the capital is retired.[338] Factors that cannot be evaluated because they are specific to each individual cooperative include (1) whether the revenues of the cooperative exceed its expenditures; (4) the particular objectives listed in a cooperative's articles of incorporation or other foundational document; (5) whether a nonprofit electric cooperative is exempt from federal income tax liability, which depends on whether it meets the requirements under Section 501(c)(12) of the Internal Revenue Code;[339] and (6) whether a cooperative would distribute its assets to profit-seeking entities upon dissolution—a factor that also may depend on state laws.[340]

It is likely that a court would find that nonprofit electric cooperatives impart economic benefits to their members by distributing electricity to them or, possibly, by issuing patronage capital to them. However, because many of the other factors that courts consider may differ for each particular cooperative, it is not possible to draw any general conclusions about whether the FTC would have Section 5 jurisdiction over these entities as "corporations."

Enforcement of Data Privacy and Security

If the FTC has Section 5 jurisdiction over a particular electric utility, it may bring an enforcement action against the utility if its privacy or security practices with regard to consumer smart meter data constitute "unfair or deceptive acts or practices in or affecting commerce."[341] The FTC Act defines an "unfair" act or practice as one that "causes or is likely to cause substantial injury to consumers which is not reasonably avoidable by consumers themselves and not outweighed by countervailing benefits to consumers or to competition."[342]

According to the FTC, an act or practice is "deceptive" if it is a material "representation, omission or practice" that is likely to mislead a consumer acting reasonably in the circumstances.[343] The history of the Commission's enforcement of consumer data privacy and security practices shows that the agency has brought complaints against entities that (1) engage in "deceptive" acts or practices by failing to comply with their stated privacy policies; or (2) employ "unfair" practices by failing to adequately secure consumer data from unauthorized parties.[344]

Often, conduct constituting a violation could fall under either category, as a failure to protect consumer data may be an unfair practice because of the unavoidable injury it causes, as well as a deceptive practice because it renders an entity's privacy policy materially misleading.

"Deceptive" Privacy Statements

A utility that fails to comply with its own privacy policy may engage in a "deceptive" act or practice under Section 5 of the FTC Act. In *Facebook, Inc.*, the FTC alleged, among other things, that the social networking site violated promises contained in its privacy policy when it made users' personal information accessible to third parties without users' consent.[345] Facebook had claimed that users could limit third-party access to their personal information on the site.

Despite this promise, applications run by users' Facebook friends were able to access the users' personal information. The Commission also charged that Facebook altered its privacy practices without users' consent, causing personal information that had been restricted by users to be available to third parties.

This change, which allegedly "caused harm to users, including, but not limited to, threats to their health and safety, and unauthorized revelation of their affiliations" constituted both a "deceptive" and an "unfair" practice in the view of the Commission.[346] Finally, the Commission alleged that Facebook had represented to users that it would not share their personal information with advertisers but had done so anyway.

In *Twitter, Inc.*, the FTC alleged that the social networking site engaged in "deceptive" acts when it violated claims made in its privacy policy about the security of consumer data by failing to "use reasonable and appropriate security measures to prevent unauthorized access to nonpublic user information." [347]

The Commission found that Twitter had permitted its administrators to access the site with easy-to-guess passwords and failed to limit the extent of administrators' access according to the requirements of their jobs. In a consent order, the company agreed not to misrepresent its privacy controls and to implement a comprehensive information security program that would be assessed by an independent third party.[348]

As smart meter data becomes valuable to third parties,[349] utilities may be tempted to sell or share this information with others to increase revenues and provide new services to their customers. If prohibited by the terms of the utility's privacy policy, it may be a "deceptive" act or practice for the utility to share a consumer's personal information with third parties without a consumer's consent.[350]

The FTC could also find deception when a utility represents that its privacy controls are capable of protecting smart meter data when, in fact, they are not.

"Unfair" Failure to Secure Consumer Data

Failure to Protect against Common Technology Threats or Unauthorized Access

The FTC may consider it an "unfair" practice when an electric utility fails to safeguard smart meter data from well-known technology threats as the data travels across the utility's communications networks. For example, in *DSW Inc.*, the FTC brought enforcement proceedings against the respondent, the owner of several shoe stores.[351] The agency alleged that the respondent failed to protect customers' credit card and check information as it was transmitted to the issuing bank for authorization. The information collected at the register traveled wirelessly to the store's computer network, and from there to the bank or check processor, which communicated its response back to the store through the same channels. The agency charged that

> [a]mong other things, respondent (1) created unnecessary risks to the information by storing it in multiple files when it no longer had a business need to keep the information; (2) did not use readily available security measures to limit access to its computer networks through wireless access points on the networks; (3) stored the information in unencrypted files that could be accessed easily by using a commonly known user ID and password; (4) did not limit sufficiently the ability of computers on one in-store network to connect to computers on other in-store and corporate networks; and (5) failed to employ sufficient measures to detect unauthorized access. As a result, a hacker could use the wireless access points on one in-store computer network to connect to, and access personal information, on the other in-store and corporate networks.[352]

Similarly, in *Cardsystems Solutions, Inc.*, the Commission brought a complaint against a credit and debit card authorization processor.[353] The FTC alleged that the respondent failed to protect its systems by neglecting to guard its network against "commonly known or reasonably foreseeable attacks" that could be avoided using low-cost methods.[354] As part of settlement agreements in *DSW* and *Cardsystems*, the respondents had to create "a comprehensive information security program" to protect consumer information that would be assessed periodically by an independent third party.[355]

Smart meters also transmit personal consumer information, often wirelessly, across several different communications networks located in various physical places.[356] Thus, it is possible that the FTC would view a utility's failure to protect smart meter data against common technology threats as an "unfair" practice if the utility could have avoided the threats by using low-cost methods such as encrypting the data; storing it in fewer places and for no longer than needed; implementing basic wireless network security; and taking other reasonable measures suggested by the agency in *DSW Inc.*

Failure to Dispose of Data Safely

A utility's failure to dispose of smart meter data safely may also constitute an "unfair" practice under Section 5. For example, in *Rite Aid Corp.*, the respondent, the owner of retail pharmacy stores, purportedly failed to safely dispose of personal information in its possession when it neglected to: "(1) implement policies and procedures to dispose securely of such information," including rendering "the information unreadable in the course of disposal; (2)

adequately train employees to dispose securely of such information; (3) use reasonable measures to assess compliance with its established policies and procedures for the disposal of such information; and (4) employ a reasonable process for discovering and remedying risks to such information."[357] The information was later found in various publicly accessible garbage dumpsters in readable form. This suggests that utilities holding smart meter data and other personal information, whether on electronic or physical media, must ensure that the methods used to destroy this data render it unreadable to third parties.

Penalties

There is no private right of action in the FTC Act. If the Commission has "reason to believe" that a violation has occurred, it may, after notice to the respondent and an opportunity for a hearing, issue an order directing the respondent to cease and desist from acts or practices that the agency finds violate the act.[358] If the respondent disobeys an order that has become final, the US Attorney General may bring an action in district court seeking the imposition of civil monetary penalties of up to $16,000 per violation ($16,000 per day for continuing violations), as well as further injunctive and equitable relief that the court deems appropriate.[359]

After a party becomes subject to a final cease and desist order under the act, the Commission may seek redress for consumers by bringing suit in state or federal court against the party if the Commission "satisfies the court that the act or practice to which the cease and desist order relates is one which a reasonable man would have known under the circumstances was dishonest or fraudulent."[360] "Such relief may include, but shall not be limited to, rescission or reformation of contracts, the refund of money or return of property, the payment of damages," and public notification of the violation, "except nothing in [15 USC. §57b(b)] is intended to authorize the imposition of any exemplary or punitive damages."[361] Once the Commission has issued a final cease and desist order (not a consent order) finding an act or practice to be deceptive, then it may bring suit in district court to obtain a civil penalty against an entity that engages in that act or practice: (1) after the order became final ("whether or not such person, partnership, or corporation was subject to such cease and desist order"); and (2) "with actual knowledge that such act or practice is unfair or deceptive and is unlawful" under Section 5 of the FTC Act.[362]

THE FEDERAL PRIVACY ACT OF 1974 (FPA)

Smart meter electricity usage data pertaining to US citizens or permanent residents that is retrievable by personal identifier from a system of records maintained by any federal "agency," including federally owned utilities, is subject to the protections contained in the Privacy Act[363] when it is maintained, collected, used, or disseminated by the agency.

Federally Owned Utilities as "Agencies"

All nine of the federally owned utilities are federal agencies covered by the Privacy Act. For the purposes of the act, the term "agency" includes, but is not limited to, "any executive department, military department, Government corporation, Government controlled corporation, or other establishment in the executive branch of the Government (including the Executive Office of the President), or any independent regulatory agency."[364] According to EIA, utilities that are part of an executive department include the four power marketing administrations in the Department of Energy (Bonneville, Southeastern, Southwestern, and Western), the International Boundary and Water Commission in the Department of State, and the Bureau of Indian Affairs and the Bureau of Reclamation in the Department of the Interior.[365] The US Army Corps of Engineers resides in the Department of Defense, which is an executive department.[366] The Tennessee Valley Authority is a government-owned corporation.[367]

Smart Meter Data as a Protected "Record"

The Privacy Act protects the type of electricity usage data gathered by smart meters, provided that the data pertains to US citizens or permanent residents, is personally identifiable, and is retrievable by the individual's name or another personal identifier. The Privacy Act "governs the collection, use, and dissemination of a 'record' about an 'individual' maintained by federal agencies in a 'system of records.'"[368] Under the statute, a "record" is "any item, collection, or grouping of information about an individual that is maintained by an agency ... that contains his name, or the identifying number, symbol, or other identifying particular assigned to the individual, such as a finger or voice print or a photograph."[369]

An "individual" is defined as "a citizen of the United States or an alien lawfully admitted for permanent residence."[370] A "system of records" is "a group of any records under the control of any agency from which information is retrieved by the name of the individual" or other personal identifier "assigned to the individual."[371]

Smart meter data held by an agency certainly fits within the broad definition of a "record" because it is a grouping of information about an individual, namely, data on that individual's electricity usage. The data is typically stored along with a consumer's account information, which usually includes a consumer's name, social security number, or other "identifying particular."[372] Thus, smart meter data would constitute a protected "record" under the Privacy Act, assuming that it pertains to a citizen of the United States or lawful permanent resident and is retrievable by a personal identifier such as a consumer's name or account number.

End Notes

[1] AMI includes the meters at the consumer's residence or business, the communications networks that send data between the consumer and utility, and the data management systems that store and process data for the utility. ELECTRIC POWER RESEARCH INST., ADVANCED METERING INFRASTRUCTURE (AMI) (2007), *available at* http://www. ferc.gov/eventcalendar/Files/20070423091846-EPRI%20-%20Advanced% 20 Metering. pdf. The primary function of AMI is to "combine interval data measurement with continuously available remote communications" to increase energy efficiency and grid reliability, and decrease expenses borne by the utility and consumer. *Id.*

[2] The Energy Independence and Security Act of 2007 (EISA) lists ten characteristics of a smart grid. These include "[i]ncreased use of digital information and controls technology to improve reliability, security, and efficiency of the electric grid"; "[d]evelopment and incorporation of demand response, demand-side resources, and energy-efficiency resources"; and "[d]eployment of "smart" technologies (real-time, automated, interactive technologies that optimize the physical operation of appliances and consumer devices) for metering, communications concerning grid operations and status, and distribution automation." EISA, P.L. 110-140, §1301, 121 Stat. 1492, 1783-84 (2007) (to be codified at 42 U.S.C. §17381).

[3] DEP'T OF ENERGY, COMMUNICATIONS REQUIREMENTS OF SMART GRID TECHNOLOGIES 1 (2010) [hereinafter DEP'T OF ENERGY COMMUNICATIONS REPORT], *available at* http://energy.gov/sites/prod/files/gcprod/documents/ Smart_Grid_ Communications_Requirements_Report_10-05-2010.pdf.

[4] *Id.* at 3, 5. These technologies include fiber optics, wireless networks, satellite, and broadband over power line. *Id.*

[5] *Id.* at 20. "Demand response is the reduction of the consumption of electric energy by customers in response to an increase in the price of electricity or heavy burdens on the system." *Id.*

[6] DEP'T OF ENERGY, DATA ACCESS AND PRIVACY ISSUES RELATED TO SMART GRID TECHNOLOGIES 5, 9 (2010) [hereinafter DEP'T OF ENERGY PRIVACY REPORT], *available at* http://energy.gov/sites/prod/files/gcprod/documents/ Broadband_ Report_Data_Privacy_10_5.pdf; *see also* ELIAS LEAKE QUINN, SMART METERING & PRIVACY: EXISTING LAW AND COMPETING POLICIES: A REPORT FOR THE COLORADO PUBLIC UTILITIES COMMISSION 1, 12 (2009) [hereinafter COLORADO PRIVACY REPORT], *available at* http://www.dora.state.co.us /puc/ docketsdecisions/ DocketFilings/09I593EG/09I-593EG_Spring2009Report-SmartGridPrivacy.pdf.

[7] DEP'T OF ENERGY COMMUNICATIONS REPORT, *supra* note 3, at 12.

[8] Companies are developing several new applications that use smart meter data to offer consumers and utilities better control over energy usage, for example by determining the energy efficiency of specific appliances within the household. DEP'T OF ENERGY PRIVACY REPORT, *supra* note 6, at 5, 9; *see also* COLORADO PRIVACY REPORT, *supra* note 6, at 1, 12.

[9] DEP'T OF ENERGY COMMUNICATIONS REPORT, *supra* note 3, at 1.

[10] *Id.* at 3.

[11] *See* NAT'L INST. OF STANDARDS AND TECH., GUIDELINES FOR SMART GRID CYBER SECURITY: VOL. 2, PRIVACY AND THE SMART GRID 14 (2010) [hereinafter NIST PRIVACY REPORT], *available at* http://csrc.nist.gov/publications/nistir/ ir7628/nistir-7628_vol2.pdf.

[12] *Id.* at 3-4, 23-24, 29.

[13] The act provides $4.5 billion for "electricity delivery and energy reliability," which includes "activities to modernize the electric grid, to include demand responsive equipment," as well as "programs authorized under title XIII of the Energy Independence and Security Act of 2007." ARRA, P.L. 111-5, 123 Stat. 115, 138-39.

[14] ARRA §405(5), (8), 123 Stat. 115, 143-44 (amendment to be codified at 42 U.S.C. §17386) (amending the Energy Independence and Security Act of 2007 (EISA) to allow for the reimbursement of up to 50% of qualifying smart grid investments instead of only 20%); *see also* EISA, P.L. 110-140, §1306, 121 Stat. 1492, 1789-91 (to be codified as amended at 42 U.S.C. §17386) (initially establishing the SGIG program).

[15] FED. ENERGY REGULATORY COMM'N, ASSESSMENT OF DEMAND RESPONSE & ADVANCED METERING 3 (2011), *available at* http://www.ferc.gov/legal/staff-reports/11-07-11-demand-response.pdf.

[16] *Id.*

[17] INST. FOR ELECTRIC EFFICIENCY, UTILITY-SCALE SMART METER DEPLOY MENTS, PLANS & PROPOSALS 1 (2011), *available at* http://www. Edison foundation.net/iee/issuebriefs/ SmartMeter_ Rollouts_0911.pdf.

[18] For additional information on the development of mandatory national smart grid privacy and cybersecurity standards by federal agencies, see MASS. INST. OF TECH., THE FUTURE OF THE ELECTRIC GRID 197-234 (2011) [hereinafter MIT GRID STUDY]; *see also* CRS Report R41886, *The Smart Grid and Cybersecurity—Regulatory Policy and Issues*, by Richard J. Campbell.

[19] According to the authors of the MIT study, cybersecurity "refers to all the approaches taken to protect data, systems, and networks from deliberate attack as well as accidental compromise, ranging from preparedness to recovery." MIT GRID STUDY, *supra* note 18, at 208. Closely related is the concept of "information privacy," which "deals with policy issues ranging from identification and collection to storage, access, and use of information." *Id.* at 219 n.viii.

[20] *See* NIST PRIVACY REPORT, *supra* note 11, at 1.

[21] *Id.* at 4, 11. Data that offers a high degree of detail is said to be "granular." *Id.*

[22] *See id.* at 4, 23-24, 29.

[23] *Id.* at 2, 9.
[24] *Id.* at 13.
[25] COLORADO PRIVACY REPORT, *supra* note 6, at 2. Some utilities may elect to receive data at less frequent intervals because "backhauling real-time or near real-time data from the billions of devices that may eventually be connected to the Smart Grid would require not only tremendous bandwidth" but also greater data storage capacities that could make the effort "economically infeasible." DEP'T OF ENERGY COMMUNICATIONS REPORT, *supra* note 3, at 20. However, the "trend" is for utilities to collect data more frequently. *See* COLORADO PRIVACY REPORT, *supra* note 6, at A-1 n.111.
[26] NIST PRIVACY REPORT, *supra* note 11, at 2, 14.
[27] *Id.* at 14. *But see* DEP'T OF ENERGY PRIVACY REPORT, *supra* note 6, at 9 (claiming, in 2010, that smart meter technology "cannot yet identify individual appliances and devices in the home in detail, but this will certainly be within the capabilities of subsequent generations of Smart Grid technologies").
[28] COLORADO PRIVACY REPORT, *supra* note 6, at 3 n.7, A-8.
[29] *Id.* at A-9.
[30] NIST PRIVACY REPORT, *supra* note 11, at 6 & n.9.
[31] *Id.* at 11.
[32] DEP'T OF ENERGY PRIVACY REPORT, *supra* note 6, at 2.
[33] NIST PRIVACY REPORT, *supra* note 11, at 11, 29; *see also* United States v. Kyllo, 190 F.3d 1041, 1043 (9th Cir. 1999), *rev'd on other grounds*, 533 U.S. 27 (2001).
[34] *Kyllo*, 190 F.3d at 1043.
[35] *See supra* notes 26-32 and accompanying text.
[36] *See supra* note 32 and accompanying text.
[37] NIST PRIVACY REPORT, *supra* note 11, at 14, 35-36.
[38] *Id.* at 27-28.
[39] *Id.* at 28.
[40] *Id.* at 31.
[41] *Id.*
[42] *Id.* at 13.
[43] *See id.* at 13, 25.
[44] *Id.* at 26-27.
[45] *Id.* at 12 (drawing a comparison to telecommunications providers' "call detail records").
[46] *Id.* at 3; DEP'T OF ENERGY COMMUNICATIONS REPORT, *supra* note 3, at 3 (stating that "integrated two-way communications ... allows for dynamic monitoring of electricity use as well as the potential for automated electricity use scheduling."). As more consumers become generators of electricity through the use of "fuel cells, wind turbines, solar roofs, and the like," the importance of two-way communication will increase. MIT GRID STUDY, *supra* note 18, at 201.
[47] DEP'T OF ENERGY COMMUNICATIONS REPORT, *supra* note 3, at 3.
[48] *Id.* at 5, 51 n.215.
[49] *Id.* at 16.
[50] *Id.*
[51] The home network will be used to provide *consumers* with near real-time data on their energy usage. *Id.* at 13-15.
[52] *Id.* Many urban installations use wireless mesh networks to carry data from the meters to the aggregation point. These networks are more reliable because each smart meter can serve as a router in the network, providing redundant network coverage. *Id.* at 18.
[53] *Id.* at 16, 19.
[54] *Id.* at 4, 19, 44.
[55] NIST PRIVACY REPORT, *supra* note 11, at 23.
[56] *Id.* at 23-24.
[57] *Id.* at 29.
[58] *See id.* at 9, 12, 33, and 36.
[59] MIT GRID STUDY, *supra* note 18, at 209, 213-16.
[60] Jack I. Lerner & Deirdre K. Mulligan, *Taking the "Long View" on the Fourth Amendment: Stored Records and the Sanctity of the Home*, 2008 STAN. TECH. L. REV. 3, ¶ 3 (2008).
[61] Additionally, as described below, there are federal statutory protections that may pertain to this data. State constitutional and statutory safeguards may also apply, but these are beyond the scope of this report.
[62] U.S. CONST. amend IV.

[63] For additional analyses of smart meters under the Fourth Amendment, see Cheryl Dancey Balough, *Privacy Implications of Smart Meters*, 86 CHI.-KENT L. REV. 161 (2011); *see also* QUINN, *supra* note 6, at 28 ("[I]nterval data of electricity consumption appears to be in something of a no-man's-land under Supreme Court Fourth Amendment jurisprudence.").

[64] California v. Ciraolo, 476 U.S. 207, 211 (1986) (citing Katz v. United States, 389 U.S. 347, 360 (1967) (Harlan, J., concurring)).

[65] Civil Rights Cases, 109 U.S. 3, 11 (1883) ("It is State action of a particular character that is prohibited. Individual invasion of individual rights is not the subject-matter of the [Fourteenth] amendment."); *see* JOHN E. NOWAK & RONALD D. ROTUNDA, CONSTITUTIONAL LAW §12.1(a)(i) (8th ed. 2010).

[66] NOWAK & ROTUNDA, *supra* note 65.

[67] Determining whether a private actor is sufficiently "public" is not clear-cut. Then Justice Rehnquist noted, "[t]he true nature of the State's involvement may not be immediately obvious, and detailed inquiry may be required in order to determine whether the test is met." Jackson v. Metropolitan Edison Co., 419 U.S. 345, 351 (1974).

[68] Burdeau v. McDowell, 256 U.S. 465, 475 (1921).

[69] *See* United States v. Jacobsen, 466 U.S. 109, 113 (1984).

[70] Marsh v. Alabama, 326 U.S. 501 (1946) (holding that privately owned property was equivalent to "community shopping center" thus private party was subject to the First and Fourteenth Amendments).

[71] *See* NOWAK & ROTUNDA, *supra* note 65, §12.2.

[72] *Jackson*, 419 U.S. at 347; *see also* Mays v. Buckeye Rural Elec. Coop., Inc., 277 F.3d 873, 880-81 (6th Cir. 2002) (holding that nonprofit cooperative utility was not a state actor under the federal constitution); Spickler v. Lee, No. 02- 1954, 2003 U.S. App. LEXIS 6227, at *2 (1st Cir. March 31, 2003) (holding that private electric utility company was not a state actor).

[73] *Jackson*, 419 U.S. at 351.

[74] *Id.* at 358-59.

[75] *Id.* at 353.

[76] *Id.* at 357.

[77] *Id.* at 351.

[78] 1 WAYNE R. LAFAVE, SEARCH AND SEIZURE §1.8, at 255 (4th ed. 2004).

[79] United States v. Howard, 752 F.2d 220, 227-28 (6th Cir. 1985).

[80] Coolidge v. New Hampshire, 403 U.S. 443, 487 (1971) (internal quotation marks omitted); *see* LAFAVE, *supra* note 78, §1.8(b).

[81] United States v. Manning, 542 F.2d 685, 686 (6th Cir. 1976).

[82] People of Dearborn Heights v. Hayes, 82 Mich. App. 253, 258 (1978).

[83] United States v. Davis, 482 F.2d 893, 897-903 (9th Cir. 1973).

[84] *Id.* at 895.

[85] *Id.* at 904.

[86] United States v. Howard, 752 F.2d 220, 228 (6th Cir. 1985).

[87] *The Supreme Court, 1986-Term—Leading Cases*, 101 HARV. L. REV. 119, 230 (1987).

[88] United States v. Attson, 900 F.2d 1427, 1430 (9th Cir. 1990) (emphasis in original).

[89] Ferguson v. City of Charleston, 532 U.S. 67, 77-78 (2001).

[90] Skinner v. Ry. Labor Executives' Ass'n, 489 U.S. 602, 620 (1989) (quoting Griffin v. Wisconsin, 483 U.S. 868, 873 (1987)).

[91] *Id.*

[92] Nat'l Treasury Employees Union v. Von Raab, 489 U.S. 656, 670 (1989).

[93] *Ferguson*, 532 U.S. at 83 (emphasis in original).

[94] *See* United States v. Attson, 900 F.2d 1427, 1431 (9th Cir. 1990); Poe v. Leonard, 282 F.3d 123, 137 (2d Cir. 2002); United States v. Elliot, 676 F. Supp. 2d 431, 435-36 (D. Md. 2009).

[95] *Attson*, 900 F.2d at 1433.

[96] *Id.*

[97] *See* Nilson v. Layton City, 45 F.3d 369, 372 (10th Cir. 1995) ("Information readily available to the public is not protected by the constitutional right to privacy."); Doe v. City of New York, 15 F.3d 264, 268 (2d Cir. 1994) ("Certainly, there is no question that an individual cannot expect to have a constitutionally protected privacy interest in matters of public record."); United States v. Ellison, 462 F.3d 557, 562 (6th Cir. 2006) (accessing license plate number from computer database held not an intrusion of a constitutionally protected area, thus not a Fourth Amendment "search"); United States v. Baxter, 492 F.2d 150, 167 (9th Cir. 1973) (holding that Fourth Amendment protections do not extend to telephone company toll and billing records); *see also*

Christopher Slobogin, *The Search and Seizure of Computers and Electronic Evidence: Transaction Surveillance by the Government*, 75 MISS. L. J. 139, 156 (2005).

[98] Slobogin, *supra* note 97.

[99] Because the focus of this report is federal law and the Fourth Amendment, a full treatment of state privacy law is beyond its scope.

[100] *In re* Public Records—Records of Municipally Operated Utility, Op. Att'y Gen. Fla. 74-35 (1974), *available at* http://www.myfloridalegal.com/ago.nsf/ Opinions/B4AED736C2272 860852566B30067371A; *see* FLA. STAT. §119.01(1) (2008) ("It is the policy of this state that all state, county, and municipal records are open for personal inspection by any person.").

[101] *See* GA. CODE ANN. §50-18-70(b) (2011); Op. Att'y Gen. Ga. 2000-4 (2000) (requiring personal utility records of certain public employees to be disclosed under public records law). Georgia defines a "public record" as "all documents, papers, letters, maps, books, tapes, photographs, computer based or generated information, or similar material prepared and maintained or received in the course of the operation of a public office or agency." GA. CODE ANN. §50-18-70(a).

[102] In South Carolina, public records include "information in or taken from any account, voucher, or contract dealing with the receipt or expenditure of public or other funds by public bodies." S.C. CODE ANN. §30-4-50 (2011). *See* Kelsey M. Swanson, *The Right to Know: An Approach to Gun Licenses and Public Access to Government Records*, 56 UCLA L. REV. 1579, 1601 (2009).

[103] OKLA. STAT. tit. 51, §24A.10 (2011).

[104] *Id.*

[105] WASH. REV. CODE §42.56.335 (2011). In Washington, the following rule applies to public utility districts and municipally owned electrical utilities: A law enforcement authority may not request inspection or copying of records of any person who belongs to a public utility district or a municipally owned electrical utility unless the authority provides the public utility district or municipally owned electrical utility with a written statement in which the authority states that it suspects that the particular person to whom the records pertain has committed a crime and the authority has a reasonable belief that the records could determine or help determine whether the suspicion might be true. Information obtained in violation of this section is inadmissible in any criminal proceeding. WASH. REV. CODE §42.56.335. The Washington Supreme Court has raised this protection to state constitutional status in *In re* Personal Restraint of Maxfield, 133 Wash. 2d 332, 344 (1997).

[106] However, the North Carolina public records law declares that "[n]othing contained herein is intended to limit public disclosure by a city or county of bill information: ... that is necessary to assist law enforcement, public safety, fire protection, rescue, emergency management, or judicial officers in the performance of their duties." N.C. GEN. STAT. §132-1.1(c)(3).

[107] Katz v. United States, 389 U.S. 347, 361 (1967) (Harlan, J., concurring).

[108] *See* Smith v. Maryland, 442 U.S. 735 (1979).

[109] *Id.*

[110] United States v. Miller, 425 U.S. 435 (1976).

[111] Kyllo v. United States, 533 U.S. 27, 33-4 (2001) ("It would be foolish to contend that the degree of privacy secured to citizens by the Fourth Amendment has been entirely unaffected by the advance of technology.").

[112] *See* Entick v. Carrington, 19 How. St. Tr. 1029 (C.P. 1765).

[113] Katz v. United States, 389 U.S. 347, 351 (1967).

[114] *See* Orin S. Kerr, *The Fourth Amendment and New Technologies: Constitutional Myths and the Case for Caution*, 102 MICH. L. REV. 801, 809-10 (2004) [hereinafter Kerr, *Fourth Amendment and New Technologies*].

[115] Orin S. Kerr, *The Case for a Third-Party Doctrine*, 107 MICH. L. REV. 561, 563 (2009) [hereinafter Kerr, *Third-Party Doctrine*]. While the third-party doctrine has supporters like Professor Kerr, this group is overshadowed by its vocal detractors. Professor LaFave described its underpinnings as "dead wrong" and that the "Court's woefully inadequate reasoning does great violence to the theory of Fourth Amendment protection which the Court developed in *Katz*." LAFAVE, *supra* note 78, §2.7(c). Justice Sotomayor lent credence to this sentiment in *United States v. Jones*, where she posited that it "may be necessary to reconsider the premise that an individual has no reasonable expectation of privacy in information voluntarily disclosed to third parties." United States v. Jones, 565 U.S. ___, 5 (Sotomayor, J., concurring in the judgment and the opinion).

[116] United States v. White, 401 U.S. 745, 750 (1971) (holding that the Fourth Amendment "affords no protection to a wrongdoer's misplaced belief that a person to whom he voluntarily confides his wrongdoing will not reveal it.") (internal quotation marks omitted).

[117] Smith v. Maryland, 442 U.S. 735 (1979).

[118] United States v. Miller, 425 U.S. 435 (1976).
[119] United States v. Willis, 759 F.2d 1486, 1498 (11th Cir. 1985).
[120] United States v. Hynson, No. 05-576, 2007 WL 2692327, at *6 (E.D. Pa. Sept. 11, 2007).
[121] *Smith*, 442 U.S. at 744.
[122] Kerr, *Third-Party Doctrine*, *supra* note 115.
[123] United States v. McIntyre, 646 F.3d 1107 (8th Cir. 2011).
[124] *Miller*, 425 U.S. at 437-438.
[125] Brief for Respondent at 4, *Miller*, 425 U.S. 435 (No. 74-1179), 1975 WL 173642, at *4 ("The Fourth Amendment is historically rooted in a concern for control over personal and private information in the face of governmental demands for access and use.") (citing Entick v. Carrington, 19 How. St. Tr. 1029 (C.P. 1765)).
[126] *Miller*, 425 U.S. at 443.
[127] *Id.*
[128] Smith v. Maryland, 442 U.S. 735 (1979).
[129] *Id.* at 737.
[130] *Id.*
[131] *Id.*
[132] *Id.* at 743-44.
[133] *Id.* at 744.
[134] United States v. Starkweather, No. 91-30354, 1992 WL 204005, at *2 (9th Cir. Aug. 24, 1992).
[135] *Id.*
[136] United States v. McIntyre, 646 F.3d 1107 (8th Cir. 2011).
[137] *Id.* at 1111.
[138] *Id.*
[139] United States v. Hamilton, 434 F. Supp. 2d 974, 980 (D. Or. 2006); Booker v. Dominion Va. Power, No. 3:09-759, 2010 U.S. Dist. LEXIS 44960, at *17 (E.D. Va. May 7, 2010); *see also* Samson v. State, 919 P.2d 171, 173 (Ala. App. 1996) (holding under state constitution that "utility records are maintained by the utility and do not constitute information in which society is prepared to recognize a reasonable expectation of privacy"); People v. Stanley, 86 Cal. Rptr. 2d 89, 94 (Cal. App. 1999) (same).
[140] *See* Duncan Kennedy, *Form and Substance in Private Law Adjudication*, 89 HARV. L. REV. 1687, 1710 (1976).
[141] Kerr, *Third-Party Doctrine*, *supra* note 115, at 564.
[142] In *Smith*, the "site of the call was immaterial for purposes of analysis" of that case. Smith v. Maryland, 442 U.S. 735, 743 (1979). Whether a person dials a telephone number from his home, a telephone booth, or any other location does not alter the nature of the activity, and thus does not affect the Fourth Amendment analysis. The privacy interests implicated are the same no matter where the call is placed. The same theory applies to bank records. It matters not where someone writes a check, or fills out a deposit slip—the privacy interest is the same.
[143] Payton v. New York, 445 U.S. 573, 589 ("The Fourth Amendment protects the individual's privacy in a variety of settings. In none is the zone of privacy more clearly defined than when bounded by the unambiguous physical dimensions of an individual's home—a zone that finds its roots in clear and specific constitutional terms: 'The right of the people to be secure in their ... houses ... shall not be violated.'") (quoting U.S. CONST. amend IV); Minnesota v. Carter, 525 U.S. 83, 99 (1998) (Kennedy, J., concurring) ("[I]t is beyond dispute that the home is entitled to special protection as the center of the private lives of our people. Security of the home must be guarded by law in a world where privacy is diminished by enhanced surveillance and sophisticated communication systems.").
[144] Silverman v. United States, 365 U.S. 505, 511 (1961).
[145] In April 2012, the Supreme Court will hear oral arguments in its most recent home privacy case, Jardines v. Florida, 73 So. 3d 34 (Fla. 2011), *cert granted*, 2012 U.S. LEXIS 7 (Jan. 6, 2012) (No. 11-564), where it will decide whether a drug sniff at the front door of a suspect's house by a trained narcotics dog is a Fourth Amendment search requiring probable cause. This case should shed further light on the parameters of privacy surrounding the home.
[146] Kyllo v. United States, 533 U.S. 27, 29 (2001).
[147] *Id.*
[148] *Id.*
[149] *Id.*
[150] *Id.* at 29-30.
[151] *Id.* at 30.

[152] *Id.*
[153] *Id.*
[154] *Id.* The Ninth Circuit held that Kyllo had not exhibited a subjective expectation of privacy in the home because he did not attempt to prevent the heat emitting from the lamps from escaping his home. United States v. Kyllo, 190 F.3d 1041, 1046 (9th Cir. 1999). Further, the panel held that even if he had a subjective expectation of privacy, it was not a reasonable one since the imager "did not expose any intimate details of Kyllo's life." *Id.* at 1047.
[155] *Kyllo*, 533 U.S. at 31.
[156] *See* Olmstead v. United States, 277 U.S. 438 (1928).
[157] Katz v. United States, 389 U.S. 347, 361 (1967) (Harlan, J., concurring). The modern formulation of the reasonable expectation of privacy test derives not from the majority opinion but from Justice Harlan's concurrence.
[158] *Kyllo*, 533 U.S. at 34.
[159] *Id.* (internal quotation marks omitted).
[160] Lerner & Mulligan, *supra* note 60, ¶ 18.
[161] United States v. Karo, 468 U.S. 705 (1984).
[162] *Id.* at 708.
[163] *Id.*
[164] *Id.* at 709-10.
[165] *Id.*
[166] *Id.* at 714.
[167] *Id.* at 714-15.
[168] *Id.* at 718.
[169] Stephanie M. Stern, *The Inviolate Home: Housing Exceptionalism in the Fourth Amendment*, 95 CORNELL L. REV. 905, 913 (2010) (citing Wilson v. Layne, 526 U.S. 603, 612 (1999)).
[170] United States v. Kyllo, 533 U.S. 27, 30 (2001).
[171] *Karo*, 468 U.S. at 705, 709-10.
[172] NIST PRIVACY REPORT, *supra* note 11, at 14 & n.35. It is unclear whether the specificity of the data from the smart meter will directly affect the constitutional analysis. *Kyllo*, 533 U.S. at 37 ("The *Fourth Amendment's* protection of the home has never been tied to measurement of the quality or quantity of information obtained."). With that said, the NIST report maintains that sufficient information about the activities inside of the home are presented to implicate a *Kyllo*, home search analysis.
[173] *Kyllo*, 533 U.S. at 34.
[174] *See* Douglas Adkins, *The Supreme Court Announces a Fourth Amendment "General Public Use" Standard for Emerging Technologies but Fails to Define It:* Kyllo v. United States, 27 DAYTON L. REV. 245 (2002).
[175] *See* United States v. Dellas, 355 F. Supp. 2d 1095, 1107 (N.D. Cal. 2005).
[176] United States v. Vela, 486 F. Supp. 2d 587, 590 (W.D. Tex. 2005).
[177] DEP'T OF ENERGY, SMART GRID SYSTEM REPORT vi (2009), *available at* http:// energy.gov/sites/prod/ files/oeprod/ DocumentsandMedia/SGSRMain_090707_lowres.pdf
[178] *Id.*
[179] United States v. Kyllo, 533 U.S. 27, 29 (2001).
[180] United States v. McIntyre, 646 F.3d 1107, 1111-12 (8th Cir. 2011).
[181] *See* Cent. Intelligence Agency v. Sims, 471 U.S. 159, 178 (1985).
[182] *See* Orin Kerr, VOLOKH CONSPIRACY, What's the Status of the Mosaic Theory After Jones?, http://volokh.com/2012/01/23/whats-the-status-of-the-mosaic-theory-after-jones/.
[183] United States v. Jones, 565 U.S. ___, 2 (2012).
[184] *Id.* at 3.
[185] *Id.* at 4.
[186] *Id.* at 13 (Alito, J., concurring in the judgment).
[187] *Id.* at 3 (Sotomayor, J., concurring in the judgment and the opinion).
[188] United States v. Maynard, 615 F.3d 544, 562 (D.C. Cir. 2010).
[189] *Id.* at 558.
[190] United States v. Knotts, 460 U.S. 276, 283-84 (1983). Because this statement was not essential to the holding, it was dictum: persuasive, but not binding.
[191] *Smith*, 442 U.S at 741 (citing Katz v. United States, 389 U.S. 347 (1967)).
[192] *Katz*, 389 U.S. at 348.

[193] *Smith*, 442 U.S. at 744 (citing United States v. Miller, 425 U.S. 435 (1976)).

[194] Kerr, *Third-Party Doctrine*, *supra* note 115, at 588.

[195] *Contra Smith*, 442 U.S. at 750 (Marshall, J., dissenting) ("[U]nless a person is prepared to forgo use of what for many has become a personal or professional necessity, he cannot help but accept the risk of surveillance. It is idle to speak of "assuming" the risk in contexts where, as a practical matter, individuals have no realistic alternative.").

[196] *In re* Restraint of Maxfield, 133 Wn.2d 332, 341 (Wash. 1997); *see also* Balough, *supra* note 63, at 185.

[197] *Cf.* United States v. Warshak, 631 F.3d 266, 288 (6th Cir. 2010) ("*Miller* involved simple business records, as opposed to the potentially unlimited variety of 'confidential communications' at issue here.").

[198] Kerr, *Fourth Amendment and New Technologies*, *supra* note 114, at 806.

[199] For more detailed information on ECPA, *see* CRS Report R41733, *Privacy: An Overview of the Electronic Communications Privacy Act*, by Charles Doyle.

[200] For a more detailed discussion of the SCA, *see* CRS Report R41733, *Privacy: An Overview of the Electronic Communications Privacy Act*, by Charles Doyle.

[201] For more detailed information on the CFAA, *see* CRS Report 97-1025, *Cybercrime: An Overview of the Federal Computer Fraud and Abuse Statute and Related Federal Criminal Laws*, by Charles Doyle.

[202] S.Rept. 99-541 at 3.

[203] 18 U.S.C. §2510(12).

[204] *See supra* note 47 and accompanying text (noting that smart meters may use a variety of communications technologies, including fiber optics, wireless networks, satellite, and broadband over power line).

[205] 18 U.S.C. §2516. Exceptions cover things such as interception with the consent of a party to the communication and interception by communication service providers as an incident to providing service.

[206] 18 U.S.C. §2511(2)(f). FISA defines electronic surveillance to include more than the interception of wire, oral, or electronic communications, 50 U.S.C. §1801(f), but places limitations on its definition based upon the location or identity of some or all of the parties to the communications involved.

[207] "Except as provided in (b) of this subsection or in subsection (5), whoever violates subsection (1) of this section shall be fined under this title or imprisoned not more than five years, or both." 18 U.S.C. §2511(4)(a).

[208] 18 U.S.C. §2511(2)(c).

[209] The list of covered criminal provisions can be found at 18 U.S.C. §2516(1), and includes offenses such as violence at international airports; animal enterprise terrorism; arson; bribery of public officials and witnesses; unlawful use of explosives; fraud by wire, radio, or television; terrorist attacks against mass transportation; sexual exploitation of children; narcotics production and trafficking; and many others.

[210] 18 U.S.C. §§2516, 2518(3).

[211] 18 U.S.C. §2517.

[212] 18 U.S.C. §2518(8).

[213] 18 U.S.C. §2518(7).

[214] *See* 50 U.S.C. §1801(a) (definition of "foreign power").

[215] For example, it extends to the collection of information necessary for the conduct of foreign affairs. *See* 50 U.S.C. §1801(e) (definition of "foreign intelligence information").

[216] 50 U.S.C. §1805(e).

[217] 50 U.S.C. §§1801-1808. FISA authorizes electronic surveillance without a FISA order in specified instances involving communications between foreign powers. 50 U.S.C. §1802.

[218] P.L. 99-508.

[219] S.Rept. 99-541 at 3.

[220] 18 U.S.C. §2701(a). Unauthorized access includes exceeding an authorization to use the facility. *Id.*

[221] 18 U.S.C. §2702.

[222] 18 U.S.C. §2703.

[223] 18 U.S.C. §2510(15).

[224] 18 U.S.C. §2510(12). Wire communications are defined as communications containing the human voice and are not implicated here. 18 U.S.C. §2510(1).

[225] *See supra* note 47 and accompanying text.

[226] Company v. United States (*In re* United States), 349 F.3d 1132, 1141 (9th Cir. 2003) (holding that definition of ECS includes service that provides drivers with the ability to make phone calls from their car for directory assistance, driving directions, or roadside assistance because those activities are intrinsically communicative).

[227] *See supra* note 8.

[228] 18 U.S.C. §2701.

229 18 U.S.C. §2510(17).
230 18 U.S.C. §2701(a). Unauthorized access includes exceeding an authorization to use the facility. *Id.*
231 18 U.S.C. §2701(b)(2).
232 18 U.S.C. §2701(b)(1).
233 18 U.S.C. §2707.
234 18 U.S.C. §2702(a)(1) ("a person or entity providing an electronic communication service to the public shall not knowingly divulge to any person or entity the contents of a communication while in electronic storage by that service").
235 18 U.S.C. §2702(b)(7).
236 *See* 18 U.S.C. §2702(b)(3).
237 18 U.S.C. §2703(a).
238 18 U.S.C. §2703(d). Some courts have held that this "reasonable grounds" standard is a less demanding standard than "probable cause." *See In re* Application of the United States, 620 F.3d 304, 313 (3d Cir. 2010) ("We also conclude that this [§2703(d)] standard is a lesser one than probable cause.").
239 18 U.S.C. §2705(a).
240 18 U.S.C. §2711(2).
241 However, if some other service provided by the utility allows the data collected by a smart meter to be stored or manipulated for the benefit of the utility's customers, it is possible that this system would fall within the definition of an RCS.
242 The SCA allows providers of an RCS to disclose stored communications with the consent of the subscriber of an RCS. 18 U.S.C. §2702(b)(3).
243 18 U.S.C. §2703(b)(1).
244 18 U.S.C. §2703(b)(1)(B).
245 18 U.S.C. §2707.
246 18 U.S.C. §1030(a)(2). For more detailed information on the CFAA, *see* CRS Report 97-1025, *Cybercrime: An Overview of the Federal Computer Fraud and Abuse Statute and Related Federal Criminal Laws*, by Charles Doyle.
247 18 U.S.C. §1030(e)(1).
248 18 U.S.C. §1030(c)(2)(A).
249 18 U.S.C. §1030(c)(2)(B).
250 18 U.S.C. §§1030(c), 3571.
251 15 U.S.C. §45(a)(1).
252 15 U.S.C. §45(a)(2).
253 *See* "Enforcement of Data Privacy and Security," *infra* p. 41; *see also* NIST PRIVACY REPORT, *supra* note 11, at 23 n.48.
254 ENERGY INFO. ADMIN., ELECTRIC POWER INDUSTRY OVERVIEW (2007) [hereinafter EIA ELECTRIC POWER OVERVIEW], *available at* http://www.eia. gov/ cneaf/electricity/page/prim2/toc2.html.
255 15 U.S.C. §45(a)(2).
256 The FTC Act does not further define "persons" or "partnerships" or impose any additional jurisdictional requirements on these entities in the way that it does for "corporations." *See* 15 U.S.C. §44.
257 15 U.S.C. §44.
258 Cal. Dental Ass'n v. FTC, 526 U.S. 756, 768 (1999) (emphasis added) (internal quotation marks omitted).
259 *Id.* at 766-69.
260 EIA ELECTRIC POWER OVERVIEW, *supra* note 254.
261 Indeed, the FTC has asserted Section 5 jurisdiction over holding companies with investor-owned electric utility subsidiaries in the past. *See, e.g., DTE Energy Co.*, 131 F.T.C. 962 (May 15, 2001) (complaint); *CMS Energy Corp.*, 127 F.T.C. 827 (June 2, 1999) (complaint). *See also In re* DTE Energy Co., FTC File No. 001 0067 (May 15, 2001) (consent order); *In re* CMS Energy Corp., FTC File No. 991 0046 (June 2, 1999) (consent order).
262 EIA ELECTRIC POWER OVERVIEW, *supra* note 254.
263 *Id.*
264 DAVID E. MCNABB, PUBLIC UTILITIES: MANAGEMENT CHALLENGES FOR THE 21ST CENTURY 165 (2005).
265 EIA ELECTRIC POWER OVERVIEW, *supra* note 254.
266 MCNABB, *supra* note 264, at 165.
267 EIA ELECTRIC POWER OVERVIEW, *supra* note 254.

[268] MCNABB, *supra* note 264, at 165.

[269] In contrast to entities that are "corporations," the FTC does not have to show that entities qualifying as "persons" are organized for profit. *See* 15 U.S.C. §44.

[270] *In re* City of Minneapolis, 105 F.T.C. 304 (May 7, 1985) (order withdrawing complaint); *In re* City of New Orleans, 105 F.T.C. 1 (Jan. 3, 1985) (order withdrawing complaint).

[271] *In re* N.C. State Bd. of Dental Exam'rs, 151 F.T.C. 607 (Feb. 3, 2011) (state action opinion); *In re* South Carolina State Bd. of Dentistry, 138 F.T.C. 229 (Sept. 12, 2003) (complaint).

[272] *In re* Mass. Board of Registration in Optometry, 110 F.T.C. 549 (June 13, 1988) (decision).

[273] *In re* Va. Bd. of Funeral Dirs. & Embalmers, 138 F.T.C. 645 (Oct. 1, 2004) (complaint).

[274] 910 F.2d 976, 979 (D.C. Cir. 1990).

[275] *Id.* at 978.

[276] *Id.* at 978-79.

[277] *Id.* at 980, 982.

[278] *See* Cal. Dental Ass'n v. FTC, 526 U.S. 756, 765-66 (1999) ("Respondent urges deference to this interpretation of the Commission's jurisdiction as reasonable. But we have no occasion to review the call for deference here, the interpretation urged in respondent's brief being clearly the better reading of the statute under ordinary principles of construction.") (internal citations omitted); *see also* Chevron U.S.A., Inc. v. NRDC, Inc., 467 U.S. 837, 842-43 (1984).

[279] 1 U.S.C. §1 (emphasis added).

[280] *See* 15 U.S.C. §44.

[281] *Chevron*, 467 U.S. at 842-43. In that case, the Court held that When a court reviews an agency's construction of the statute which it administers, it is confronted with two questions. First, always, is the question whether Congress has directly spoken to the precise question at issue. If the intent of Congress is clear, that is the end of the matter; for the court, as well as the agency, must give effect to the unambiguously expressed intent of Congress. If, however, the court determines Congress has not directly addressed the precise question at issue, the court does not simply impose its own construction on the statute, as would be necessary in the absence of an administrative interpretation. Rather, if the statute is silent or ambiguous with respect to the specific issue, the question for the court is whether the agency's answer is based on a permissible construction of the statute. *Id.*

[282] Todd H. Cohen, *Double Vision: The FTC, State Regulation, and Deciding What's Best for Consumers*, 59 GEO. WASH. L. REV. 1249, 1267 (1991) ("In sum, the *California State Board of Optometry* court relied on federalism principles to justify protecting state interests. The court extended the judicially-created *Parker* state action doctrine to cover FTC trade regulation rules and applied the clear statement doctrine to prevent the FTC from invalidating a state law as unfair without additional congressional action.").

[283] 491 U.S. 58 (1989).

[284] *California Optometry*, 910 F.2d 976, 980 (D.C. Cir. 1990) (internal quotation marks omitted).

[285] *Will*, 491 U.S. at 60.

[286] *Id.* at 64.

[287] *Id.* at 65 (citations omitted).

[288] Representative Covington, the sponsor of the act, explained during floor debate on the measure that Section 5 "embraces within the scope of that section every kind of person, natural or artificial, who may be engaged in interstate commerce."51 CONG. REC. 14,928 (1914). Despite this remark, courts have not taken such a broad view of the FTC's jurisdiction under the act. Even the Supreme Court has held that there are some limits on the entities covered by Section 5. *See* Cal. Dental Ass'n v. FTC, 526 U.S. 756, 766-67 (1999) (requiring, for jurisdiction, that a "proximate relation" must exist between the activities of a nonprofit and the benefit it provides to its members, and implying that the activities must confer "more than *de minimis* or merely presumed economic benefits" on the members).

[289] *See California Optometry*, 910 F.2d at 980-81 ("This rule of statutory construction serves to ensure that the States' sovereignty interests are adequately protected by the political process.").

[290] *Id.* at 980. For more information on the factors that courts consider when making this determination, see FED. TRADE COMM'N, REPORT OF THE STATE ACTION TASK FORCE (2003), *available at* http://www.ftc.gov/os/2003/09/ stateactionreport.pdf.

[291] *See* Cohen, *supra* note 282, at 1267.

[292] Although this report focuses on the FTC's consumer law cases under Section 5 ("unfair or deceptive acts or practices"), and not its antitrust cases ("unfair methods of competition"), both types of prohibited activities

share the same phrase for the purposes of determining the agency's jurisdiction: "persons, partnerships, or corporations." *See* 15 U.S.C. §45(a)(2).

[293] *See In re* Mass. Board of Registration in Optometry, 110 F.T.C. 549 (June 13, 1988) (decision) (citations omitted).

[294] *California Optometry*, 910 F.2d at 980 (citations omitted).

[295] *Id.* at 980 (citation omitted).

[296] *See, e.g.*, *In re* N.C. State Bd. of Dental Exam'rs, 151 F.T.C. 607 (Feb. 3, 2011) (state action opinion); *In re* Mass. Board of Registration in Optometry, 110 F.T.C. 549 (June 13, 1988) (decision).

[297] For more information on the factors that courts consider when making this determination, see FED. TRADE COMM'N, REPORT OF THE STATE ACTION TASK FORCE (2003), *available at* http://www.ftc.gov/os/2003/09/stateactionreport.pdf.

[298] This report does not consider whether any constitutional implications would result if the FTC, an independent executive branch agency, brought an enforcement proceeding against another executive branch agency. *See generally* Michael Eric Herz, *When Can the Federal Government Sue Itself?*, 32 WM. & MARY L. REV. 893 (1991).

[299] EIA ELECTRIC POWER OVERVIEW, *supra* note 254. Among these utilities are the Tennessee Valley Authority, the four power marketing administrations in the Department of Energy, and the Army Corps of Engineers. *Id.*

[300] *Id.*

[301] *See supra* notes 269-97 and accompanying text.

[302] 5 U.S.C. §552a.

[303] *See* "The Federal Privacy Act of 1974," *infra* p. 45.

[304] 15 U.S.C. §44.

[305] *In re* Minn. Rural Health Coop., FTC File No. 051 0199 (Dec. 28, 2010) (decision and order).

[306] *In re* Heublein, Inc., 96 F.T.C. 385 (Oct. 7, 1980) (final order).

[307] *See* DEP'T OF ENERGY, CASE STUDY – NATIONAL RURAL ELECTRIC COOPERATIVE ASSOCIATION SMART GRID INVESTMENT GRANT 1, *available at* http://energy.gov/sites/prod/files/oeprod/DocumentsandMedia/ NRECA_case_study.pdf.

[308] EIA ELECTRIC POWER OVERVIEW, *supra* note 254.

[309] *Id.* "Net margins" is the term given to "revenues in excess of the cost of providing service." *Id.*

[310] *See, e.g.*, Cent. Rural Electric Coop., Patronage Capital, http://www.crec.coop/CREC Advantage/Patronage Capital/ tabid/711/Default.aspx ("Allocated patronage capital appears as an entry on the permanent financial records of the cooperative and reflect [sic] your equity or ownership in CREC. When patronage capital is retired, a check or bill credit is issued to you and your equity in the cooperative is reduced. ... When considering a retirement, the board analyzes the financial health of the cooperative and will not authorize a retirement that will adversely affect the financial integrity of the cooperative."); Fall River Rural Electric Coop., Patronage Capital, http://www.frrec.com/myAccount/ patronage Capital.aspx ("The Cooperative's Board of Directors retires patronage capital when finances allow, often on an annual basis. The oldest patronage capital is retired first. Fall River currently retires patronage capital on a rotation of approximately 20 years."); Kauai Island Util. Coop., Member Patronage Capital Information, http://www.kiuc.coop/member_patcap-qa.htm ("A portion of Patronage Capital may be periodically paid to the members upon approval of the Board of Directors and our lenders."); Sulphur Springs Valley Electric Coop., Inc., Patronage Capital Credits, http://www.ssvec.org/?page_id=583 ("Capital credits represent your share of the Cooperative's margins – margins are the operating revenue remaining after operating expenses. The amount assigned in your name depends on your energy purchases. To calculate this, we divide your annual energy purchase by the Cooperative's operating income for the year. The more electricity you buy, the more capital credits you earn.").

[311] 15 U.S.C. §44 (emphasis added).

[312] 526 U.S. 756, 759-60, 767 (1999).

[313] *Id.* at 766 (internal citations omitted).

[314] *Id.*

[315] *Id.* at 766-67.

[316] *Id.* at 768.

[317] 638 F.2d 443, 446 (1980).

[318] *Id.* at 448. The court noted in passing that the AMA's articles of incorporation stated that one purpose of the organization was to "safeguard the material interests of the medical profession." *Id.*

[319] 405 F.2d 1011, 1015 (8th Cir. 1969).

[320] *See id.* at 1017. The court also remarked that at least one case had established that "even though a corporation's income exceeds its disbursements its nonprofit character is not necessarily destroyed." *Id.*

[321] *Id.* at 1020, 1022.

[322] *Id.* at 1020.

[323] *Id.*

[324] *Id.*

[325] *Id.* at 1019.

[326] This analysis assumes that a court would extend the holdings of the applicable case law, which covered entities organized as nonprofit corporations and professional associations, to include entities organized as nonprofit electric cooperatives.

[327] Many cooperatives provide other services to their communities that could constitute "economic benefits." The National Rural Electric Cooperative Association notes that, "In addition to electric service, many electric co-ops are involved in community development and revitalization projects" that include "small business development and jobs creation, improvement of water and sewer systems, and assistance in delivery of health care and educational services." Nat'l Rural Electric Coop. Ass'n, Member Directory, http://www.nreca.coop/members/MemberDirectory/Pages/ default.aspx.

[328] *See* sources cited *supra* note 310.

[329] Cal. Dental Ass'n v. FTC, 526 U.S. 756, 759-60, 767 (1999).

[330] Am. Med. Ass'n v. FTC, 638 F.2d 443, 448 (1980).

[331] *See, e.g.*, Cent. Rural Electric Coop., Patronage Capital, http://www.crec. coop/CRECAd vantage/Patronage Capital/tabid/711/Default.aspx ("These margins represent an interest-free loan of operating capital by the membership to the cooperative.").

[332] *See, e.g.*, Kauai Island Util. Coop., Member Patronage Capital Information, http://www. kiuc.coop/ member_ patcap qa.htm (characterizing the retirement of patronage capital as a "refund").

[333] 15 U.S.C. §44.

[334] *See* sources cited *supra* note 310.

[335] *See id.*

[336] *See* Nat'l Rural Electric Coop. Ass'n, Seven Cooperative Principles, http://www.nreca. coop/ members/ SevenCoopPrinciples/Pages/default.aspx (describing "Members' Economic Participation").

[337] Whether electricity service and patronage capital, which are clearly benefits, constitute "economic benefits" within the meaning of the Supreme Court's holding in *California Dental Ass'n* is a separate question.

[338] *See* sources cited *supra* note 310.

[339] I.R.C. §501(c)(12).

[340] *See* Cmty. Blood Bank v. FTC, 405 F.2d 1011, 1020 (8th Cir. 1969).

[341] 15 U.S.C. §45(a)(1). For more details on FTC enforcement of consumer data privacy and security under Section 5, see CRS Report RL34120, *Federal Information Security and Data Breach Notification Laws*, by Gina Stevens.

[342] 15 U.S.C. §45(n).

[343] *In re* Cliffdale Assocs., Inc., 103 F.T.C. 110, 174 (1984) (policy statement at end of opinion).

[344] *See Consumer Privacy: Hearing Before the S. Comm. on Commerce, Sci., and Transp.*, 11th Cong. (2010) (statement of Jon D. Leibowitz, Chairman, Fed. Trade Comm'n) (describing the FTC's enforcement activity in the areas of consumer data privacy and security), *available at* http://www.ftc.gov/os/testimony/ 100727consumerprivacy.pdf. The FTC recently released a preliminary report on the consumer privacy implications of new technologies. FED. TRADE COMM'N, PROTECTING CONSUMER PRIVACY IN AN ERA OF RAPID CHANGE: A PROPOSED FRAMEWORK FOR BUSINESSES AND POLICYMAKERS (2010), *available at* http://www.ftc.gov/os/2010/12/ 101201privacy report.pdf.

[345] FTC File No. 092 3184 (Nov. 29, 2011) (complaint).

[346] *Id.*

[347] FTC File No. 092 3093 (Mar. 2, 2011) (complaint).

[348] FTC File No. 092 3093 (Mar. 2, 2011) (decision and order)

[349] NIST PRIVACY REPORT, *supra* note 11, at 14, 35-36.

[350] As suggested below, it may also be an "unfair" practice, regardless of whether the utility has a privacy policy.

[351] FTC File No. 052 3096 (Mar. 7, 2006) (complaint).

[352] *Id.*

[353] FTC File No. 052 3148 (Sept. 5, 2006) (complaint).

[354] *Id.*

[355] *See, e.g.*, *In re* Cardsystems Solutions, Inc., FTC File No. 052 3148 (Sept. 5, 2006) (decision and order).

[356] NIST PRIVACY REPORT, *supra* note 11, at 23.

[357] FTC File No. 072 3121 (Nov. 12, 2010) (complaint).

[358] 15 U.S.C. §45(b). The Commission may seek a preliminary injunction in district court if it "has reason to believe" that an entity subject to the Commission's jurisdiction "is violating, or is about to violate, any provision of law enforced" by the FTC, and such an injunction would be in the public interest. 15 U.S.C. §53(b). In "proper cases the Commission may seek, and after proper proof, the court may issue, a permanent injunction." *Id.*

[359] 15 U.S.C. §45(l). The size of the civil monetary penalty was last adjusted for inflation in 2009. 16 C.F.R. §1.98.

[360] 15 U.S.C. §57b(a)(2).

[361] 15 U.S.C. §57b(b).

[362] 15 U.S.C. §45(m)(1)(B).

[363] 5 U.S.C. §552a. The federally owned utilities primarily sell electricity to nonprofit electric utilities on the wholesale markets rather than distribute electricity directly to consumers. EIA ELECTRIC POWER OVERVIEW, *supra* note 254. As these utilities provide only about 1% of total sales of electricity to end user consumers, *id.*, they may be unlikely to acquire consumer smart meter data, which is typically transmitted to distribution utilities. However, as the smart grid becomes more interconnected, more utilities at different points in the smart grid may come into possession of this data. NIST PRIVACY REPORT, *supra* note 11, at 23.

[364] *See* 5 U.S.C. §552(f)(1). The act also covers data in a "system of records" operated by a government contractor on behalf of a federal agency. *See* 5 U.S.C. §552a(m).

[365] EIA ELECTRIC POWER OVERVIEW, *supra* note 254.

[366] DEP'T OF THE ARMY CORPS OF ENG'RS, CIVIL WORKS STRATEGIC PLAN 1 (2004), *available at* http://www.corpsresults.us/pdfs/cw_strat.pdf. It is also a "Major Command within the Army." *Id.*

[367] Tenn. Valley Auth., About TVA, http://www.tva.com/abouttva/index.htm.

[368] *See* CRS Report RL34120, *Federal Information Security and Data Breach Notification Laws*, by Gina Stevens (citations omitted).

[369] 5 U.S.C. §552(a)(4).

[370] 5 U.S.C. §552a(a)(2).

[371] 5 U.S.C. §552a(a)(5).

[372] NIST PRIVACY REPORT, *supra* note 11, at 26-27.

In: Privacy: Select Issues and Laws for the 21st Century
Editor: Doris B. Delrio
ISBN: 978-1-62618-429-9

Chapter 2

DRONES IN DOMESTIC SURVEILLANCE OPERATIONS: FOURTH AMENDMENT IMPLICATIONS AND LEGISLATIVE RESPONSES*

Richard M. Thompson II

SUMMARY

The prospect of drone use inside the United States raises far-reaching issues concerning the extent of government surveillance authority, the value of privacy in the digital age, and the role of Congress in reconciling these issues.

Drones, or unmanned aerial vehicles (UAVs), are aircraft that can fly without an onboard human operator. An unmanned aircraft system (UAS) is the entire system, including the aircraft, digital network, and personnel on the ground. Drones can fly either by remote control or on a predetermined flight path; can be as small as an insect and as large as a traditional jet; can be produced more cheaply than traditional aircraft; and can keep operators out of harm's way. These unmanned aircraft are most commonly known for their operations overseas in tracking down and killing suspected members of Al Qaeda and related organizations. In addition to these missions abroad, drones are being considered for use in domestic surveillance operations, which might include in furtherance of homeland security, crime fighting, disaster relief, immigration control, and environmental monitoring.

Although relatively few drones are currently flown over U.S. soil, the Federal Aviation Administration (FAA) predicts that 30,000 drones will fill the nation's skies in less than 20 years. Congress has played a large role in this expansion. In February 2012, Congress enacted the FAA Modernization and Reform Act (P.L. 112-95), which calls for the FAA to accelerate the integration of unmanned aircraft into the national airspace system by 2015. However, some Members of Congress and the public fear there are insufficient safeguards in place to ensure that drones are not used to spy on American citizens and unduly infringe upon their fundamental privacy. These observers caution that the FAA is primarily charged with ensuring air traffic safety, and is not adequately prepared to handle the issues of privacy and civil liberties raised by drone use.

---

* This is an edited, reformatted and augmented version of Congressional Research Service, Publication No. R42701, dated September 6, 2012.

This report assesses the use of drones under the Fourth Amendment right to be free from unreasonable searches and seizures. The touchstone of the Fourth Amendment is reasonableness. A reviewing court's determination of the reasonableness of drone surveillance would likely be informed by location of the search, the sophistication of the technology used, and society's conception of privacy in an age of rapid technological advancement. While individuals can expect substantial protections against warrantless government intrusions into their homes, the Fourth Amendment offers less robust restrictions upon government surveillance occurring in public places and perhaps even less in areas immediately outside the home, such as in driveways or backyards. Concomitantly, as technology advances, the contours of what is reasonable under the Fourth Amendment may adjust as people's expectations of privacy evolve.

In the 112th Congress, several measures have been introduced that would restrict the use of drones at home. Senator Rand Paul and Representative Austin Scott introduced the Preserving Freedom from Unwarranted Surveillance Act of 2012 (S. 3287, H.R. 5925), which would require law enforcement to obtain a warrant before using drones for domestic surveillance, subject to several exceptions. Similarly, Representative Ted Poe's Preserving American Privacy Act of 2012 (H.R. 6199) would permit law enforcement to conduct drone surveillance pursuant to a warrant, but only in investigation of a felony.

INTRODUCTION

The prospect of drone use in domestic surveillance operations has engendered considerable debate among Americans of various political ideologies.[1] Opponents of drone surveillance have complained that the use of unmanned aircraft on American soil infringes upon fundamental privacy interests and the ability to freely associate with others.[2] Some are specifically concerned about the possibility of turning military technology inward to surveil American citizens.[3] Proponents have responded by emphasizing their potential benefits, which may include protecting public safety, patrolling our nation's borders, and investigating and enforcing environmental and criminal law violations.[4]

The tension between security and privacy interests is not new, but has been heightened by the explosion of surveillance technology in recent decades. Police officers who were once relegated to naked eye observations may soon have, or in some cases already possess, the capability to see through walls or track an individual's movements from the sky.[5]

One might question, then: What is the proper balance between the necessity of the government to keep people safe and the privacy needs of individuals? As some polls suggest, while the public supports drone usage in certain circumstances, they are less enthusiastic about using them as part of routine law enforcement activity.[6]

The Fourth Amendment to the United States Constitution safeguards Americans' privacy and prevents excessive government intrusion by prohibiting "unreasonable searches and seizures."[7] Courts have long grappled with how to apply the text of this eighteenth century provision to twentieth century technologies.

Although the Supreme Court has the final say in the interpretation of the Fourth Amendment and other constitutional safeguards,[8] Congress and, in many cases, the President are free to institute more stringent restrictions upon government surveillance operations.[9]

This report first explores the potential uses of drones in the domestic sphere by federal, state, and local governments. It then surveys current Fourth Amendment jurisprudence, including cases surrounding privacy in the home, privacy in public spaces, location tracking, manned aerial surveillance, and those involving the national border.

Next, it considers how existing jurisprudence may inform current and proposed drone uses. It then describes the various legislative measures introduced in the 112th Congress to address the legal and policy issues surrounding drones. Finally, it briefly identifies several alternative approaches that may constrain the potential scope of drone surveillance.

Background, Uses, and Drone Technology

Drones, also known as unmanned aerial vehicles (UAVs), are aircraft that do not carry a human operator and are capable of flight under remote control or autonomous programming.[10] An unmanned aircraft system (UAS) is the entire system, including the aircraft, digital network, and personnel on the ground.[11] Drones can range from the size of an insect—sometimes called nano drones or micro UAVs—to the size of a traditional jet.[12]

Drones are perhaps most commonly recognized from their missions abroad, including to target and kill suspects members of Al Qaeda and related groups, but they might be used for a variety of other purposes, including for both commercial and law enforcement activities within the United States. In fact, the FAA predicted that 30,000 unmanned aircraft could be flying in U.S. skies in less than 20 years.[13] One reason for this expansion has been a push by Congress for a faster integration of UAVs into U.S. airspace.[14] Most recently, as part of the FAA Modernization and Reform Act of 2012, Congress mandated that the Federal Aviation Administration (FAA) "develop a comprehensive plan to safely accelerate the integration of civil unmanned aircraft systems into the national airspace system."[15] This plan shall provide for integration of UAVs by September 2015.

Drones have been employed domestically by federal, state, and local governments in a range of circumstances. The Department of Homeland Security (DHS) uses them to police the nation's borders to deter unlawful border crossings by unauthorized aliens, criminals, and terrorists, and to detect and interdict the smuggling of weapons, drugs, and other contraband into the country.[16] Within DHS, Customs and Border Protection's (CBP's) Office of Air and Marine (OAM) has flown missions to support federal and state agencies such as the Federal Bureau of Investigation (FBI), the Department of Defense (DOD), Immigration and Customs Enforcement (ICE), the U.S. Secret Service, and the Texas Rangers.[17] According to a recent disclosure by the FAA, several local police departments, state and private colleges, and small cities and towns have also received FAA Certificates of Authorization (COAs) to fly unmanned aircraft domestically.[18] Recently, a police force in North Dakota conducted the nation's first drone-assisted arrest.[19] DHS, in conjunction with local law enforcement agencies, has been testing drone capabilities in a host of other situations including detecting radiation, monitoring a hostage situation, tracking a gun tossed by a fleeing suspect, firefighting, and finding missing persons.[20]

Currently, drones can be outfitted with high-powered cameras,[21] thermal imaging devices,[22] license plate readers,[23] and laser radar (LADAR).[24] In the near future, law enforcement organizations might seek to outfit drones with facial recognition or soft biometric recognition, which can recognize and track individuals based on attributes such as height, age, gender, and skin color.[25] As explained below, the relative sophistication of drones contrasted with traditional surveillance technology may influence a court's decision whether domestic drone use is lawful under the Fourth Amendment.

FOURTH AMENDMENT JURISPRUDENCE

The Fourth Amendment's story is one of continuity and change. Core values such as privacy and protection from excessive and arbitrary government intrusion are always within its sweep. A continuing question, though, is how the demands of its protection apply to an ever-changing society in which new and pervasive forms of technology are increasingly common. Although there are numerous rules and exceptions throughout the Supreme Court's Fourth Amendment jurisprudence, this section will explore those most pertinent to domestic drone use.

In short, the Fourth Amendment regulates when, where, and how the government may conduct searches and seizures. The Amendment provides, in relevant part: "The right of the people to be secure in their persons, houses, papers, and effects, against unreasonable searches and seizures, shall not be violated[.]"[26] The Fourth Amendment does not apply to all government acts, but only to those that constitute a search. So when does government monitoring constitute a Fourth Amendment "search" for which a warrant is generally required? Initially, courts' assessment focused on the specific area being investigated. Consider the 1928 case *Olmstead v. United States*.[27] There, the Supreme Court held that police wiretaps of the defendant's home telephone did not constitute a Fourth Amendment search because the police did not trespass onto Olmstead's property to intercept his conversation.[28] The Court's thinking at the time was that if the person's home, tangible property, or papers were not physically invaded, then no search in the constitutional sense occurred. Almost 40 years later, the Court shifted focus from property to privacy interests.[29] In *Katz v. United States*, decided in 1967, the Court held that an FBI agent's use of a bug to listen to the private conversations of Mr. Katz while in a telephone booth violated his Fourth Amendment rights.[30] Although he was in a public telephone booth and there was no physical invasion, the Court noted that what a person "seeks to preserve private, even in an area accessible to the public, may be constitutionally protected."[31] One of the modern Fourth Amendment tests relied upon by courts in assessing whether government monitoring constitutes a "search" derives from Justice Harlan's concurrence in *Katz*. It considers whether the person has a subjective expectation of privacy in the area to be searched and whether society is prepared to deem that expectation reasonable.[32]

Although the Court said in *Katz* that the Fourth Amendment "protects people not places,"[33] Justice Harlan noted that determining what "protection it affords people ... requires reference to a '*place*.'"[34] And as Justice Scalia observed when writing for a majority of the Court in *United States v. Jones*, a Fourth Amendment search occurs, "at a minimum," where "the Government obtains information by physically intruding on a constitutionally protected area."[35] The majority in *Jones* indicated that the reasonable expectation of privacy test was never intended to replace the property-based approach used in earlier cases, but merely augment it.[36] So where do individuals enjoy the most Fourth Amendment protection? The least? Why does the location dictate the level of protection? And how does technology affect society's expectation of privacy?

When analyzing domestic drone use under the Fourth Amendment, a reviewing court may be informed by cases surrounding privacy in the home, privacy in public spaces, location tracking, manned aerial surveillance, those involving the national border, and warrantless searches under the special needs doctrine.

Privacy in the Home

The home has always held a central place in American life, and remains the area accorded the greatest Fourth Amendment protection.[37] The Fourth Amendment protects this zone of privacy by ensuring that "the right of the people to be secure in their ... houses ... against unreasonable search and seizure, shall not be violated[.]"[38] In most instances, the Supreme Court has rigorously adhered to this safeguard.[39] For instance, although police officers may make a warrantless arrest of an individual for a felony offense committed in public,[40] they may not step inside his home without a warrant, barring any recognized exception.[41]

In addition to a physical entry and search of the home, police are likewise prohibited from using certain technology to pierce this zone of privacy. In *Kyllo v. United States*, government agents used a thermal-imaging device to determine heat patterns inside the home of Danny Kyllo.[42] The Court began with the presumption that a warrantless search of a home is unreasonable.[43] Ultimately, the Court protected this "realm of guaranteed privacy" by holding that obtaining information about the inside of a home that could not otherwise be obtained except by entering the home, through the use of technology not in "general public use," is a "search" covered by the Fourth Amendment.[44]

The home, however, does not provide an absolute shield against government surveillance. As Justice Harlan emphasized in *Katz*, "[A] man's home is, for most purposes, a place where he expects privacy, but objects, activities, or statements that he exposes to the plain view of outsiders are not 'protected' because no intention to keep them to himself has been exhibited." Indeed, in certain instances, police may use their natural senses to conduct warrantless searches of the inside of a home.[45] To fall under this exception—known as the "plain view" doctrine—the police must be in a lawful vantage point when they conduct the surveillance, and the incriminating nature of the evidence must be readily apparent.[46]

Curtilage and Open Fields

Once an individual moves from the confines of the home, he is entitled to different Fourth Amendment considerations. Depending on a host of varying factors, areas outside of the home may be considered "curtilage" or "open fields." [47] The curtilage is the area immediately surrounding the home—an area the Court has granted similar protections as the inside of the home.[48] To determine if an area is curtilage, a court will look at how close the area is to the home; whether the area is within a fence surrounding the home; how the area is used; and whether the area is protected from observation by passersby.[49] Although an area may be deemed curtilage—as with the home—it is not veiled with unconditional constitutional protection. As the Court noted in one aerial surveillance case:

> The Fourth Amendment protection of the home has never been extended to require law enforcement officers to shield their eyes when passing by a home on public thoroughfares. Nor does the mere fact that an individual has taken measures to restrict some views of his activities preclude an officer's observations from a public vantage point where he has a right to be and which renders the activities clearly visible.[50]

On the other hand, the area outside the curtilage is sometimes considered "open fields," which "do not provide the setting for those intimate activities that the Amendment is intended to shelter from governmental interference or surveillance,"[51] and thus are not given similar Fourth Amendment protections. Differentiating between the two is no easy task. In one case, for example, the Ninth Circuit Court of Appeals determined that the defendant's driveway was not curtilage as he had taken no affirmative steps to block it from observation by passers-by.[52] Furthermore, in the fly-over cases discussed *infra*, the Supreme Court has permitted similar searches in both open fields and the curtilage, to some extent eliminating any constitutional difference between the two.

Manned Aerial Surveillance

In a series of cases that provide the closest analogy to UAVs, the Supreme Court addressed the use of *manned* aircraft to conduct domestic surveillance over residential and industrial areas. In each, the Court held that the fly-over at issue was not a search prohibited by the Fourth Amendment, as the areas surveilled were open to public view.

In *California v. Ciraolo*, police received a tip that an individual was growing marijuana in his backyard next to his suburban home.[54] Because two fences blocked their view of the yard, officers flew a fixed-wing aircraft at an altitude of 1,000 feet over the property to conduct a visual inspection. From this vantage point, the officers readily identified with the naked eye marijuana plants growing in the defendant's yard. The Court held that the defendant's expectation of privacy in the area immediately surrounding his home was not reasonable, since "what a person knowingly exposes to the public ... is not a subject of Fourth Amendment protection."[55] "Any member of the public flying in this airspace who glanced down could have seen everything these officers observed," the Court remarked.[56] Much weight was placed on the fact that the plane was at all times in navigable airspace as defined by federal statute.[57]

Similarly, in *Florida v. Riley*, local police received a tip that an individual was growing marijuana in a greenhouse located 10 to 20 feet away from his mobile home.[58] The officers could not see the contents of the greenhouse from the ground, so they flew a helicopter over the defendant's backyard at an altitude of 400 feet. While overhead, an officer saw marijuana plants through a crack in the greenhouse roof. Because the helicopter, like the plane in *Ciraolo*, was in navigable airspace—where any member of the public could have flown—the Court did not consider this a search for which a warrant was required.[59]

In the final case of the series, *Dow Chemical v. United States*, the Court was asked whether a theory of "industrial curtilage" would prevent a government agency from conducting aerial surveillance over a 2,000-acre commercial plant.[60] There, after Dow Chemical Co. refused access to the Environmental Protection Agency (EPA), the EPA hired a commercial aerial photographer to take photos of the facility using a precision aerial mapping camera. Having ruled out the argument that the areas surrounding an industrial complex are entitled to the same protection as similar areas surrounding a home, the Court concluded that photographing the plant from navigable airspace was not a search.[61]

Government Tracking

Like the aerial surveillance cases, individuals have reduced—and in some contexts no—Fourth Amendment protection from government tracking of their travel in public places. This has permitted the government to conduct warrantless tracking of a vehicle's movements while traveling on public streets. However, once people enter a private residence, the tracking must cease. Also, using technology to perform pervasive tracking might not meet Fourth Amendment muster.

Consider, for example, these two government tracking cases, *United States v. Knotts* and *United States v. Karo*.[62] In both cases, the government hid a location monitoring device in an item that was then given to the suspects. In *Knotts*, the police tracked the suspect's movements solely while traveling on public roadways.[63] The Court held that people have no reasonable expectation of privacy in their movements on public streets. As such, no Fourth Amendment search occurred, thus no warrant was required. By contrast, in *Karo*, the police tracked a beeper device on public streets *and* while the beeper was in a private residence—a "location not open to visual surveillance."[64] "Indiscriminate monitoring of property that has been withdrawn from public view," the Court declared, "would present far too serious a threat to privacy interests in the home to escape entirely some sort of Fourth Amendment oversight."[65] The Court held the search unlawful.

Although surveillance in public is generally not considered a search, pervasive tracking may cross the line. Take, for instance, the Supreme Court's recent decision in the GPS tracking case *United States v. Jones*.[66] In that case, the Court held that the attachment and monthlong tracking of a GPS device on an individual's vehicle constituted a trespass, and hence a Fourth Amendment search.[67] The Court grounded its decision in the property-based approach to assessing what constitutes a "search" under the Fourth Amendment, which had been more prevalent in the late 19th and early 20th century cases involving relatively unsophisticated technology.

The Court's focus on whether the attachment of a tracking device constitutes a trespass triggering Fourth Amendment protections is not necessarily applicable to drone surveillance. However, in two separate concurring opinions that together made up five members of the Court, an alternative framework was proposed that may have more far-reaching implications for the domestic use of UAVs.

Justice Alito, concurring in the Court's judgment, and joined by Justices Ginsburg, Breyer, and Kagan, would have held that "the use of longer term GPS monitoring in investigations of most offenses impinges on expectations of privacy. For such offenses, society's expectation has been that law enforcement agents and others would not— and indeed, in the main, simply could not—secretly monitor and catalogue every single movement of an individual's car for a very long period." Justice Sotomayor, joining the controlling opinion in *Jones*, but also concurring separately, noted that although following people for a short period of time conveys little information about them, tracking an individual for an extended period "reflects a wealth of detail about her familial, political, professional, religious, and sexual associations."[69] Thus, the length of time an individual is kept under surveillance and the breadth of data collected through such surveillance may inform a reviewing court whether a particular surveillance practice constitutes a Fourth Amendment search.[70]

Border Searches

Even more so than surveillance of public places generally, law enforcement agencies are granted significant deference to conduct surveillance at or near American borders. The federal government has a significant interest in protecting American borders from crossings by persons attempting to enter unlawfully, drug trafficking, and, perhaps most importantly, the transit of weapons and persons seeking to do harm to American people and infrastructure.

Congress has granted federal law enforcement agencies significant search powers at the border.

Section 287 of the Immigration and Nationality Act (INA), codified at 8 U.S.C. § 1357, authorizes immigration officers to conduct warrantless searches of any vessel within a reasonable distance from the United States border and any vehicle within 25 miles from a border for the "purpose of patrolling the border to prevent the illegal entry of aliens into the United States."[71] Similarly, 19 U.S.C. § 482 authorizes customs officers to search vehicles and persons on which or whom they have reasonable cause to believe are carrying goods unlawfully into the United States.[72]

The Supreme Court has likewise acknowledged this federal interest in the borders, observing that "[t]he Government's interest in preventing the entry of unwanted persons and effects is at its zenith at the international border."[73] Again, the touchstone in every Fourth Amendment case is whether the search is *reasonable*.[74]

The Court observed in *United States v. Montoya De Hernandez* that "the Fourth Amendment balance of reasonableness is qualitatively different at the international border."[75] "Routine searches," the Court continued, "are not subject to any requirement of reasonable suspicion, probable cause, or warrant."[76] "Routine" searches have included pat downs for weapons or contraband,[77] the use of drug sniffing dogs,[78] and the inspection of luggage.[79] By contrast, "non-routine" searches are those that go beyond a limited intrusion, and require the government official to have (at a minimum) "reasonable suspicion" of wrongdoing.[80] Prolonged detentions,[81] strip searches,[82] and body cavity searches[83] have all been considered non-routine searches.

Unlike searches directly at the border, the Court has shown more reticence in granting law enforcement unfettered discretion to conduct searches near, but not directly at, the border. In *Almeida-Sanchez v. United States*, the defendant's vehicle was stopped and searched by U.S. Border Patrol agents 25 miles north of the U.S.-Mexico border.[84] The agents had neither a warrant nor probable cause, nor even reasonable suspicion, to conduct the search. The government argued that the search was permissible under § 287 of the Immigration and Nationality Act.

A federal statute, the Court noted, cannot trump the Constitution. The Court refused to permit this suspicionless search, as it was conducted neither at the border nor at its "functional equivalent."[85]

Warrants, Suspicionless Searches, and Special Needs

The baseline rule in Fourth Amendment cases is that police must obtain a warrant to search an individual or their property in all but a few limited instances.[86] This rule ensures that an independent judicial officer, rather than a police officer in the field, is determining whether there is probable cause to conduct a search or seizure.[87] Over time, however, the Court has loosened this warrant requirement in instances where a strict showing of individualized suspicion of probable cause would hinder the government from addressing health and safety concerns.[88] In two lines of overlapping cases—administrative searches and "special needs" cases—the Court has balanced the individual's privacy interest against the government's interest to determine if a warrant or any individualized suspicion is required.[89] These two theories permit law enforcement to conduct dragnet searches in certain instances.

Suspicionless general searches are ones "in which the government searches or seizes every person, place, or thing in a specific location or involved in a specific activity based only on a showing of a generalized government interest."[90] Suspicionless searches have been conducted at the national border,[91] private businesses[92] and police roadblocks.[93] In the roadblock cases, the Court has balanced the government's interest against the individual's privacy interest to determine whether police may stop and question drivers without a warrant or any suspicion of criminal wrongdoing. In *Michigan Dep't of State Police v. Sitz*, the Court upheld the suspicionless stopping and examination of drivers for intoxication at sobriety checkpoints.[94] The Court reasoned that the high incidence of drunk driving balanced against the minimal intrusion on drivers permitted suspicionless checkpoints. In *City of Indianapolis v. Edmund*, however, law enforcement was not permitted to set up a drug interdiction checkpoint. [95] The Court held that searches such as this violated the Fourth Amendment when their "primary purpose" is "to uncover evidence of ordinary criminal wrongdoing."[96] Justice O'Connor observed that if this type of roadblock were allowed "the Fourth Amendment would do little to prevent such intrusions from becoming a routine part of American life."[97]

Application of Fourth Amendment to Drones

As evidenced by the foregoing, the constitutionality of domestic drone surveillance may depend upon the context in which such surveillance takes place. Whether a targeted individual is at home, in his backyard, in the public square, or near a national border will play a large role in determining whether he is entitled to privacy. Equally important is the sophistication of the technology used by law enforcement and the duration of the surveillance. Both of these factors will likely inform a reviewing court's reasoning as to whether the government's surveillance constitutes an unreasonable search in violation of the Fourth Amendment.

Location of Search

Based on existing case law, it is reasonable to assume that surveillance of an individual while in his home—an area accorded the greatest Fourth Amendment protection—using technology not in general public use would be an unlawful search absent a search warrant. The Supreme Court in *Kyllo* was particularly concerned about law enforcement's use of powerful equipment to peer inside an individual's home. Currently, UAVs carry high-megapixel cameras and thermal imaging, and will soon have the capacity to see through walls and ceilings.[98] These technologies are not generally available to the public, and under current jurisprudence, their use by law enforcement would probably constitute a search covered by the Fourth Amendment. However, the use of low-powered cameras or other unsophisticated technology to view people and objects in plain view while in their home might not trigger Fourth Amendment protections. The rationale for this notion is that officers are not required to avert their eyes when they see illegal activity in plain view, especially when the subject of the search has taken no affirmative efforts to hide their activity from public view.

Moving beyond the home, it is unclear whether circumstances exist in which the area immediately surrounding the home—for instance, a backyard, a swimming pool, a deck, or a porch—would receive similar protections as the interior of the home if surveilled by drones or other aerial vehicles.[99] Although the Supreme Court has recited on many occasions that a person located in a home's curtilage is accorded similar privacy protections as when inside the home, the aerial surveillance cases arguably constitute an exception to this general principle. In the two aerial cases, *Riley* and *Ciraolo*, the area surveilled was within close proximity of the home, yet the police surveillance at altitudes of 400 and 1,000 feet were not considered a search.

Based on the aerial surveillance cases, it may be reasonable to presume a warrant would *not* be required (nor, perhaps, any suspicion, for that matter) to conduct drone surveillance of most public places for a relatively short period of time. The Supreme Court remarked in *Ciraolo* that the "Fourth Amendment simply does not require the police traveling in the public airways at [1,000 feet] to obtain a warrant to observe what is visible to the naked eye."[100] However, the rarity of drone flights may distinguish their use from surveillance by the piloted aircraft used in the three aerial cases decided by the Court. All three of these cases were premised on the fact that each aircraft was flying in navigable airspace, and that these flights were not "sufficiently rare" to provide a reasonable expectation of privacy in the area to be searched. To this point, Justice White remarked in *Riley* that "there is nothing in the record or before us to suggest that helicopters flying at 400 feet are sufficiently rare in this country to lend substance to respondent's claim that he reasonably anticipated that his greenhouse would not be subject to observation from that altitude."[101] Presently, use of UAVs in U.S. airspace is considerably less common. The FAA has issued only approximately 300 licenses for drone use in U.S. airspace.[102] The general public would likely find it exceedingly unusual for a drone to fly over their homes taking surveillance photographs. This rarity might factor into a reviewing court's determination of whether individuals have a legitimate expectation of privacy from various forms of drone surveillance while in a public place.[103]

The federal government's authority to use unmanned aircraft is undoubtedly at its maximum near U.S. borders. One of the federal government's only affirmative duties is to protect citizens from external harm.[104] This includes securing the borders. The Court has hesitated from interfering with the performance of this duty, and it would in all likelihood demonstrate the same deference when it comes to the use of UAVs. Moreover, the Supreme Court's rulings in border cases have all involved active searches—either a physical search of a vehicle or stopping and questioning a vehicle's passenger. Surveillance by UAVs, on the other hand, may be considered more passive and therefore may be even less likely to run afoul of Fourth Amendment requirements. Drone surveillance does not require any physical manipulation of a person or his things. UAVs also do not require the seizure of a person for any period of time (though drone surveillance may lead to law enforcement physically apprehending a person who is seen engaging in suspected illegal activity). However, the Court has shown some reticence about giving law enforcement carte blanche search power at the border. Roving vehicle patrols and indiscriminate searches in *Almeida-Sanchez v. United States* and *United States v. Brignoni-Ponce* were deemed unconstitutional.[105] It is unclear whether this reticence would extend to drone surveillance along the border if it were to become significantly widespread.

Technology Used

Like location, the technology used by UAVs may be a decisive factor considered by courts in determining whether individual's have a legitimate expectation of privacy in the object or area of the challenged drone search. Technological developments make it increasingly easy to share and acquire personal information about others, oftentimes without their direct knowledge or consent. As surveillance technology advances and becomes ever-present in Americans' lives, people's conception of privacy may tend to oscillate. Justice Scalia, writing for the majority in *Kyllo v. United States*, remarked on this trend:

> It would be foolish to contend that the degree of privacy secured to citizens by the Fourth Amendment has been entirely unaffected by the advance of technology. For example, ... the technology enabling human flight has exposed to public view (and hence, we have said, to official observation) uncovered portions of the house and its curtilage that once were private. The question we confront today is what limits there are upon this power of technology to shrink the realm of guaranteed privacy.[106]

Justice Alito, joined by three other justices in his *United States v. Jones* concurrence, likewise observed:

> The *Katz* test rests on the assumption that this hypothetical reasonable person has a well-developed and stable set of privacy expectations. But technology can change those expectations. Dramatic technological change may lead to periods in which popular expectations are in flux and may ultimately produce significant changes in popular attitudes. New technology may provide increased convenience or security at the expense of privacy, and many people may find the tradeoff worthwhile. And even if the public does not welcome the diminution of privacy that new technology entails, they may eventually reconcile themselves to this development as inevitable.[107]

The crucial question, then, is whether drones have the potential to be significantly more invasive than traditional surveillance technologies such as manned aircraft or low-powered cameras— technologies that have been upheld in previous cases. In this vein, some have asked whether using sophisticated digital platforms on a drone is any different from attaching the same instrument to a lamppost or traditional aircraft.[108] Take, for example, the tracking of license plates. Currently, many states and municipalities employ automatic license plate readers (ALPRs), which are usually mounted on police vehicles or stationary objects along the streets, take a snapshot of a license plate as a car drives by, and store this information in a large database for possible later use by law enforcement.[109] It is alleged that these devices can be used to track a person's movements when police aggregate the data from a multitude of ALPR stations.[110] A majority of the reviewing federal circuit courts have held that a person has no reasonable expectation of privacy in his license plate number.[111]

However, it appears that no federal court has addressed the constitutionality of the use ALPRs (whether attached to a drone, manned vehicle, or a stationary device), as opposed to plate numbers collected by a human observer. Nonetheless, the question remains whether attaching an ALPR—or any similar sophisticated technology—to a drone would alter the constitutionality of its use by law enforcement. Some say yes, arguing that the sophistication of drone technology in and of itself "present[s] a unique threat to privacy."[112] Drones are smaller, can fly longer, and can be built more cheaply than traditional aircraft. For instance, defense firm Lockheed Martin's Stalker—a small, electrically powered drone—can be recharged from the ground using a laser.[113] It now has a flight time of more than 48 hours. As this technology advances, it is reported that some drones could theoretically "stay in the air forever."[114] Unlike a stationary license plate tracker or video camera, drones can lock on a target's every move for days, and possibly weeks and months. This ability to closely monitor an individual's movements with pinpoint accuracy may raise more significant constitutional concerns than some other types of surveillance technology.

Furthermore, the technology and sophistication of drones may mark a considerable departure from the traditional technologies used in the three manned aerial surveillance cases decided by the Supreme Court. First, all three holdings in *Ciraolo*, *Riley*, and *Dow Chemical* were premised on naked-eye searches. Chief Justice Burger remarked in *Dow Chemical*: "It may well be, as the government concedes, that surveillance of private property using highly sophisticated surveillance equipment not generally available to the public, such as satellite technology, might be constitutionally proscribed absent a warrant."[115] As noted above, the sophistication of surveillance technology available to drones, such as facial recognition or laser radar which can "see" through walls, may lead some to question the relevance of prior Fourth Amendment jurisprudence concerning more rudimentary forms of surveillance technology.

The sophistication of drones also has the ability to break down any practical privacy safeguard. In the pre-computer age, the greatest privacy protections were neither constitutional nor statutory, but practical. Putting officers everywhere in the community cost too much for local police departments. This acted as a natural barrier to excessive police presence. Drones are not hindered by similar limitations. This is similar to the expansion of GPS technology observed by the five concurring justices in *United States v. Jones*. There, Justice Sotomayor, writing for herself, noted that because GPS technology was cheaper and performed in a surreptitious manner, it "evades the ordinary checks that constrain abusive law enforcement practices: limited police resources and community hostility."[116] Justice Alito sounded a similar note in *Jones*: "Traditional surveillance for any extended period of time was difficult and costly and therefore rarely undertaken. [GPS devices] make long-term monitoring relatively easy and cheap."[117] Instead of putting more officers in the field, a police force could put drones in the sky for potentially less expense. Already, drones with video capabilities can be purchased from private vendors for a few hundred dollars.[118] This access to inexpensive technology may significantly reduce budgetary concerns that once checked the government from widespread surveillance.

The duration and pervasiveness of drone surveillance—two factors closely associated with the technology employed by law enforcement—may also influence a court's Fourth Amendment analysis. Consider the Fifth Circuit Court of Appeal's ruling in *United States v. CuevasSanchez*.[119] In that case, federal law enforcement agents suspected the defendant was using his home as a drop house for drug traffickers. After obtaining a court order, the agents installed a video camera on a utility pole overlooking the defendant's 10-foot high fence surrounding his back yard. The officers observed the removal of drugs from the gas tanks of several cars parked in the defendant's yard. Based on these observations, the defendant was arrested whereupon the police seized a large amount of marijuana. At trial, the defendant moved to suppress the evidence on the basis that the warrant was defective. However, the court first addressed whether the video surveillance was a search under the Fourth Amendment. In determining that the video surveillance was a search, the panel noted that this "was not a one-time overhead flight or a glance over the fence by a passer-by. ... It does not follow that *Ciraolo* authorizes any type of surveillance whatever just because one type of minimally-intrusive aerial observation is possible."[120] Drones have the capability to stay in the air for long periods of time and can hover in one location. Similar to the mounted camera in *Cuevas-Sanchez*, this permits law enforcement to employ drones in prolonged surveillance operations. This capability may sway a court's determination of whether certain types of warrantless drone surveillance are compatible with the Fourth Amendment.

Warrant Requirement and Suspicionless Drone Searches

Applying the Fourth Amendment to drones requires application of the threshold question: was there a search? Again, this will depend on all the factors discussed above—the area of the search, the technology used, and whether society would respect the target's expectation of privacy in the place searched. If a reviewing court concludes that the drone surveillance was not a search, neither a warrant nor any degree of individualized suspicion would be required. If, however, the court concluded there was a search, then a court would ask whether a warrant is required, if one of the exceptions apply, and what level of suspicion, if any, is necessary to uphold the search.

Unless a meaningful distinction can be made between drone surveillance and more traditional forms of government tracking, existing jurisprudence suggests that a reviewing court would likely uphold drone surveillance conducted with no individualized suspicion when conducted for purposes other than strict law enforcement. The Supreme Court has hesitated from interfering in what they see as the executive's function in protecting the health and safety of the American population. As Chief Justice Rehnquist noted in the *Sitz*, the Court does not want

> to transfer from politically accountable officials to the courts the decision as to which among reasonable alternative law enforcement techniques should be employed to deal with serious public danger. ... [F]or purposes of Fourth Amendment analysis, the choice among such reasonable alternatives remains with the governmental officials who have a unique understanding of, and a responsibility for, limited public resources, including a finite number of police officers.[121]

The Court may defer to law enforcement officials in the drone context also. There are countless instances where the government may seek to utilize drones for health and safety purpose that go beyond mere law enforcement. These may include firefighting, search and rescue missions, traffic safety enforcement, or environmental protection. If, on other hand, surveillance is conducted primarily to enforce the law, a warrant may be required, unless one of the exceptions to the warrant requirement applies.

LEGISLATIVE PROPOSALS IN THE 112TH CONGRESS TO CONSTRAIN DOMESTIC USE OF DRONES

Although the Supreme Court is the final arbiter of the Constitution, Congress and the President can provide for greater regulation of drones than the Fourth Amendment requires. Congress has taken such steps over the years to address government surveillance of communications in transit (commonly known as wiretapping),[122] communications in storage such as e-mails,[123] bank records,[124] and health records,[125] among a host of other private information.

Several measures have been introduced in the 112th Congress that would restrict the domestic use of drones, and establish arguably greater constraints on their usage than the Fourth Amendment requires. Several bills were prompted by a general concern for potential privacy intrusions by federal and state law enforcement and executive agencies. Others seek to curb specific instances of surveillance, such as that conducted by the Environmental Protection Agency (EPA).

Preserving Freedom from Unwarranted Surveillance Act of 2012 (H.R. 5925, S. 3287)

Representative Austin Scott and Senator Rand Paul recently introduced similar legislation in the House and Senate, respectively, entitled the Preserving Freedom from Unwarranted Surveillance Act of 2012 (H.R. 5925, S. 3287).[126]

These bills would require any entity acting under the authority of the federal government to obtain a warrant based upon probable cause before conducting drone surveillance to investigate violations of criminal law or regulations. There are, however, several exceptions to this warrant requirement: (1) to prevent or deter illegal entry of any persons or illegal substances into the United States; (2) when a law enforcement officer possesses reasonable suspicion that under particular circumstances, swift action to prevent imminent danger to life is necessary; or (3) when the Secretary of Homeland Security determines credible intelligence indicates a high risk of a terrorist attack by a specific individual or organization. Both bills create a right to sue for any violation of its prohibitions.

However, only S. 3287 includes an express provision prohibiting unlawfully obtained evidence from being used at trial.

Preserving American Privacy Act of 2012 (H.R. 6199)

Similarly, Representative Ted Poe's Preserving American Privacy Act of 2012 (H.R. 6199) would restrict the domestic use of drones.[127] It would only permit use of drones by law enforcement pursuant to a warrant and in the investigation of a felony. Any search would be subject to the same limitations and exceptions as apply in the jurisdiction where the search is conducted. There is an express exclusionary provision so that evidence obtained in violation of the act would be inadmissible in a federal criminal prosecution. Such evidence would also be excluded from administrative hearings. Additionally, no federal agency may permit a private entity from monitoring an individual. The bill has an exception for searches conducted within 25 miles of the national border.

Farmers Privacy Act of 2012 (H.R. 5961) and Other Restrictions on EPA Drone Use

Representative Shelley Moore Capito introduced the Famers Privacy Act of 2012, which would prohibit the EPA from conducting aerial surveillance of agricultural lands unless the EPA has consent from the farmer, has provided public notice, or has obtained a certificate of reasonable suspicion from the United States District Court for the District of Columbia.[128] During debate on the 2012 Farm Bill, Senators Mike Johanns and Barbara Boxer filed competing amendments regarding EPA unmanned aerial surveillance. Senator Johanns's amendment would have banned the EPA from using aerial surveillance to inspect or record images of farming operations.[129] Senator Boxer's amendment would have permitted the EPA to conduct fly-overs if it was more cost-effective than ground inspections and if state officials were notified of such flights.[130] Neither amendment was ultimately adopted.

Alternative Proposals

In addition to the above legislation, observers have contemplated a number of other proposals in to restrict or regulate domestic drone surveillance. In instances where the Fourth Amendment does not require a warrant, Congress could potentially require that law enforcement obtain an area warrant. This warrant not need state the exact location of the search, but could describe a general area to be surveilled. Another possible option, applicable in situations where a warrant is not required under the Fourth Amendment (*e.g.*, certain instances of aerial surveillance of public places) would be for Congress to require law enforcement to procure enough evidence to establish probable cause that a crime has been committed or evidence of crime will be found in the place to be searched, but forego the warrant requirement. Additionally, Congress could create a similar cause of action for privacy violations caused by drone surveillance as contained in 18 U.S.C. § 2712, which creates a civil remedy for violations of the Wiretap Act, the Stored Communications Act, and certain provisions of the Foreign Intelligence Surveillance Act of 1978.

Congress could also limit the admissibility of evidence in a criminal prosecution to situations where its acquisition was the purpose of the drone search. For instance, if police are permitted to conduct drone surveillance for a search and rescue mission and inadvertently observe a violation of criminal law or regulation, the evidence would not be admissible in a criminal prosecution or administrative proceeding.

CONCLUSION

The introduction of drones into American airspace raises many legal and policy questions. For instance, how far can the government go in its attempts to maintain security and ensure that laws are enforced? What level of privacy should Americans expect in an age where technology facilitating the acquisition of personal information expands at a phenomenal pace? Currently, there is a vast body of Fourth Amendment law that governs the circumstances in which law enforcement must obtain a warrant before conducting surveillance. However, the sheer sophistication of drone technology and the sensors they can carry may remove drones from this traditional Fourth Amendment framework.

Beyond the courts and the Constitution, what role should Congress and the President play in regulating the introduction of drones inside the United States? As the integration of drones for domestic surveillance operations quickly accelerates, these questions and others will be posed to the American people and their political leaders.

End Notes

1 The term "domestic drone surveillance" as used in this report is designed to cover a wide range of government uses including, but not limited to, investigating and deterring criminal or regulatory violations; conducting health and safety inspections; performing search and rescue missions; patrolling the national borders; and conducting environmental investigations.

2 Letter from Representatives Edward J. Markey and Joe Barton, Co-Chairmen of the Congressional Bi-Partisan Privacy Caucus, to Michael P. Huerta, Acting Administrator of the Federal Aviation Administration (April 19, 2012) ("[I]n addition to benefits, there is also the potential for drone technology to enable invasive and pervasive surveillance without adequate privacy protections."), *available at* http://markey.house.gov/sites/markey. house.gov/files/documents/4-19-12.Letter%20FAA%20Drones%20.pdf; AMERICAN CIVIL LIBERTIES UNION, PROTECTING PRIVACY FROM AERIAL SURVEILLANCE: RECOMMENDATIONS FOR GOVERNMENT USE OF DRONE AIRCRAFT 1 (2011), *available at* https://www.aclu.org/files/assets/protectingprivacyfrom aerialsurveillance.pdf.

3 Mark Brunswick, *Spies in the sky signal new age of surveillance*, STARTRIBUNE (July 22, 2012, 6:26 a.m.), *available at* http://www.startribune.com/local/163304886.html?refer=y.

4 Some state and local officials have expressed interest in employment of drones for public safety and law enforcement purposes. *See, e.g.*, Brianne Carter, *Gov. Bob McDonnell supports drones policing Virginia*, ABC NEWS (May 30, 2012), *available at* http://www.wjla.com/ articles/2012/05/gov-bob-mcdonnell-supports-drones-policing-virginia76464.html; *Unmanned Aircraft Systems Within the Homeland: Security Game Changer? Hearing Before the Subcomm. on Oversight, Investigations, and Management of the H. Comm. on Homeland Sec.*, 112th Cong. 3 (2012) (statement of William R. McDaniel, Chief Deputy, Montgomery County Sheriff's Office, Conroe, TX) ("UAV systems for public safety agencies are extremely viable, effective, and economical means to enhance the public safety response to critical incidents.").

5 The Supreme Court remarked in *Kyllo v. United States*, 533 U.S. 27, 37 (2001): The ability to 'see' through walls and other opaque barriers is a clear, and scientifically feasible, goal of law enforcement research and development. The National Law Enforcement and Corrections Technology Center, a program within the United States Department of Justice, features on its Internet Website projects that include a 'Radar-Based

Through-the-Wall Surveillance System,' 'Handheld Ultrasound Through the Wall Surveillance,' and a 'Radar Flashlight' that 'will enable law officers to detect individuals through interior building walls.'

[6] *U.S. Supports Some Domestic Drone Use, But Public Registers Concern About Own Privacy* 1, Monmouth University Polling Institute (June 12, 2012), *available at* http://www.monmouth.edu.

[7] U.S. CONST. amend IV.

8 Cooper v. Aaron, 358 U.S. 1, 18 (1958) ("[Marbury v. Madison] declared the basic principle that the federal judiciary is supreme in the exposition of the law of the Constitution, and that principle has ever since been respected by this Court and the Country as a permanent and indispensable feature of our constitutional system.").

[9] In reaction to the Supreme Court's ruling in *United States v. Miller*, 425 U.S. 435 (1976), that the privacy of an individual's bank records were generally not protected by the Fourth Amendment, Congress enacted the Right to Financial Privacy Act, P.L. 95-630, 92 Stat. 3697 (codified at 12 U.S.C. § 3401-3422), creating a statutory protection for such records.

[10] DEP'T OF DEFENSE, DICTIONARY OF MILITARY AND ASSOCIATED TERMS 331 (2012). Unless expressly mentioned, the terms "unmanned aerial vehicle," "UAV," "unmanned aircraft system," "UAS," and "drone" are used interchangeably in this report.

[11] *Id.*

[12] See CRS Report R42136, *U.S. Unmanned Aerial Systems*, by Jeremiah Gertler, for a description of the various types of drones currently operated in the United States.

[13] FEDERAL AVIATION ADMINISTRATION, FAA AEROSPACE FORECAST: FISCAL YEARS 2010-2030, at 48 (2010), *available at* http://www.faa.gov/data_research/aviation/ aerospace_forecasts/2010-2030/media/2010%20Forecast%20Doc.pdf. The FAA has noted that "Federal agencies are planning to increase their use of UAS's. State and local governments envision using UAS's to aid in law enforcement and firefighting. Potential commercial uses are also possible, for example, in real estate photography or pipeline inspection. UAS's could perform some manned aircraft missions with less noise and fewer emissions." *Id.*

[14] *See, e.g.*, Intelligence Reform and Terrorism Prevention Act of 2004, P.L. 108-458, § 5102, 118 Stat. 3638, 3732 (requesting that DHS test the feasibility of using unmanned aircraft to patrol the northern border of the United States).

[15] FAA Modernization and Reform Act of 2012, P.L. 112-95, § 332, 126 Stat. 11, 73.

[16] *See* CRS Report RS21698, *Homeland Security: Unmanned Aerial Vehicles and Border Surveillance*, by Chad C. Haddal and Jeremiah Gertler.

[17] The OAM mission is to "protect the American people and the Nation's critical infrastructure through the coordinated use of integrated air and marine forces." DEP'T OF HOMELAND SECURITY, OFFICE OF INSPECTOR GENERAL, CBP'S USE OF UNMANNED AIRCRAFT SYSTEMS IN THE NATION'S BORDER SECURITY 2 (2012). These forces are used to "detect, interdict, and prevent acts of terrorism and the unlawful movement of people, illegal drugs, and other contraband toward or across U.S. borders." *Id.*

[18] There are over 300 total, including those issued to the following entities: City of Herrington, KS; Cornell University; Department of Energy Idaho National Laboratory; Eastern Gateway College Community College—Steubenville, OH; Miami-Dade Police Department; Mississippi Department of Marine Resources; North Little Rock Police Department, AR; Ogden Police Department, UT; Ohio University; Seattle Police Department; Texas A&M—Texas Engineering Experiment Station; Texas Department of Public Safety; Texas State University; University of Connecticut; University of Florida; U.S. Department of Agriculture Agricultural Research Service; Utah State University; Virginia Tech. *See* Unmanned Aircraft Systems, Federal Aviation Administration, http://www.faa.gov/ about/initiatives/uas/.

[19] *New age of surveillance, supra* note 3.

[20] Brian Bennett, *Drones Tested as Tools for Police and Firefighters*, LOS ANGELES TIMES (August 5, 2012 5:00 A.M.), http://www.latimes.com/news/nationworld/nation/la-na-drones-testing-20120805,0,6483617.story.

[21] The U.S. Army recently acquired a 1.8 gigapixel camera for use on its drones. This camera offers 900 times the pixels of a 2 megapixel camera found in some cell phones. It can track objects on the ground 65 miles away from an altitude of 20,000 feet. *US Army unveils 1.8 gigapixel camera helicopter drone*, BBC NEWS (December 29, 2011 6:11 p.m.), http://www.bbc.com/news/technology-16358851.

[22] Infrared cameras, also known as thermal imaging, can see objects through walls based on the relative levels of heat produced by the objects. *See* Draganflyer X6, Thermal Infrared Camera, http://www.draganfly.com/uav-helicopter/ draganflyer-x6/features/flir-camera.php.

[23] This sensor can recognize and permit drones to track vehicles based on license plate numbers. Customs and Border Protection Today, Unmanned Aerial Vehicles Support Border Security (July 2004), http://www.cbp.gov/xp/ CustomsToday/2004/Aug/other/aerial_vehicles.xml.

[24] This sensor produces three-dimensional images, and has the capability to see through trees and foliage. U.S. ARMY, UAS CENTER FOR EXCELLENCE, "EYES OF THE ARMY" US ARMY ROADMAP FOR UNMANNED AIRCRAFT SYSTEMS 2010- 2035, at 83 (2010).

[25] *See* Clay Dillow, *Army Developing Drones that Can Recognize Your Face from a Distance*, POPSCI (September 28, 2011), 5:01 p.m.), *available at* http://www.popsci.com/technology/ article/2011-09/army-wants-drones-can-recognizeyour-face-and-read-your-mind. As for weaponization, a sheriff's office in Texas has recently acquired a 50-pound ShadowHawk Helicopter that can carry a 40mm grenade launcher and a 12-gauge shotgun. *Talk of drones patrolling U.S. skies spawns anxiety*, USA TODAY (June 19, 2012 9:13 A.M.), http://www.usatoday.com/news/washington/story/ 2012-06-19/drone-backlash/55682654/1. The sheriff's office denied that these lethal weapons would be used, but is reportedly contemplating use of rubber bullets and tear gas on their drones. *Groups Concerned Over Arming Domestic Drones*, CBS DC (May 23, 2012 1:18 P.M.), http://washington.cbslocal. com/2012/05/23/groups-concerned-overarming-of-domestic-drones/. Although beyond the scope of this report, it should be noted that excessive force claims are analyzed under the Fourth Amendment's protection against unreasonable seizures. *See* Graham v. Connor, 490 U.S. 386, 395 (1989) ("Where, as here, the excessive force claim arises in the context of an arrest or investigatory stop of a free citizen, it is most properly characterized as one invoking the protections of the Fourth Amendment, which guarantees citizens the right 'to be secure in their persons ... against unreasonable ... seizures.'").

[26] U.S. CONST. amend IV.

[27] Olmstead v. United States, 277 U.S. 438, 466 (1928).

[28] *Id.*

[29] Katz v. United States, 389 U.S. 347, 351 (1967).

[30] *Id.* at 359.

[31] *Id.* at 351.

[32] *Id.* at 361 (Harlan, J., concurring).

[33] *Id.* at 351.

[34] *Id.* at 361 (Harlan, J., concurring); *see also* Oliver v. United States, 466 U.S. 170 (1984). We have frequently acknowledged that privacy interests are not coterminous with property rights. E. g., United States v. Salvucci, 448 U.S. 83, 91 (1980). However, because "property rights reflect society's explicit recognition of a person's authority to act as he wishes in certain areas, [they] should be considered in determining whether an individual's expectations of privacy are reasonable." Rakas v. Illinois, 439 U.S. 128, 153 (1978) (Powell, J., concurring). Indeed, the Court has suggested that, insofar as "[one] of the main rights attaching to property is the right to exclude others, ... one who owns or lawfully possesses or controls property will in all likelihood have a legitimate expectation of privacy by virtue of this right to exclude." *Id.*, at 144, n. 12. *Oliver*, 466 U.S. at 189-90.

[35] United States v. Jones, 132 S. Ct. 945, 950 n.3 (2012).

[36] *Id.*

[37] DANIEL SOLOVE, UNDERSTANDING PRIVACY 59 (2008).

[38] U.S. CONST. amend IV.

[39] Silverman v. United States, 365 U.S. 505, 512 (1961) ("At the very core stands the right of a man to retreat into his own home and be free from unreasonable government intrusion.").

[40] United States v. Watson, 423 U.S. 411 (1976).

[41] Payton v. New York, 445 U.S. 573, 603 (1980). This protection not only covers traditional houses, but apartments, Clinton v. Virginia, 377 U.S 158 (1963), and motel rooms, Stoner v. California, 376 U.S. 483 (1964).

[42] Kyllo v. United States, 533 U.S. 27, 29-30 (2001).

[43] *Id.* at 31.

[44] *Id.* at 34.

[45] In one case, police observation of marijuana plants through a crack in the house's siding did not constitute an unlawful search. *United States v. Hammett*, 236 F.3d 1054, 1061 (9th Cir. 2001). In another, the court held that the police officer's observation of contraband through the front dining room window was not unlawful. *United States v. Taylor*, 90 F.3d 903, 909 (4th Cir. 1996).

[46] Coolidge v. New Hampshire, 403 U.S. 443, 466 (1971).

[47] United States v. Hester, 365 U.S 57 (1924) (distinguishing between the doctrines of curtilage and open fields).

[48] The Court has defined curtilage as "the area to which extends the intimate activity associated with the 'sanctity of a man's home and the privacies of life.'" Oliver v. United States, 466 U.S. 170, 180 (1984) (quoting Boyd v. United States, 116 U.S. 616, 630 (1886)).
[49] United States v. Dunn, 480 U.S. 294, 301 (1987).
[50] California v. Ciraolo, 476 U.S. 207, 213 (1986).
[51] Dow Chemical Co. v. United States, 476 U.S. 227, 234-35 (1986) (quoting *Oliver*, 466 U.S. at 179).
[52] Maisano v. Welcher, 940 F.2d 499 (9th Cir. 1991).
[53] *Ciraolo*, 476 U.S. at 213.
[54] *Id.* at 207.
[55] *Id.* at 213.
[56] *Id.* at 213-214. It should be noted that although the police did take photographs with a 35-millimeter camera, the warrant relied on naked-eye observations and not the photographs. Thus, the holding was based on the naked-eye observations, unaided by the camera.
[57] *Id.* at 213 (citing 49 U.S.C. § 1304).
[58] Florida v. Riley, 488 U.S. 445, 448 (1989).
[59] *Id.*
[60] *Dow Chemical Co.*, 476 U.S. 227.
[61] *Id.* at 239
[62] United States v. Knotts, 460 U.S. 276 (1983); United States v. Karo, 468 U.S. 705 (1984).
[63] *Knotts*, 460 U.S. at 279. The Court reiterated that its analysis was based on the fact that the beeper was tracked within the vicinity of a home, not actually in the home. *Id*
[64] *Karo*, 468 U.S. at 714.
[65] *Id.* at 715.
[66] United States v. Jones, 132 S. Ct. 945 (2012).
[67] *Id.* at 949. *See generally* CRS Report R42511, *United States v. Jones: GPS Monitoring, Property, and Privacy*, by Richard M. Thompson II.
[68] *Jones*, 132 S. Ct. at 955 (Sotomayor, J., concurring).
[69] *Id.*
[70] Although the two concurring opinions in *Jones* arguably do not constitute binding precedent, lower courts have combined them as a possible alternative holding. *See* United States v. Hanna, No. 11-20678-CR, 2012 WL 279435, at *3 (S.D. Fla. Jan. 3, 2012) (analyzing the issue of Fourth Amendment standing to contest GPS surveillance under both the trespass theory and *Katz*'s privacy test); State v. Zahn, No. 25584, 2012 WL 862707 (S.D. Mar. 14, 2012) (holding that both the trespass approach and the mosaic theory can apply to GPS tracking); *but see* United States v. Bradshaw, No. 1:11-CR-257, 2012 WL 774964 (N.D. Ohio Mar. 8, 2012) (noting that the *Jones* majority did not adopt the mosaic theory).
[71] 8 U.S.C. 1357.
[72] 19 U.S.C. § 482. In the 112th Congress, the House of Representatives introduced H.R. 1505, which would enlarge CBP's authority to secure U.S. borders on federal land. H.R. 1505; *see also* John S. Adams, *Border bill would expand Homeland Security powers*, USA TODAY (September 26, 2011).
[73] United States v. Flores-Montano, 541 U.S. 149, 152 (2004).
[74] Cady v. Dombrowski, 413 U.S. 433, 439 (1973).
[75] United States v. Montoya De Hernandez, 473 U.S. 531, 538 (1985).
[76] *Id.*
[77] United States v. Beras, 183 F.3d 22, 24 (1st Cir. 1999) (ruling that pat down of defendant's legs was routine search).
[78] United States v. Kelly, 302 F.3d 291, 294-95 (5th Cir. 2002).
[79] United States v. Okafor, 285 F.3d 842 (9th Cir. 2002).
[80] *Montoya De Hernandez*, 473 U.S. at 541.
[81] *Id.*
[82] United States v. Asbury, 586 F.2d 973, 975 (1978).
[83] United States v. Ogberaha, 771 F.2d 655, 657 (2d Cir. 1985).
[84] Almeida-Sanchez v. United States, 413 U.S. 266, 267-68 (1973).
[85] *Id.* at 272-73 ("For example, searches at an established station near the border, at a point marking the confluence of two or more roads that extend from the border, might be functional equivalents from border searches. For another example, a search of the passengers and cargo of an airplane arriving at a St. Louis airport after a nonstop flight from Mexico would clearly be the functional equivalent of a border search."). Like *Almeida-*

Sanchez, Border Patrol agents in *United States v. Brignoni-Ponce* stopped an individual's vehicle as part of a roving patrol solely because the occupants appeared to be of Mexican descent, with no proof of illegal activity. *United States v. Brignoni-Ponce*, 422 U.S. 873, 874-75 (1975). Again, the Court struck down this practice of suspicionless stops, remarking that "[i]n the context of border area stops, the reasonableness requirement of the Fourth Amendment demands something more than the broad and unlimited discretion sought by the Government. Roads near the border carry not only aliens seeking to enter the country illegally, but a large volume of legitimate traffic as well." *Id.* at 882.

[86] Mincey v. Arizona, 437 U.S. 385, 390 (1978) (citation omitted).

[87] Johnson v. Untied States, 333 U.S. 10, 14 (1948) ("The right of officers to thrust themselves into a home is also a grave concern, not only to the individual but to a society which chooses to dwell in reasonable security and freedom from surveillance. When the right of privacy must reasonably yield to the right of search is, as a rule, to be decided by a judicial officer, not by a policeman or government enforcement agent."). Probable cause is found when, looking at the "totality-of-the-circumstances" there "is a fair probability that contraband or evidence of a crime will be found in a particular place." Illinois v. Gates, 462 U.S. 213, 238 (1983).

[88] Eve Brensike Primus, *Disentangling Administrative Searches*, 111 COLUM. L. REV. 254, 256 (2011).

[89] Nat'l Treasury Employees Union v. Von Raab, 489 U.S. 656, 665-66 (1989).

[90] Primus, *supra* note 88, at 263.

[91] United States v. Martinez-Fuerte, 428 U.S. 543, 566 (1976).

[92] United States v. Biswell, 406 U.S 311, 317 (inspection of gun dealer's storeroom) ("We have little difficulty in concluding that where, as here, regulatory inspections further urgent federal interest, and the possibilities of abuse and the threat to privacy are not of impressive dimensions, the inspection may proceed without a warrant where specifically authorized by statute.").

[93] Mich. Dep't of State Police v. Sitz, 496 U.S. 444, 455 (1990).

[94] *Id.* at 455.

[95] City of Indianapolis v. Edmund, 531 U.S. 32 (2000).

[96] *Id.* at 42.

[97] *Id.*

[98] EYES OF THE ARMY, *supra* note 24.

[99] *See generally,* Paul McBride, *Beyond Orwell: The Application of Unmanned Aircraft Systems in Domestic Surveillance Operations*, 74 J. Air. L. & Com. 627, 655-56 ("This implies that although the curtilage does not benefit from the absolute protection afforded to the interior of the home, there is a close relationship between the two, and that technology directed at the home and its curtilage will be subjected to a more skeptical analysis than would be applied in a case involving open fields or industrial areas.").

[100] California v. Ciraolo, 476 U.S. 207, 215 (1986).

[101] Florida v. Riley, 488 U.S. 445, 451-52 (1989).

[102] Federal Aviation Administration, *supra* note 18.

[103] *Ciraolo*, 476 U.S. at 212. However, in determining society's privacy expectations, a reviewing court might also take into consideration the proliferation of aerial mapping such as Google Maps and Google Earth conducted by private actors. *See generally* Google Maps, Street View, http://www.google.com/streetview.

[104] U.S. CONST. art. IV, § 4 ("The United States shall guarantee to every State in this Union a Republican Form of Government, and shall protect each of them against Invasion[.]").

[105] Almeida-Sanchez v. United States, 413 U.S. 266 (1973); *United States v. Brignoni-Ponce*, 422 U.S. 873 (1975).

[106] Kyllo v. United States, 533 U.S. 27, 33-34 (2001).

[107] United States v. Jones, 132 S. Ct. 945, 962 (2012) (Alito, J., concurring).

[108] Stanford Law Review Symposium, *Drones—Privacy Paradox: Privacy and its Conflicting Values* (February 2, 2012), http://cyberlaw.stanford.edu/multimedia/drones-privacy-paradox-privacy-and-its-conflicting-values-video.

[109] *ACLU Seeks Details on Automatic License Plate Readers in Massive Nationwide Request,* AMERICAN CIVIL LIBERTIES UNION (July 31, 2012), http://www.aclu.org/technology-and-liberty/aclu-seeks-details-automatic-licenseplate-readers-massive-nationwide-reque-4.

[110] *Id.*

[111] *See, e.g.*, Olabisiomotosho v. City of Houston, 185 F.3d 521, 529 (5th Cir. 1999) ("A motorist has no privacy interest in her license plate number. Like the area outside the cartilage [sic] of a dwelling, a car's license plate number is constantly open to the plain view of passersby.") (internal citation and quotation marks omitted); United States v. Ellison, 462 F.3d 557, 562 (6th Cir. 2006) ("No argument can be made that a motorist seeks to keep the information on his license plate private. The very purpose of a license plate number, like that of a

Vehicle Identification Number, is to provide identifying information to law enforcement officials and others."); United States v. Castaneda, 494 F.3d 1146, 1151 (9th Cir. 2007); United States v. Walraven, 892 F.2d 972, 974 (10th 1989).

[112] *Using Unmanned Aircraft Systems Within the Homeland: Security Game Changer? Hearing Before the Subcomm. on Oversight, Investigations, and Management of the H. Comm. on Homeland Sec.*, 112th Cong. 3 (2012) (statement of Amie Stepanovich, Counsel, Electronic Privacy Information Center).

[113] Mark Brown, *Lockheed uses ground-based laser to recharge drone mid-flight*, WIRED (July 12, 2012), *available at* http://www.wired.co.uk/news/archive/2012-07/12/lockheed-lasers.

[114] *Id.* Lockheed has reportedly been working on extending flight times from days to months. *Id.*

[115] *Dow Chemical*, 476 U.S. at 238.

[116] United States v. Jones, 132 S. Ct. 945, 956 (Sotomayor, J., concurring) (internal quotation marks omitted).

[117] *Id.*

[118] *See, e.g.*, Apple Store, Parrot AR.Drone 2.0, http://store.apple.com/us/product/H8859ZM/A/ parrot-ar-drone-2-0. This aircraft, is remote-controlled by an iPhone or iPad, and has a high-definition camera that can take both pictures and videos. *Id.*

119 United States v. Cuevas-Sanchez, 821 F.2d 248 (5th Cir. 1987).

[120] *Id.* at 251.

[121] Mich. Dep't of State Police v. Sitz, 496 U.S. 444, 453-54 (1990).

[122] Omnibus Crime Control and Safe Streets Act of 1968, P.L. 90-351, 87 Stat. 197, 211 (codified at 18 U.S.C. § 2510- 2522).

[123] Electronic Communications Privacy Act of 1986, P.L. 99-508, 100 Stat. 1848 (codified at 18 U.S.C. § 2701-2712).

[124] Right to Financial Privacy Act, P.L. 95-630, 92 Stat. 3697 (codified at 12 U.S.C. § 3401-3422).

[125] Health Insurance Portability and Accountability Act of 1996, P.L. 104-191, 110 Stat. 1936.

[126] H.R. 5925, S. 3287, 112th Cong. 2d Sess. (2012).

[127] H.R. 6199, 112th Cong. 2d Sess. (2012).

[128] H.R. 5961, 112th Cong. 2 (2012). Legislative action was sparked by claims that the EPA was conducting aerial inspections of Midwestern farms with a drone. It was reported that an EPA inspector flew a drone over the farm looking for clean water violations from manure run-off into streams. David A. Fahrenthold, *Reining in the Rumors about EPA 'drones,'* WASH. POST (June 18, 5:05 P.M.), *available at* http://www.washingtonpost.com/politics/reiningin-the-rumors-about-epa-drones/2012/06/16/gJQAw WjkhV _story.html. After several weeks, it was discovered that the fly-overs were conducted by manned aircraft not drones, but this revelation did not quell the debate over the use of drones for such purposes.

[129] S.Amdt. 2372.

[130] S.Amdt. 2456.

In: Privacy: Select Issues and Laws for the 21st Century
Editor: Doris B. Delrio
ISBN: 978-1-62618-429-9

Chapter 3

UNITED STATES V. JONES: GPS MONITORING, PROPERTY, AND PRIVACY*

Richard M. Thompson II

SUMMARY

In *United States v. Jones*, 132 S. Ct. 945 (2012), all nine Supreme Court Justices agreed that Jones was *searched* when the police attached a Global Positioning System (GPS) device to the undercarriage of his car and tracked his movements for four weeks. The Court, however, splintered on what constituted the search: the attachment of the device or the long-term monitoring. The majority held that the *attachment* of the GPS device and an attempt to obtain information was the violation; Justice Alito, concurring, argued that the *monitoring* was a violation of Jones's reasonable expectation of privacy; and Justice Sotomayor, also concurring, agreed with them both, but would provide further Fourth Amendment protections. This report will examine these three decisions in an effort to find their place in the body of existing Fourth Amendment law pertaining to privacy, property, and technology.

In *Jones*, the police attached a GPS tracking device to the bottom of Jones's car and monitored his movements for 28 days. At trial, the prosecution relied on Jones's movements to a stash house to tie him to a drug conspiracy. Jones was convicted and given a life sentence. The United States Court of Appeals for the District of Columbia Circuit reversed, holding that the evidence was unlawfully obtained under the Fourth Amendment. The Supreme Court agreed. The majority, speaking through Justice Scalia, explained that a physical intrusion into a constitutionally protected area, coupled with an attempt to obtain information, can constitute a violation of the Fourth Amendment. Although the Court's landmark decision in *Katz v. United States*, 389 U.S. 347 (1967), supposedly altered the focus of the Fourth Amendment from property to privacy, the majority argued that it left untouched traditional spheres of Fourth Amendment protection—a person and his house, papers, and effects. Because the police had invaded

* This is an edited, reformatted and augmented version of Congressional Research Service, Publication No. R42511, dated April 30, 2012.

Jones's property—his car, which is an *effect*—that was all the Court needed to hold that a constitutional search had occurred.

The majority's test, however, provides little guidance in instances where the government need not physically install a device to conduct surveillance, for instance, by using cell phones or preinstalled GPS devices in vehicles.

To understand how the Court may rule on these technologies, one must look to the two concurrences, which provide a more global interpretation of the Fourth Amendment. Justice Alito, writing for a four-member concurrence, would have applied the *Katz* privacy formulation, asserting that longer-term monitoring constitutes an invasion of privacy, whereas short-term monitoring does not. He left it to future courts to distinguish between the two.

Justice Sotomayor's concurrence appears to provide the most protection, finding that both the trespass approach and the privacy-based approach should be utilized. She also questioned the rule that any information provided to a third party, which occurs in many commercial transactions like banking or computing, should lose all privacy protections.

Although all three opinions concluded that the government's action in *Jones* was a search, none expressly required that police get a warrant in future GPS tracking cases. (The government forfeited the argument.) Further, there is no clear indication of the level of suspicion—probable cause, reasonable suspicion, or something less—that is required to attach a GPS unit and monitor the target's movements. Additionally, there have been several bills filed in the 112th Congress, including Senator Patrick J. Leahy's Electronic Communications Privacy Act Amendment Act of 2011 (S. 1011) and Senator Ron Wyden's and Representative Jason Chaffetz's identical legislation, S. 1212 and H.R. 2168, the Geolocational Privacy and Surveillance Act (GPS bill), that would require a warrant based upon probable cause to access geolocation information.

INTRODUCTION

There is little doubt that technology is fast becoming intertwined with our jobs, our social life, and even our most private interactions with each other. This phenomenon creates friction among many compelling interests. The first is a clash between two contrasting values: the desire for privacy and the longing to be connected through the newest and most advanced technology. To a certain extent, as one advances, the other must necessarily recede. Meanwhile, courts are tasked with determining the balance between government's law enforcement needs and the people's privacy. The Fourth Amendment to the U.S. Constitution provides the measuring stick to determine this balance. The amendment ensures "[t]he right of the people to be secure in their persons, houses, papers, and effects, against unreasonable searches and seizures, shall not be violated."[1] Its primary function is to prohibit government intrusion upon the privacy and property rights of the people. When new technology is involved, achieving this balance is not an easy undertaking.

United States v. Jones presented such a challenge to the Supreme Court. The question posed was whether the installation and month-long monitoring of a GPS device attached to Jones's car constituted a violation of the Fourth Amendment's prohibition against "unreasonable searches and seizures."[2] This usage of the Global Positioning System (GPS)[3] is not unusual in criminal investigations,[4] but up to that point longer-term monitoring had not been directly tested by the Court. Thus, many observers awaited the *Jones* ruling for its potential impact not only on government monitoring programs, but also on general Fourth Amendment cases involving prolonged government surveillance.

In prior government tracking cases,[5] the Court applied the test from *Katz v. United States*, which addresses whether the individual had a reasonable expectation of privacy in the area to be searched.[6] Because the police in *Jones* physically invaded his property to attach the GPS device—whereas in the previous cases they had not—the Court declined to apply *Katz*, but instead based its decision on a trespass theory.[7] The trespass theory asks whether there was a physical intrusion onto a constitutionally protected area coupled with an attempt to obtain information.[8] In *Jones*, there was, so the Court applied this more limited test and held that a search occurred. Though the majority bypassed the *Katz* approach, Justice Alito, concurring with Justices Breyer, Ginsburg, and Kagan, would have applied *Katz*.[9] Long-term surveillance, Justice Alito wrote, violated Jones's reasonable expectation of privacy under *Katz*. Justice Sotomayor agreed with both the majority and Alito's concurrence, but called for additional protection by questioning the viability of the third-party doctrine, which holds that any information voluntarily given to a third party loses all privacy protections.[10]

This report will analyze all three opinions in an attempt to determine how *Jones* might affect future use of GPS tracking and other government surveillance techniques. First, it will briefly recount the facts that led to Jones's prosecution, his appeal, and the Supreme Court's review. Next, it will analyze the majority's property-based test, evaluating it against similar Fourth Amendment case law. Additionally, this section will raise issues concerning the possible impact of this approach on similar search and seizure cases. Next, the report will examine both Justice Alito's and Justice Sotomayor's concurrences and their potential impact on cases involving technology. Because the Court did not express whether a warrant is required, the report will posit several theories on how this issue may be resolved in the future.

UNITED STATES V. JONES: A PROPERTY-BASED APPROACH TO THE FOURTH AMENDMENT

In 2004, a Joint Task Force of the FBI and the District of Columbia Metropolitan Police Department suspected Antoine Jones was part of a drug distribution ring.[11] Based on information obtained from wiretaps, a pen register,[12] and video surveillance, the task force obtained a warrant to monitor Jones's Jeep with a GPS tracking device. According to the terms of the warrant, the officers had 10 days to install it and were required to do it in the District of Columbia. The officers installed the device on the 11th day in Maryland while the Jeep was parked in a public parking lot.[13] For the next four weeks the device tracked Jones's every movement, creating 2,000 pages of monitoring data.[14] During this time, the device tracked Jones's movements to and from a known stash house.

Jones was indicted for conspiracy to distribute and possession with intent to distribute cocaine. At trial, the prosecution relied heavily on Jones's movements derived from the GPS to connect him with a larger drug ring.[15] He moved to dismiss this information as a warrantless search under the Fourth Amendment. The United States District Court for the District of Columbia excluded the data derived when his car was parked in his garage but allowed into evidence all of his public movements.[16] Jones was ultimately convicted and sentenced to life imprisonment.[17] The United States Court of Appeals for the District of Columbia Circuit reversed, holding that the GPS data were derived in violation of Jones's reasonable expectation of privacy under the Fourth Amendment.[18] The Supreme Court then granted a writ of certiorari, agreeing to review Jones's case.

Most observers assumed the Supreme Court would, like the D.C. Circuit Court of Appeals, apply the reasonable expectation of privacy test developed in *Katz v. United States* to determine if the tracking was a Fourth Amendment search. Under the *Katz* test, a search in the constitutional sense has occurred if the individual had an actual expectation of privacy in the area to be searched that society would deem reasonable.[19] Since 1967, when *Katz* was handed down, the Court had developed a body of case law applying this privacy-based formulation of the Fourth Amendment.[20]

The *Jones* majority, led by Justice Scalia, took a different route.[21] It held that the *attachment* of the GPS device, coupled with its use to monitor Jones's movements, was a constitutional search.[22] The Fourth Amendment ensures that "[t]he right of the people to be secure in their persons, houses, papers, and effects, against unreasonable searches and seizures, shall not be violated."[23] Because Jones's vehicle is an *effect*—listed in the text of the Fourth Amendment—the police's physical intrusion by attaching the GPS for tracking purposes constituted a *search*.[24] This theory hinges on common law trespass as it was known in 1791 (when the Fourth Amendment was adopted). It does not rely on *Katz*, nor any subjective conception of privacy. The majority contended that Jones's rights should not strictly depend on whether his reasonably expected zone of privacy was pierced.[25] Rather, the majority asserted, property rights also define an individual's right to be free from government intrusion.

Justice Alito, in concurrence, contended that the majority's reliance on "18th-century tort law" which "might have provided grounds in 1791 for a suit based on trespass to chattels," "strains the language of the Fourth Amendment; it has little if any support in current Fourth Amendment case law; and it is highly artificial."[26] Justice Alito would have instead applied the *Katz* formulation.[27]

This criticism prompts two central questions: (1) Does the majority's property-based approach enjoy textual, historical, or jurisprudential support?; and (2) What effect will this approach have on other areas of government investigations?

The seeds for the property-based approach were planted in England in *Entick v. Carrington*, a case considered by many as an ancestor of the Fourth Amendment.[28] There, the English court forbade government agents from searching through Entick's home, looking for papers intended to prove his seditious writing. The agents had a general warrant to search the home, but the warrant lacked a specific description of the area to be searched and the items to be seized. Lord Camden declared that no government agent nor any other person may enter the property of another without permission, even if no harm is done.[29] This theory carried over to the colonies and prompted the framers to include a prohibition against unreasonable searches and seizures when drafting the Bill of Rights.[30] Under this common law trespass approach, the key inquiry is not necessarily the content of the information obtained by the police, but rather their method of retrieving it. The *Jones* Court had no doubts that the attachment of the GPS device (which required a trespass of Jones's car) would have been a search when the Fourth Amendment was adopted—when *Entick* was fresh in the framers' minds.[31]

Although property certainly controlled Fourth Amendment thinking during the infancy of the Fourth Amendment, its control waned in later years. *Olmstead v. United States* provides an example. There, federal agents installed several wiretaps on the telephone wires coming from Olmstead's house.[32] In upholding this electronic eavesdropping, the Court ruled that the Fourth Amendment applied only when there was an official search or seizure of a person, his tangible papers and effects, and an "actual physical invasion" of the individual's home.[33] Because the installation of the wiretap did not require the agents to trespass onto Olmstead's property, the Court held that it was not a search or seizure under the Fourth Amendment.[34]

Forty years later, the Court began its shift away from this property-centric approach. In *Warden v. Hayden*, the Court noted the property-based approach had been discredited over the years, and that privacy should be the focus of the inquiry under the Fourth Amendment.[35] Subsequently, the Court decided *Katz v. United States*, where it held an electronic surveillance of Katz's conversations while he was in a public telephone booth was impermissible, despite the fact that no property rights were involved.[36] The "Fourth Amendment protects people, not places," the Court declared, and any search that invaded a person's "reasonable expectation of privacy" should be considered a search in the constitutional sense.[37]

This seemingly conflicting line of cases left many wondering whether property and privacy could coexist under the Fourth Amendment. The Court attempted to reconcile these two lines in *Soldal v. County of Cook*.[38] There, while under the supervision of local police, a landlord had his tenant's trailer home towed from the rented lot.[39] The tenant sued the police under Section 1983, a civil rights statute, for a violation of his Fourth Amendment right to be free from unreasonable seizure. The Seventh Circuit Court of Appeals denied the tenant's claim, holding that any Fourth Amendment violation must be supported by some invasion of privacy.[40] The police did not invade the tenant's privacy, but only his possessory interest in the property, enough for the court to hold the Fourth Amendment inapplicable. Instead, the panel noted that the due process clause was the proper avenue of relief for a "pure deprivation of property."[41]

The Supreme Court disagreed, ruling that the police action was a seizure notwithstanding the lack of a privacy interest at stake.[42] The Court took pains to note that privacy-based cases like *Katz* and *Warden* had not "snuffed out the previously recognized protection for property under the Fourth Amendment," but instead had "demonstrated that property is not the sole measure of Fourth Amendment violations."[43] The Court noted that the amendment does not protect possessory interests in all kinds of property, such as an open field not closely connected with a person's home, but certainly covers things specifically listed in the constitutional text—persons, houses, papers, and effects.[44]

This idea that the Fourth Amendment protects both privacy and property independently is infused throughout the majority opinion in *Jones*. As Justice Scalia noted, *Katz* did not *supplant* the common law trespass approach, but merely *supplemented* it.[45] But is a simple trespass alone enough to constitute a violation? The Court answered no: in addition to the physical intrusion, there must be "an attempt to find something or to obtain information."[46] Also, not every police trespass will be a constitutional search. The government must intrude upon an area enumerated in the text of the amendment (person, houses, papers, and effects).[47] This leaves several questions. If a car is an effect, what other personal property may be covered under this approach? Will computer data constitute an *effect*? Will an e-mail constitute an electronic *paper*? If a police officer walks onto one's porch, is that an invasion of his *house*? There are no easy answers to these questions.

Additionally, because the Court focused on the attachment of the device and the property interests involved, there remain questions of whether prolonged tracking with a device is permissible under the Fourth Amendment if there is no trespass.

As the majority noted, "[s]ituations involving merely transmission of electronic signals without trespass would *remain* subject to *Katz* analysis."[48] Justice Alito's and Sotomayor's concurrences in *Jones* may be scrutinized for how the Court might handle these scenarios under *Katz*.[49]

THE IMPLICATIONS OF JONES AND TECHNOLOGY

As more cell phones and cars are outfitted with GPS tracking technologies, police need not physically attach a device to track its movements. Because the *Jones* majority opinion is based on a *physical* trespass into a constitutionally protected area, it seemingly will not apply where GPS is preinstalled. Justices Alito, and his four-Justice concurrence, and Sotomayor, concurring separately, provide insight into how a future court may apply the Fourth Amendment to evolving technologies.[50] These opinions rely, to a certain extent, on the mosaic theory first discussed in the D.C. Circuit opinion, which says that tracking a person's public movements over a long duration is constitutionally unacceptable even if tracking each of the movements individually may be permitted. Whether this approach will garner a majority on the Court is unclear. However, at a minimum, these concurrences have engendered discussion in the lower courts, with several courts citing the mosaic theory as a viable alternative.[51]

The question then becomes how much weight should the Alito and Sotomayor concurring opinions be accorded?[52] There is no *one* rule to answer this question.[53] Generally, there are two types of concurrences in Supreme Court opinions. The first is the true concurrence, in which the Justice concurs in the judgment, but disagrees with the reasoning.[54] Justice Alito's opinion exemplifies that type of concurrence; he agreed that the surveillance constituted a Fourth Amendment search, but would have decided the case under the traditional reasonable expectation of privacy test instead of the trespass test. The second category is the simple concurrence, where the Justice agrees with the judgment and the reasoning of the majority,[55] but also poses possible new theories that may not be directly relevant to that particular case, but can be used later to move the law in a particular direction.[56] Justice Sotomayor's opinion seems to fit this latter category. Although these two concurrences chart somewhat different courses in their strategy and reasoning, when combined they appear to command five votes on the Court—a potential majority.[57]

Justice Alito's Concurrence: A *Katz*-Based Approach

Justice Alito spends most of his concurrence attempting to counter the majority's common law trespass theory.[58] He argued that Scalia's reversion to the law as it stood in 1791 was unwise, and a return to the much-criticized property approach.[59] The focus of this report, however, is Justice Alito's discussion of long-term GPS tracking under *Katz*'s reasonable expectation of privacy test.

Before coming up on appeal, the D.C. Circuit below examined whether Jones's whereabouts over the month-long period of tracking were *exposed* to the public.[60] A person's movements are not *actually* exposed, the court answered, because the likelihood that anyone could actually follow someone for a month is highly improbable.[61] Further, the movements are not *constructively* exposed because in many instances the whole is greater than the sum of the parts.[62] This last proposition is premised on the mosaic theory. The mosaic theory supposes that tracking the whole of one's movements over an extended period of time reveals significantly more about that person than each individual trip does in isolation.[63] For instance, police cannot infer much about a person from *one* trip to the liquor store. However, a *daily* trip to the same liquor store would provide greater insight into the person's habits. The government has employed this theory in the national security context for protecting intelligence sources and methods of obtaining information.[64] The thrust of the argument is that unless a person has a broad view of the situation in question, he will not understand the importance of a single piece of evidence.[65] Thus, with GPS tracking, following someone for one trip may not say much about a person, but following his every movement for an extended period presumably reveals considerably more.

United States v. Knotts created an obstacle to the panel's adoption of the mosaic theory.[66] In *Knotts*, the Supreme Court held that a person has no reasonable expectation of privacy in his movements on public streets.[67] The Court, however, did not foreclose the argument that, even if traveling on public roadways, pervasive or intrusive police activity may violate the Fourth Amendment.[68] The Court suggested it would revisit the issue if police were to use "dragnet-type law enforcement practices."[69] Although the purport of this phrase is somewhat obscure, the D.C. Circuit understood it to mean that 24-hour surveillance of a single individual was sufficient for it to apply.[70] As such, the panel ruled that the previous tracking cases were not controlling, allowing it to apply the mosaic theory.[71] Based on this application, the court granted Jones's motion to dismiss all location evidence obtained from the GPS device.

As noted earlier, Justice Scalia and the majority did not apply the mosaic theory. Instead they grounded their decision in a common law trespass theory.[72] Justice Alito, on the other hand, wanted to confront directly this question of how technology affected a society's expectations of privacy. He first posited that the ubiquity of cell phones, video monitoring, and other technologies in modern life shapes the average person's expectation of privacy—presumably reducing that expectation.[73] Based on his understanding of *Katz*, Alito would have asked whether the use of GPS tracking involved an intrusion a reasonable person would not have expected. Under his approach, "relatively short-term monitoring of a person's movements on public streets accords with expectations of privacy that our society has recognized as reasonable."[74] However, the use of "longer term" GPS monitoring will in most instances violate the Fourth Amendment.[75] Justice Alito declined to create a rule for determining at what point police tracking crosses this constitutional line. He concluded that four weeks of tracking was a search.[76]

Because of the limited nature of Justice Alito's discussion, it is difficult to discern precisely which theory he employed. It is arguable that he and the three other Justices implicitly support the mosaic theory. To say that short-term monitoring is permissible, but longer-term monitoring is not, indicates there is something about the aggregation of a person's movements that prompted these Justices to deem it a Fourth Amendment search.[77] It could also be argued that Justice Alito's concurrence did not accept the mosaic theory, but instead applied the probabilistic model of Fourth Amendment theory.[78] This theory supposes that when government conducts an investigation in a way that would surprise an individual, or "interferes with customs and social expectations," it violates a reasonable expectation of privacy.[79] Justice Alito categorizes the *Katz* test as looking at the "privacy expectations of the hypothetical reasonable person"—a hypothetical person who has "a well-developed and stable set of privacy expectations."[80] Justice Alito notes that in precomputer days, the police had the time and resources to track only persons of exceptional interest to the police. He seems to accord much importance in the belief that the hypothetical reasonable person would be surprised to learn that the police would be tracking their every movement for a month-long period—an act beyond society's expectations.

Justice Sotomayor's Concurrence: The Broadest Reading of the Fourth Amendment

As far as Fourth Amendment rights are concerned, Justice Sotomayor provided the broadest interpretation in *Jones* by joining the majority's trespass approach, openly supporting Justice Alito's privacy-based approach,[81] and putting into question the continuing viability of the third-party doctrine—a theory many believe creates the largest gap in privacy protection, especially in the realm of technology.

Whereas it is unclear whether Justices Alito, Breyer, Kagan, and Ginsburg support the mosaic theory, Justice Sotomayor maintained that this theory should directly guide the Court's determination of a person's privacy expectations in their public movements.[82] She noted that "GPS monitoring generates a precise, comprehensive record of a person's public movements that reflects a wealth of detail about her familial, political, professional, religious, and sexual associations."[83] As part and parcel of the mosaic theory, she contended that an individual's awareness that the government may be constantly watching can chill one's freedom of speech and association under the First Amendment.[84] Although the police might obtain the same evidence through traditional surveillance, there is something about the technology that troubled Justice Sotomayor. She seemed concerned that there will no longer be a logistical barrier between the government and the people. Police now have access to a cheap technology that can produce a significant amount of data. The Court must consider this a search—presumably requiring a warrant—to provide adequate oversight over the executive branch.[85] This idea seems to coincide with Justice Jackson's well-worn saying that courts prefer that searches be overseen by a "neutral and detached magistrate instead of being judged by the officer engaged in the often competitive enterprise of ferreting out crime."[86]

Additionally, Justice Sotomayor called for a reexamination of the third-party doctrine. This doctrine supposes that any information a person voluntarily conveys to a third party is no longer entitled to Fourth Amendment protection, as the person cannot have a reasonable expectation that the third party will guard the privacy in that information.[87] This rule has been used to justify access to bank records,[88] the telephone numbers a person dials,[89] electric billing records,[90] and cell phone billing records.[91] Some argue that when individuals give documents to a third party, usually in a commercial transaction, they consent to the release of such information to the government,[92] or at a minimum assume the risk that the person trusted with the information would hand it over.[93] Justice Sotomayor suggests that perhaps this theory should not be permitted to reach its logical extent in the digital age, in which people convey a wealth of personal information to third parties.[94] She contends that the Fourth Amendment rules should not require a person to keep secret any information the person does not want the government to obtain. In the end, she leaves it to another day to reevaluate the third-party doctrine in an age where most private information is handed over in the course of commercial transactions. In the meantime, Justice Sotomayor believed the physical intrusion theory was enough to resolve the case.[95]

WARRANT REQUIREMENT AFTER JONES

All nine Justices agreed that tracking a person for four months is a constitutional search. Where there is little agreement among Court observers, though, is what level of suspicion is required to conduct GPS monitoring or whether a warrant is required.[96] Because the government failed to argue that a warrant was not required or that something less than probable cause would be enough to conduct this surveillance, the Court considered the arguments forfeited.[97] Thus, to determine if a warrant or something less will be required in future cases, general Fourth Amendment principles must suffice until the courts provide further guidance.

The "ultimate touchstone" of the Fourth Amendment is reasonableness, as required by the history and text of the prohibition against "unreasonable searches and seizures."[98] That is to say, once a court determines a *search* has occurred, it must then inquiry whether it was reasonable. In most instances, the Supreme Court has required the government to obtain a warrant based upon probable cause for a search to be considered reasonable.[99] A review of the cases, however, shows that this rule is not ironclad, and that the exceptions are commonplace.[100]

Some commentators argue that the automobile exception could apply to the use of a GPS tracking device.[101] The automobile exception—one of the warrantless search exceptions—evolved from the exigency requirement.[102] It was first formulated in the 1925 case of *Carroll v. United States*, in which the Court permitted the police, who had probable cause to suspect that the defendant's car was carrying bootlegged liquor, to conduct a warrantless vehicle search.[103] The Court noted that it was not practicable to obtain a warrant for evidence secreted on a "ship, motor boat, wagon or automobile" because the vehicle can be "quickly moved out of the locality or jurisdiction."[104] In later cases, the Court developed a second rationale for the automobile exception, reasoning that drivers have a diminished expectation of privacy when in their vehicles.[105] This is based on the notion that cars travel on public thoroughfares where the driver and occupants are in plain view of the public.[106] Further, cars and drivers alike are subject to extensive government regulation,[107] and vehicles must undergo periodic inspections.[108]

As noted in *Carroll*, because a vehicle can be moved quickly from the jurisdiction, requiring a warrant to attach a GPS device may not be feasible.[109] Also, tracking someone's public movements may not be as invasive as searching through a person's belongings as is currently permitted under the traditional automobile exception.[110] On the reverse side, police will generally know in advance when they intend to use a GPS device, thereby negating the presumed exigency that is linked with cars. A court could hold that warrants are generally required for GPS devices, unless a true exigency existed beyond that presumed in general automobile cases, for example, in a case of kidnapping or a fleeing suspect.

Additionally, some commentators believe that the general reasonableness standard may apply, vitiating a need for a warrant.[111] These theories suppose that the intrusion on the individual is minimal and the government interest significant. In line with this reasoning, one observer posited that a *Terry*-type standard would be sufficient—that is, that the police must have reasonable suspicion to conduct a search, but need neither probable cause nor a warrant.[112] A court would review the reasonableness after the fact, unlike warrants, where the review comes before the search.

CONCLUSION

Nine Justices are seemingly in agreement that, based on the facts of *Jones*, the attachment of a GPS device to the bottom of Jones's car and tracking him for a month-long period was a constitutional search. Presented with a different set of facts, the Court's unanimity may disintegrate. For instance, if the police need not attach the device, but it is preinstalled, for example, in a cell phone or a navigation system in a car, the outcome may differ. Further, even though this surveillance was considered a search, the Court gave no guidance on whether a warrant is required or what quantum of suspicion is enough to use GPS monitoring.

That said, it is within the power of Congress or state legislatures to propose their own requirements. The federal Constitution sets the minimum constitutional standard. Legislatures (state or federal) may create more protection of privacy and property. Congress has done this on several occasions, most notably in the field of communications with the wiretap statutes.[113] When technology is in flux, one may argue that the institutional capabilities of a legislature may be the better venue to develop these rules.[114] Justice Alito suggested this approach in his *Jones* concurrence: "In circumstances involving dramatic technological change, the best solution to privacy concerns may be legislative. A legislative body is well situated to gauge changing public attitudes, to draw detailed lines, and to balance privacy and public safety in a comprehensive way."[115]

There has been legislative activity in recent Congresses to update privacy laws to cover new technologies such as GPS. Senator Leahy has introduced the Electronic Communications Privacy Act Amendments Act of 2011 (S. 1011), which would prohibit the government from accessing or using a device to acquire geolocation information, unless it obtains a warrant based upon probable cause or a court order under Title I or Title IV of the Foreign Intelligence Surveillance Act (FISA) of 1978.[116] Similarly, Senator Ron Wyden and Representative Jason Chaffetz have introduced identical legislation, S. 1212 and H.R. 2168, entitled the Geolocational Privacy and Surveillance Act, or GPS bill, which would make it unlawful for law enforcement to intercept or use a person's location unless they obtained a warrant based upon probable cause or one of the limited exceptions applied.[117]

With each advance in technology, the courts and Congress are asked to balance a host of competing interests including privacy, property, technology, and the needs of law enforcement. It will take future cases and statutes to better delineate a proper balance.

End Notes

[1] U.S. Const. amend. IV.
[2] United States v. Jones, 132 S. Ct. 945, 948 (2012).
[3] GPS is a network of 24 government satellites that constantly send out radio signals and allow a receiver on Earth to determine its position. Aaron Renenger, *Satellite Tracking and the Right to Privacy*, 53 HASTINGS L. J. 549, 550 (2002).
[4] John Ganz, *It's Already Public: Why Federal Officers Should Not Need Warrants to Use GPS Vehicle Tracking Devices*, 95 CRIM. L. & CRIMINOLOGY 1325, 1330 (2005).
[5] United States v. Knotts, 460 U.S. 276, 278-79 (1983) (holding that use of tracking device while suspect was on public thoroughfares was not a violation of the Fourth Amendment as he had no reasonable expectation of privacy in his public movements); United States v. Karo, 468 U.S. 705, 718 (1984) (holding that use of tracking of device while in private home was a violation of the Fourth Amendment).
[6] This reasonable expectation of privacy test was formulated by Justice Harlan in his *Katz* concurrence. Katz v. United States, 389 U.S. 347, 361 (1967) (Harlan, J., concurring).
[7] *Jones*, 132 S. Ct. at 952.
[8] *Id.* at 951 n.5.
[9] *Id.* at 958 (Alito, J., concurring).
[10] *Id.* at 957 (Sotomayor, J., concurring).
[11] *Id.* at 948.
[12] A pen register is a device that determines the outgoing telephone numbers dialed from a telephone. 18 U.S.C. § 3127(3).
[13] Since the device was attached one day late and in the wrong jurisdiction, the installation was considered warrantless.
[14] *Id.*
[15] *Id.* at 948-49.
[16] United States v. Jones, 451 F. Supp. 2d 71, 88 (D. D.C. 2006).
[17] *Jones*, 132 S. Ct. at 949.
[18] United States v. Maynard, 615 F.3d 544, 555 (D.C. Cir. 2010). Because Jones's case was consolidated with other codefendants on appeal, it was entitled *United States v. Maynard* before the D.C. Circuit Court of Appeals. It was subsequently changed back to *United States v. Jones* when reviewed by the Supreme Court.
[19] Katz v. United States, 389 U.S. 347, 361 (1967) (Harlan, J., concurring).
[20] *See* Kyllo v. United States, 533 U.S. 27, 32 (2001) ("In assessing when a search is not a search, we have applied somewhat in reverse the principle first enunciated in *Katz v. United States*, 389 U.S. 347, 19 L. Ed. 2d 576, 88 S. Ct. 507 (1967)); California v. Ciraolo, 476 U.S. 207, 215 (1986) ("The touchstone of Fourth Amendment analysis is whether a person has a 'constitutionally protected reasonable expectation of privacy.' Katz v. United States, 389 U.S. 347, 360 (1967) (Harlan, J., concurring).")).
[21] The majority consisted of Chief Justice Roberts, and Justices Thomas, Kennedy, and Sotomayor. In addition to joining the majority opinion, Justice Sotomayor also wrote a concurring opinion explored below.
[22] *Jones*, 132 S. Ct. at 949.
[23] U.S. CONST. amend IV.
[24] *Jones*, 132 S. Ct. at 949.
[25] *Id.* at 950.

The Government contends that the Harlan standard shows that no search occurred here, since Jones had no "reasonable expectation of privacy" in the area of the Jeep accessed by Government agents (its underbody) and in the locations of the Jeep on the public roads, which were visible to all. But we need not address the Government's contentions, because Jones's Fourth Amendment rights do not rise or fall with the Katz formulation. At bottom, we must "assur[e] preservation of that degree of privacy against government that existed when the Fourth Amendment was adopted."

[26] *Id.* at 958 (Alito, J., concurring).
[27] *Id.*
[28] Entick v. Carrington, 95 Eng. Rep. 807 (C.P. 1765); *see* Ricardo J. Bascaus, *Property and Probable Cause: The Fourth Amendment's Principled Protection of Privacy*, 60 RUTGERS L. REV. 575, 581-82 (2008).
[29] Entick v. Carrington, 95 Eng. Rep. 807 (C.P. 1765).
[30] *See* Amil Akir, *Fourth Amendment First Principles*, 107 HARV. L. REV. 757, 767 (1994).
[31] *Jones*, 132 S. Ct. at 950.

[32] Olmstead v. United States, 277 U.S. 438, 456-57 (1928).
[33] *Id.* at 466.
[34] *Id.*
[35] Warden, Maryland Penitentiary v. Hayden, 387 U.S. 294, 304 (1967) ("We have recognized that the principal object of the Fourth Amendment is the protection of privacy rather than property, and have increasingly discarded fictional and procedural barriers rested on property concepts.").
[36] Katz v. United States, 389 U.S. 347, 359 (1967).
[37] *Id.* at 351, 360 (Harlan, J., concurring).
[38] Soldal v. County of Cook, 506 U.S. 56 (1992).
[39] *Id.* at 58.
[40] Soldal v. County of Cook, 942 F.2d 1073, 1078 (7th Cir. 1991).
[41] *Id.*
[42] *Soldal*, 506 U.S. at 65.
[43] *Id.* at 64.
[44] *Id.* at 64 n.7.
[45] *Jones*, 132 S. Ct. at 950-951.
[46] *Id.* at 951 n.5. It is not clear from the majority opinion whether a mere attempt to obtain information is enough, or if the attempt must be successful. In one phrasing the Court requires "installation of a GPS device on a target's vehicle, and its *use* of that device....," *Id.* at 949 (emphasis added), and in another it requires a trespass plus "an *attempt* to find or to obtain information." *Id.* at 951 n.5 (emphasis added). A reasonable interpretation is that an attempt is enough: if the police were to come into a person's home looking for evidence, but found nothing, this would probably qualify under the majority's approach.
[47] *Id.* at 953 n.8.
[48] *Id.* at 953.
[49] The importance of these concurrences was noted by an FBI attorney: "[E]ven though its not technically holding, we have to anticipate how it's going to go down the road." Julia Angwin, *FBI Turns Off Thousands of GPS Devices After Supreme Court Ruling* (Feb. 25, 2012, 3:36 PM), http://blogs.wsj.com/digits/2012/02/25/fbi-turns-off-thousands-ofgps-devices-after-supreme-court.
[50] Jones, 132 S. Ct. at 854 (Sotomayor, J., concurring); 132 S. Ct. at 957 (Alito, J., concurring).
[51] United States v. Hanna, No. 11-20678-CR, 2012 WL 279435, at *3 (S.D. Fla. Jan. 3, 2012) (analyzing the issue of Fourth Amendment standing under both the trespass theory and *Katz*'s privacy test); United States v. Bradshaw, No. 1:11-CR-257, 2012 WL 774964 (N.D. Ohio Mar. 8, 2012) (noting that the *Jones* majority did not adopt the mosaic theory); State v. Zahn, No. 25584, 2012 WL 862707 (S.D. Mar. 14, 2012) (holding that both the trespass approach and the mosaic theory can apply to GPS tracking).
[52] This dialogue between concurring justices and those they are trying to persuade lies at the heart of the common law system—a case-by-case discussion between judges, lawyers, and the public about the progression of the law. RICHARD A. POSNER, THE FEDERAL COURTS: CRISIS AND REFORM 236 (1985).
[53] Igor Kirman, *Standing Apart to Be a Part: The Precedential Value of Supreme Court Concurring Opinions*, 95 COLUM L. REV. 2083, 2096-2101 (1995) (explaining that some courts will presume precedential value in a concurring opinion while others will presume no precedential value).
[54] Lewis A. Kornhauser & Lawrence G. Sager, *The One and the Many: Adjudication in Collegial Courts*, 81 CAL. L. REV. 1 (1993).
[55] Kirman, *supra* note 53, 2119.
[56] Scott C. Idleman, *A Prudential Theory of Judicial Candor*, 73 TEX. L. REV. 1307, 1371 (1995).
[57] Mark Tushnet, *Themes in Warren Court Biographies*, 70 N.Y.U. L. REV. 748, 763 (1995).
[58] *Jones*, 132 S. Ct. at 957 (Alito, J., concurring) Justice Alito contended that the Court melded the two distinct acts of *search* and *seizure* into one to develop its holding; that this approach is merely a return to the much-criticized *Olmstead*, when property controlled; that there are no 18th century analogs to GPS; and that the attachment would not suffice even under common tort law. *Id.*
[59] *Jones*, 132 S. Ct. at 958-59 (Alito, J., concurring).
[60] United States v. Maynard, 615 F.3d 544, 558 (D.C. Cir. 2010).
[61] *Id.* at 558.
[62] *Id.*
[63] *Id.* at 561-62.
[64] Cen. Int. Agency v. Sims, 471 U.S. 159, 178 (1985).
[65] *Id.* at 178.

[66] United States v. Knotts, 460 U.S. 276, 281 (1983).
[67] *Knotts*, 460 U.S. at 281.
[68] *Id.* at 283.
[69] *Id.* This phrase was dicta, meaning it was not essential to the case; thus it is persuasive, but not binding on lower courts.
[70] *Maynard*, 615 F.3d at 556.
[71] *Id.* at 558.
[72] *Jones*, 132 S. Ct. at 951. The Court did not repudiate the mosaic theory, but instead did not reach the question of whether this privacy-based theory would apply; the property-based approach was sufficient to resolve the case.
[73] *Id.* at 958 (Alito, J., concurring). Query whether the reasonable expectation of privacy test is designed to test what privacy the average person would expect. *See* Orin Kerr, *The Fourth Amendment and New Technologies*, 102 MICH. L. REV. 801, 838 (2004) ("A 'reasonable expectation of privacy' has not been equated with the expectation of privacy of a reasonable person; rather, it has been used as a term of art based heavily on property law principles.").
[74] *Jones*, 132 S. Ct. at 964 (Alito, J., concurring).
[75] *Id.*
[76] *Id.*
[77] The mosaic theory need not be cabined to only the GPS tracking scenario. It could apply in other contexts such as smart electric meters, Internet searches, or any other activity in which surveillance of activity over a long period of time can be aggregated to produce an in-depth look into the subject's daily activities, belief systems, etc. CRS Report R42338, *Smart Meter Data: Privacy and Cybersecurity*, by Brandon J. Murrill, Edward C. Liu, and Richard M. Thompson II.
[78] Orin Kerr, *What's the Status of the Mosaic Theory After Jones?*, THE VOLOKH CONSPIRACY (Jan. 23, 2012, 1:59 PM), http://volokh.com/2012/01/23/whats-the-status-of-the-mosaic-theory-after-jones/.
[79] Orin S. Kerr, *Four Models of Fourth Amendment Protection*, 60 STAN. L. REV. 503, 509 (2007).
[80] *Jones*, 132 S. Ct. at 962 (Alito, J., concurring).
[81] Although she could not join his opinion, Justice Sotomayor clearly supported Justice Alito's reasoning. *Jones*, 132 S. Ct. at 956 (Sotomayor, J., concurring) ("As Justice Alito incisively observes ...."; "I agree with Justice Alito....").
[82] *Id.*
[83] *Id.*
[84] *Id.*
[85] *Id.*
[86] Johnson v. United States, 333 U.S. 10, 14 (1948).
[87] United States v. Miller, 425 U.S. 435, 443 (1976). "The Fourth Amendment does not prohibit the obtaining of information revealed to a third party and conveyed by him to Government authorities, even if the information is revealed on the assumption that it will be used only for a limited purpose and the confidence placed in the third party will not be betrayed."
[88] *Miller*, 425 U.S. at 435.
[89] Smith v. Maryland, 442 U.S. 735 (1979).
[90] United States v. McIntyre, 646 F.3d 1107 (8th Cir. 2011).
[91] United States v. Hynson, No. 05-576, 2007 WL 2692327, at *6 (E.D. Pa. Sept. 11, 2007).
[92] *See* Orin S. Kerr, *The Case for a Third-Party Doctrine*, 107 MICH. L. REV. 561, 565 (2009).
[93] *Smith*, 442 U.S. at 744 ("Because the depositor [in *Miller*] 'assumed the risk' of disclosure, the Court held that it would be unreasonable for him to expect his financial records to remain private.").
[94] *Jones*, 132 S. Ct. at 957 (Sotomayor, J., concurring).
[95] *Id.*
[96] *See* Peter Swire, *A Reasonableness Approach to Searches After the Jones GPS Tracking Case*, 64 STAN. L. REV. ONLINE 57 (2012); Daniel J. Solove, *United States v. Jones and the Future of Privacy Law: The Potential Far-Reaching Implications of the GPS Surveillance Case*, 90 CRIM. L. REPER. 632 (2012); Tom Goldstein, Why Jones is still less of a pro-privacy decision than most thought, SCOTUSblog (Jan. 30, 2012, 10:53 AM), http://www.scotusblog.com/2012/01/why-jones-is-still-less-of-a-pro-privacy-decision-than-most-thought/.
[97] *Jones*, 132 S. Ct. at 954.
[98] Brigham City v. Stuart, 547 U.S. 398, 403 (2006); Nat'l Treasury Employees Union v. Von Raab, 489 U.S. 656, 665 (1989); California v. Acevedo, 500 U.S. 565, 581 (1991) (Scalia, J., concurring in the judgment).
[99] Mincey v. Arizona, 437 U.S. 385, 390 (1978) (quoting Katz v. United States, 389 U.S. 347, 357 (1967)).

[100] The Court often states that "[t]he Fourth Amendment proscribes all unreasonable searches and seizures, and it is a cardinal principle that 'searches conducted outside the judicial process, without prior approval by judge or magistrate, are *per se* unreasonable under the Fourth Amendment—subject only to a few specifically established and well-delineated exceptions.'" United States v. Ross, 456 U.S. 798, 825 (1982) (quoting Katz v. United States, 389 U.S. 347, 357 (1967)). One scholar aptly commented on this rule:

In fact, these exceptions are neither few nor well-delineated. There are over twenty exceptions to the probable cause or the warrant requirement or both. They include searches incident to arrest (exceptions to both); automobile searches (exception to warrant requirement); border searches (both); searches near the border (warrant and sometimes both); administrative searches (probable cause exception); administrative searches of regulated businesses (warrant); stop and frisk (both); plain view, open field seizures and prison "shakedowns" (both, because they are not covered by the fourth amendment at all); exigent circumstances (warrant); search of a person in custody (both); search incident to nonarrest when there is probable cause to arrest (both); fire investigations (warrant); warrantless entry following arrest elsewhere (warrant); boat boarding for document checks (both); consent searches (both); welfare searches (both, because not a "search"); inventory searches (both); driver's license and vehicle registration checks (both); airport searches (both); searches at courthouse doors (both); the new "school search" (both); and finally the standing doctrine which, while not strictly an exception to fourth amendment requirements, has that effect by causing the courts to ignore fourth amendment violations.

Craig M. Bradley, *Two Models of the Fourth Amendments*, 83 MICH. L. REV. 1468, 1473-74 (1985) (internal citations omitted).

[101] Goldstein, *supra* note 96.

[102] Carol A. Chase, *Privacy Takes a Back Seat: Putting the Automobile Exception Back on Track after Several Wrong Turns*, 41 B.C. L. REV. 71, 75 (1999).

[103] Carroll v. United States, 267 U.S. 132 (1925).

[104] *Id.* at 153.

[105] United States v. Chadwick, 433 U.S. 1, 12-13 (1977).

[106] Cardwell v. Lewis, 417 U.S. 583, 590 (1974).

[107] Cady v. Dombrowski, 413 U.S. 433, 441 (1973) ("All States require vehicles to be registered and operators to be licensed. States and localities have enacted extensive and detailed codes regulating the condition and manner in which motor vehicles may be operated on public streets and highways.").

[108] South Dakota v. Opperman, 428 U.S. 364, 367-8 (1976).

[109] *See* Orin Kerr, Jones, *the Automobile Exception, and the Warrant Requirement*, THE VOLOKH CONSPIRACY (Feb. 2, 2012 12:45 AM), http://volokh.com/2012/02/02/jones-the-automobile-exception-and-the-warrant-requirement/.

[110] *Id.*

[111] *See* Swire, *supra* note 96; Goldstein, *supra* note 96.

[112] Swire, *supra* note 96.

[113] Kerr, *supra* note 73, at 839. For an in-depth look at the statutory regulation of communication surveillance, see CRS Report R41733, *Privacy: An Overview of the Electronic Communications Privacy Act*, by Charles Doyle.

[114] *Id.* at 857.

The difference favors legislatures when technology is in flux because the privacy implications of particular rules can fluctuate as technology advances. To ensure that the law maintains its intended balance, it needs mechanisms that can adapt to technological change. Legislatures are up to the task; courts generally are not. Legislatures can experiment with different rules and make frequent amendments; they can place restrictions on both public and private actors; and they can even "sunset" rules so that they apply only for a particular period of time. The courts cannot. As a result, Fourth Amendment rules will tend to lack the flexibility that a regulatory response to new technologies may require.... The statutory framework that governs Internet privacy demonstrates the flexibility and creative potential of legislative approaches.

Id. at 871.

[115] *Jones*, 132 S. Ct. at 964 (Alito, J., concurring).

[116] S. 1011, 112th Cong., 1st Sess. (2011).

[117] S. 1212, H.R. 2168, 112th Cong., 1st Sess. (2011).

In: Privacy: Select Issues and Laws for the 21st Century
Editor: Doris B. Delrio
ISBN: 978-1-62618-429-9

Chapter 4

GOVERNMENT COLLECTION OF PRIVATE INFORMATION: BACKGROUND AND ISSUES RELATED TO THE USA PATRIOT ACT REAUTHORIZATION*

Edward C. Liu and Charles Doyle

SUMMARY

Congress enacted the USA PATRIOT Act soon after the 9/11 terrorist attacks. The most controversial sections of the act facilitate the federal government's collection of more information, from a greater number of sources, than had previously been authorized in criminal or foreign intelligence investigations. The Foreign Intelligence Surveillance Act (FISA), the Electronic Communications Privacy Act (ECPA), and the national security letter (NSL) statutes were all bolstered. With the changes came greater access to records showing an individual's spending and communication patterns as well as increased authority to intercept e-mail and telephone conversations and to search homes and businesses. In some cases, evidentiary standards required to obtain court approval for the collection of information were lowered. Other approaches included expanding the scope of information subject to search, adding flexibility to the methods by which information could be collected, and broadening the purposes for which information may be sought.

Some perceived the changes as necessary to unearth terrorist cells and update investigative authorities to respond to the new technologies and characteristics of ever-shifting threats. Others argued that authorities granted by the USA PATRIOT Act and subsequent measures could unnecessarily undermine constitutional rights over time. In response to such concerns, sunset provisions were established for many of the changes.

Subsequent legislation made most of these changes permanent. However, a number of authorities affecting the collection of foreign intelligence information are still temporary. Three such provisions (the lone wolf, roving wiretap, and business record sections of FISA) are set to expire on June 1, 2015. Additionally, provisions added by the FISA Amendments

* This is an edited, reformatted and augmented version of the Congressional Research Service Publication, CRS Report for Congress R40980, dated June 16, 2011.

Act of 2008, relating to the use of foreign intelligence tools to target individuals while they are reasonably believed to be abroad, will expire on December 31, 2012.

INTRODUCTION

Shortly after the 9/11 terrorist attacks, Congress enacted the USA PATRIOT Act, in part, to "provid[e] enhanced investigative tools" to "assist in the prevention of future terrorist activities and the preliminary acts and crimes which further such activities."[1] To that end, the act eased restrictions on the government's ability to collect information regarding people's activities and conversations, both in domestic criminal investigations and in the realms of foreign intelligence gathering and national security. The changes are perceived by many to be necessary in light of the new breed of threats in a post-9/11 world.[2] The expanded authorities also prompted concerns regarding the appropriate balance between national security interests and civil liberties.[3] In part for that reason, the changes were revisited and modified in subsequent measures.[4]

This report discusses the history of constitutional interpretations and legislative responses relevant to the collection of private information for criminal investigation, foreign intelligence gathering, and national security purposes. Next, it summarizes the relevant statutory frameworks and changes made by the USA PATRIOT Act and subsequent measures. It then examines congressional oversight, judicial review, and "minimization procedures" designed to limit the extent of government intrusions where possible. Finally, it discusses several related matters likely to play a role in the legislative debate surrounding reauthorization of the expiring provisions.

CONSTITUTIONAL LIMITATIONS

Constitutional limitations restrict the government's ability to access private information. The Fourth Amendment to the U.S. Constitution is particularly relevant. To the extent that government activity burdens individuals' freedom of speech and related rights, the First Amendment may also play a role.

Fourth Amendment

The Fourth Amendment to the U.S. Constitution provides a right "of the people to be secure in their persons, houses, papers, and effects, against unreasonable searches and seizures."[5] Many of the government activities discussed in this report have the potential to constitute a search as that term is defined in Fourth Amendment jurisprudence. Namely, government action constitutes a search when it intrudes upon a person's "reasonable expectation of privacy," which requires both that an "individual manifested a subjective expectation of privacy in the searched object" and that "society is willing to recognize that expectation as reasonable."[6]

Thus, the Fourth Amendment ultimately limits the government's ability to conduct a range of activities, such as physical searches of homes or offices and listening to phone conversations. As a general rule, the Fourth Amendment requires the government to demonstrate "probable cause" and obtain a warrant (unless a recognized warrant exception applies) before conducting a search.[7]

This rule applies most clearly in criminal investigations. For example, an officer conducting a criminal investigation typically may not search a person's belongings without first obtaining a warrant that describes the property for which sufficient evidence justifies a search.

The extent to which the Fourth Amendment warrant requirement applies to the government's collection of information for intelligence gathering and other purposes unrelated to criminal investigations is unclear. Although the surveillance of wire or oral communications for criminal law enforcement purposes was held to be subject to the warrant requirement of the Fourth Amendment in 1967,[8] neither the Supreme Court nor Congress sought to regulate the use of such surveillance for national security purposes at that time. Several years later, the Supreme Court invalidated warrantless electronic surveillance of domestic organizations for national security purposes, but indicated that its conclusion might differ if the electronic surveillance targeted foreign powers or their agents.[9] A lower court has since upheld the statutory scheme governing the gathering of foreign intelligence information against a Fourth Amendment challenge, despite an assumption that orders issued pursuant to the statute might not constitute "warrants" for Fourth Amendment purposes.[10] The Supreme Court has not yet directly addressed the issue. However, even if the warrant requirement was found not to apply to searches for foreign intelligence or national security purposes, such searches would presumably be subject to the general Fourth Amendment "reasonableness" test.[11]

In contrast with its rulings on surveillance, the Supreme Court has not historically applied the protections of the Fourth Amendment to documents held by third parties. In 1976, it held that financial records in the possession of third parties could be obtained by the government without a warrant.[12] Later, it likewise held that the installation and use of a pen register—a device used to capture telephone numbers dialed—does not constitute a Fourth Amendment search.[13] The reasoning was that individuals have a lesser expectation of privacy with regard to information held by third parties.

First Amendment

The First Amendment to the U.S. Constitution restricts government efforts to prohibit the free exercise of religion or to abridge free speech, freedom of the press, the right to peaceful assembly, or the right to petition for redress of grievances.[14] Two First Amendment concerns arise with regard to electronic surveillance, access to records, and related investigatory activities. One addresses direct restrictions on speech that may accompany government collection of private information, such as non-disclosure requirements accompanying orders compelling government access to business records, discussed *infra.* A second concern is that overly broad authorities permitting government intrusion may lead to a "chilling" (i.e., stifling) effect on public discourse.[15] Some post-9/11 laws address the latter issue directly, for example by prohibiting investigations based solely on a person's First Amendment activities.[16] Despite safeguards, there is concern that post-9/11 authorities may have been used to circumvent First Amendment limitations on analogous authorities.[17]

History of Congressional Action

Congress addressed the federal government's access to private information following key Supreme Court decisions interpreting the Fourth Amendment. In 1968, it enacted legislation, Title III of the Omnibus Crime Control and Safe Streets Act, which outlawed the unauthorized interception of wire or oral communications and authorized interception under court supervision for law enforcement purposes.[18] Later, it passed the Electronic Communications Privacy Act (ECPA), which incorporated and modernized Title III to cover electronic as well as wire and oral communications.[19]

In the years following the Supreme Court's 1972 ruling on surveillance (the "*Keith* case"), Congress actively examined the intelligence practices of past presidential administrations and found that every administration since Franklin D. Roosevelt engaged in electronic surveillance without prior judicial approval.[20] It also found that the authority was sometimes abused.[21] Partly in light of these findings, Congress enacted the Foreign Intelligence Surveillance Act (FISA)[22] to create a statutory framework for the use of electronic surveillance to collect foreign intelligence information.

Similarly, in response to the Supreme Court's rulings regarding the Fourth Amendment's non- application to documents held by third parties, Congress enacted the Right to Financial Privacy Act (RFPA)[23] to constrain government authorities' access to individuals' financial records. Although these privacy protections are subject to a foreign intelligence exception,[24] government authorities were not authorized to compel financial institutions to secretly turn over financial records until 1986.[25] That year, the FBI was also given authority, in the form of FBI-issued "national security letters," to access customer records held by telephone companies and other communications service providers in specified instances justified by a national security rationale.[26] Two additional national security letter authorities were enacted in the mid-1990s. The first provided access to credit and financial records of federal employees with security clearances.[27] The second gave the FBI access to credit agency records in order to facilitate the identification of financial institutions utilized by the target of an investigation.[28]

Intelligence gathering laws were expanded during the same time period. In 1994, FISA was amended to cover physical searches for foreign intelligence purposes.[29] Four years later, Congress amended FISA to permit the Foreign Intelligence Surveillance Court to issue orders authorizing (1) the use of pen registers and trap and trace devices to track calling patterns;[30] and (2) the production of some business records not available through existing national security letter authorities.[31]

The USA PATRIOT Act,[32] enacted in 2001, represented a broad expansion of existing statutory authorities. It eliminated barriers to cooperation between law enforcement and foreign intelligence investigations, modified surveillance authorities under both FISA and ECPA, and created a fifth category of national security letters. Many of these provisions were made temporary, subject to sunset in 2005.[33]

In 2004, Congress enacted the Intelligence Reform and Terrorism Prevention Act. Among other things, the act amended FISA to allow targeting so-called "lone wolves" or individuals believed to be engaged in terrorism, but who were not linked to a known terrorist organization.[34] The "lone wolf" provision was given an expiration date to match that which applied to many of the USA PATRIOT Act provisions.

The next year, Congress reauthorized the USA PATRIOT Act, making the majority of its expiring provisions permanent.[35] However, two of its most controversial provisions, discussed *infra*, together with the 2004 lone wolf provision, were given a new sunset date of December 31, 2009.36 Since then, these three provisions have been repeatedly extended prior to expiration, with a current sunset date of June 1, 2015.[37]

In 2005, President Bush acknowledged that he had authorized a Terrorist Surveillance Program (TSP), which captured some international communications apparently without judicial or statutory authority. As discussed *infra*, Congress subsequently enacted the Protect America Act in 2007 to address issues raised in response to the TSP. The Protect America Act expired in 2008, but was replaced with provisions in the FISA Amendments Act of 2008, which are currently set to sunset on December 31, 2012.

STATUTORY FRAMEWORK

The applicable statutory regime or procedural rules differ according to the purpose for which the federal government collects private information. In criminal law enforcement investigations, the Federal Rules of Criminal Procedure, ECPA, and other provisions in Title 18 of the U.S. Code apply. In contrast, the collection of foreign intelligence information is governed by FISA. Finally, five national security statutes, discussed *infra*, regulate the issuance of national security letters. Statutes in these areas provide analogous authorities for various government activities but require that different standards and procedures be satisfied.

Federal Rules of Criminal Procedure and Subpoena Authorities

In criminal cases, federal officials ordinarily gain access to spaces, documents, and other private materials pursuant to a warrant (during investigation) or a subpoena (during prosecution). In criminal investigations, Federal Rule of Criminal Procedure 41 provides procedures applicable to search warrants to obtain evidence of a crime; contraband, fruits of crime, or other items illegally possessed; or property "designed for use, intended for use, or used in committing a crime."[38]

During the indictment phase, federal grand juries have the power to investigate the possibility that a federal crime has been committed within the judicial district in which they are convened and enjoy the benefit of the subpoena power of the court within whose district they sit.[39] However, grand jury subpoenas are limited. Namely, like criminal search warrants, their purpose must have a criminal nexus.

Other subpoena authorities include those issued during the discovery or trial phases of a criminal prosecution and those issued by federal agencies pursuant to specific statutes.[40] Although they are analogous to authorities relied upon to acquire third party documents in national security or foreign intelligence gathering investigations, agency administrative subpoenas and grand jury subpoenas are unlikely to provide an alternative means to acquire third party documents in a national security investigation and thus have not been a significant issue in post 9/11 legislation.[41]

Electronic Communications Privacy Act (ECPA)

The Electronic Communications Privacy Act (ECPA) provides three sets of general prohibitions accompanied by law enforcement exceptions that operate under judicial supervision.[42] These address (1) the interception of wire, oral or electronic communications (wiretapping);[43] (2) access to the content of stored electronic communications and to communications transaction records;[44] and (3) the use of trap and trace devices and pen registers (essentially in and out secret "caller id" devices).[45]

ECPA generally prohibits interception of wire, oral, or electronic communications by means of an electronic, mechanical or other device but sets forth a number of exceptions to the general prohibition.[46] It limits the types of criminal cases in which electronic surveillance may be used and requires court orders authorizing electronic surveillance to be supported by probable cause to believe that the target is engaged in criminal activities, that normal investigative techniques are insufficient, and that the facilities that are the subject of surveillance will be used by the target.[47] It also limits the use and dissemination of information intercepted.[48] In addition, when an interception order expires, authorities must notify those whose communications have been intercepted.[49] Moreover, it declares that the FISA and ECPA procedures are the exclusive means for accomplishing electronic surveillance as defined in FISA and for intercepting wire, oral, or electronic communications.[50]

Whereas provisions governing interception of communications in criminal investigations reflect a concern for Fourth Amendment requirements,[51] portions of ECPA which address stored communications and the use of pen registers and trap and trace devices are less demanding and reflect Supreme Court jurisprudence suggesting that third party business records and communications entrusted to third parties are not typically protected.[52] Government authorities may have access to communications stored with providers, and related communications records, under a search warrant, subpoena, or court order,[53] or when voluntarily surrendered by providers in emergency circumstances.[54] However, as with the interception of communications, ECPA limits the government's use and dissemination of information and requires that targets be notified.[55]

Foreign Intelligence Surveillance Act (FISA)

FISA governs the gathering of information about foreign powers, including international terrorist organizations such as al Qaeda, and their agents.[56] Although it is often discussed in relation to the prevention of terrorism, it applies to the gathering of foreign intelligence information for other purposes.[57]

Although some exceptions apply,[58] government agencies typically must obtain authorization from the Foreign Intelligence Surveillance Court (FISC), a neutral judicial decision maker, when gathering foreign intelligence information pursuant to FISA. Orders issued by the FISC authorize federal officials to conduct electronic surveillance[59] or physical searches;[60] utilize pen registers and trap and trace devices;[61] access specified business records and other tangible things;[62] or target U.S. persons reasonably believed to be abroad.[63]

Although requiring a nexus to a foreign power or foreign intelligence is a common theme, different standards apply for each type of FISA order. For electronic surveillance orders, FISA currently requires that an application include, among other things, a "statement of the facts and circumstances relied upon" to justify the government's belief that a target is a foreign power or its agent.[64] It must also describe the identity, if known, or a description of the specific target of the electronic surveillance and the nature and location of each of the facilities or places at which the electronic surveillance will be directed, if known.[65] When the nature and location are unknown, the FISC must direct the relevant officials to provide notice to the FISC of specific information within 10 days of the date on which surveillance begins to be directed at a new facility or place.[66] FISA also requires that less intrusive means of information gathering be used before an electronic surveillance order may be granted. Specifically, an application for an order authorizing electronic surveillance must include a certification that the information sought under the order is foreign intelligence information, and that the information may not reasonably be obtained by normal investigative techniques, together with a statement of the basis upon which such certifications rest.[67] Relatedly, an application for an electronic surveillance order must specify proposed "minimization procedures."[68]

For physical searches, the government typically must provide, among other things, "the identity, if known, or a description of the target of the search," and "a statement of the facts and circumstances relied upon by the applicant to justify the applicant's belief that ... the target of the physical search is a foreign power or an agent of a foreign power."[69]

For FISA orders authorizing pen registers and trap and trace devices, although limited exceptions apply,[70] an application generally must certify that "the information likely to be obtained is foreign intelligence information not concerning a United States person or is relevant to an ongoing investigation to protect against international terrorism or clandestine intelligence activities."[71]

Finally, for orders to access records and other tangible things, FISA currently requires both "a statement of facts showing that there are reasonable grounds to believe that the tangible things sought are relevant to a [foreign intelligence, international terrorism, or espionage investigation]" and an "enumeration of minimization procedures" to be applied.[72] These provisions also include recipient non-disclosure provisions, grounds for recipients to challenge such production or non- disclosure requirements, and government reporting requirements.[73]

Many of these statutes include a requirement intended to safeguard individuals' freedom of speech and other First Amendment protections. In particular, investigations generally must not be based solely on a U.S. citizen's exercise of his or her First Amendment rights.[74]

National Security Letter Statutes

Five federal statutes require businesses—namely communications providers, financial institutions, and consumer credit entities—to produce specified records to federal officials in national security investigations.[75] Absent a statutory prohibition or some other specific legal impediment, federal authorities are free to request, and to receive voluntarily, access to third party business records. These national security letter (NSL) statutes are designed to carve out narrow national security exceptions to prohibitions on government information gathering in ECPA, the Right to Financial Privacy Act, and the Fair Credit Reporting Act.

Unlike with warrants in criminal investigations or orders issued under FISA, NSLs are issued directly by federal officials, without approval by any judicial body. They are analogous to orders for tangible things issued in intelligence gathering investigations pursuant to FISA because they are a demand for business records and their use is confined to national security investigations. Yet unlike FISA orders, they are not issued by a court and are available for only the records of three narrow categories of businesses. Moreover, the FBI issues tens of thousands of NSLs a year,[76] while the FISA court approves only a handful of tangible-item orders a year.[77]

Only the FBI may issue NSLs under the communications provider, financial institution, and the narrower of the two consumer credit agency statutes. Authority under the other consumer credit agency statute is available to the agencies of the intelligence community, and authority under the National Security Act extends to both intelligence and law enforcement agencies.

The information available under each of the statutes varies. The National Security Act statute reaches an extensive array of financial and consumer credit records, but only applies to federal employees and individuals who have consented to disclosure of the information.[78] The more sweeping consumer credit statute extends to any consumer information held by a consumer credit reporting agency but only when sought in connection with an investigation into international terrorism.[79] The communications provider NSL statute applies to provider transaction records concerning customers' names, addresses, length of service, and billing records sought in connection with an inquiry into international terrorism or clandestine intelligence activities.[80] The more circumspect of the consumer credit NSL statutes covers credit agency records concerning consumers' names, current and former addresses, current and former places of employment, and the identification of financial institutions in which they have or had accounts—sought in connection with an inquiry into international terrorism and clandestine intelligence activities.[81] The financial institution NSL statute reaches customer transaction records of banks, credit unions, and a long list of other businesses that often deal in cash (pawn shops, casinos, car dealerships, jewelers, etc.), again sought in connection with an inquiry into international terrorism and clandestine intelligence activities.[82]

NSL recipients may be bound by nondisclosure requirements under each of the statutes.[83] A federal statute also provides recipients with the ability to seek judicial review of any secrecy requirement imposed and of the NSL itself.[84] However, this statutory judicial review mechanism has been altered by the Second Circuit's decision in *John Doe, Inc. v. Mukasey*, discussed *infra* at "Judicial Oversight," which held that these nondisclosure provisions would violate the First Amendment unless the agency first petitions and convinces a court that there is a risk that disclosure would endanger national security or foreign relations.[85]

CHANGES MADE BY THE USA PATRIOT ACT AND SUBSEQUENT MEASURES

The USA PATRIOT Act and subsequent measures made far-reaching changes expanding the government's authority to collect private information pursuant to FISA, ECPA, and the NSL statutes.[86] Absent congressional intervention, three of the amendments to FISA—the lone wolf, roving wiretap, and business record provisions—will expire on February 28, 2011.

Lowering of the Wall Between Criminal Investigations and Foreign Intelligence Gathering

The USA PATRIOT Act lowered somewhat the wall traditionally separating criminal investigation from foreign intelligence gathering. Prior to the act, FISA required that foreign intelligence gathering be the sole or primary purpose of an investigation; thus, activities conducted with an additional rationale of criminal investigation were required to adhere to criminal procedure requirements. Section 218 of the act amended the standard to require that foreign intelligence gathering be a "significant" rather than "the [sole]" purpose of surveillance or a search for which a court order is sought under FISA.[87] Thus, the presence of ancillary criminal investigation purposes no longer eliminates the ability to rely on FISA authorities, so long as a significant foreign intelligence purpose also exists. Relatedly, as discussed *infra*, the USA PATRIOT Act and subsequent measures increased the scope of international terrorism-related activities which now fall within the ambit of the federal criminal code.

The act also attempted to improve communication between foreign intelligence and criminal law enforcement agencies. To that end, it includes several provisions that authorize information sharing. For example, section 504 authorizes federal officers to consult with criminal law enforcement officers regarding information obtained from a physical search in order "to coordinate efforts to investigate or protect against" various national security threats.[88]

Expansion of Persons Subject to Investigation

Several post-9/11 measures addressed threshold or definitional issues affecting the range of persons whose communications, records, or effects might be investigated as part of foreign intelligence gathering. The controversial 2004 lone wolf provision, one of the three expiring provisions, is especially significant. It expanded the definition of "agent of a foreign power" in FISA to include a non-U.S. person who "knowingly engages in sabotage or international terrorism, or activities that are in preparation therefor, for or on behalf of a foreign power."[89] Because FISA orders—including those for surveillance, physical searches, pen registers, trap and trace devices, and business records—require evidence indicating that a target is a foreign power or its agent, the broadened definition makes the authorities applicable to targets for which a link to an international terrorist organization or other foreign power is not yet supported by probable cause.[90]

Another important expansion followed in the wake of revelations regarding the Terrorist Surveillance Program. Two measures, discussed in greater detail *infra*,[91] eased federal officials' ability to gather foreign intelligence information between persons in the United States and others thought to be located outside of the United States. In the first, now expired, measure, Congress exempted "surveillance directed at a person reasonably believed to be located outside of the United States" from the definition of "electronic surveillance" under FISA.[92] Although this made it unnecessary to obtain a FISA order to conduct such surveillance, Congress simultaneously established temporary procedures governing the capture of communications for specified groups of targets reasonably believed to be located overseas.[93] The second measure provides separate authorities with differing standards for targeting non-U.S. persons and U.S. persons reasonably believed to be located outside the United States. [94]

Finally, by authorizing the collection of information believed to be *relevant* to a national security or foreign intelligence investigation, the USA PATRIOT Act and its successors in several instances widened the circle of persons whose communications or effects might fall within the ambit of authorities for intelligence gathering.[95] Authorities had previously limited that circle to persons believed to be agents of foreign powers.

Expansion of Electronic Surveillance Authorities

The USA PATRIOT Act amended electronic surveillance authorities in ECPA and FISA. The amendments to ECPA primarily address matters other than the interception of the content of communications. However, the act did add several terrorism-related offenses to the list of federal crimes that may serve as the basis for an interception order.[96] It also authorizes intercepting officers to share information with various federal intelligence and law enforcement officials[97] and provides explicit disciplinary provisions for intentional violations by federal employees.[98]

Moreover, section 217 created a new exception to ECPA's general prohibition on the interception of electronic communications. The exception permits law enforcement officials to intercept the communications of an intruder into someone else's computer or computer system with the consent of system's owner or operator.[99] The exception is limited to the trespasser's communications to, through, and from the invaded system.

An additional important amendment to ECPA broadened the stored communication language in an effort to treat stored voice mail in the same manner as e-mail.[100] Finally, section 220 amended ECPA to permit nationwide service of search warrants of material held by service providers,[101] and section 212 amended it to allow for emergency disclosures by service providers.[102]

Likewise, the USA PATRIOT Act and its progeny made several changes to FISA's electronic surveillance authorities. The so-called "roving wiretap" provision, section 206 of the USA PATRIOT Act, permits roving or multipoint wiretaps where the Foreign Intelligence Surveillance Court finds that the actions of the target of the application for electronic surveillance under FISA may have the effect of thwarting the identification of a specific communications or other common carrier, landlord, custodian, or specified person to whom the order to furnish information, facilities, or technical assistance in connection with the wiretap should be directed.[103] As amended by P.L. 109-177, this finding must be based upon specific facts provided in the application.[104] In addition, section 207 of the USA PATRIOT Act extended the duration of FISA wiretaps and extensions thereof.[105]

Section 225 added a new provision to FISA that bars suits against any wire or electronic service provider, custodian, landlord, or other person that furnishes information, facilities, or technical assistance in connection with electronic surveillance pursuant to a FISC order or with a request for emergency assistance under FISA.[106]

Expansion of Authorities to Conduct Physical Searches

"Physical searches," as defined by FISA, are analogous to searches authorized by warrants in criminal investigations.[107] The most notable amendment specific to FISA provisions governing orders for physical searches, made by section 207 of the USA PATRIOT Act, increased the maximum duration of physical search orders targeting persons other than a foreign power.[108] The maximum duration of such orders was 45 days but is now 120 days for searches targeting an agent of a foreign power and 90 days for other targets.[109]

Expansion of Authorities for Pen Registers and Trap and Trace Devices

The USA PATRIOT Act amended both FISA and ECPA provisions relevant to the use of pen register and trap and trace devices. The most notable amendment to FISA was made in section 214. Previously, the use of pen registers and similar devices could be authorized only for investigations to gather foreign intelligence information or information concerning international terrorism. Section 214 broadened the purposes for which the devices may be authorized by allowing their use in "any investigation to obtain foreign intelligence information not concerning a United States person or to protect against international terrorism or clandestine intelligence activities."[110] However, it prohibits any investigation involving a United States person that is "conducted solely upon the basis of activities protected by the first amendment to the Constitution."[111]

Section 216 amended the ECPA to authorize courts to issue orders for the use of pen registers and trap and trace devices anywhere within the United States.[112] The statute previously limited their application to the issuing court's jurisdiction. It also authorizes the use of such devices to capture source and addressee information for computer conversations (e.g., e-mail) as well as telephone conversations.[113]

Expanded Access to Records and Other Tangible Things

As mentioned, the USA PATRIOT Act focused in part on the statutory tools available in anti- terrorism investigations. Some of those tools enable agents to unearth documents that reveal the paper trail of crime and of the activities of international terrorist organizations and other foreign powers and their agents—grand jury, administrative, and judicial subpoenas; search warrants; court orders under the Electronic Communications Privacy Act (ECPA) and the Foreign Intelligence Surveillance Act (FISA); and national security letters (NSLs). The most important changes were made to FISA and the national security letter statutes. The USA

The law now permits a delayed notification for 30 days or more for such warrants. In addition, the period of delay may be renewed and extended for intervals of 90 days or more if there is reason to believe that immediate notification will "result in (A) endangering the life or physical safety of an individual; (B) flight from prosecution; (C) destruction of or tampering with evidence; (D) intimidation of potential witnesses; or (E) otherwise seriously jeopardizing an investigation."[138]

In FY2008, federal courts issued 763 delayed notice warrants, most often for 90 days.[139] Drug cases accounted for 474 of the initial warrants and for 369 of the 528 extensions granted; terrorism cases accounted for three of the warrants and two of the extensions.[140] Thus, even when there is a criminal nexus, delayed notice search warrants do not appear to be a regular employed investigative tool in national security investigations.

JUDICIAL OVERSIGHT AND MINIMIZATION PROCEDURES

Congress relies on three types of safeguards to protect against abuse of the new authority established by the USA PATRIOT Act and its successors: congressional oversight, judicial oversight, and minimization procedures.

Congressional Oversight

Measures following the USA PATRIOT Act established various reporting and notification requirements, presumably to provide transparency regarding the use of enhanced authorities. For example, section 6002 of the FISA Amendments Act of 2004, P.L. 108-458, requires the Attorney General, on a semiannual basis, to report to relevant committees regarding the use of various FISA authorities, Foreign Intelligence Surveillance Court decisions, and related matters for each preceding six-month period.[141]

Congress instituted additional reporting requirements when it reauthorized and made permanent many USA PATRIOT Act provisions in 2005. For example, section 114 of the USA PATRIOT Improvement and Reauthorization Act of 2005 enhanced congressional oversight of delayed notice search warrants by requiring that no later than 30 days after the expiration or denial of such a warrant, the issuing or denying judge notify the Administrative Office of the U.S. Courts of (1) an application for a delayed notice search warrant; (2) whether the warrant was either granted, modified, or denied; (3) the length of time of the delay in giving notice; and (4) the offense specified in the warrant or the application.[142] In addition, it requires the Director of the Administrative Office to submit an annual report to Congress summarizing the use of delayed notice warrants.[143]

Similarly, section 209 of the 2005 reauthorization measure instituted a semi-annual reporting requirement, whereby the Attorney General must report to the Senate Judiciary Committee and the House and Senate Intelligence Committees regarding physical searches conducted pursuant to FISA, and must submit to those committees and the House Judiciary Committee a report with statistical information concerning the number of emergency physical search orders authorized or denied by the Attorney General.[144] Likewise, section 128 requires that the Judiciary Committees receive full reports on the use of the FISA's pen register and trap and trace authority every six months.[145]

Judicial Oversight

Notification requirements facilitate judicial oversight as well. For example, section 216 of the USA PATRIOT Act requires law enforcement officers to submit a detailed report to the court authorizing the search describing information collected via pen registers and trap and trace devices.[146] The requirement was likely a response to objections that e-mail header information, now authorized to be collected, can be more revealing than a telephone number.

Congress and the courts have also addressed individuals' direct access to judicial review. For example, section 223 of the USA PATRIOT Act amended ECPA to authorize a cause of action against the United States for willful violation by federal employees of the stored communications and records provisions, of the court-ordered interception provisions, and of the FISA electronic surveillance, physical search, pen register, or trap and trace device provisions.[147]

The federal courts have in some cases determined that insufficient access to judicial review raises constitutional problems. In the context of national security letters, the U.S. Court of Appeals for the Second Circuit, in *John Doe, Inc. v. Mukasey*,[148] held that the current gag order and accompanying judicial review provisions only survive First Amendment scrutiny if the government takes specified actions. Namely, it must promptly petition for judicial review (at the recipient's option) and convince the district court that the proposed secrecy provision is narrowly crafted to meet the statutorily identified adverse consequences of disclosure.[149] The *John Doe, Inc.* court also found unconstitutional the statutory requirement (18 U.S.C. § 3511(b)) that a reviewing court give conclusive weight to the government's certification that disclosure might have adverse consequences.[150]

Judicial review of nondisclosure orders accompanying FISA tangible items orders would seem to stand on different footing. The First Amendment defect in the NSL provisions is the want of prompt judicial involvement. The nondisclosure orders under FISA are issued by the FISC, a neutral judicial body, and consequently would seem to suffer no such malady. The statute, however, establishes an intricate procedure under which a recipient must wait a year before filing a motion to modify or set aside a nondisclosure requirement.[151] Petitions, which survive a screening process designed to weed out frivolous challenges, may be granted only if the judge concludes that there is no reason to believe that disclosure would endanger national security or individual safety or would interfere with a diplomatic relations or a criminal, counter-terrorism, or counter-intelligence investigation.[152] As in the NSL statute provision to which the Second Circuit objected,[153] the government's certification of a possible adverse impact on national security or diplomatic relations is conclusive.[154] If a petition is denied, a renewed petition may not be filed until a year later.[155]

Although FISA does not say so in so many words, the recipient of a FISA order who disobeys an order of the court probably stands in contempt of court.[156] It may be assumed that FISA court- issued orders would be beyond reproach on First Amendment grounds when issued. Yet, the time bars on release from a gag order for which the need has passed might be thought troubling. The time bars notwithstanding, however, a recipient might find an effective avenue for timely review by refusing to comply with the order to produce followed by a challenge to the gag order at the subsequent show cause or habeas hearing.

Minimization Procedures

Minimization means different things in different contexts. In an abstract sense, it means capturing, keeping, using, and passing on to others no more information than is necessary to satisfy the purposes for which the statutory authority to do so was given. Under ECPA, it means procedures to minimize the interception of communications other than those for which the Title III order was granted.[157] Under FISA, minimization means, roughly, procedures to curtail the interception of the communications of Americans consistent with national security needs.[158] FISA also has provisions governing the use of FISA-generated evidence in subsequent federal or state proceedings under which district courts may review the legality of the use of FISA authority and suppress the resulting evidence when appropriate.[159] As discussed *supra*, in addition to requiring minimization procedures specific to an investigation, both ECPA and FISA also place general limitations on the use of authorities and the information collected. For example, ECPA restricts the use and dissemination of information collected.[160]

Today, the national security letter statutes have no comparable provisions, although most have dissemination limits.[161] Section 119 of the USA PATRIOT Improvement and Reauthorization Act of 2005 directed the Attorney General to report on the feasibility of establishing national security letter minimization procedures.[162] A report prepared by the Justice Department's inspector general discussed efforts of the Justice Department to formulate such procedures and reservations concerning the initial proposals.[163] The inspector general has also testified that such procedures are needed and overdue, but acknowledged that the task has proven challenging.[164] He expressed the view that the national security letter minimization procedures should address "collection of information through national security letters, how the FBI can upload national security information in FBI databases, the dissemination of NSL information, the appropriate tagging and tracking of national security letter derived information in FBI databases and files, and the time period for retention of national security letter obtained information."[165]

Unlike the NSL statutes, section 215 of the USA PATRIOT Act, as amended, has an explicit minimization component, which calls for procedures governing the retention and dissemination of records and other tangible things collected pursuant to FISA orders.[166] The Justice Department, however, failed to reach internal consensus on issues such as "the time period for retention of information, definitional issues of 'U.S. person identifying information,' and whether to include procedures for addressing material received in response to, but beyond the scope of, the FISA Court order; uploading information into FBI databases; and handling large or sensitive data collections."[167] Accordingly, it issued interim procedures, which the inspector general concluded "do not adequately address the intent and requirements of the [law] for minimization requirements."[168]

RELATED MATTERS

A few key ancillary matters are likely to be raised in the legislative debate surrounding reauthorization of the USA PATRIOT Act and related authorities. One is the increasingly murky relationship between intelligence gathering authorities and the federal criminal code. Provisions enacted in the wake of the Terrorist Surveillance Program, including retroactive immunity for communications providers and authorities regarding persons located outside the United States that are set to expire in 2012 may also be explored.

Nexus between Intelligence Gathering and Federal Criminal Statutes

Despite some lessening of traditional divisions between criminal law enforcement and foreign intelligence gathering resulting from the USA PATRIOT Act and subsequent measures, the purpose of government activity, and the resulting statutory framework, continues to have important consequences for the scope and nature of information collection likely to be authorized.

Searches and surveillance in criminal investigations must be justified by indicia of criminal conduct.[169] In contrast, a significant purpose of an electronic surveillance or a physical search conducted pursuant to FISA must be the collection of foreign intelligence information,[170] and those activities must be supported by probable cause to believe both (1) that the person targeted by the order is a foreign power or its agent, and (2) that the subject of the search (i.e., the telecommunications at which the surveillance is directed or place to be searched) is owned, possessed, in transit to or from, or is being or is about to be used by the target.[171] Likewise, the use of national security letters is generally limited to investigations of international terrorism or for clandestine intelligence activities.

Thus, the presence of a criminal law enforcement rationale is significant. Federal intelligence agents may avail themselves of grand jury subpoenas and other criminal law enforcement tools when there is a nexus to a criminal offense. The existence of that nexus often depends upon the reach of federal substantive anti-terrorism law. Federal law prohibits certain violent acts of terrorism such as aircraft sabotage and the use of weapons of mass destruction.[172] It also condemns misconduct committed in anticipation of violent acts of terrorism such as providing material support to terrorism organizations or accepting military training from terrorist organizations.[173] Moreover, terrorist offenses often serve as an element of other federal crimes such as racketeering or supply the basis for expanded procedural options in areas such as the statute of limitations.[174] For example, federal law extends the general five-year statute of limitations for prosecution of a federal crime to eight years when the offense is one defined as a federal crime of terrorism.[175]

Two federal statutes, both amended by the USA PATRIOT Act, outlaw providing material support for terrorists. One prohibits providing support for federal crimes of terrorism or similar offenses;[176] the other providing support for designated terrorist organizations.[177] The second declares in part that "[w]hoever knowingly provides material support or resources to a foreign terrorist organization, or attempts or conspires to do so, shall be fined under this title or imprisoned not more than 15 years, or both."[178] Conviction requires proof that the defendant either knew that the organization had been designated a foreign terrorist organization or that it engaged in terrorism.[179] It does not require the government to prove that the support was provided with the intent to further the organization's illicit activities.[180] In 2010, in a challenge to the second material support provision, the Supreme Court held that it was not unconstitutionally vague and did not violate the First Amendment, as applied to training or expert advice provided in coordination with or at the direction of a terrorist group.[181]

In addition to the racketeering and statute of limitation provisions, federal crimes of terrorism appear in a number of federal statutes. In some instances, the presence of a federal crime of terrorism is an element of the offense.[182] In others, investigation of a federal crime of terrorism constitutes an exception to an otherwise applicable privacy restriction.[183] As a general rule, the Sentencing Guidelines recommend more severe sentences for federal crimes of terrorism.[184]

In addition to the material support crime, federal law uses an alternative terrorism cross reference with at least equal regularity. Namely, 18 U.S.C. § 2331 provides an element for some offenses, such as one which makes it a federal crime to commit bribery affecting port security with the intent to commit international or domestic terrorism.[185] It too supplies the grounds for an exception to otherwise binding privacy restrictions.[186] And, several federal crimes are more severely punished when they are committed in furtherance of international or domestic terrorism.[187]

The difference between the two cross references is one of specificity on one hand and a terrorism nexus on the other. 18 U.S.C. § 2332b(g)(5)(B) provides a relatively limited list of specific federal crimes that need not necessarily be committed in a terrorist context.[188] 18 U.S.C. § 2331, on the other hand, includes any federal, state, or foreign crime of violence, but only if committed for terrorist purposes.[189] The domestic terrorism definition of section 2331 originated in the USA PATRIOT Act.[190] Critics have suggested that its want of specificity threatens possible misuse against political dissents.[191]

Aftermath of the Terrorist Surveillance Program (TSP)

In late 2005, the *New York Times* reported that the federal government had "monitored the international telephone calls and international e-mail messages of hundreds, perhaps thousands, of people in the United States without warrants."[192] Subsequently, President Bush acknowledged that, after the attacks of September 11, 2001, he had authorized the National Security Agency to "intercept international communications into and out of the United States" by "persons linked to al Qaeda or related terrorist organizations" based upon "his constitutional authority to conduct warrantless wartime electronic surveillance of the enemy,"[193] despite the general rule that electronic surveillance by the federal government is unlawful unless conducted pursuant to the Foreign Intelligence Surveillance Act (FISA) or Title III of the Omnibus Crime Control and Safe Streets Act (Title III).[194] Now discontinued, the TSP appears to have been active from shortly after September 11, 2001, to some time in January of 2007.[195]

Following these revelations, Congress enacted the Protect America Act, P.L. 110-55, and the FISA Amendments Act of 2008, P.L. 110-261. They addressed several issues raised in public discussions regarding the TSP. Two provisions likely to arise in the current legislative debate include (1) retroactive immunity for telecommunications providers who played a role in the TSP; and (2) temporary provisions applying different procedures and standards to targets under FISA depending upon the person's nationality and geographic location.

Retroactive Immunity for Telecommunications Providers

After private citizens and interest groups became aware of the TSP, they filed dozens of lawsuits alleging various statutory and constitutional violations by the telecommunications companies that participated in the program.[196] During litigation, the government moved for the dismissal of the cases on the basis of the state secrets privilege, which bars the disclosure during litigation of information that, "in the interest of national security, should not be divulged."[197] While the district court left open the possibility that the privilege might lead to dismissal at a later date, it declined to dismiss the suits before the discovery stage in the litigation.[198]

Insofar as many of the details of the TSP remain classified, it is likely that assertions of the state secrets privilege would have been central to the disposition of the civil suits against telecommunications providers. However, the enactment of the 2008 FISA Amendments Act provided the Attorney General with the authority to seek the dismissal of these lawsuits.[199] Under the 2008 law, no civil case against a covered telecommunications company could proceed if the Attorney General certified that any assistance given by the defendant was given in connection with the TSP between September 11, 2001, and January 17, 2007, and the defendant received written assurances that the TSP was authorized by the President and determined to be lawful.[200] Dismissal was required if the court found that the certified facts were supported by "substantial evidence." In September of 2008, Attorney General Mukasey made the necessary certification and moved to dismiss the civil suits against the telecommunications providers.[201] In June of 2009, the consolidated suits were dismissed after the district court found the certification to be supported by substantial evidence.[202] That decision was appealed to the Ninth Circuit, and is currently pending.

Were Congress to act subsequently to repeal the retroactive immunity provided by the FAA, the defendants might argue that such a repeal violates their due process rights[203] or the constitutionally required separation of powers.[204] However, courts have generally only upheld such claims where the party was in possession of a final, unreviewable judgment. Although, at this time, the cases have been dismissed by the district court, that dismissal has not been reduced to a final, unreviewable judgment as it is currently being reviewed by the Ninth Circuit. Therefore, legislative modification of the retroactive immunity enjoyed by these defendants under the FISA Amendments Act remains a possibility.

Provisions Expiring in 2012

After the TSP activities were concluded in 2007, Congress enacted the Protect America Act, which established a mechanism for the acquisition, via a certification by the Director of National Intelligence (DNI) and the Attorney General but without a court order, of foreign intelligence information concerning a person reasonably believed to be outside the United States.[205] This temporary authority ultimately expired after approximately six months, on February 16, 2008. Several months later, the Congress enacted the FISA Amendments Act of 2008, which created separate procedures for targeting non-U.S. persons and U.S. persons reasonably believed to be outside the United States under a new Title VII of FISA.[206] Title VII is set to expire on December 31, 2012.

Pursuant to Title VII, non-U.S. persons reasonably believed to be abroad may be targeted to acquire foreign intelligence information pursuant to a joint Attorney General/Director of National Intelligence (DNI) authorization if certain criteria are met.[207] The authority may not be used for reverse targeting—in situations where the true focus of the collection effort is a person in the United States.[208] Title VII requires a FISC order to authorize the targeting U.S. persons reasonably believed to be abroad.[209] The targeting procedures, minimization procedures, and supporting certifications by the Attorney General and the DNI, applicable to the targeting of non- U.S. persons reasonably believed to be outside the United States, are subject to judicial review by the FISC. In addition, electronic communications service providers directed by the Attorney General and the DNI to provide assistance in connection with such acquisitions from targeted non-U.S. persons may challenge such directives before the FISC, with appeal to the Foreign Intelligence Surveillance Court of Review, and, if necessary, to the Supreme Court. Probable cause determinations, minimization procedures, and certifications with respect to the targeting of U.S. persons reasonably believed to be outside the United States are also subject to judicial review.

Upon enactment of Title VII, a number of organizations brought suit challenging the joint authorization procedure for surveillance of non-U.S. persons reasonably believed to be abroad. The suit alleged that this authority violated the targets' Fourth Amendment rights. Although the case was originally dismissed for lack of standing, the Second Circuit ruled, in March of 2011, that the organizations had suffered sufficient injury, based on the financial costs they incurred in order to avoid their reasonable fear of being subject to surveillance under Title VII. Consequently, the case has been remanded to the trial court to address the merits of the plaintiffs' Fourth Amendment challenge.[210]

CONCLUSION

As with previous USA PATRIOT Act reauthorization debates, the slated expiration of FISA amendments in 2011 (and provisions concerning persons reasonably believed to be abroad in 2012) may prompt an examination of authorities for government collection of private information. As mentioned, bills introduced in the 111th Congress (before a key expiration date was temporarily extended) propose significant changes to existing authorities. Congress is likely to revisit those proposals when it considers a longer-term extension of expiring provisions.

Arguments raised in the debate in the 111th Congress reflect fundamental questions regarding the level of government intrusion necessary to ensure the country's safety. Referring to the expiring provisions, the U.S. Department of Justice asserts that the expanded authorities have proven to be important and effective intelligence gathering tools.[211] Thus, although it is "willing to consider" proposals to modify authorities to provide additional privacy protections, the Justice Department warns that care should be taken to ensure that any changes to existing authorities "do not undermine the effectiveness of [the expiring FISA amendments]."[212]

Countervailing arguments assert that amendments enacted following the 9/11 terrorist attacks undermined citizens' civil liberties unnecessarily.[213] Specifically, they argue that the broader the authorities for the collection of foreign intelligence information, the greater the likelihood that U.S. citizens' private conversations or documents will be swept within the scope of an authorized investigation. For example, a concern might be that the authority for "roving wiretaps" increases the likelihood that innocent conversations involving U.S. citizens will be the subject of electronic surveillance. Likewise, at least one commentator asserts that national security letters have a "too diffuse" focus, which leads to anecdotal evidence showing that "their effectiveness is disproportionately small compared with the extent of ... the invasion of privacy they represent."[214]

Reflecting the arguments on both sides, the legislative debate is likely to address ways in which the need for rigorous investigative tools might be balanced with the safeguarding of constitutional guarantees.

End Notes

[1] Uniting and Strengthening America by Providing Appropriate Tools Required to Intercept and Obstruct Terrorism (USA PATRIOT) Act of 2001, P.L. 107-56; H.Rept. 107-236, pt. 1, at 41 (2001).

[2] *See, e.g., Reauthorizing the USA PATRIOT Act: Ensuring Liberty and Security: Hearing Before the S. Judiciary Comm.*, 111th Cong. (Sept. 23, 2009) (statement of Kenneth L. Wainstein, Partner, O'Melveny & Myers and former Ass't Atty'y Gen. for National Security).

[3] *See, e.g., Unchecked National Security Letter Powers and Our Civil Liberties: Hearing Before the House Perm. Select Comm. on Intelligence*, 110th Cong. (Mar. 28, 2007) (statement of Lisa Graves, then Deputy Director, Center for National Security Studies).

[4] *See, e.g.*, USA PATRIOT Improvement and Reauthorization Act of 2005, P.L. 109-177; An act to amend the USA PATRIOT Act to extend the sunset of certain provisions of that act to July 1, 2006, P.L. 109-160; USA PATRIOT Act Additional Reauthorizing Amendments Act of 2006, P.L. 109-178; Protect America Act of 2007, P.L. 110-55; FISA Amendments Act of 2008, P.L. 110-261.

[5] U.S. Const. amend. IV.

[6] Kyllo v. United States, 533 U.S. 27, 33 (2001) (citing California v. Ciraolo, 476 U.S. 207, 211 (1986)).

[7] *See, e.g.*, Atwater v. City of Lago Vista, 532 U.S. 318, 354 (2001) (recognizing a warrant exception for arrest of an individual who commits a crime in an officer's presence, as long as the arrest is supported by probable cause). Probable cause is "a fluid concept—turning on the assessment of probabilities in particular factual contexts." Illinois v. Gates, 462 U.S. 213, 232 (1983). For example, for issuance of a search warrant, probable cause requires an issuing magistrate to determine, based on specific evidence, whether there exists a "fair probability" that, for example, an area contains contraband. *Id.* at 238. Exceptions to the warrant requirement include, for example, "exigent circumstances" where people's lives are at risk or illegal items in "plain view" during a search authorized for other items.

[8] Katz v. United States, 389 U.S. 347, 353 (1967), *overruling* Olmstead v. United States, 277 U.S. 438 (1928).

[9] United States v. U.S. District Court, 407 U.S. 297, 313-14, 321-24 (1972) (also referred to as the Keith case, so named for the District Court judge who initially ordered disclosure of unlawful warrantless electronic surveillance to the defendants). *See also* In re Directives, 551 F.3d 1004, 1011 (Foreign Intell. Surveillance Ct. Rev. 2008) (holding that the foreign intelligence surveillance of targets reasonably believed to be outside of the U.S. qualifies for the "special needs" exception to the warrant requirement).

[10] In re Sealed Case, 310 F.3d 717, 738-46 (Foreign Intell. Surveillance Ct. Rev. 2002).

[11] The "general reasonableness," or "totality-of-the circumstances," test requires a court to determine the constitutionality of a search or seizure "by assessing, on the one hand, the degree to which [a search or seizure] intrudes upon an individual's privacy and, on the other, the degree to which it is needed for the promotion of legitimate governmental interests." Samson v. California, 547 U.S. 843, 848 (2006).

[12] United States v. Miller, 425 U.S. 435 (1976).

[13] Smith v. Maryland, 442 U.S. 735, 745-46 (1979).

[14] U.S. Const. amend. I.

[15] *See U.S. District Court*, 407 U.S. at 314 ("The price of lawful public dissent must not be a dread of subjection to an unchecked surveillance power. Nor must the fear of unauthorized official eavesdropping deter vigorous citizen dissent and discussion of Government action in private conversation. For private dissent, no less than open public discourse, is essential to our free society.").

[16] *See, e.g.*, 50 U.S.C. § 1842(c).

[17] *See, e.g.*, Office of the Inspector General, Department of Justice, *A Review of the FBI's Use of Section 215 Orders for Business Records in 2006*, Mar. 2008, http://www.usdoj.gov/ oig/special/s0803a/final.pdf, at 5

(expressing concern that the FBI had issued a national security letter after the FISA court had twice declined to grant an order for the same material due to First Amendment objections).

[18] P.L. 90-351, 18 U.S.C. §§ 2510-2520 (1970 ed. Supp.IV).

[19] P.L. 99-508, 18 U.S.C. §§ 2510-2520 (1988 ed. Supp.II).

[20] *See* S. Rept. 95-604(I), at 7, 1978 U.S.C.C.A.N. 3904, 3908.

[21] The report of a congressional committee convened to examine intelligence gathering after Watergate stated: "Too many people have been spied upon by too many government agencies and too much information has been collected. The government has often undertaken the secret surveillance of citizens on the basis of their political beliefs, even when those beliefs posed no threat of violence or illegal acts on behalf of a hostile foreign power. The Government, operating primarily through secret informants, but also using other intrusive techniques such as wiretaps, microphone 'bugs', surreptitious mail opening, and break-ins, has swept in vast amounts of information about the personal lives, views, and associations of American citizens." *See Intelligence Activities and the Rights of Americans, Final Report of the Select Committee to Study Governmental Operations with respect to Intelligence Activities and the Rights of Americans, United States Senate, Book II*, S. Rept. 94-755, at 5 (1976) (hereinafter Church Committee Final Report). *See also Supplementary Detailed Staff Reports on Intelligence Activities and the Rights of Americans, Church Committee Final Report,, Book III*, S. Rept. 94-755, at 271-351.

[22] P.L. 95-511, 50 U.S.C. § 1801 *et seq.*

[23] P.L. 95-630, § 1114, 12 U.S.C. § 3401 *et seq.*

[24] 12 U.S.C. § 3414(a)(1)(A), (B).

[25] P.L. 99-569, § 404, 12 U.S.C. § 3414(a)(5)(A).

[26] Electronic Communications Privacy Act, P.L. 99-508, § 201(a), 18 U.S.C. § 2709.

[27] P.L. 103-359, § 802, 50 U.S.C. § 436.

[28] P.L. 104-93, § 601(a), 15 U.S.C. § 1681u.

[29] P.L. 103-359, § 807(a)(3), 50 U.S.C. §§ 1821-1829.

[30] Pen registers capture the numbers dialed on a telephone line; trap and trace devices identify the originating number of an incoming call on a particular phone line. See 18 U.S.C. § 3127(3)-(4).

[31] P.L. 105-272, §§ 601, 602.

[32] P.L. 107-56.

[33] *Id*. at § 224.

[34] P.L. 108-458, § 6001.

[35] P.L. 109-177, § 102(a).

[36] *Id.* at §§ 102(b), 103.

[37] Three of these extensions were relatively short term. Department of Defense Appropriations Act, 2010, P.L. 111-118, § 1004 (extending the expiration date to February 28, 2010); P.L. 111-141 (extending the date to February 28, 2011); and P.L. 112-3 (extending the date to May 27, 2011). However, the last enactment extended the three provisions for four years. P.L. 112-14 (extending the date to June 1, 2015).

[38] Fed. R. Crim. Pro. 41(c). *See also* 18 U.S.C. § 3103a (adding to the grounds provided in Rule 41 that "a warrant may be issued to search for or seize any property that constitutes evidence of a criminal offense in violation of the laws of the United States," and permitting delayed notice of a search in some circumstances). In general, statutes in Title 18 of the U.S. Code governing searches and seizures in criminal cases incorporate relevant sections of Federal Rule of Criminal Procedure 41 by reference. *See, e.g.,* 18 U.S.C. § 3103 (incorporating the grounds for which a search warrant may be issued). However, some provisions add statutory requirements. *See, e.g.,* 18 U.S.C. § 3109 (adding procedures for breaking doors or windows to execute a search warrant).

[39] United States v. Williams, 504 U.S. 36, 48 (1992).

[40] For example, administrative subpoenas are available for use in the investigation by the Drug Enforcement Administration; by federal agency inspectors general; and in health care fraud, child abuse, and presidential protection investigations. *See* 21 U.S.C. § 876; 5 U.S.C. App. (III) § 6; 18 U.S.C. § 3486.

[41] Subpoena authorities are unlikely to substitute for authorities applicable in national security investigations. For administrative subpoenas, one reason is that relevant statutes do not impose a gag order component; thus, national security information might be compromised. More importantly, national security investigations and the type of investigations in which such subpoenas may be used will only rarely coincide. However, criminal investigations in which grand jury subpoenas are sought may intersect with foreign intelligence investigations under FISA in situations involving criminal conduct that also has national security implications, such as international terrorism or espionage.

[42] See CRS Report 98-326, *Privacy: An Overview of Federal Statutes Governing Wiretapping and Electronic Eavesdropping*, by Gina Stevens and Charles Doyle, for a more detailed discussion of the federal laws governing wiretapping and electronic eavesdropping, along with appendices including copies of the texts of ECPA and FISA.

[43] 18 U.S.C. §§ 2510-2522.

[44] 18 U.S.C. §§ 2701-2712.

[45] 18 U.S.C. §§ 3121-3127. Pen registers capture the numbers dialed on a telephone line; trap and trace devices identify the originating number of a call on a particular phone line. *See* 18 U.S.C. § 3127(3)-(4).

[46] 18 U.S.C. § 2511.

[47] 18 U.S.C. §§ 2516, 2518(3).

[48] 18 U.S.C. § 2517.

[49] 18 U.S.C. § 2518(8).

[50] 18 U.S.C. § 2511(2)(f). FISA defines electronic surveillance to include more than the interception of wire, oral, or electronic communications, 50 U.S.C. § 1801(f), but places limitations on its definition based upon the location or identity of some or all of the parties to the communications involved.

[51] Berger v. New York, 388 U.S. 41 (1967); Katz v. United States, 389 U.S. 347 (1967); S. Rept. 90-1097, at 66 (1967).

[52] Smith v. Maryland, 442 U.S. 735 (1979); United States v. Miller, 425 U.S. 435 (1976); S. Rept. 99-541, at 3 (1986).

[53] 18 U.S.C. § 2503. But communications held by electronic communications providers for less than 180 days require a warrant, 18 U.S.C. § 2703(a).

[54] 18 U.S.C. § 2702.

[55] 18 U.S.C. §§ 2517, 2518(8).

[56] *See* 50 U.S.C. § 1801(a) (definition of "foreign power").

[57] For example, it extends to the collection of information necessary for the conduct of foreign affairs. See 50 U.S.C. § 1801(e) (definition of "foreign intelligence information").

[58] For example, FISA provides for emergency authorization of electronic surveillance or a physical search by the Attorney General in some circumstances, while an order is sought. 50 U.S.C. §§ 1805(e) and 1824(e), respectively. It also allows physical searches to be conducted in absence of a court order for periods of up to one year where the target is a foreign nation or component of a foreign nation, a faction of a foreign nation or nations not substantially composed of U.S. persons, or an entity openly acknowledged by a foreign government or governments to be directed and controlled by such government or governments, as long as the Attorney General: (1) certifies that the physical search is directed solely at a foreign power, there is no substantial likelihood that the search will "involve the premises, information, material, or property of a United States person," and proposed minimization procedures meet specified standards; and (2) fulfills various reporting requirements regarding minimization procedures. 50 U.S.C. § 1822. *See also* 50 U.S.C. § 1802 (electronic surveillance of such foreign powers for up to one year without a court order).

[59] 50 U.S.C. §§ 1801-1808. FISA authorizes electronic surveillance without a FISA order in specified instances involving communications between foreign powers. 50 U.S.C. § 1802.

[60] 50 U.S.C. §§ 1822-1826.

[61] 50 U.S.C. §§ 1841-1846.

[62] 50 U.S.C. §§ 1861-1862.

[63] 50 U.S.C. §§ 1881b, 1881c. As discussed *infra*, FISA also currently includes a statutory framework for targeting non-U.S. persons abroad to acquire foreign intelligence information pursuant to a joint Attorney General/Director of National Intelligence (DNI) authorization in specified circumstances. 50 U.S.C. § 1881a.

[64] 50 U.S.C. § 1804(a)(4).

[65] 50 U.S.C. §§ 1804(a)(2); 1805(c)(1)(A) and (B).

[66] 50 U.S.C. § 1805(a)(3).

[67] 50 U.S.C. § 1804(a)(7)(C) and (E).

[68] *Id.* at § 1804(a)(5). Minimization procedures, examined in greater detail *infra*, are safeguards which limit the government's use of collected information.

[69] 50 U.S.C. § 1823(a).

[70] The exceptions authorize: (1) emergency authorization by the Attorney General for up to 48 hours, if specified criteria are met, while an application for a FISC order is pursued; and (2) the installation and use of pen registers and trap and trace devices for up to 15 calendar days following a congressional declaration of war). 50 U.S.C. §§ 1843, 1844.

[71] 50 U.S.C. § 1842(c).

[72] 50 U.S.C. § 1861(b)(2).

[73] 50 U.S.C. §§ 1861-1862.

[74] *See, e.g.*, 50 U.S.C. §§ 1805(a)(2)(A) (electronic surveillance), 1824(a)(2)(A) (physical searches),1842(c) (pen register or trap and trace device).

[75] The NSL statutes are: 18 U.S.C. § 2709 of ECPA; section 1114(a)(5) of the Right to Financial Privacy Act (12 U.S.C. § 3414(a)(5)); sections 626 and 627 of the Fair Credit Reporting Act (15 U.S.C. §§1681u and 1681v); and section 802 of the National Security Act of 1947 (50 U.S.C. § 436). For a more detailed discussion of the NSL statutes and the proposals to amend them see, CRS Report RL33320, *National Security Letters in Foreign Intelligence Investigations: Legal Background and Recent Amendments*, by Charles Doyle, and CRS Report R40887, *National Security Letters: Proposed Amendments in the 111th Congress*, by Charles Doyle.

[76] According to reports by the Department of Justice Inspector General's Office, the FBI issued 39,346 NSL requests in 2003, 56,507 in 2004, 47,221 in 2005, and 49,425 in 2006. Office of the Inspector General, U.S. Department of Justice, *A Review of the Federal Bureau of Investigation's Use of National Security Letters* (March 2008) at 110.

[77] The Justice Department reported that the FISA court issued 13 tangible item orders in 2008 and 17 in 2007, Letters dated May 14, 2009 from Ass't Att'y Gen. Ronald Weich to Vice-President Biden, Senators Reid and McConnell, Speaker Pelosi, and Congressmen Hoyer and Boehner, http://www.justice.gov/nsd/foia/reading_room/2008fisa-ltr.pdf.

[78] 50 U.S.C. § 436.

[79] 15 U.S.C. § 1681v.

[80] 18 U.S.C. § 2709.

[81] 15 U.S.C. § 1681u.

[82] 12 U.S.C. § 3414(a)(5).

[83] The terms "nondisclosure requirements," "secrecy requirements," and "gag orders" are used interchangeably throughout this report.

[84] 18 U.S.C. § 3511.

[85] John Doe, Inc. v. Mukasey, 549 F.3d 861, 883 (2d Cir. 2008).

[86] Expansions were also made to some related authorities. For example, the USA PATRIOT Act and subsequent legislation amended the grand jury secrecy rule to permit prosecutors to disclose grand jury information to federal, state, local, or foreign law enforcement or intelligence officials under certain circumstances.

[87] 50 U.S.C. § 1804(a)(7)(B) (electronic surveillance); 50 U.S.C. § 1823(a)(7)(B) (physical searches).

[88] 50 U.S.C. § 1806(k)(1) (electronic surveillance); 50 U.S.C. § 1825 (physical searches).

[89] *Id.* at § 6001(a); 50 U.S.C. § 1801(b)(1)(C).

[90] *But see* Letter from Assistant Attorney General Ronald Weich to Hon. Patrick J. Leahy, at 5 (Sept. 14, 2009), http://judiciary.senate.gov/resources/documents/ 111thCongress/ upload/091409WeichtoLeahy.pdf (indicating that the lone wolf provision has not yet been relied upon in a federal investigation). For more information regarding the lone wolf provision and the other expiring amendments to FISA, see CRS Report R40138, *Amendments to the Foreign Intelligence Surveillance Act (FISA) Extended Until June 1*, 2015, by Edward C. Liu.

[91] *See* discussion regarding the aftermath of the Terrorist Surveillance Program.

[92] The Protect America Act of 2007, P.L. 110-55.

[93] *Id.*

[94] The FISA Amendments Act of 2008, P.L. 110-261.

[95] *See, e.g.*, P.L. 109-177, § 106(b), 50 U.S.C. §§ 1861-1863; P.L. 107-56, § 505(a)(3), 18 U.S.C. § 2709.

[96] P.L. 107-56, §§ 201, 202, 18 U.S.C. § 2516(1).

[97] P.L. 107-56, § 203(b), 18 U.S.C. §§ 2510(19), 2517(1).

[98] P.L. 107-56, § 223(a), 18 U.S.C. § 2520(f).

[99] P.L. 107-56, § 217, 18 U.S.C. §§ 2511(2)(i), 2510(21).

[100] P.L. 107-56, § 209, 18 U.S.C. §§ 2703, 2510(14).

[101] P.L. 107-56, § 220, 18 U.S.C. §§ 2711, 2703.

[102] P.L. 107-56, § 212, 18 U.S.C. § 2702.

[103] 50 U.S.C. § 1805(c)(2)(B).

[104] *Id.*

[105] P.L. 107-56, § 207, 50 U.S.C. § 1805(e).

[106] P.L. 107-56, § 225, 50 U.S.C. § 1805(i). This section was expanded by section 314(a)(2)(D) of the Intelligence Authorization Act for Fiscal Year 2002, P.L. 107-108, to cover those who provide such assistance in connection with a FISA order authorizing a physical search or emergency assistance.

[107] The definition of "physical search" in FISA incorporates the standard—"reasonable expectation of privacy"—which typically triggers the Fourth Amendment warrant requirement in criminal investigations. *See* 50 U.S.C. § 1821(5) (defining "physical search" as: "any physical intrusion within the United States into premises or property (including examination of the interior of property by technical means) that is intended to result in a seizure, reproduction, inspection, or alteration of information, material, or property, *under circumstances in which a person has a reasonable expectation of privacy and a warrant would be required for law enforcement purposes*, but does not include (A) "electronic surveillance" ... or (B) the acquisition by the United States Government of foreign intelligence information from international or foreign communications, or foreign intelligence activities conducted in accordance with otherwise applicable Federal law ....") (emphasis added).

[108] P.L. 107-56, §207, 50 U.S.C. § 1824(d). The maximum duration of a physical search order targeting a foreign power was and is one year.

[109] *Id.*

[110] P.L. 107-56, §214, 50 U.S.C. § 1842(a)(1).

[111] *Id.*

[112] P.L. 107-56, §216, 18 U.S.C. § 3123(a).

[113] 18 U.S.C. §§ 3121, 3123.
[114] P.L. 107-56, §§ 328(g), 505.
[115] *See, e.g.*, 18 U.S.C. § 2709 (2000 ed.). A textual comparison of the NSL statutes now and prior to the USA PATRIOT Act appears as an appendix in CRS Report R40887, *National Security Letters: Proposed Amendments in the 111th Congress*, by Charles Doyle.
[116] *See, e.g,*, 18 U.S.C. § 2709.
[117] Office of the Inspector General, U.S. Department of Justice, *A Review of the Federal Bureau of Investigation's Use of National Security Letters* (March 2007) (*IG Rept. I*) at 43-5; Office of the Inspector General, U.S. Department of Justice, *A Review of the Federal Bureau of Investigation's Use of National Security Letters* (March 2008) (*IG Rept. II*) at 114-16.
[118] *IG Rept. I* at 46.
[119] *Id.* at 124. Second IG's report indicated it was too soon to tell whether the FBI had eliminated the problems identified in the first report, *IG Rept. II* at 161.
[120] 50 U.S.C. §§ 1861-1862 (2000 ed.).
[121] 50 U.S.C. § 1861(a)(1).
[122] 50 U.S.C. §§ 1861-1863.
[123] 50 U.S.C. § 1861(a).
[124] P.L. 109-177, §§ 102(b), 106A.
[125] Office of the Inspector General, U.S. Department of Justice, *A Review of the Federal Bureau of Investigation's Use of Section 215 Orders for Business Records* (March 2007) (*IG 215 Rept. I*); Office of the Inspector General, U.S. Department of Justice, *A Review of the Federal Bureau of Investigation's Use of Section 215 Orders for Business Records* in 2006 (March 2008) (*IG 215 Rept. II*).
[126] *IG 215 Rept.I* at 16-7.
[127] *Id.* at 17; 50 U.S.C. § 1842(d)(2)(C).
[128] *IG 215 Rept. I* at 17; *IG 215 Rept. II* at 15.
[129] *IG 215 Rept. II* at 57.
[130] *Id.*
[131] *Id.* at 58.
[132] 50 U.S.C. § 1861(b) (2000 ed., Supp. I).
[133] 50 U.S.C. § 1861(b).
[134] 50 U.S.C. § 1861(b)(2).
[135] Fed. R. Crim. P. 41(f).
[136] 18 U.S.C. § 3103a(b).
[137] See United States v. Pangburn, 983 F.2d 449 (2d Cir. 1993); United States v. Freitas, 800 F.2d 1451 (9th Cir. 1986); United States v. Simmons, 206 F.3d 392 (4th Cir. 2000).
[138] 18 U.S.C. §§ 3103a(b), 2705(b). In other Fourth Amendment cases, the Supreme Court has identified the destruction of evidence, threats to individual safety, and risk of the suspect's flight as among the permissible exigent circumstances justify delayed notice. *See, e.g.,* Wilson v. Arkansas, 514 U.S. 927, 936 (1995).
[139] Administrative Office of the United States Courts, *Report of the Director of the Administrative Office of the United States Courts on Applications for Delayed-Notice Search Warrants and Extensions*, EC-2350, 155 Cong. Rec. S7555 (daily ed. July 15, 2009) at 1-2.
[140] *Id.* at 6.
[141] P.L. 108-458, § 6002, 50 U.S.C. 1801 note.
[142] P.L. 109-177, § 114, 18 U.S.C. § 3103a(d)(1).
[143] *Id.*
[144] P.L. 109-177, § 109(a), 50 U.S.C. § 1826.
[145] P.L. 109-177, § 128(b), 50 U.S.C. § 1846(a).
[146] P.L. 107-56, § 216, 18 U.S.C. § 3123(a)(3).
[147] P.L. 107-56, § 223(c), 18 U.S.C. §§ 2510(19), 2712.
[148] 549 F.3d 861 (2d. Cir. 2008).
[149] For national security letters, such consequences include danger to the national security or to individual safety, or interference with diplomatic relations or with a criminal counter-intelligence, or counter-terrorism investigation. In a criminal context, disclosure of an officer's purpose to execute a warrant may be excused if disclosure is likely to result in adverse consequences such as the loss of evidence, flight of a suspect, or a danger to individual safety, Wilson v. Arkansas, 514 U.S. 927, 935-36 (1995).
[150] *Mukasey*, 549 F.3d at 883.
[151] 50 U.S.C. § 1861(f).
[152] 50 U.S.C. § 1861(f)(2).
[153] 549 F.3d 861, 882-83 (2d Cir. 2008) ("the fiat of a governmental official, though senior in rank and doubtless honorable in the execution of official duties, cannot displace the judicial obligation to enforce constitutional requirements").
[154] 50 U.S.C. § 1861(f)(2)(C)(ii).

[155] 50 U.S.C. § 1861(f)(2)(C)(iii).
[156] *Cf.*, 18 U.S.C. §§ 401, 402.
[157] 18 U.S.C. § 2518(5).
[158] 50 U.S.C. § 1801(h).
[159] 50 U.S.C. §§ 1806, 1825.
[160] 18 U.S.C. §§ 2517, 2518(8).
[161] 18 U.S.C. § 2709(d); 12 U.S.C. § 3414(a)(5)(B); 15 U.S.C. § 1681u(f); 50 U.S.C. § 436(e).
[162] P.L. 109-177, § 119(f).
[163] *IG Rept. II* at 64-72.
[164] *Reauthorizing the USA Patriot Act: Hearings Before the Senate Comm. on the Judiciary*, 111th Cong. (2009) (statement of U.S. Department of Justice Inspector General Glenn A. Fine).
[165] *Id.*
[166] 50 U.S.C. § 1861(g).
[167] *IG 215 Rept. II* at 76.
[168] *Id.* at 87.
[169] *See* Fed. R. Crim. P. 41(c); 18 U.S.C. § 2518(3).
[170] *See, e.g.*, 50 U.S.C. § 1804(a)(7)(B) (2008). Prior to 2001, the statute had required that "the purpose" of a FISA warrant be foreign intelligence collection.
[171] 50 U.S.C. § 1805(a)(2)(A) and (B) (electronic surveillance); 50 U.S.C. § 1824(a)(2) (physical search). In contrast, federal criminal search warrants require probable cause to believe that instrumentalities, evidence, or fruits of a crime will be found in the place to be searched. See Fed. R. Crim. P. 41(c).
[172] 18 U.S.C. § 32 (destruction aircraft or aircraft facilities); 18 U.S.C. § 2332a (use of weapons of mass destruction)
[173] 18 U.S.C. § 2339B (providing material support); 18 U.S.C. § 2339D (military training). While section 2339B covers attempted violations, section 2339D does not.
[174] 18 U.S.C. §§ 1961-1962 (racketeering); 18 U.S.C. § 3286 (statute of limitations).
[175] 18 U.S.C. § 2332b(g)(5) classifies over forty federal offenses as "federal crimes of terrorism."
[176] 18 U.S.C. § 2339A.
[177] 18 U.S.C. § 2339B. Neither section explicitly covers material support of the families of terrorist suicide bombers.
[178] 18 U.S.C. § 2339B(a)(1).
[179] More precisely, it requires that it had been designated or that the organization has or is engaged in terrorist activity as defined in 8 U.S.C. § 1182(a)(3)(B), or in terrorism as defined in 22 U.S.C. § 2656f(d)(2).
[180] Holder v. Humanitarian Law Project, 130 S. Ct. 2705, 2717 (2010).
[181] *Id.* at 2719-2720, 2729-2730.
[182] 18 U.S.C. § 2283 (transportation of explosives or weapons of mass destruction knowing they are intended to be used commit a federal crime of terrorism) and § 2284 (transportation of a terrorist who intends to commit, or is in flight following commission of, a federal crime of terrorism).
[183] 20 U.S.C. §§ 1232g(j), 9573(e) (court orders for access to confidential educational records).
[184] U.S.S.G. § 3A1.4.
[185] 18 U.S.C. § 226.
[186] 20 U.S.C. § 1232g(j), § 9573(e) (court orders for access to confidential educational records).
[187] *E.g.*, 18 U.S.C. § 1001 (false statements), § 1028 (fraud relating to identification documents), § 1505 (obstruction of administrative proceedings).
[188] 18 U.S.C. § 2332b(g)(5) consists of two elements: a terrorism element ("an offense that is calculated to influence or affect the conduct of government by intimidation or coercion, or to retaliate against government conduct," 18 U.S.C. § 2332b(g)(5)(A)) and one listing specific federal crimes ("an offense that ... is a violation of [specified sections]," 18 U.S.C. § 2332b(g)(5)(B)). Most statutes cross reference only to section 2332b(g)(5)(B).
[189] *See* 18 U.S.C. § 2331(1) (defining "international terrorism"); 18 U.S.C. § 2331(5) (defining "domestic terrorism").
[190] P.L. 107-56, § 802.
[191] *See e.g., How the USA PATRIOT Act Will permit Governmental Infringement upon the Privacy of Americans in the Name of "Intelligence" Investigations*, 150 U. Pa. L. Rev. 1651, 1688-692 (2002).
[192] James Risen and Eric Lichtblau, *Bush Lets U.S. Spy on Callers Without Courts, N.Y. Times*, Dec. 16, 2005, at 1.
[193] U.S. Department of Justice, *Legal Authorities Supporting the Activities of the National Security Agency Described by the President*, at 5, 17, Jan. 19, 2006, http://www.usdoj.gov/opa/whitepaperonnsalegalauthorities.pdf. *See also* CRS Report R40888, *Presidential Authority to Conduct Warrantless Electronic Surveillance to Gather Foreign Intelligence Information*, by Elizabeth B. Bazan and Jennifer K. Elsea.
[194] The "procedures in [Title III of the Omnibus Crime Control and Safe Streets Act] and the Foreign Intelligence Surveillance Act of 1978 shall be the *exclusive means* by which electronic surveillance, as defined in section

101 of FISA, and the interception of domestic wire, oral, and electronic communications may be conducted." 18 U.S.C. § 2511(2)(f) (emphasis added).

[195] S.Rept. 110-209, at 4. *See also* Letter from Attorney General Gonzales to Senate Judiciary Committee Chairman Patrick Leahy and Senator Arlen Specter (January 17, 2007).

[196] *Id.* at 7.

[197] United States v. Reynolds, 345 U.S. 1, 10 (1953).

[198] Hepting v. AT&T, 439 F. Supp. 2d 974, 994 (N.D. Cal. 2006).

[199] 50 U.S.C. § 1885a.

[200] Alternatively, the Attorney General can certify that the alleged assistance was not in fact provided by the defendant. 50 U.S.C. § 1885a(a)(5).

[201] *See* Public Certification of the Attorney General of the U.S., In re Nat'l Security Telecommunications Records Litigation, MDL Dkt. No. 06-1791-VRW (N.D. Cal. Sep. 19, 2008) (on file with author).

[202] In re NSA Telcoms. Records Litig., 633 F. Supp. 2d 949 (N.D. Cal. 2009).

[203] Chase Sec. Corp. v. Donaldson, 325 U.S. 304, 315-316 (1945) (noting in dicta that "some rules of law probably could not be changed retroactively without hardship and oppression" to the extent that it would be considered a violation of the Due Process Clause).

[204] See Plaut v. Spendthrift Farm, Inc., 514 U.S. 211 (1995) (federal law that reopened final judgment in cases where statute of limitations barred claim was a violation of the separation of powers).

[205] P.L. 110-55, 50 U.S.C. §§ 1805a-1805c.

[206] P.L. 110-261, § 101, 50 U.S.C. §§ 1881-1881g.

[207] 50 U.S.C. § 1881a.

[208] 50 U.S.C. § 1881a(b)(2).

[209] 50 U.S.C. §§ 1881b and 1881c.

[210] Amnesty Int'l v. Clapper, 2011 U.S. App. LEXIS 5699 (2d Cir. Mar. 21, 2011) reversing Amnesty Int'l United States v. McConnell, 646 F. Supp. 2d 633 (S.D.N.Y., 2009). But see In re Directives Pursuant to Section 105b of the Foreign Intelligence Surveillance Act, 551 F.3d 1004, 1009-1016 (U.S. Foreign Intell. Surveil Ct. Rev. 2008) (upholding similar joint authorization procedure under the Protect America Act in the face of a Fourth Amendment challenge brought by telecommunications provider).

[211] Letter from the U.S. Department of Justice to Hon. Patrick J. Leahy (Sept. 14, 2009), http://judiciary.senate.gov/resources/documents/111thCongress/upload/ 091409WeichtoLeahy.pdf.

[212] *Id.*

[213] *See e.g., Restoring the Rule of Law: Hearing Before the Senate Comm. on the Judiciary, Subcomm. on the Constitution*, 110th Cong. (Sept. 16, 2008) (statement of Suzanne E. Spaulding, Esq.).

[214] *Unchecked National Security Letter Powers and Our Civil Liberties: Hearing Before the House Perm. Select Comm. on Intelligence*, 110th Cong. (Mar. 28, 2007) (statement of Lisa Graves, then Deputy Director, Center for National Security Studies).

In: Privacy: Select Issues and Laws for the 21st Century
Editor: Doris B. Delrio
ISBN: 978-1-62618-429-9

Chapter 5

PRIVACY: AN OVERVIEW OF THE ELECTRONIC COMMUNICATIONS PRIVACY ACT*

Charles Doyle

SUMMARY

This report provides an overview of federal law governing wiretapping and electronic eavesdropping under the Electronic Communications Privacy Act (ECPA). It also appends citations to state law in the area and the text of ECPA.

It is a federal crime to wiretap or to use a machine to capture the communications of others without court approval, unless one of the parties has given his prior consent. It is likewise a federal crime to use or disclose any information acquired by illegal wiretapping or electronic eavesdropping. Violations can result in imprisonment for not more than five years; fines up to $250,000 (up to $500,000 for organizations); civil liability for damages, attorneys' fees and possibly punitive damages; disciplinary action against any attorneys involved; and suppression of any derivative evidence. Congress has created separate, but comparable, protective schemes for electronic communications (e.g., email) and against the surreptitious use of telephone call monitoring practices such as pen registers and trap and trace devices.

Each of these protective schemes comes with a procedural mechanism to afford limited law enforcement access to private communications and communications records under conditions consistent with the dictates of the Fourth Amendment. The government has been given narrowly confined authority to engage in electronic surveillance, conduct physical searches, and install and use pen registers and trap and trace devices for law enforcement purposes under ECPA and for purposes of foreign intelligence gathering under the Foreign Intelligence Surveillance Act.

---

* This is an edited, reformatted and augmented version of the Congressional Research Service Publication, CRS Report for Congress R41733, dated October 9, 2012.

INTRODUCTION

This is an outline of the Electronic Communications Privacy Act (ECPA).[1] ECPA consists of three parts. The first, sometimes referred to as Title III, outlaws the unauthorized interception of wire, oral, or electronic communications.[2] It also establishes a judicial supervised procedure to permit such interceptions for law enforcement purposes.[3] The second, the Stored Communications Act, focuses on the privacy of, and government access to, stored electronic communications.[4] The third creates a procedure for governmental installation and use of pen registers as well as trap and trace devices.[5] It also outlaws such installation or use except for law enforcement and foreign intelligence investigations.[6]

BACKGROUND

At common law, "eavesdroppers, or such as listen under walls or windows, or the eaves of a house, to hearken after discourse, and thereupon to frame slanderous and mischievous tales, are a common nuisance and presentable at the court-leet; or are indictable at the sessions, and punishable by fine and finding of sureties for [their] good behavior."[7] Although early American law proscribed common law eavesdropping, the crime was little prosecuted and by the late nineteenth century had "nearly faded from the legal horizon."[8] With the invention of the telegraph and telephone, however, state laws outlawing wiretapping or indiscretion by telephone and telegraph operators preserved the spirit of the common law prohibition in this country.

Congress enacted the first federal wiretap statute as a temporary measure to prevent disclosure of government secrets during World War I.[9] Later, it proscribed intercepting and divulging private radio messages in the Radio Act of 1927,[10] but did not immediately reestablish a federal wiretap prohibition. By the time of the landmark Supreme Court decision in *Olmstead*, however, at least forty-one of the forty-eight states had banned wiretapping or forbidden telephone and telegraph employees and officers from disclosing the content of telephone or telegraph messages or both.[11]

Olmstead was a Seattle bootlegger whose Prohibition Act conviction was the product of a federal wiretap. He challenged his conviction on three grounds, arguing unsuccessfully that the wiretap evidence should have been suppressed as a violation of either his Fourth Amendment rights, his Fifth Amendment privilege against self-incrimination, or the rights implicit in the Washington state statute that outlawed wiretapping.

For a majority of the Court, writing through Chief Justice Taft, Olmstead's Fourth Amendment challenge was doomed by the absence of "an official search and seizure of his person, or such a seizure of his papers or his tangible material effects, or an actual physical invasion of his house or curtilage[12] for the purposes of making a seizure."[13]

Chief Justice Taft pointed out that Congress was free to provide protection which the Constitution did not.[14] Congress did so in the 1934 Communications Act by expanding the Radio Act's proscription against intercepting and divulging radio communications so as to include intercepting and divulging radio or wire communications.[15]

The Federal Communications Act outlawed wiretapping, but it said nothing about the use of machines to surreptitiously record and transmit face to face conversations.[16] In the absence of a statutory ban the number of surreptitious recording cases decided on Fourth Amendment grounds surged and the results began to erode *Olmstead*'s underpinnings.[17]

Erosion, however, came slowly. Initially the Court applied *Olmstead*'s principles to the electronic eavesdropping cases. Thus, the use of a dictaphone to secretly overhear a private conversation in an adjacent office offended no Fourth Amendment precepts because no physical trespass into the office in which the conversation took place had occurred.[18] Similarly, the absence of a physical trespass precluded Fourth Amendment coverage of the situation where a federal agent secretly recorded his conversation with a defendant held in a commercial laundry in an area open to the public.[19] On the other hand, the Fourth Amendment did reach the government's physical intrusion upon private property during an investigation, as for example when they drove a "spike mike" into the common wall of a row house until it made contact with a heating duct for the home in which the conversation occurred.[20]

The spike mike case presented something of a technical problem, because there was some question whether the spike mike had actually crossed the property line of the defendant's town house when it made contact with the heating duct. The Court declined to rest its decision on the technicalities of local property law, and instead found that the government's conduct had intruded upon privacy of home and hearth in a manner condemned by the Fourth Amendment.[21]

Each of these cases focused upon whether a warrantless trespass onto private property had occurred, that is, whether the *means* of conducting a search and seizure had been so unreasonable as to offend the Fourth Amendment. Yet in each case, the object of the search and seizure had been not those tangible papers or effects for which the Fourth Amendment's protection had been traditionally claimed, but an intangible, a conversation. This enlarged view of the Fourth Amendment could hardly be ignored, for "[i]t follows from ... *Silverman* ... that the Fourth Amendment may protect against the overhearing of verbal statements as well as against the more traditional seizure of papers and effects."[22]

Soon thereafter the Court repudiated the notion that the Fourth Amendment's protection was contingent upon some trespass to real property in *Katz v. United States.*[23] Katz was a bookie convicted on the basis of evidence gathered by an electronic listening and recording device set up outside the public telephone booth that Katz used to take and place bets. The Court held that the gateway for Fourth Amendment purposes stood at that point where an individual should to able to expect that his or her privacy would not be subjected to unwarranted governmental intrusion.[24]

One obvious consequence of Fourth Amendment coverage of wiretapping and other forms of electronic eavesdropping is the usual attachment of the Amendment's warrant requirement. To avoid constitutional problems and at the same time preserve wiretapping and other forms of electronic eavesdropping as a law enforcement tool, some of the states established a statutory system under which law enforcement officials could obtain a warrant, or equivalent court order, authorizing wiretapping or electronic eavesdropping.

The Court rejected the constitutional adequacy of one of the more detailed of these state statutory schemes in *Berger v. New York.*[25] The statute was found deficient because of its failure to require:

- a particularized description of the place to be searched;
- a particularized description of the crime to which the search and seizure related;

- a particularized description of the conversation to be seized;
- limitations to prevent general searches;
- termination of the interception when the conversation sought had been seized;
- prompt execution of the order;
- return to the issuing court detailing the items seized; and
- any showing of exigent circumstances to overcome the want of prior notice.[26]

Berger helped persuade Congress to enact Title III of the Omnibus Crime Control and Safe Streets Act of 1968, a comprehensive wiretapping and electronic eavesdropping statute that not only outlawed both activities in general terms but that also permitted federal and state law enforcement officers to use them under strict limitations designed to meet the objections in *Berger*.[27]

A decade later another Supreme Court case persuaded Congress to supplement Title III with a judicially supervised procedure for the use of wiretapping and electronic eavesdropping in foreign intelligence gathering situations. When Congress passed Title III there was some question over the extent of the President's inherent powers to authorize wiretaps—without judicial approval—in national security cases. As a consequence, the issue was simply removed from the Title III scheme.[28]

After the Court held that the President's inherent powers were insufficient to excuse warrantless electronic eavesdropping on purely domestic threats to national security,[29] Congress considered it prudent to augment the foreign intelligence gathering authority of the United States with the Foreign Intelligence Security Act of 1978 (FISA).[30] The FISA provides a procedure for judicial review and authorization of electronic surveillance and other forms of information gathering for foreign intelligence purposes.

Two other Supreme Court cases influenced the development of federal law in the area. In *United States v. Miller*,[31] the Court held that a customer had no Fourth Amendment protected expectation of privacy in the records his bank created concerning his transactions with them. These third party records were therefore available to the government under a subpoena ducestecum rather than a more narrowly circumscribed warrant.[32] In *Smith v. Maryland*,[33] it held that no warrant was required for the state's use of a pen register or trap and trace device, if the device merely identified the telephone numbers for calls made and received from a particular telephone. No Fourth Amendment search or seizure occurred, the Court held, since the customer had no justifiable expectation of privacy in information which he knew or should have known the telephone company might ordinarily capture for billing or service purposes.[34]

In 1986, Congress enacted the Electronic Communications Privacy Act (ECPA).[35] ECPA consists of three parts: a revised Title III;[36] the Stored Communications Act (SCA);[37] and provisions governing the installation and use of pen registers as well as trap and trace devices.[38] Congress has adjusted the components of ECPA and FISA, over the years. It has done so sometimes in the interests of greater privacy; sometimes in the interest of more effective law enforcement or foreign intelligence gathering; often with an eye to some combination of those interests. Prominent among its enactments are:

- the USA PATRIOT Act;[39]
- the Intelligence Authorization Act for Fiscal Year 2002;[40]

- the 21st Century Department of Justice Appropriations Authorization Act;[41]
- the Department of Homeland Security Act;[42]
- the USA PATRIOT Improvement and Reauthorization Act;[43] and
- the Foreign Intelligence Surveillance Act of 1978 Amendments Act of 2008 (2008 FISA Amendments Act).[44]

TITLE III: PROHIBITIONS

In Title III, ECPA begins the proposition that unless provided otherwise, it is a federal crime to engage in wiretapping or electronic eavesdropping; to possess wiretapping or electronic eavesdropping equipment; to use or disclose information obtained through illegal wiretapping or electronic eavesdropping; or to disclose information secured through court-ordered wiretapping or electronic eavesdropping, in order to obstruct justice.[45]

Illegal Wiretapping and Electronic Eavesdropping

First among these is the ban on illegal wiretapping and electronic eavesdropping that covers:

- any person who
- intentionally
- intercepts, or endeavors to intercept,
- wire, oral, or electronic communications
- by using an electronic, mechanical, or other device
- unless the conduct is specifically authorized or expressly not covered, *e.g.*
    - one of the parties to the conversation has consented to the interception,
    - the interception occurs in compliance with a statutorily authorized (and ordinarily judicially supervised) law enforcement or foreign intelligence gathering interception,
    - the interception occurs as part of providing or regulating communication services,
    - certain radio broadcasts, and
    - in some places, spousal wiretappers.[46]

Person

The prohibition applies to "any employee, or agent of the United States or any State or political subdivision thereof, and any individual, partnership, association, joint stock company, trust, or corporation."[47]

Intentional

Conduct can only violate Title III if it is done "intentionally," inadvertent conduct is no crime; the offender must have done on purpose those things which are outlawed.[48] He need not be shown to have known, however, that his conduct was unlawful.[49]

Jurisdiction

Subsection 2511(1) contains two interception bars—one, 2511(1)(a), simply outlaws intentional interception; the other, 2511(1)(b), outlaws intentional interception when committed under any of five jurisdictional circumstances with either an implicit or explicit nexus to interstate or foreign commerce.[50] Congress adopted the approach because of concern that its constitutional authority might not be sufficient to ban instances of electronic surveillance that bore no discernable connection to interstate commerce or any other of Congress's enumerated constitutional powers. So it enacted a general prohibition, and as a safety precaution, a second provision more tightly tethered to specific jurisdictional factors.[51] The Justice Department has honored that caution by employing subparagraph (b) to prosecute the interception of oral communications, while using subparagraph (a) to prosecute other forms of electronic eavesdropping.[52]

Interception

Interception "means the aural or other acquisition of the contents" of various kinds of communications by means of "electronic, mechanical or other devices."[53] Although logic might suggest that interception occurs only in the place where the communication is captured, the cases indicate that interception occurs as well where the communication begins, is transmitted, or is received.[54] Yet, it does not include instances when an individual simply reads or listens to a previously intercepted communication, regardless of whether additional conduct may implicate the prohibitions on use or disclosure.[55]

Once limited to aural acquisitions, ECPA enlarged the definition of "interception" by adding the words "or other acquisition" so that it is no longer limited to interceptions of communications that can be heard.[56] The change complicates the question of whether the wiretap, stored communications, or trap and trace portions of the ECPA govern the legality of various means of capturing information relating to a communication. The analysis might seem to favor wiretap coverage when it begins with an examination of whether an "interception" has occurred. Yet, there is little consensus over when an interception occurs; that is, whether "interception" as used in section 2511 contemplates surreptitious acquisition, either contemporaneous with transmission, or whether such acquisition may occur anytime before the initial cognitive receipt of the contents by the intended recipient, or under some other conditions.[57]

The USA PATRIOT Act resolved some of the statutory uncertainty concerning voice mail when it removed voice mail from the wiretap coverage of Title III (striking the phrase "and such term includes any electronic storage of such communication" from the definition of "wire communications" in Title III (18 U.S.C. 2510(1)) and added stored *wire* communications to the stored communications coverage of 18 U.S.C. 2703.[58]

Content

The interceptions proscribed in Title III are confined to those that capture a communication's "content," that is, "information concerning [its] substance, purport, or meaning."[59] Trap and trace devices and pen registers once captured only information relating to the source and addressee of a communication, not its content. That is no longer the case. The "post-cut-through dialed digit features" of contemporary telephone communications now transmit communications in such a manner that the use of ordinary pen register or trap and trace devices will capture both non-content and content.[60] As a consequence, a few courts have held, either as a matter of statutory construction or constitutional necessity, that the authorities must rely on a Title III wiretap order rather than a pen register/trap and trace order if such information will be captured.[61]

By Electronic, Mechanical, or Other Device

The statute does not cover common law "eavesdropping," but only interceptions "by electronic, mechanical or other device."[62] The term includes computers,[63] but it is defined so as not to include hearing aids or extension telephones in normal use (use in the "ordinary course of business").[64] Whether an extension phone has been installed and is being used in the ordinary course of business or in the ordinary course of law enforcement duties, so that it no longer constitutes an interception device for purposes of Title III and comparable state laws has proven a somewhat vexing question.[65]

Although often intertwined with the consent exception discussed below, the question generally turns on the facts in a given case.[66] When the exemption is claimed as a practice in the ordinary course of business, the interception must be for a legitimate business reason, it must be routinely conducted, and at least in some circuits employees must be notified that their conversations are being monitored.[67] Similarly, "Congress most likely carved out an exception for law enforcement officials to make clear that the routine and almost universal recording of phone lines by police departments and prisons, as well as other law enforcement institutions, is exempt from the statute."[68] The exception contemplates administrative rather than investigative monitoring,[69] which must nevertheless be justified by a lawful, valid law enforcement concern.[70]

Wire, Oral, or Electronic Communications

An interception is only a violation of Title III if the conversation or other form of captured communication is among those kinds which the statute protects, in oversimplified terms—if it is a telephone (wire), face to face (oral), or computer (electronic) communication. Thus, Title III does cover silent video surveillance.[71]

Title III does not cover all wire, oral or electronic communications. "Oral communications," by definition, includes only those face to face conversations for which the speakers have a justifiable expectation of privacy.[72] "Wire communications" are limited to those that are at some point involve voice communications (i.e., only aural transfers).[73] The term "electronic communications" encompasses radio and data transmissions generally, but excludes certain radio transmissions which can be innocently captured without great difficulty.[74] Even when a radio transmission meets the definition, Title III's general exemption may render its capture innocent.[75]

Endeavoring to Intercept

Although the statute condemns attempted wiretapping and electronic eavesdropping ("endeavoring to intercept"),[76] the provisions appear to have escaped use, interest, or comment heretofore, perhaps because the conduct most likely to constitute preparation for an interception—possession of wiretapping equipment—is already a separate crime.[77]

Exemptions: Consent Interceptions

Consent interceptions are common, controversial and have a history all their own. The early bans on divulging telegraph or telephone messages had a consent exception.[78] The Supreme Court upheld consent interceptions against Fourth Amendment challenge both before and after the enactment of Title III.[79] The argument in favor of consent interceptions has always been essentially that a speaker risks the indiscretion of his listeners and holds no superior legal position simply because a listener elects to record or transmit his statements rather than subsequently memorializing or repeating them.[80] Wiretapping or electronic eavesdropping by either the police or anyone else with the consent of at least one party to the conversation is not unlawful under the federal statute.[81] These provisions do no more than shield consent interceptions from the sanctions of federal law; they afford no protection from the sanctions of state law. Many of the states recognize comparable exceptions, but some only permit interception with the consent of *all* parties to a communication.[82]

Under federal law, consent may be either explicitly or implicitly given. For instance, someone, who uses a telephone other than his or her own and has been told by the subscriber that conversations over the instrument are recorded, has been held to have implicitly consented to interception when using the instrument.[83] This is not to say that subscriber consent alone is sufficient, for it is the parties to the conversation whose privacy is protected.[84] Although consent may be given in the hopes of leniency from law enforcement officials or as an election between unpalatable alternatives, it must be freely given and not secured coercively.[85]

Private consent interceptions may not be conducted for a criminal or tortious purpose.[86] Some state wiretap laws do not recognize a one party consent exception. There, interception with the consent of but one party to the conversation is a violation of state law. But the federal exception is available as long as the *purpose* of the interception was neither criminal nor tortious—though the *means* may have been.[87] At one time, the limitation encompassed interceptions for criminal, tortious, *or* otherwise injurious purposes, but ECPA dropped the reference to injurious purposes for fear that First Amendment values might be threatened should the clause be read to outlaw consent interceptions conducted to embarrass.[88]

Exemptions: Publicly Accessible Radio Communications

Radio communications which can be inadvertently heard or are intended to be heard by the public are likewise exempt. These include not only commercial broadcasts, but ship and aircraft distress signals, tone-only pagers, marine radio and citizen band radio transmissions, and interceptions necessary to identify the source of any transmission, radio or otherwise, disrupting communications satellite broadcasts.[89]

Exemptions: Government Officials

Government officials have the benefit of an exemption when executing a Title III eavesdropping order;[90] acting in an emergency situation pending issuance of a court order;[91] acting under the authority of Title III in the case of communications of an intruder in a communications system acting with the approval of the system provider;[92] acting under the authority of the Foreign Intelligence Surveillance Act,[93] or acting pursuant to the authority according them the use of pen registers and trap and trace devices.[94]

Exemptions: Communication Service Providers

A further exemption applies to those who supply communications services: the telephone company, switchboard operators, and the like. The exemption permits interception in the name of improved service; to allow a service provider to itself against fraud;[95] to assist federal and state officials operating under a judicially supervised interception order,[96] and for the regulatory activities of the Federal Communications Commission.[97]

Domestic Exemptions

A few courts recognize a "vicarious consent" exception under which a custodial parent may secretly record the conversations of his or her minor child in the interest of protecting the child.[98] Although rejected by most,[99] a handful of federal courts have held that Title III does not preclude one spouse from wiretapping or electronically eavesdropping upon the other,[100] a result other courts have sometimes reached through the telephone extension exception discussed above.[101]

Illegal Disclosure of Information Obtained by Wiretapping or Electronic Eavesdropping

Title III has three disclosure offenses. The first is a general prohibition focused on the products of an unlawful interception:

- any person [who]
- intentionally
- discloses or endeavors to disclose to another person
- the contents of any wire, oral, or electronic communication
- having reason to know
- that the information was obtained through the interception of a wire, oral, or electronic communication
- in violation of 18 U.S.C. 2511(1)
- is subject to the same sanctions and remedies as the wiretapper or electroniceavesdropper.[102]

This is true of the wiretapper or electronic eavesdropper and of all those who, aware of the information's illicit origins, disclose it. The defendant must be shown to have known that the interception occurred and that the interception was unlawful.[103] There are exceptions. When the illegally secured information relates to a matter of usual public concern, the First Amendment precludes a prosecution for disclosure under §2511(c).[104] Moreover, the legislative history indicates that Congress did not intend to punish the disclosure of intercepted information that is public knowledge. Less clear is whether the limitation is confined to information commonly known at the time of capture, or more likely, information of which the public was generally aware at the time of disclosure.[105] Finally, the results of electronic eavesdropping authorized under Title III may be disclosed and used for law enforcement purposes[106] and for testimonial purposes.[107]

Title III makes it a federal crime to disclose intercepted communications under two other circumstances. It is a federal crime to disclose, with an intent to obstruct criminal justice, any information derived from lawful police wiretapping or electronic eavesdropping, *i.e.*:

- any person [who]
- intentionally discloses, or endeavors to disclose, to any other person
- the contents of any wire, oral, or electronic communication
- intercepted by means authorized by sections:
    - 2511(2)(a)(ii) (communication service providers, landlords, etc. who assist police setting up wiretaps or electronic eavesdropping devices)
    - 2511(2)(b) (FCC regulatory activity)
    - 2511(2)(c) (police one party consent)
    - 2511(2)(e) (Foreign Intelligence Surveillance Act)
    - 2516 (court-ordered, police wiretapping or electronic surveillance)
    - 2518 (emergency wiretaps or electronic surveillance)
- knowing or having reason to know that
- the information was obtained through the interception of such a communication
- in connection with a criminal investigation
- having obtained or received the information in connection with a criminal investigation
- with intent to improperly obstruct, impede, or interfere with a duly authorized criminal investigation
- is subject to the same sanctions and remedies as one who illegally wiretaps.[108]

Offenders face the criminal and civil liability as those who wiretap.[109]

This second disclosure proscription applies to efforts to obstruct justice by revealing information gleaned from either federal wiretaps. It may also apply to state wiretaps. It covers information generated from a court-ordered wiretap authorized under §2516. Section 2516 authorizes both federal and state court-ordered wiretaps.[110] On the other hand, strictly speaking, §2516 permits state wiretapping when "authorized" by state law.[111] The courts might conclude that Congress would have spoken more clearly, if it intended to make it a federal crime to obstruct state criminal prosecutions by the disclosing of information derived from a state wiretap.

A third disclosure proscription applies only to electronic communications service providers "who intentionally divulge the contents of the communication while in transmission" to anyone other than sender and intended recipient.[112] The prohibition comes with its own exemptions for divulgence—when one of the parties to the communications consents, when Title III authorizes disclosure of a court approved interception, when necessary for transmission of the communication, or when it involves inadvertent discovery of information relating to the commission of a crime.[113] Although subsection 2511(3) provides no specific sanctions, violators would presumably be exposed to criminal liability under the general disclosure proscription, 18 U.S.C. 2511(1)(c), and to civil liability under 18 U.S.C. 2520.[114]

Illegal Use of Information Obtained by Unlawful Wiretapping or Electronic Eavesdropping

The prohibition on the use of information secured from illegal wiretapping or electronic eavesdropping mirrors its disclosure counterpart:

- any person [who]
- intentionally
- uses or endeavors to use to another person
- the contents of any wire, oral, or electronic communication
- having reason to know
- that the information was obtained through the interception of a wire, oral, orelectronic communication
- in violation of 18 U.S.C. 2511(1)
- is subject to the same sanctions and remedies as the wiretapper or electroniceavesdropper.[115]

The available case law under the use prohibition of paragraph 2511(1)(d) is scant, and the section has rarely been invoked except in conjunction with the disclosure prohibition of paragraph 2511(1)(c).[116] The wording of the two is clearly parallel, the legislative history describes them in the same breath,[117] and they are treated alike for law enforcement purposes.[118]

A few courts had recognized an exception to the disclosure-use bans of subsection 2511(1) when law enforcement officials disclose or use the results of an illegal interception in which they had played no role.[119] The criminal and civil liability that attend unlawful use of intercepted communications in violation of paragraph 2511(1)(d) are the same as for unlawful disclosure in violation of paragraphs 2511(1)(c) or 2511(1)(e), or for unlawful interception under paragraphs 2511(1)(a) or 2511(1)(b).[120]

Shipping, Manufacturing, Distributing, Possessing or Advertising Wire, Oral, or Electronic Communication Interception Devices

The proscriptions for possession and trafficking in wiretapping and eavesdropping devices are even more demanding than those that apply to the predicate offense itself. There are exemptions for service providers,[121] government officials and those under contract with the government,[122] but there is no exemption for equipment designed to be used by private individuals, lawfully but surreptitiously.[123] Nevertheless, inoperable equipment, though designed to intercept, may not be considered equipment "which can be used to intercept" and consequently may not serve as the basis for a conviction under §2512.[124]

Section 2512's three prohibitions feature several common elements, declaring that:

- any person who
- intentionally
- either

(a)

- sends through the mail or sends or carries in interstate or foreign commerce
- any electronic, mechanical, or other device
- knowing or having reason to know
- that the design of such device renders it primarily useful
- for the purpose of the surreptitious interception of wire, oral, or electronic communications; or

(b)

- manufactures, assembles, possesses, or sells
- any electronic, mechanical, or other device
- knowing or having reason to know
- that the design of such device renders it primarily useful
- for the purpose of the surreptitious interception of wire, oral, or electronic communications, and
- that such device or any component thereof has been or will be sent through the mail or transported in interstate or foreign commerce; or

(c)

- places in any newspaper, magazine, handbill, or other publication or disseminates electronically
- any advertisement of—
  - any electronic, mechanical, or other device
  - knowing or having reason to know
  - that the design of such device renders it primarily useful
  - for the purpose of the surreptitious interception of wire, oral, or electronic communications; or
  - any other electronic, mechanical, or other device
  - where such advertisement promotes the use of such device
  - for the purpose of the surreptitious interception of wire, oral, or electronic communications
- knowing the content of the advertisement and knowing or having reason to know
- that such advertisement will be sent through the mail or transported in interstate or foreign commerce

shall be imprisoned for not more than five years and/or fined not more than $250,000 (not more than $500,000 for organizations).[125]

The legislative history lists among the items Congress considered "primarily useful for the purpose of the surreptitious interception of communications: the martini olive transmitter, the spike mike, the infinity transmitter, and the microphone disguised as a wristwatch, picture frame, cuff link, tie clip, fountain pen, stapler, or cigarette pack."[126]

Questions once raised over whether §2512 covers equipment designed to permit unauthorized reception of scrambled satellite television signals have been resolved.[127] Each of the circuits to consider the question has now concluded that §2512 outlaws such devices,[128] but simple possession does not give rise to a private cause of action.[129]

TITLE III: GOVERNMENT ACCESS

The prohibitions in each of ECPA's three parts—chapter 119 (Title III), chapter 121 (Stored Communications Act), and chapter 206 (pen registers and trap and trace devices)—yield to the need for government access, usually under judicial supervision.

Law Enforcement Wiretapping and Electronic Eavesdropping

Title III exempts federal and state law enforcement officials from its prohibitions on the interception of wire, oral, and electronic communications under three circumstances: (1) pursuant to or in anticipation of a court order,[130] (2) with the consent of one of the parties to the communication;[131] and (3) with respect to the communications of an intruder within an electronic communications system.[132]

To secure a Title III interception order as part of a federal criminal investigation, a senior Justice Department official must approve the application for the court order authorizing the interception of wire or oral communications.[133] The procedure is only available where there is probable cause to believe that the wiretap or electronic eavesdropping will produce evidence of one of a long, but not exhaustive, list of federal crimes,[134] or of the whereabouts of a "fugitive from justice" fleeing from prosecution of one of the offenses on the predicate offense list.[135] Any federal prosecutor may approve an application for a court order under section 2518 authorizing the interception of email or other electronic communications and the authority extends to any federal felony rather than more limited list of federal felonies upon which a wiretap or bug must be predicated.[136]

At the state level, the principal prosecuting attorney of a state or any of its political subdivisions may approve an application for an order authorizing wiretapping or electronic eavesdropping based upon probable cause to believe that it will produce evidence of a felony under the state laws covering murder, kidnaping, gambling, robbery, bribery, extortion, drug trafficking, or any other crime dangerous to life, limb or property. State applications, court orders and other procedures must at a minimum be as demanding as federal requirements.[137]

Applications for a court order authorizing wiretapping and electronic surveillance include:

- the identity of the applicant and the official who authorized the application;
- a full and complete statement of the facts including
  - details of the crime,
  - a particular description of the nature, location and place where the interception is to occur,[138]
  - a particular description of the communications to be intercepted, and
  - the identities (if known) of the person committing the offense and of the persons whose communications are to be intercepted;
- a full and complete statement of the alternative investigative techniques used or an explanation of why they would be futile or dangerous;

- a statement of the period of time for which the interception is to be maintained and if it will not terminate upon seizure of the communications sought, a probable cause demonstration that further similar communications are likely to occur;
- a full and complete history of previous interception applications or efforts involving the same parties or places;
- in the case of an extension, the results to date or explanation for the want of results; and
- any additional information the judge may require.[139]

Before issuing an order authorizing interception, the court must find:

- probable cause to believe that an individual is, has or is about to commit one or more of the predicate offenses;
- probable cause to believe that the particular communications concerning the crime will be seized as a result of the interception requested;
- probable cause to believe that "the facilities from which, or the place where, the wire, oral, or electronic communications are to be intercepted are being used, or are about to be used, in connection with the commission of such offense, or are leased to, listed in the name of, or commonly used by such person";[140] and
- that normal investigative procedures have been or are likely to be futile or toodangerous."[141]

Subsections 2518(4) and (5) demand that any interception order include:

- the identity (if known) of the persons whose conversations are to be intercepted;
- the nature and location of facilities and place covered by the order;
- a particular description of the type of communication to be intercepted and an indication of the crime to which it relates;
- the individual approving the application and the agency executing the order;
- the period of time during which the interception may be conducted and an indication of whether it may continue after the communication sought has been seized;
- an instruction that the order shall be executed
  - as soon as practicable, and
  - so as to minimize the extent of innocent communication seized;[142] and
- upon request, a direction for the cooperation of communications providers and others necessary or useful for the execution of the order.[143]

Compliance with these procedures may be postponed briefly until after the interception effort has begun, upon the approval of senior Justice Department officials in emergency cases involving organized crime or national security threatening conspiracies or involving the risk of death or serious injury.[144]

The court orders remain in effect only as long as required but not more than 30 days. After 30 days, the court may grant 30 day extensions subject to the procedures required for issuance of the original order.[145] During that time the court may require progress reports at such intervals as it considers appropriate.[146] Intercepted communications are to be recorded and the evidence secured and placed under seal (with the possibility of copies for authorized law enforcement disclosure and use) along with the application and the court's order.[147]

Within 90 days of the expiration of the order those whose communications have been intercepted are entitled to notice, and evidence secured through the intercept may be introduced into evidence with 10 days' advance notice to the parties.[148]

Title III also describes conditions under which information derived from a court ordered interception may be disclosed or otherwise used. It permits disclosure and use for official purposes by:

- other law enforcement officials including foreign officials;[149]
- federal intelligence officers to the extent that it involves foreign intelligenceinformation;[150]
- other American or foreign government officials to the extent that it involves the threat of hostile acts by foreign powers, their agents, or international terrorists.[151]

It also allows witnesses testifying in federal or state proceedings to reveal the results of a Title III tap,[152] provided the intercepted conversation or other communication is not privileged.[153]

Without a Title III order and without offending Title III, authorities may intercept the wire, oral, or electronic communications, it they have the consent of one of the parties to the communication.[154] As noted earlier, consent may be either explicitly or implicitly given. For instance, someone who uses a telephone other than his or her own and has been told by the subscriber that conversations over the instrument are recorded has been held to have implicitly consented to interception when using the instrument.[155] This is not to say that subscriber consent alone is sufficient, for it is the parties to the conversation whose privacy is designed to be protected.[156] Although consent may be given in the hopes of leniency from law enforcement officials or as an election between unpalatable alternatives, it must be freely given and not secured coercively.[157]

Little judicial or academic commentary accompanies the narrow "computer trespasser" justification for governmental interception of electronic communications in paragraph 2511(2)(i).[158] The paragraph originated as a temporary provision in the USA PATRIOT Act,[159] and seems designed to enable authorities to track intruders who would surreptitiously use the computer systems of others to cover their trail.[160]

TITLE III: CONSEQUENCES OF A VIOLATION

Criminal Penalties

Interception, use, or disclosure in violation of Title III is generally punishable by imprisonment for not more than five years and/or a fine of not more than $250,000 for individuals and not more than $500,000 for organizations.[161] The same penalties apply to the unlawful capture of cell phone and cordless phone conversations, since the Homeland

Security Act[162] repealed the reduced penalty provisions that at one time applied to the unlawful interceptions using radio scanners and the like.[163] There is a reduced penalty, however, for filching satellite communications as long as the interception is not conducted for criminal, tortious, nor mercenary purposes: unauthorized interceptions are broadly proscribed subject to an exception for unscrambled transmissions[164] and are subject to the general five-year penalty, but interceptions for neither criminal, tortious, nor mercenary purposes subject offenders to only civil punishment.[165] Equipment used to wiretap or eavesdrop in violation of Title III is subject to confiscation by the United States, either in a separate civil proceeding or a part of the prosecution of the offender.[166]

In addition to exemptions previously mentioned, Title III provides a defense to criminal liability based on good faith.[167]

Civil Liability

Victims of a violation of Title III may be entitled to equitable relief, damages (equal to the greater of actual damages, $100 per day of violation, or $10,000),[168] punitive damages, reasonable attorney's fees and reasonable litigation costs.[169] A majority of federal courts hold that a court may decline to award damages, attorneys' fees and costs, but a few still consider such awards mandatory.[170] In addition, a majority hold that governmental entities other than the United States may be liable for violations of section 2520[171] and that law enforcement officers enjoy a qualified immunity from suit under section 2520.[172]

The cause of action created in section 2520 is subject to a good faith defense.[173] Efforts to claim the defense by anyone other than government officials or someone working at their direction have been largely unsuccessful.[174] Moreover, as addressed more extensively below, the 2008 Foreign Intelligence Surveillance Amendments Act, under some circumstances, bars any state or federal cause of action against anyone who assists the government with the installation or use of a means of electronic eavesdropping or electronic surveillance.[175]

Civil Liability of the United States

The USA PATRIOT Act authorizes a cause of action against the United States for willful violations of Title III, the Foreign Intelligence Surveillance Act or the provisions governing stored communications in 18 U.S.C. 2701-2712.[176] Successful plaintiffs are entitled to the greater of $10,000 or actual damages, and reasonable litigation costs.[177]

Administrative Action

Upon a judicial or administrative finding of a Title III violation suggesting possible intentional or willful misconduct on the part of a federal officer or employee, the federal agency or department involved may institute disciplinary action. It is required to explain to its Inspector General's office if it declines to do so.[178]

Attorney Discipline

At one time, the American Bar Association (ABA) considered it ethical misconduct for an attorney to intercept or record a conversation without the consent of all of the parties to the conversation, ABA Formal Op. 337 (1974). The reaction of state regulatory authorities with the power to discipline professional misconduct was mixed. Some agreed with the ABA.[179] Some agreed with the ABA, but expanded the circumstances under which recording could be conducted within ethical bounds.[180] Some disagreed with the ABA view.[181] The ABA has since repudiated its earlier position, ABA Formal Op. 01-422 (2001). Attorneys who engage in *unlawful* wiretapping or electronic eavesdropping will remain subject to professional discipline in every jurisdiction.[182] In light of the ABA's change of position, courts and bar associations have had varied reactions to *lawful* wiretapping or electronic eavesdropping by members of the bar.[183]

Exclusion of Evidence

When the federal wiretap statute prohibits disclosure, the information is inadmissible as evidence before any federal, state, or local tribunal or authority.[184] Individuals whose conversations have been intercepted or against whom the interception was directed[185] have standing to claim the benefits of the section 2515 exclusionary rule through a motion to suppress under 18 U.S.C. 2518(10)(a). Paragraph 2518(10)(a) bars admission as long as the evidence is the product of (1) an unlawful interception, (2) an interception authorized by a facially insufficient court order, or (3) an interception executed in manner substantially contrary to the order authorizing the interception. Mere technical noncompliance is not enough; the defect must be of a nature that substantially undermines the regime of court-supervised interception for law enforcement purposes.[186]

Although the Supreme Court has held that section 2515 may require suppression in instances where the Fourth Amendment exclusionary rule would not,[187] some of the lower courts have recognized the applicability of the good faith exception to the Fourth Amendment exclusionary rule in section 2515 cases.[188] Other courts have held, moreover, that the fruits of an unlawful wiretapping or electronic eavesdropping may be used for impeachment purposes.[189]

The admissibility of tapes or transcripts of tapes of intercepted conversations raise a number of questions quite apart from the legality of the interception. As a consequence of the prerequisites required for admission, privately recorded conversations are more likely to be found inadmissible than those recorded by government officials. Admissibility will require the party moving for admission to show that the tapes or transcripts are accurate, authentic and trustworthy.[190] For some courts this demands a showing that, "(1) the recording device was capable of recording the events offered in evidence; (2) the operator was competent to operate the device; (3) the recording is authentic and correct; (4) changes, additions, or deletions have not been made in the recording; (5) the recording has been preserved in a manner that is shown to the court; (6) the speakers on the tape are identified; and (7) the conversation elicited was made voluntarily and in good faith, without any kind of inducement."[191]

STORED COMMUNICATIONS ACT (SCA)

SCA: Prohibitions

In its original form Title III was ill-suited to ensure the privacy of those varieties of modern communications which are equally vulnerable to intrusion when they are at rest as when they are in transmission. Surreptitious "access" is as least as great a threat as surreptitious "interception" to the patrons of electronic mail (email), electronic bulletin boards, voice mail, pagers, and remote computer storage.

Accordingly, ECPA, in the Stored Communications Act (SCA), bans surreptitious access to communications at rest, although it does so beyond the confines that apply to interception, 18 U.S.C. 2701 - 2711. These separate provisions afford protection for email, voice mail, and other electronic communications only somewhat akin to that available for telephone and face to face conversations under 18 U.S.C. 2510-2522. The SCA has two sets of proscriptions: a general prohibition and a second applicable to only certain communications providers. The general proscription makes it a federal crime to:

- intentionally
- either
  - access without authorization or
  - exceed an authorization to access
- a facility through which an electronic communication service is provided
- and thereby obtain, alter, or prevent authorized access to a wire or electronic communication while it is in electronic storage in such system, 18 U.S.C.2701(a).[192]

The prohibition extends only to "intentional" violations, that is, violations where the defendant had as a conscious objective the forbidden conduct and proscribed result.[193] The offense has three essential components: access, to a facility through which service is supplied, and consequences (obtain, alter, prevent access to a wire or electronic communication). The first requires either unauthorized access or access in excess of authorization. The third requires either acquisition or alteration of an electronic communication or denial of access to it. The courts have encountered little difficulty in determining whether a defendant's conduct constitutes obtaining, altering, or preventing access to a communication. They have divided, however, over cases in which the defendant was granted access to a communication but used access for the purposes other than that for which it was authorized.[194] The question is less divisive when the grant of access is expressly limited[195] or when an individual with authorized access provides an outsider with his user name and password.[196]

The "facility through which an electronic communication service is provided" need not be one made available to the public; but includes as well facilities through which a private employer provides electronic communication services to his employees.[197]

The section only protects communications while "in electronic storage" in a facility through which electronic communications service is provided. "Electronic storage" is defined to encompass temporary, intermediate storage incidental to transmission as well as backup storage.[198] The definition is not always easily applied.[199]

Section 2701's prohibitions yield to several exceptions and defenses. First, the section itself declares that:

Subsection (a) of this section does not apply with respect to conduct authorized—

(1) by the person or entity providing a wire or electronic communications service;
(2) by a user of that service with respect to a communication of or intended for that user; or
(3) in section 2703 [requirements for government access],
2704 [backup preservation] or
2518 [court ordered wiretapping or electronic eavesdropping] of this title.[200]

Second, there are the good faith defenses provided by section 2707:

A good faith reliance on—

(1) a court warrant or order, a grand jury subpoena, a legislative authorization, or a statutory authorization (including a request of a governmental entity under section 2703(f) of this title) [relating to an official request for a service provider preserve evidence];
(2) a request of an investigative or law enforcement officer under section 2518(7) of this title [relating to emergency wiretapping and electronic eavesdropping]; or
(3) a good faith determination that section 2511(3) of this title [relating to the circumstances under which an electronic communications provider may divulge the contents of communication][201] permitted the conduct complained of

is a complete defense to any civil or criminal action brought under this chapter or any other law. 18 U.S.C. 2707(e).

Third, there is the general immunity from civil liability afforded providers under subsection 2703(e):

[N]o cause of action shall lie in any court against any provider of wire or electronic communication service, its officers, employees, agents, or other specified persons for providing information, facilities, or assistance in accordance with the terms of a court order, warrant, subpoena, statutory authorization, or certification under this chapter.

A second set of prohibitions appears in section 2702 and supplements those in section 2701. Section 2702 bans the disclosure of the content of electronic communications and records relating to them by those who provide the public with electronic communication service or remote computing service. The section forbids providers to disclose the content of certain communications to anyone[202] or to disclose related records to governmental entities.[203]

Public electronic communication service (ECS) providers to the public must keep confidential the content of any "communication while in electronic storage by that service."[204] Public remote computer service (RCS) providers must keep confidential the content of "any communication which is carried or maintained on that service—(A) on behalf of, and received by means of electronic transmission from (or created by means of computer processing of communications received by means of electronic transmission from), a subscriber or customer of such service; (B) solely for the purpose of providing storage or computer processing services to such subscriber or customer, if the provider is not authorized to access the contents of any such communications for purposes of providing any services other than storage or computer processing."[205]

Both sets of providers must keep confidential any "record or other information pertaining to a subscriber to or customer of such service (not including the contents of communications covered by paragraph (1) or (2)) to any government entity."[206]

Section 2702 comes with its own set of exceptions which permit disclosure of the contents of a communication:

(1) to an addressee or intended recipient of such communication or an agent of such addressee or intended recipient;
(2) as otherwise authorized in section 2517 [relating to disclosures permitted under Title III], 2511(2)(a)[relating to provider disclosures permitted under Title III for protection of provider property or incidental to service], or 2703 [relating to required provider disclosures pursuant to governmental authority] of this title;
(3) with the lawful consent of the originator or an addressee or intended recipient of such communication, or *the subscriber in the case of remote computing service*;
(4) to a person employed or authorized or whose facilities are used to forward such communication to its destination;
(5) as may be necessarily incident to the rendition of the service or to the protection of the rights or property of the provider of that service;
(6) to the National Center for Missing and Exploited Children, in connection with a report submitted thereto under section 227 of the Victims of Child Abuse Act of 1990;
(7) to a law enforcement agency—(A) if the contents—(i) were inadvertently obtained by the service provider; and (ii) appear to pertain to the commission of a crime;
(8) to a Federal, State, or local government entity, if the provider, in good faith, believes that an emergency involving danger of death or serious physical injury to any person requires disclosure without delay of communications relating to the emergency.[207]

The record disclosure exceptions are similar.[208]

The Ninth Circuit in *Quon* noted that the exception in paragraph 2702(b)(3)(disclosure "with the lawful consent of the originator or an addressee or intended recipient of such communication, or *the subscriber in the case of remote computing service*) permits RCS providers to disclose the contents of otherwise protected communications does not afford ECS providers the same exception.[209] Thus, the service provider violated the SCA when it supplied the Ontario Police Department (the subscriber) with the text of Sergeant Quon's pager messages.[210]

SCA: Government Access

The circumstances and procedural requirements for law enforcement access to stored wire or electronic communications and transactional records are less demanding than those under Title III.[211] They deal with two kinds of information—often in the custody of the communications service provider rather than of any of the parties to the communication—communications records and the content of electronic or wire communications. The Stored Communications Act provides two primary avenues for law enforcement access: permissible provider disclosure (section 2702) and required provided access (section 2703).[212] As noted earlier in the general discussion of section 2702, a public electronic communication service (ECS) provider or a public remote computing service (RCS) provider may disclose the content of a customer's communication without the consent of a communicating party to a law enforcement agency in the case of inadvertent discovery of information relating to commission of a crime,[213] or to any government entity in an emergency situation.[214] ECS and RCS providers may also disclose communications records to any governmental entity in an emergency situation.[215] Federal, state, and local agencies, regardless of the nature of their missions, all qualify as governmental entities for purposes of section 2702.[216]

Section 2702 authorizes voluntary disclosure. Section 2703 speaks to the circumstances under which ECS and RCS providers may be required to disclose communications content and related records. Section 2703 distinguishes between recent communications and those that have been in electronic storage for more than 180 days.[217] The section insists that government entities resort to a search warrant to compel providers to supply the content of wire or electronic communications held in electronic storage for less than 180 days.[218] It permits them to use a warrant, subpoena, or a court order authorized in subsection 2703(d) to force content disclosure with respect to communications held for more than 180 days.[219]

A subsection 2703(d) court order may be issued by a federal magistrate or by a judge qualified to issue an order under Title III.[220] It need not be issued in the district in which the provider is located.[221]

The person whose communication is disclosed is entitled to notice, unless the court authorizes delayed notification because contemporaneous notice might have an adverse impact.[222] Government supervisory officials may certify the need for delayed notification in the case of a subpoena.[223] Traditional exigent circumstances and a final general inconvenience justification form the grounds for delayed notification in either case:

- endangering the life or physical safety of an individual;
- flight from prosecution;
- destruction of or tampering with evidence;
- intimidation of potential witnesses; or
- otherwise seriously jeopardizing an investigation or unduly delaying a trial.[224]

Subsection 2703(d) authorizes issuance of an order when the governmental entity has presented specific and articulable facts sufficient to establish reasonable grounds to believe that the contents are relevant and material to an ongoing criminal investigation.[225] Some courts have held that this "reasonable grounds" standard is a *Terry* standard, a less demanding standard than "probable cause," and that under some circumstances this standard may be constitutionally insufficient to justify government access to provider held email.[226] A Sixth Circuit panel has held that the Fourth Amendment precludes government access to the content of stored communications (email) held by service providers in the absence of a warrant, subscriber consent, or some other indication that the subscriber has waived his or her expectation of privacy.[227] Where the government instead secures access through a subpoena or court order as section 2703 permits, the evidence may be subject to both the Fourth Amendment exclusionary rule and the exceptions to the rule.[228]

The SCA has two provisions which require providers to save customer communications at the government's request. One is found in subsection 2703(f). It requires ECS and RCS providers to preserve "records and other evidence in its possession," at the request of a governmental entity pending receipt of a warrant, court order, or subpoena.[229] Whether providers are bound to preserve emails and other communications that come into their possession both before and after receipt of the request is unclear.[230]

The second preservation provision is more detailed. It permits a governmental entity to insist that providers preserve backup copies of the communications covered by a subpoena or subsection 2703(d) court order. It gives subscribers the right to challenge the relevancy of the information sought.[231] It might also be read to require the preservation of the content of communications received by the provider both before and after receipt of the order, but the requirement that copies be made within two days of receipt of the order seems to preclude such an interpretation.[232]

Section 2703 provides greater protection to communication content than to provider records relating to those communications. Under subsection 2703(c), a governmental entity may require a ECS or RCS provider to disclose records or information pertaining to a customer or subscriber— other than the content of a communication—under a warrant, a court order under subsection 2703(d), or with the consent of the subject of the information.[233] An administrative, grand jury or trial subpoena is sufficient, however, for a limited range of customer or subscriber related information.[234] The customer or subscriber need not be notified of the record disclosure in either case.[235]

The district courts have been divided for some time over the question of what standard applies when the government seeks cell phone location information from a provider, either current or historical.[236] The Third Circuit has held that while issuance of an order under subsection 2703(d) does not require a showing of probable cause as a general rule, the circumstances of a given case may require it.[237]

In *United States v. Jones*,[238] five members of the Supreme Court seemed to suggest that a driver has a reasonable expectation that authorities must comply with the demands of the Fourth Amendment before acquiring access to information that discloses the travel patterns of his car over an extended period of time. There, the Court unanimously agreed that the agents' attachment of a tracking device to Jones' car and long-term capture of the resulting information constituted a Fourth Amendment search.[239] For four Justices, placement of the device constituted a physical intrusion upon a constitutionally protected area.[240] For four others, long-term tracking constituted a breach of Jones' reasonable expectation of privacy.[241] For the ninth Justice, the activity constituted a Fourth Amendment search under either rationale.[242] It remains to be seen whether the Supreme Court's decision in *Jones* will contribute to resolution of the issue.[243]

SCA: Consequences

Breaches of the unauthorized access prohibitions of section 2701 expose offenders to possible criminal, civil, and administrative sanctions. Violations committed for malicious, mercenary, tortious or criminal purposes are punishable by imprisonment for not more than five years (not more than 10 years for a subsequent conviction) and/or a fine of not more than $250,000 (not more than $500,000 for organizations); lesser transgressions, by imprisonment for not more than one year (not more than five years for a subsequent conviction) and/or a fine of not more than $100,000.[244] Victims of a violation of subsection 2701(a) have a cause of action for equitable relief, reasonable attorneys' fees and costs, and damages equal to the amount of any offender profits added to the total of the victim's losses (but not less than $1,000 in any event).[245]

Violations by the United States may give rise to a cause of action and may result in disciplinary action against offending officials or employees under the same provisions that apply to U.S. violations of Title III,[246] Unlike violations of Title III, however, there is no statutory prohibition on disclosure or use of the information through a violation of section 2701;[247] nor is there a statutory rule for the exclusion of evidence as a consequence of a violation.[248] Yet, violations of SCA, which also constitute violations of the Fourth Amendment, will trigger both the Fourth Amendment exclusionary rule and the exceptions to that rule.[249]

No criminal penalties attend a violation of voluntary provider disclosure prohibitions of section 2702. Yet, ECS and RCS providers—unable to claim the benefit of one of the section's exceptions, of the good faith defense under subsection 2707(e), or of the immunity available under subsection 2703(e)—may be liable for civil damages, costs and attorneys' fees under section 2707 for any violation of section 2702.[250]

PEN REGISTERS AND TRAP AND TRACE DEVICES (PR/T&T)

PR/T&T: Prohibitions

A trap and trace device identifies the source of incoming calls, and a pen register indicates the numbers called from a particular instrument.[251] Since they did not allowed the user to overhear the "contents" of the phone conversation or to otherwise capture the content of a communication, they were not considered interceptions within the reach of Title III prior to the enactment of ECPA.[252] Although Congress elected to expand the definition of interception, it chose to regulate these devices beyond the boundaries of Title III for most purposes.[253] Nevertheless, the Title III wiretap provisions apply when, due to the nature of advances in telecommunications technology, pen registers and trap and trace devices are able to capture wire communication "content."[254]

The USA PATRIOT Act enlarged the coverage of sections 3121-3127 to include sender/addressee information relating to email and other forms of electronic communications.[255]

Subsection 3121(a) outlaws installation or use of a pen register or trap and trace device, except under one of seven circumstances:

- pursuant to a court order issued under sections 3121-3127;
- pursuant to a Foreign Intelligence Surveillance Act (FISA) court order;[256]
- with the consent of the user;
- when incidental to service;
- when necessary to protect users from abuse of service;
- when necessary to protect providers from abuse of service;[257] or
- in an emergency situation.[258]

PR/T&T: Government Access

Federal government attorneys and state and local police officers may apply for a court order authorizing the installation and use of a pen register and/or a trap and trace device upon certification that the information that it will provide is relevant to a pending criminal investigation.[259]

An order authorizing installation and use of a pen register or trap and trace device must:

- specify
  - the person (if known) upon whose telephone line the device is to be installed,
  - the person (if known) who is the subject of the criminal investigation,
  - the telephone number, (if known) the location of the line to which the device is to be attached, and geographical range of the device,
  - a description of the crime to which the investigation relates;
- upon request, direct carrier assistance pursuant to section 3124;
- terminate within 60 days, unless extended;
- involve a report of particulars of the order's execution in Internet cases; and
- impose necessary nondisclosure requirements.[260]

The order may be issued by a judge of "competent jurisdiction" over the offense under investigation, including a federal magistrate judge.[261] Senior Justice Department or state prosecutors may approve the installation and use of a pen register or trap and trace device prior to the issuance of court authorization in emergency cases that involve either an organized crime conspiracy, an immediate danger of death or serious injury, a threat to national security, or a serious attack on a "protected computer."[262] Emergency use must end within 48 hours, or sooner if an application for court approval is denied.[263]

Federal authorities have applied for court orders, under the Stored Communications Act (18 U.S.C. 2701-2712) and the trap and trace authority of 18 U.S.C. 3121-3127, seeking to direct communications providers to supply them with the information necessary to track cell phone users in conjunction with an ongoing criminal investigation. Thus far, their efforts have met with mixed success.[264]

PRT&T: Consequences

The use or installation of pen registers or trap and trace devices by anyone other than the telephone company, service provider, or those acting under judicial authority is a federal crime, punishable by imprisonment for not more than a year and/or a fine of not more than $100,000 ($200,000 for an organization).[265] Subsection 3124(e) creates a good faith defense for reliance upon a court order under subsection 3123(b), an emergency request under subsection 3125(a), "a legislative authorization, or a statutory authorization."[266] There is no accompanying exclusionary rule, and consequently a violation of section 3121 will not serve as a basis to suppress any resulting evidence.[267]

Moreover, unlike violations of Title III, there is no requirement that the target of an order be notified upon the expiration of the order; nor is there a separate federal private cause of action for victims of a pen register or trap and trace device violation.[268] One court, in order to avoid First Amendment concerns, has held that the statute precludes imposing permanent gag orders upon providers.[269] Nevertheless permitting providers to disclose the existence of an order to a target does not require them to do so. Some of the states have established a separate criminal offense for unlawful use of a pen register or trap and trace device,[270] yet most of these seem to follow the federal lead and have not established a separate private cause of action for unlawful installation or use of the devices.[271]

ELECTRONIC COMMUNICATIONS PRIVACY ACT (TEXT)

Chapter 119 ("Title III")

18 U.S.C. 2510. Definitions

As used in this chapter—

(1) "wire communication" means any aural transfer made in whole or in part through the use of facilities for the transmission of communications by the aid of wire, cable, or other like connection between the point of origin and the point of reception (including the use of such connection in a switching station) furnished or operated by any person engaged in providing or operating such facilities for the transmission of interstate or foreign communications or communications affecting interstate or foreign commerce;

(2) "oral communication" means any oral communication uttered by a person exhibiting an expectation that such communication is not subject to interception under circumstances justifying such expectation, but such term does not include any electronic communication;

(3) "State" means any State of the United States, the District of Columbia, the Commonwealth of Puerto Rico, and any territory or possession of the United States;

(4) "intercept" means the aural or other acquisition of the contents of any wire, electronic, or oral communication through the use of any electronic, mechanical, or other device;

(5) "electronic, mechanical, or other device" means any device or apparatus which can be used to intercept a wire, oral, or electronic communication other than—

(a) any telephone or telegraph instrument, equipment or facility, or any component thereof, (i) furnished to the subscriber or user by a provider of wire or electronic communication service in the ordinary course of its business and being used by the subscriber or user in the ordinary course of its business or furnished by such subscriber or user for connection to the facilities of such service and used in the ordinary course of its business; or (ii) being used by a provider of wire or electronic communication service in the ordinary course of its business, or by an investigative or law enforcement officer in the ordinary course of his duties;

(b) a hearing aid or similar device being used to correct subnormal hearing to not better than normal;

(6) "person" means any employee, or agent of the United States or any State or political subdivision thereof, and any individual, partnership, association, joint stock company, trust, or corporation;

(7) "Investigative or law enforcement officer" means any officer of the United States or of a State or political subdivision thereof, who is empowered by law to conduct investigations of or to make arrests for offenses enumerated in this chapter, and any attorney authorized by law to prosecute or participate in the prosecution of such offenses;

(8) "contents," when used with respect to any wire, oral, or electronic communication, includes any information concerning the substance, purport, or meaning of that communication;

(9) "Judge of competent jurisdiction" means—

(a) a judge of a United States district court or a United States court of appeals; and

(b) a judge of any court of general criminal jurisdiction of a State who is authorized by a statute of that State to enter orders authorizing interceptions of wire, oral, or electronic communications;

(10) "communication common carrier" has the meaning given the term in section 3 of the Communications Act of 1934;

(11) "aggrieved person" means a person who was a party to any intercepted wire, oral, or electronic communication or a person against whom the interception was directed;

(12) "electronic communication" means any transfer of signs, signals, writing, images, sounds, data, or intelligence of any nature transmitted in whole or in part by a wire, radio, electromagnetic, photoelectronic or photo optical system that affects interstate or foreign commerce, but does not include—

(A) any wire or oral communication;

(B) any communication made through a tone-only paging device;

(C) any communication from a tracking device (as defined in section 3117 of this title); or

(D) electronic funds transfer information stored by a financial institution in a communications system used for the electronic storage and transfer of funds;

(13) "user" means any person or entity who—

(A) uses an electronic communication service; and

(B) is duly authorized by the provider of such service to engage in such use;

(14) "electronic communications system" means any wire, radio, electromagnetic, photo optical or photo electronic facilities for the transmission of wire or electronic communications, and any computer facilities or related electronic equipment for the electronic storage of such communications;

(15) "electronic communication service" means any service which provides to users thereof the ability to send or receive wire or electronic communications;

(16) "readily accessible to the general public" means, with respect to a radio communication, that such communication is not—

(A) scrambled or encrypted;

(B) transmitted using modulation techniques whose essential parameters have been withheld from the public with the intention of preserving the privacy of such communication;

(C) carried on a subcarrier or other signal subsidiary to a radio transmission;

(D) transmitted over a communication system provided by a common carrier, unless the communication is a tone only paging system communication; or
(E) transmitted on frequencies allocated under part 25, subpart D, E, or F of part 74, or part 94 of the Rules of the Federal Communications Commission, unless, in the case of a communication transmitted on a frequency allocated under part 74 that is not exclusively allocated to broadcast auxiliary services, the communication is a two-way voice communication by radio;

(17)"electronic storage" means—
(A) any temporary, intermediate storage of a wire or electronic communication incidental to the electronic transmission thereof; and
(B) any storage of such communication by an electronic communication service for purposes of backup protection of such communication;

(18)"aural transfer" means a transfer containing the human voice at any point between and including the point of origin and the point of reception.

(19)"foreign intelligence information", for purposes of section 2517(6) of this title, means—
(A) information, whether or not concerning a United States person, that relates to the ability of the United States to protect against—
(i) actual or potential attack or other grave hostile acts of a foreign power or an agent of a foreign power;
(ii) sabotage or intentional terrorism by a foreign power or an agent of a foreign power; or
(iii) clandestine intelligence activities by and intelligence service or network of a foreign power or by an agent of a foreign power; or
(B) information, whether or not concerning a United States person, with respect to a foreign power or foreign territory that relates to—
(i) the national defense or the security of the United States; or
(ii) the conduct of the foreign affairs of the United States.

(20)"protected computer" has the meaning set forth in section 1030; and

(21)"computer trespasser"—
(A) means a person who accesses a protected computer without authorization and thus has no reasonable expectation of privacy in any communication transmitted to, through, or from the protected computer; and
(B) does not include a person known by the owner or operator of the protected computer to have an existing contractual relationship with the owner or operator of the protected computer for access to all or part of the protected computer.

18 U.S.C. 2511. Interception and Disclosure of Wire, Oral, or Electronic Communications Prohibited

(1) Except as otherwise specifically provided in this chapter any person who—
(a) intentionally intercepts, endeavors to intercept, or procures any other person to intercept or endeavor to intercept, any wire, oral, or electronic communication;
(b) intentionally uses, endeavors to use, or procures any other person to use or endeavor to use any electronic, mechanical, or other device to intercept any oral communication when—

(i) such device is affixed to, or otherwise transmits a signal through, a wire, cable, or other like connection used in wire communication; or
(ii) such device transmits communications by radio, or interferes with the transmission of such communication; or
(iii) such person knows, or has reason to know, that such device or any component thereof has been sent through the mail or transported in interstate or foreign commerce; or
(iv) such use or endeavor to use (A) takes place on the premises of any business or other commercial establishment the operations of which affect interstate or foreign commerce; or (B) obtains or is for the purpose of obtaining information relating to the operations of any business or other commercial establishment the operations of which affect interstate or foreign commerce; or
(v) such person acts in the District of Columbia, the Commonwealth of Puerto Rico, or any territory or possession of the United States;

(c) intentionally discloses, or endeavors to disclose, to any other person the contents of any wire, oral, or electronic communication, knowing or having reason to know that the information was obtained through the interception of a wire, oral, or electronic communication in violation of this subsection;

(d) intentionally uses, or endeavors to use, the contents of any wire, oral, or electronic communication, knowing or having reason to know that the information was obtained through the interception of a wire, oral, or electronic communication in violation of this subsection; or

(e) (i) intentionally discloses, or endeavors to disclose, to any other person the contents of any wire, oral, or electronic communication, intercepted by means authorized by sections 2511(2)(a)(ii), 2511(2)(b)-(c), 2511(2)(e), 2516, and 2518 of this chapter, (ii) knowing or having reason to know that the information was obtained through the interception of such a communication in connection with a criminal investigation, (iii) having obtained or received the information in connection with a criminal investigation, and (iv) with intent to improperly obstruct, impede, or interfere with a duly authorized criminal investigation, shall be punished as provided in subsection (4) or shall be subject to suit as provided in subsection (5).

(2)

(a)

(i) It shall not be unlawful under this chapter for an operator of a switchboard, or an officer, employee, or agent of a provider of wire or electronic communication service, whose facilities are used in the transmission of a wire or electronic communication, to intercept, disclose, or use that communication in the normal course of his employment while engaged in any activity which is a necessary incident to the rendition of his service or to the protection of the rights or property of the provider of that service, except that a provider of wire communication service to the public shall not utilize service observing or random monitoring except for mechanical or service quality control checks.

(ii) Notwithstanding any other law, providers of wire or electronic communication service, their officers, employees, and agents, landlords, custodians, or other persons, are authorized to provide information, facilities, or technical assistance to persons authorized by law to intercept wire, oral, or electronic communications or to conduct electronic surveillance, as defined in section 101 of the Foreign Intelligence Surveillance Act of 1978, if such provider, its officers, employees, or agents, landlord, custodian, or other specified person, has been provided with—

[P.L. 110-261, Sec. 101(c)(1)] (A) a court order directing such assistance *or a court order pursuant to section 704 of the Foreign Intelligence Surveillance Act of 1978* signed by the authorizing judge,
[P.L. 110-261, Sec. 403(b)(2)(C)] *Effective December 31, 2012 ... (C) except as provided in section 404, section 2511(2) (A)(ii)(A) of title 18, United States Code, is amended by striking "or a court order pursuant to section 704 of the Foreign Intelligence Surveillance Act of 1978."*
[P.L. 110-261, Sec. 404(b)(3)] *Challenge of directives; protection from liability; use of information— Notwithstanding any other provision of this Act or of the Foreign Intelligence Surveillance Act of 1978 (50 U.S.C. 1801 et seq.) ... (E) section 2511(2)(a)(ii)(A) of title 18, United States Code, as amended by section 101(c)(1), shall continue to apply to an order issued pursuant to section 704 of the Foreign Intelligence Surveillance Act of 1978, as added by section 101(a)[50 U.S.C. 1881c];* or

(B) a certification in writing by a person specified in section 2518(7) of this title or the Attorney General of the United States that no warrant or court order is required by law, that all statutory requirements have been met, and that the specified assistance is required, setting forth the period of time during which the provision of the information, facilities, or technical assistance is authorized and specifying the information, facilities, or technical assistance required. No provider of wire or electronic communication service, officer, employee, or agent thereof, or landlord, custodian, or other specified person shall disclose the existence of any interception or surveillance or the device used to accomplish the interception or surveillance with respect to which the person has been furnished a court order or certification under this chapter, except as may otherwise be required by legal process and then only after prior notification to the Attorney General or to the principal prosecuting attorney of a State or any political subdivision of a State, as may be appropriate. Any such disclosure, shall render such person liable for the civil damages provided for in section 2520. No cause of action shall lie in any court against any provider of wire or electronic communication service, its officers, employees, or agents, landlord, custodian, or other specified person for providing information, facilities, or assistance in accordance with the terms of a court order, statutory authorization, or certification under this chapter.

(iii)If a certification under subparagraph (ii)(B) for assistance to obtain foreign intelligence information is based on statutory authority, the certification shall identify the specific statutory provision and shall certify that the statutory requirements have been met.

(b) It shall not be unlawful under this chapter for an officer, employee, or agent of the Federal Communications Commission, in the normal course of his employment and in discharge of the monitoring responsibilities exercised by the Commission in the enforcement of chapter 5 of title 47 of the United States Code, to intercept a wire or electronic communication, or oral communication transmitted by radio, or to disclose or use the information thereby obtained.

(c) It shall not be unlawful under this chapter for a person acting under color of law to intercept a wire, oral, or electronic communication, where such person is a party to the communication or one of the parties to the communication has given prior consent to such interception.

(d) It shall not be unlawful under this chapter for a person not acting under color of law to intercept a wire, oral, or electronic communication where such person is a party to the communication or where one of the parties to the communication has given prior consent to such interception unless such communication is intercepted for the purpose of committing any criminal or tortious act in violation of the Constitution or laws of the United States or of any State.

(e) Notwithstanding any other provision of this title or section 705 or 706 of the Communications Act of 1934, it shall not be unlawful for an officer, employee, or agent of the United States in the normal course of his official duty to conduct electronic surveillance, as defined in section 101 of the Foreign Intelligence Surveillance Act of 1978, as authorized by that Act.

(f) Nothing contained in this chapter or chapter 121 or 206 of this title, or section 705 of the Communications Act of 1934, shall be deemed to affect the acquisition by the United States Government of foreign intelligence information from international or foreign communications, or foreign intelligence activities conducted in accordance with otherwise applicable Federal law involving a foreign electronic communications system, utilizing a means other than electronic surveillance as defined in section 101 of the Foreign Intelligence Surveillance Act of 1978, and procedures in this chapter or chapter 121 and the Foreign Intelligence Surveillance Act of 1978 shall be the exclusive means by which electronic surveillance, as defined in section 101 of such Act, and the interception of domestic wire, oral, and electronic communications may be conducted.

(g) It shall not be unlawful under this chapter or chapter 121 of this title for any person—

(i) to intercept or access an electronic communication made through an electronic communication system that is configured so that such electronic communication is readily accessible to the general public;

(ii) to intercept any radio communication which is transmitted—

(I) by any station for the use of the general public, or that relates to ships, aircraft, vehicles, or persons in distress;

(II) by any governmental, law enforcement, civil defense, private land mobile, or public safety communications system, including police and fire, readily accessible to the general public;

(III) by a station operating on an authorized frequency within the bands allocated to the amateur, citizens band, or general mobile radio services; or

(IV) by any marine or aeronautical communications system;

(iii) to engage in any conduct which—

(I) is prohibited by section 633 of the Communications Act of 1934; or

(II) is excepted from the application of section 705(a) of the Communications Act of 1934 by section 705(b) of that Act;

(iv) to intercept any wire or electronic communication the transmission of which is causing harmful interference to any lawfully operating station or consumer electronic equipment, to the extent necessary to identify the source of such interference; or

(v) for other users of the same frequency to intercept any radio communication made through a system that utilizes frequencies monitored by individuals engaged in the provision or the use of such system, if such communication is not scrambled or encrypted.

(h) It shall not be unlawful under this chapter—

(i) to use a pen register or a trap and trace device (as those terms are defined for the purposes of chapter 206 (relating to pen registers and trap and trace devices) of this title); or

(ii) for a provider of electronic communication service to record the fact that a wire or electronic communication was initiated or completed in order to protect such provider, another provider furnishing service toward the completion of the wire or electronic communication, or a user of that service, from fraudulent, unlawful or abusive use of such service.

(i) It shall not be unlawful under this chapter for a person acting under color of law to intercept the wire or electronic communications of a computer trespasser transmitted to, through, or from the protected computer, if—

(I) the owner or operator of the protected computer authorizes the interception of the computer trespasser's communications on the protected computer;

(II) the person acting under color of law is lawfully engaged in an investigation;

(III) the person acting under color of law has reasonable grounds to believe that the contents of the computer trespasser's communications will be relevant to the investigation; and

(IV) such interception does not acquire communications other than those transmitted to or from the computer trespasser.

(3)

(a) Except as provided in paragraph (b) of this subsection, a person or entity providing an electronic communication service to the public shall not intentionally divulge the contents of any communication (other than one to such person or entity, or an agent thereof) while in transmission on that service to any person or entity other than an addressee or intended recipient of such communication or an agent of such addressee or intended recipient.

(b) A person or entity providing electronic communication service to the public may divulge the contents of any such communication—

(i) as otherwise authorized in section 2511(2) (a) or 2517 of this title;

(ii) with the lawful consent of the originator or any addressee or intended recipient of such communication;

(iii) to a person employed or authorized, or whose facilities are used, to forward such communication to its destination; or

(iv) which were inadvertently obtained by the service provider and which appear to pertain to the commission of a crime, if such divulgence is made to a law enforcement agency.

(4)

(a) Except as provided in paragraph (b) of this subsection or in subsection (5), whoever violates subsection (1) of this section shall be fined under this title or imprisoned not more than five years, or both.

(b) Conduct otherwise an offense under this subsection that consists of or relates to the interception of a satellite transmission that is not encrypted or scrambled and that is transmitted—

(i) to a broadcasting station for purposes of retransmission to the general public; or

(ii) as an audio subcarrier intended for redistribution to facilities open to the public, but not including data transmissions or telephone calls, is not an offense under this subsection unless the conduct is for the purposes of direct or indirect commercial advantage or private financial gain.

(c) [Redesignated (b)]

(5)

(a)

(i) If the communication is—

(A) a private satellite video communication that is not scrambled or encrypted and the conduct in violation of this chapter is the private viewing of that communication and is not for a tortious or illegal purpose or for purposes of direct or indirect commercial advantage or private commercial gain; or

(B) a radio communication that is transmitted on frequencies allocated under subpart D of part 74 of the rules of the Federal Communications Commission that is not scrambled or encrypted and the conduct in violation of this chapter is not for a tortious or illegal purpose or for purposes of direct or indirect commercial advantage or private commercial gain, then the person who engages in such conduct shall be subject to suit by the Federal Government in a court of competent jurisdiction.

(ii) In an action under this subsection—

(A) if the violation of this chapter is a first offense for the person under paragraph (a) of subsection (4) and such person has not been found liable in a civil action under section 2520 of this title, the Federal Government shall be entitled to appropriate injunctive relief; and

(B) if the violation of this chapter is a second or subsequent offense under paragraph (a) of subsection (4) or such person has been found liable in any prior civil action under section 2520, the person shall be subject to a mandatory $500 civil fine.

(b) The court may use any means within its authority to enforce an injunction issued under paragraph (ii)(A), and shall impose a civil fine of not less than $500 for each violation of such an injunction.

18 U.S.C. 2512. Manufacture, Distribution, Possession, and Advertising of Wire, Oral, or Electronic Communication Intercepting Devices Prohibited

(1) Except as otherwise specifically provided in this chapter, any person who intentionally—

(a) sends through the mail, or sends or carries in interstate or foreign commerce, any electronic, mechanical, or other device, knowing or having reason to know that the design of such device renders it primarily useful for the purpose of the surreptitious interception of wire, oral, or electronic communications;

(b) manufactures, assembles, possesses, or sells any electronic, mechanical, or other device, knowing or having reason to know that the design of such device renders it primarily useful for the purpose of the surreptitious interception of wire, oral, or electronic communications, and that such device or any component thereof has been or will be sent through the mail or transported in interstate or foreign commerce; or

(c) places in any newspaper, magazine, handbill, or other publication or disseminates by electronic means any advertisement of—

(i) any electronic, mechanical, or other device knowing or having reason to know that the design of such device renders it primarily useful for the purpose of the surreptitious interception of wire, oral, or electronic communications; or

(ii) any other electronic, mechanical, or other device, where such advertisement promotes the use of such device for the purpose of the surreptitious interception of wire, oral, or electronic communications,

knowing the content of the advertisement and knowing or having reason to know that such advertisement will be sent through the mail or transported in interstate or foreign commerce, shall be fined under this title or imprisoned not more than five years, or both.

(2) It shall not be unlawful under this section for—

(a) a provider of wire or electronic communication service or an officer, agent, or employee of, or a person under contract with, such a provider, in the normal course of the business of providing that wire or electronic communication service, or

(b) an officer, agent, or employee of, or a person under contract with, the United States, a State, or a political subdivision thereof, in the normal course of the activities of the United States, a State, or a political subdivision thereof, to send through the mail, send or carry in interstate or foreign commerce, or manufacture, assemble, possess, or sell any electronic, mechanical, or other device knowing or having reason to know that the design of such device renders it primarily useful for the purpose of the surreptitious interception of wire, oral, or electronic communications.

(3) It shall not be unlawful under this section to advertise for sale a device described in subsection (1) of this section if the advertisement is mailed, sent, or carried in interstate or foreign commerce solely to a domestic provider of wire or electronic communication service or to an agency of the United States, a State, or a political subdivision thereof which is duly authorized to use such device.

18 U.S.C. 2513. Confiscation of Wire, Oral, or Electronic Communication Interception Devices

Any electronic, mechanical, or other device used, sent, carried, manufactured, assembled, possessed, sold, or advertised in violation of section 2511 or section 2512 of this chapter may be seized and forfeited to the United States. All provisions of law relating to (1) the seizure, summary and judicial forfeiture, and condemnation of vessels, vehicles, merchandise, and baggage for violations of the customs laws contained in title 19 of the United States Code, (2) the disposition of such vessels, vehicles, merchandise, and baggage or the proceeds from the sale thereof, (3) the remission or mitigation of such forfeiture, (4) the compromise of claims, and (5) the award of compensation to informers in respect of such forfeitures, shall apply to seizures and forfeitures incurred, or alleged to have been incurred, under the provisions of this section, insofar as applicable and not inconsistent with the provisions of this section; except that such duties as are imposed upon the collector of customs or any other person with respect to the seizure and forfeiture of vessels, vehicles, merchandise, and baggage under the provisions of the customs laws contained in title 19 of the United States Code shall be performed with respect to seizure and forfeiture of electronic, mechanical, or other intercepting devices under this section by such officers, agents, or other persons as may be authorized or designated for that purpose by the Attorney General.

18 U.S.C. 2515. Prohibition of Use as Evidence of Intercepted Wire or Oral Communications

Whenever any wire or oral communication has been intercepted, no part of the contents of such communication and no evidence derived therefrom may be received in evidence in any trial, hearing, or other proceeding in or before any court, grand jury, department, officer, agency, regulatory body, legislative committee, or other authority of the United States, a State, or a political subdivision thereof if the disclosure of that information would be in violation of this chapter.

18 U.S.C. 2516. Authorization for Interception of Wire, Oral, or Electronic Communications

(1) The Attorney General, Deputy Attorney General, Associate Attorney General, or any Assistant Attorney General, any acting Assistant Attorney General, or any Deputy Assistant Attorney General or acting Deputy Assistant Attorney General in the Criminal Division or National Security Division specially designated by the Attorney General, may authorize an application to a Federal judge of competent jurisdiction

for, and such judge may grant in conformity with section 2518 of this chapter an order authorizing or approving the interception of wire or oral communications by the Federal Bureau of Investigation, or a Federal agency having responsibility for the investigation of the offense as to which the application is made, when such interception may provide or has provided evidence of—

(a) any offense punishable by death or by imprisonment for more than one year under sections 2122 and 2274 through 2277 of title 42 of the United States Code (relating to the enforcement of the Atomic Energy Act of 1954), section 2284 of title 42 of the United States Code (relating to sabotage of nuclear facilities or fuel), or under the following chapters of this title: chapter 10 (relating to biological weapons) chapter 37 (relating to espionage), chapter 55 (relating to kidnapping), chapter 90 (relating to protection of trade secrets), chapter 105 (relating to sabotage), chapter 115 (relating to treason), chapter 102 (relating to riots), chapter 65 (relating to malicious mischief), chapter 111 (relating to destruction of vessels), or chapter 81 (relating to piracy);

(b) a violation of section 186 or section 501(c) of title 29, United States Code (dealing with restrictions on payments and loans to labor organizations), or any offense which involves murder, kidnapping, robbery, or extortion, and which is punishable under this title;

(c) any offense which is punishable under the following sections of this title: section 37 (relating to violence at international airports), section 43 (relating to animal enterprise terrorism), section 81 (arson within special maritime and territorial jurisdiction), section 201 (bribery of public officials and witnesses), section 215 (relating to bribery of bank officials), section 224 (bribery in sporting contests), subsection (d), (e), (f), (g), (h), or (i) of section 844 (unlawful use of explosives), section 1032 (relating to concealment of assets), section 1084 (transmission of wagering information), section 751 (relating to escape), section 832 (relating to nuclear and weapons of mass destruction threats), section 842 (relating to explosive materials), section 930 (relating to possession of weapons in Federal facilities), section 1014 (relating to loans and credit applications generally; renewals and discounts), section 1114 (relating to officers and employees of the United States), section 1116 (relating to protection of foreign officials), sections 1503, 1512, and 1513 (influencing or injuring an officer, juror, or witness generally), section 1510 (obstruction of criminal investigations), section 1511 (obstruction of State or local law enforcement), section 1591 (sex trafficking of children by force, fraud, or coercion), section 1751 (Presidential and Presidential staff assassination, kidnapping, and assault), section 1951 (interference with commerce by threats or violence), section 1952 (interstate and foreign travel or transportation in aid of racketeering enterprises), section 1958 (relating to use of interstate commerce facilities in the commission of murder for hire), section 1959 (relating to violent crimes in aid of racketeering activity), section 1954 (offer, acceptance, or solicitation to influence operations of employee benefit plan), section 1955 (prohibition of business enterprises of gambling), section 1956 (laundering of monetary instruments), section 1957 (relating to engaging in monetary transactions in property derived from specified unlawful activity), section 659 (theft from interstate shipment), section 664 (embezzlement from pension and welfare funds), section 1343 (fraud by wire, radio, or television), section 1344 (relating to bank fraud), section 1992 (relating to terrorist attacks against mass transportation), sections 2251 and 2252 (sexual exploitation of children), section 2251A (selling or buying of children), section 2252A (relating to material constituting or containing child pornography), section 1466A (relating to child obscenity), section 2260 (production of sexually explicit depictions of a minor for importation into the United States), sections 2421, 2422, 2423, and 2425 (relating to transportation for illegal sexual activity and related crimes), sections 2312, 2313, 2314, and 2315 (interstate transportation of stolen property), section 2321 (relating to trafficking in certain motor vehicles or motor vehicle parts), section 2340A (relating to torture), section 1203 (relating to hostage taking), section 1029 (relating to fraud and related activity in connection with access devices), section 3146 (relating to penalty for failure to appear), section 3521(b)(3) (relating to witness relocation and assistance), section 32 (relating to destruction of aircraft or aircraft facilities), section 38 (relating to aircraft parts fraud), section 1963 (violations with respect to racketeer influenced and corrupt organizations), section 115 (relating to threatening or retaliating against a Federal official), section 1341 (relating to mail fraud), a felony violation of section 1030 (relating to computer fraud and abuse), section 351 (violations with respect to congressional, Cabinet, or Supreme Court assassinations, kidnapping, and assault), section 831 (relating to prohibited transactions involving nuclear materials), section 33 (relating to destruction of motor vehicles or motor vehicle facilities), section 175 (relating to biological weapons), section 175c (relating to variola virus), section 956 (conspiracy to harm persons or property overseas), section a felony violation of section 1028 (relating to production of false identification documentation), section 1425 (relating to the procurement of citizenship or nationalization unlawfully), section 1426 (relating to the reproduction of naturalization or citizenship papers), section 1427 (relating to the sale of naturalization or citizenship papers), section 1541 (relating to passport issuance without authority), section 1542 (relating to false statements in passport applications), section 1543 (relating to forgery or false use of passports), section 1544 (relating to misuse of passports), or section 1546 (relating to fraud and misuse of visas, permits, and other documents); section 555 (relating to construction or use of international border tunnels);

(d) any offense involving counterfeiting punishable under section 471, 472, or 473 of this title;

(e) any offense involving fraud connected with a case under title 11 or the manufacture, importation, receiving, concealment, buying, selling, or otherwise dealing in narcotic drugs, marihuana, or other dangerous drugs, punishable under any law of the United States;

(f) any offense including extortionate credit transactions under sections 892, 893, or 894 of this title;

(g) a violation of section 5322 of title 31, United States Code (dealing with the reporting of currency transactions), or section 5324 of title 31, United States Code (relating to structuring transactions to evade reporting requirement prohibited);

(h) any felony violation of sections 2511 and 2512 (relating to interception and disclosure of certain communications and to certain intercepting devices) of this title;
(i) any felony violation of chapter 71 (relating to obscenity) of this title;
(j) any violation of section 60123(b) (relating to destruction of a natural gas pipeline), section 46502 (relating to aircraft piracy), the second sentence of section 46504 (relating to assault on a flight crew with dangerous weapon), or section 46505(b)(3) or (c) (relating to explosive or incendiary devices, or endangerment of human life, by means of weapons on aircraft) of title 49;
(k) any criminal violation of section 2778 of title 22 (relating to the Arms Export Control Act);
(l) the location of any fugitive from justice from an offense described in this section;
(m) a violation of section 274, 277, or 278 of the Immigration and Nationality Act (8 U.S.C. 1324, 1327, or 1328) (relating to the smuggling of aliens);
(n) any felony violation of sections 922 and 924 of title 18, United States Code (relating to firearms);
(o) any violation of section 5861 of the Internal Revenue Code of 1986 (relating to firearms);
(p) a felony violation of section 1028 (relating to production of false identification documents), section 1542 (relating to false statements in passport applications), section 1546 (relating to fraud and misuse of visas, permits, and other documents, section 1028A (relating to aggravated identity theft)) of this title or a violation of section 274, 277, or 278 of the Immigration and Nationality Act (relating to the smuggling of aliens); or
(q) any criminal violation of section 229 (relating to chemical weapons): or sections 2332, 2332a, 2332b, 2332d, 2332f, 2332g, 2332h 2339, 2339A, 2339B, 2339C, or 2339D of this title (relating to terrorism);
(r) any criminal violation of section 1 (relating to illegal restraints of trade or commerce), 2 (relating to illegal monopolizing of trade or commerce), or 3 (relating to illegal restraints of trade or commerce in territories or the District of Columbia) of the Sherman Act (15 U.S.C. 1, 2, 3); or
(s) any conspiracy to commit any offense described in any subparagraph of this paragraph.

(2) The principal prosecuting attorney of any State, or the principal prosecuting attorney of any political subdivision thereof, if such attorney is authorized by a statute of that State to make application to a State court judge of competent jurisdiction for an order authorizing or approving the interception of wire, oral, or electronic communications, may apply to such judge for, and such judge may grant in conformity with section 2518 of this chapter and with the applicable State statute an order authorizing, or approving the interception of wire, oral, or electronic communications by investigative or law enforcement officers having responsibility for the investigation of the offense as to which the application is made, when such interception may provide or has provided evidence of the commission of the offense of murder, kidnapping, gambling, robbery, bribery, extortion, or dealing in narcotic drugs, marihuana or other dangerous drugs, or other crime dangerous to life, limb, or

property, and punishable by imprisonment for more than one year, designated in any applicable State statute authorizing such interception, or any conspiracy to commit any of the foregoing offenses.

(3) Any attorney for the Government (as such term is defined for the purposes of the Federal Rules of Criminal Procedure) may authorize an application to a Federal judge of competent jurisdiction for, and such judge may grant, in conformity with section 2518 of this title, an order authorizing or approving the interception of electronic communications by an investigative or law enforcement officer having responsibility for the investigation of the offense as to which the application is made, when such interception may provide or has provided evidence of any Federal felony.

18 U.S.C. 2517. Authorization for Disclosure and Use of Intercepted Wire, Oral, or Electronic Communications

(1) Any investigative or law enforcement officer who, by any means authorized by this chapter, has obtained knowledge of the contents of any wire, oral, or electronic communication, or evidence derived therefrom, may disclose such contents to another investigative or law enforcement officer to the extent that such disclosure is appropriate to the proper performance of the official duties of the officer making or receiving the disclosure.

(2) Any investigative or law enforcement officer who, by any means authorized by this chapter, has obtained knowledge of the contents of any wire, oral, or electronic communication or evidence derived therefrom may use such contents to the extent such use is appropriate to the proper performance of his official duties.

(3) Any person who has received, by any means authorized by this chapter, any information concerning a wire, oral, or electronic communication, or evidence derived therefrom intercepted in accordance with the provisions of this chapter may disclose the contents of that communication or such derivative evidence while giving testimony under oath or affirmation in any proceeding held under the authority of the United States or of any State or political subdivision thereof.

(4) No otherwise privileged wire, oral, or electronic communication intercepted in accordance with, or in violation of, the provisions of this chapter shall lose its privileged character.

(5) When an investigative or law enforcement officer, while engaged in intercepting wire, oral, or electronic communications in the manner authorized herein, intercepts wire, oral, or electronic communications relating to offenses other than those specified in the order of authorization or approval, the contents thereof, and evidence derived therefrom, may be disclosed or used as provided in subsections (1) and (2) of this section. Such contents and any evidence derived therefrom may be used under subsection (3) of this section when authorized or approved by a judge of competent jurisdiction where such judge finds on subsequent application that the contents were otherwise intercepted in accordance with the provisions of this chapter. Such application shall be made as soon as practicable.

(6) Any investigative or law enforcement officer, or attorney for the Government, who by any means authorized by this chapter, has obtained knowledge of the contents of any wire, oral, or electronic communication, or evidence derived therefrom, may disclose such contents to any Federal law enforcement, intelligence, protective, immigration,

national defense, or national security official to the extent that such contents include foreign intelligence or counterintelligence (as defined in section 3 of the National Security act of 1947 (50 U.S.C. 401a), or foreign intelligence information (as defined in subsection (19) of section 2510 of this title), to assist the official who is to receive that information in the performance of his official duties. Any Federal official who receives information pursuant to this provision may use that information only as necessary in the conduct of that person's official duties subject to any limitations on the unauthorized disclosure of such information.

(7) Any investigative or law enforcement officer, or other Federal official in carrying out official duties as such Federal official, who by any means authorized by this chapter, has obtained knowledge of the contents of any wire, oral, or electronic communication, or evidence derived therefrom, may disclose such contents or derivative evidence to a foreign investigative or law enforcement officer to the extent that such disclosure is appropriate to the proper performance of the official duties of the officer making or receiving the disclosure, and foreign investigative or law enforcement officers may use or disclose such contents or derivative evidence to the extent such use or disclosure is appropriate to the proper performance of their official duties.

(8) Any investigative or law enforcement officer, or other Federal official in carrying out official duties as such Federal official, who by any means authorized by this chapter, has obtained knowledge of the contents of any wire, oral, or electronic communication, or evidence derived therefrom, may disclose such contents or derivative evidence to any appropriate Federal, State, local, or foreign government official to the extent that such contents or derivative evidence reveals a threat of actual or potential attack or other grave hostile acts of a foreign power of an agent of as foreign power, domestic or international sabotage, domestic or international terrorism, or clandestine intelligence gathering activities by an intelligence service or network of a foreign power or by an agent of a foreign power, within the United States or elsewhere, for the purpose of preventing or responding to such a threat. Any official who receives information pursuant to this provision may use that information only as necessary in the conduct of that person's official duties subject to any limitations on the unauthorized disclosure of such information, and any State, local, or foreign official who receives information pursuant to this provision may use that information only consistent with such guidelines as the Attorney General and Director of Central Intelligence shall jointly issue.

18 U.S.C. 2518. Procedure for Interception of Wire, Oral, or Electronic Communications

(1) Each application for an order authorizing or approving the interception of a wire, oral, or electronic communication under this chapter shall be made in writing upon oath or affirmation to a judge of competent jurisdiction and shall state the applicant's authority to make such application. Each application shall include the following information:

(a) the identity of the investigative or law enforcement officer making the application, and the officer authorizing the application;

(b) a full and complete statement of the facts and circumstances relied upon by the applicant, to justify his belief that an order should be issued, including (i) details as to the particular offense that has been, is being, or is about to be committed, (ii) except as provided in subsection (11), a particular description of the nature and location of the facilities from which or the place where the communication is to be intercepted, (iii) a particular description of the type of communications sought to be intercepted, (iv) the identity of the person, if known, committing the offense and whose communications are to be intercepted;

(c) a full and complete statement as to whether or not other investigative procedures have been tried and failed or why they reasonably appear to be unlikely to succeed if tried or to be too dangerous;

(d) a statement of the period of time for which the interception is required to be maintained. If the nature of the investigation is such that the authorization for interception should not automatically terminate when the described type of communication has been first obtained, a particular description of facts establishing probable cause to believe that additional communications of the same type will occur thereafter;

(e) a full and complete statement of the facts concerning all previous applications known to the individual authorizing and making the application, made to any judge for authorization to intercept, or for approval of interceptions of, wire, oral, or electronic communications involving any of the same persons, facilities or places specified in the application, and the action taken by the judge on each such application; and

(f) where the application is for the extension of an order, a statement setting forth the results thus far obtained from the interception, or a reasonable explanation of the failure to obtain such results.

(2) The judge may require the applicant to furnish additional testimony or documentary evidence in support of the application.

(3) Upon such application the judge may enter an ex parte order, as requested or as modified, authorizing or approving interception of wire, oral, or electronic communications within the territorial jurisdiction of the court in which the judge is sitting (and outside that jurisdiction but within the United States in the case of a mobile interception device authorized by a Federal court within such jurisdiction), if the judge determines on the basis of the facts submitted by the applicant that—

(a) there is probable cause for belief that an individual is committing, has committed, or is about to commit a particular offense enumerated in section 2516 of this chapter;

(b) there is probable cause for belief that particular communications concerning that offense will be obtained through such interception;

(c) normal investigative procedures have been tried and have failed or reasonably appear to be unlikely to succeed if tried or to be too dangerous;

(d) except as provided in subsection (11), there is probable cause for belief that the facilities from which, or the place where, the wire, oral, or electronic communications are to be intercepted are being used, or are about to be used, in connection with the commission of such offense, or are leased to, listed in the name of, or commonly used by such person.

(4) Each order authorizing or approving the interception of any wire, oral, or electronic communication under this chapter shall specify—
 (a) the identity of the person, if known, whose communications are to be intercepted;
 (b) the nature and location of the communications facilities as to which, or the place where, authority to intercept is granted;
 (c) a particular description of the type of communication sought to be intercepted, and a statement of the particular offense to which it relates;
 (d) the identity of the agency authorized to intercept the communications, and of the person authorizing the application; and
 (e) the period of time during which such interception is authorized, including a statement as to whether or not the interception shall automatically terminate when the described communication has been first obtained. An order authorizing the interception of a wire, oral, or electronic communication under this chapter shall, upon request of the applicant, direct that a provider of wire or electronic communication service, landlord, custodian or other person shall furnish the applicant forthwith all information, facilities, and technical assistance necessary to accomplish the interception unobtrusively and with a minimum of interference with the services that such service provider, landlord, custodian, or person is according the person whose communications are to be intercepted. Any provider of wire or electronic communication service, landlord, custodian or other person furnishing such facilities or technical assistance shall be compensated therefor by the applicant for reasonable expenses incurred in providing such facilities or assistance. Pursuant to section 2522 of this chapter, an order may also be issued to enforce the assistance capability and capacity requirements under the Communications Assistance for Law Enforcement Act.

(5) No order entered under this section may authorize or approve the interception of any wire, oral, or electronic communication for any period longer than is necessary to achieve the objective of the authorization, nor in any event longer than thirty days. Such thirty-day period begins on the earlier of the day on which the investigative or law enforcement officer first begins to conduct an interception under the order or ten days after the order is entered. Extensions of an order may be granted, but only upon application for an extension made in accordance with subsection (1) of this section and the court making the findings required by subsection (3) of this section. The period of extension shall be no longer than the authorizing judge deems necessary to achieve the purposes for which it was granted and in no event for longer than thirty days. Every order and extension thereof shall contain a provision that the authorization to intercept shall be executed as soon as practicable, shall be conducted in such a way as to minimize the interception of communications not otherwise subject to interception under this chapter, and must terminate upon attainment of the authorized objective, or in any event in thirty days. In the event the intercepted communication is in a code or foreign language, and an expert in that foreign language or code is not reasonably available during the interception period, minimization may be accomplished as soon as practicable after such interception. An interception under this chapter may be conducted in whole or in part by Government personnel, or by an individual operating under a contract with the Government,

acting under the supervision of an investigative or law enforcement officer authorized to conduct the interception.

(6) Whenever an order authorizing interception is entered pursuant to this chapter, the order may require reports to be made to the judge who issued the order showing what progress has been made toward achievement of the authorized objective and the need for continued interception. Such reports shall be made at such intervals as the judge may require.

(7) Notwithstanding any other provision of this chapter, any investigative or law enforcement officer, specially designated by the Attorney General, the Deputy Attorney General, the Associate Attorney General, or by the principal prosecuting attorney of any State or subdivision thereof acting pursuant to a statute of that State, who reasonably determines that—

(a) an emergency situation exists that involves—

(i) immediate danger of death or serious physical injury to any person,

(ii) conspiratorial activities threatening the national security interest, or

(iii) conspiratorial activities characteristic of organized crime, that requires a wire, oral, or electronic communication to be intercepted before an order authorizing such interception can, with due diligence, be obtained, and

(b) there are grounds upon which an order could be entered under this chapter to authorize such interception, may intercept such wire, oral, or electronic communication if an application for an order approving the interception is made in accordance with this section within forty-eight hours after the interception has occurred, or begins to occur. In the absence of an order, such interception shall immediately terminate when the communication sought is obtained or when the application for the order is denied, whichever is earlier. In the event such application for approval is denied, or in any other case where the interception is terminated without an order having been issued, the contents of any wire, oral, or electronic communication intercepted shall be treated as having been obtained in violation of this chapter, and an inventory shall be served as provided for in subsection (d) of this section on the person named in the application.

(8)

(a) The contents of any wire, oral, or electronic communication intercepted by any means authorized by this chapter shall, if possible, be recorded on tape or wire or other comparable device. The recording of the contents of any wire, oral, or electronic communication under this subsection shall be done in such way as will protect the recording from editing or other alterations. Immediately upon the expiration of the period of the order, or extensions thereof, such recordings shall be made available to the judge issuing such order and sealed under his directions. Custody of the recordings shall be wherever the judge orders. They shall not be destroyed except upon an order of the issuing or denying judge and in any event shall be kept for ten years. Duplicate recordings may be made for use or disclosure pursuant to the provisions of subsections (1) and (2) of section 2517 of this chapter for investigations. The presence of the seal provided for by this subsection, or a satisfactory explanation for the absence thereof, shall be a prerequisite for the use or disclosure of the contents of any wire, oral, or electronic communication or evidence derived therefrom under subsection (3) of section 2517.

(b) Applications made and orders granted under this chapter shall be sealed by the judge. Custody of the applications and orders shall be wherever the judge directs. Such applications and orders shall be disclosed only upon a showing of good cause before a judge of competent jurisdiction and shall not be destroyed except on order of the issuing or denying judge, and in any event shall be kept for ten years.

(c) Any violation of the provisions of this subsection may be punished as contempt of the issuing or denying judge.

(d) Within a reasonable time but not later than ninety days after the filing of an application for an order of approval under section 2518(7)(b) which is denied or the termination of the period of an order or extensions thereof, the issuing or denying judge shall cause to be served, on the persons named in the order or the application, and such other parties to intercepted communications as the judge may determine in his discretion that is in the interest of justice, an inventory which shall include notice of—

(1) the fact of the entry of the order or the application;

(2) the date of the entry and the period of authorized, approved or disapproved interception, or the denial of the application; and

(3) the fact that during the period wire, oral, or electronic communications were or were not intercepted.

The judge, upon the filing of a motion, may in his discretion make available to such person or his counsel for inspection such portions of the intercepted communications, applications and orders as the judge determines to be in the interest of justice. On an ex parte showing of good cause to a judge of competent jurisdiction the serving of the inventory required by this subsection may be postponed.

(9) The contents of any wire, oral, or electronic communication intercepted pursuant to this chapter or evidence derived therefrom shall not be received in evidence or otherwise disclosed in any trial, hearing, or other proceeding in a Federal or State court unless each party, not less than ten days before the trial, hearing, or proceeding, has been furnished with a copy of the court order, and accompanying application, under which the interception was authorized or approved. This ten-day period may be waived by the judge if he finds that it was not possible to furnish the party with the above information ten days before the trial, hearing, or proceeding and that the party will not be prejudiced by the delay in receiving such information.

(10)

(a) Any aggrieved person in any trial, hearing, or proceeding in or before any court, department, officer, agency, regulatory body, or other authority of the United States, a State, or a political subdivision thereof, may move to suppress the contents of any wire or oral communication intercepted pursuant to this chapter, or evidence derived therefrom, on the grounds that

(i) the communication was unlawfully intercepted;

(ii) the order of authorization or approval under which it was intercepted is insufficient on its face; or

(iii) the interception was not made in conformity with the order of authorization or approval. Such motion shall be made before the trial, hearing, or proceeding unless there was no opportunity to make such motion or the person was not aware of the grounds of the motion. If the motion is granted, the contents of the intercepted wire or oral communication, or evidence derived therefrom, shall be treated as having been obtained in violation of this chapter. The judge, upon the filing of such motion by the aggrieved person, may in his discretion make available to the aggrieved person or his counsel for inspection such portions of the intercepted communication or evidence derived therefrom as the judge determines to be in the interests of justice.

(b) In addition to any other right to appeal, the United States shall have the right to appeal from an order granting a motion to suppress made under paragraph (a) of this subsection, or the denial of an application for an order of approval, if the United States attorney shall certify to the judge or other official granting such motion or denying such application that the appeal is not taken for purposes of delay. Such appeal shall be taken within thirty days after the date the order was entered and shall be diligently prosecuted.

(c) The remedies and sanctions described in this chapter with respect to the interception of electronic communications are the only judicial remedies and sanctions for nonconstitutional violations of this chapter involving such communications.

(11)The requirements of subsections (1) (b)(ii) and (3) (d) of this section relating to the specification of the facilities from which, or the place where, the communication is to be intercepted do not apply if—

(a) in the case of an application with respect to the interception of an oral communication—

(i) the application is by a Federal investigative or law enforcement officer and is approved by the Attorney General, the Deputy Attorney General, the Associate Attorney General, an Assistant Attorney General, or an acting Assistant Attorney General;

(ii) the application contains a full and complete statement as to why such specification is not practical and identifies the person committing the offense and whose communications are to be intercepted; and

(iii) the judge finds that such specification is not practical; and

(b) in the case of an application with respect to a wire or electronic communication—

(i) the application is by a Federal investigative or law enforcement officer and is approved by the Attorney General, the Deputy Attorney General, the Associate Attorney General, an Assistant Attorney General, or an acting Assistant Attorney General;

(ii) the application identifies the person believed to be committing the offense and whose communications are to be intercepted and the applicant makes a showing that there is probable cause to believe that the person's actions could have the effect of thwarting interception from a specified facility;

(iii) the judge finds that such showing has been adequately made; and

(iv) the order authorizing or approving the interception is limited to interception only for such time as it is reasonable to presume that the person identified in the application is or was reasonably proximate to the instrument through which such communication will be or was transmitted.

(12) An interception of a communication under an order with respect to which the requirements of subsections (1) (b)(ii) and (3) (d) of this section do not apply by reason of subsection (11)(a) shall not begin until the place where the communication is to be intercepted is ascertained by the person implementing the interception order. A provider of wire or electronic communications service that has received an order as provided for in subsection (11)(b) may move the court to modify or quash the order on the ground that its assistance with respect to the interception cannot be performed in a timely or reasonable fashion. The court, upon notice to the government, shall decide such a motion expeditiously.

18 U.S.C. 2519. Reports Concerning Intercepted Wire, Oral, or Electronic Communications

(1) In January of each year, any judge who has issued an order (or an extension thereof) under section 2518 that expired during the preceding year, or who has denied approval of an interception during that year, shall report to the Administrative Office of the United States Courts—

(a) the fact that an order or extension was applied for;

(b) the kind of order or extension applied for (including whether or not the order was an order with respect to which the requirements of sections 2518(1) (b)(ii) and 2518(3) (d) of this title did not apply by reason of section 2518(11) of this title);

(c) the fact that the order or extension was granted as applied for, was modified, or was denied;

(d) the period of interceptions authorized by the order, and the number and duration of any extensions of the order;

(e) the offense specified in the order or application, or extension of an order;

(f) the identity of the applying investigative or law enforcement officer and agency making the application and the person authorizing the application; and

(g) the nature of the facilities from which or the place where communications were to be intercepted.

(2) In March of each year the Attorney General, an Assistant Attorney General specially designated by the Attorney General, or the principal prosecuting attorney of a State, or the principal prosecuting attorney for any political subdivision of a State, shall report to the Administrative Office of the United States Courts—

(a) the information required by paragraphs (a) through (g) of subsection (1) of this section with respect to each application for an order or extension made during the preceding calendar year;

(b) a general description of the interceptions made under such order or extension, including (i) the approximate nature and frequency of incriminating communications intercepted, (ii) the approximate nature and frequency of other communications intercepted, (iii) the approximate number of persons whose communications were intercepted, (iv) the number of orders in which encryption was encountered and whether such encryption prevented law enforcement from obtaining the plain text of communications intercepted pursuant to such order, and (v) the approximate nature, amount, and cost of the manpower and other resources used in the interceptions;

(c) the number of arrests resulting from interceptions made under such order or extension, and the offenses for which arrests were made;

(d) the number of trials resulting from such interceptions;

(e) the number of motions to suppress made with respect to such interceptions, and the number granted or denied;

(f) the number of convictions resulting from such interceptions and the offenses for which the convictions were obtained and a general assessment of the importance of the interceptions; and

(g) the information required by paragraphs (b) through (f) of this subsection with respect to orders or extensions obtained in a preceding calendar year.

(3) In June of each year the Director of the Administrative Office of the United States Courts shall transmit to the Congress a full and complete report concerning the number of applications for orders authorizing or approving the interception of wire, oral, or electronic communications pursuant to this chapter and the number of orders and extensions granted or denied pursuant to this chapter during the preceding calendar year. Such report shall include a summary and analysis of the data required to be filed with the Administrative Office by subsections (1) and (2) of this section. The Director of the Administrative Office of the United States Courts is authorized to issue binding regulations dealing with the content and form of the reports required to be filed by subsections (1) and (2) of this section.

18 U.S.C. 2520. Recovery of Civil Damages Authorized

(a) In general.—Except as provided in section 2511(2) (a)(ii), any person whose wire, oral, or electronic communication is intercepted, disclosed, or intentionally used in violation of this chapter may in a civil action recover from the person or entity other than the United States which engaged in that violation such relief as may be appropriate.

(b) Relief.—In an action under this section, appropriate relief includes—

(1) such preliminary and other equitable or declaratory relief as may be appropriate;

(2) damages under subsection (c) and punitive damages in appropriate cases; and

(3) a reasonable attorney's fee and other litigation costs reasonably incurred.

(c) Computation of damages.—(1) In an action under this section, if the conduct in violation of this chapter is the private viewing of a private satellite video communication that is not scrambled or encrypted or if the communication is a radio communication that is transmitted on frequencies allocated under subpart D of part 74 of the rules of the Federal Communications Commission that is not scrambled or encrypted and the conduct is not for a tortious or illegal purpose or for purposes of direct or indirect commercial advantage or private commercial gain, then the court shall assess damages as follows:

(A) If the person who engaged in that conduct has not previously been enjoined under section 2511(5) and has not been found liable in a prior civil action under this section, the court shall assess the greater of the sum of actual damages suffered by the plaintiff, or statutory damages of not less than $50 and not more than $500.

(B) If, on one prior occasion, the person who engaged in that conduct has been enjoined under section 2511(5) or has been found liable in a civil action under this section, the court shall assess the greater of the sum of actual damages suffered by the plaintiff, or statutory damages of not less than $100 and not more than $1000.

(2) In any other action under this section, the court may assess as damages whichever is the greater of—

(A) the sum of the actual damages suffered by the plaintiff and any profits made by the violator as a result of the violation; or

(B) statutory damages of whichever is the greater of $100 a day for each day of violation or $10,000.

(d) Defense.—A good faith reliance on—

(1) a court warrant or order, a grand jury subpoena, a legislative authorization, or a statutory authorization;

(2) a request of an investigative or law enforcement officer under section 2518(7) of this title; or

(3) a good faith determination that section 2511(3) or 2511(2)(i) of this title permitted the conduct complained of; is a complete defense against any civil or criminal action brought under this chapter or any other law.

(e) Limitation.—A civil action under this section may not be commenced later than two years after the date upon which the claimant first has a reasonable opportunity to discover the violation.

(f) Administrative Discipline.—If a court or appropriate department or agency determines that the United States or any of its departments or agencies has violated any provision of this chapter, and the court finds that the circumstances surrounding the violation raise serious questions about whether or not an officer or employee of the United States acted willfully or intentionally with respect to the possible violation, the department or agency shall, upon receipt of a true and correct copy of the decision and findings of the court or appropriate department or agency promptly initiate a proceeding to determine whether disciplinary action against the officer or employee is warranted. If the head of the department or agency involved determines that disciplinary action is not warranted, he or she shall notify the Inspector General with jurisdiction over the department or agency concerned and shall provide the Inspector General with the reasons for such determination.

(g) Improper Disclosure Is Violation.—Any willful disclosure or use by an investigative or law enforcement officer or governmental entity of information beyond the extent permitted by section 2517 is a violation of this chapter for purposes of section 2510(a).

18 U.S.C. 2521. Injunction against Illegal Interception

Whenever it shall appear that any person is engaged or is about to engage in any act which constitutes or will constitute a felony violation of this chapter, the Attorney General may initiate a civil action in a district court of the United States to enjoin such violation. The court shall proceed as soon as practicable to the hearing and determination of such an action, and may, at any time before final determination, enter such a restraining order or prohibition, or take such other action, as is warranted to prevent a continuing and substantial injury to the United States or to any person or class of persons for whose protection the action is brought. A proceeding under this section is governed by the Federal Rules of Civil Procedure, except that, if an indictment has been returned against the respondent, discovery is governed by the Federal Rules of Criminal Procedure.

18 U.S.C. 2522. Enforcement of the Communications Assistance for Law Enforcement Act

(a) Enforcement by court issuing surveillance order.—If a court authorizing an interception under this chapter, a State statute, or the Foreign Intelligence Surveillance Act of 1978 (50 U.S.C. 1801 et seq.) or authorizing use of a pen register or a trap and trace device under chapter 206 or a State statute finds that a telecommunications carrier has failed to comply with the requirements of the Communications Assistance for Law Enforcement Act, the court may, in accordance with section 108 of such Act, direct that the carrier comply forthwith and may direct that a provider of support services to the carrier or the manufacturer of the carrier's transmission or switching equipment furnish forthwith modifications necessary for the carrier to comply.

(b) Enforcement upon application by Attorney General.—The Attorney General may, in a civil action in the appropriate United States district court, obtain an order, in accordance with section 108 of the Communications Assistance for Law Enforcement Act, directing that a telecommunications carrier, a manufacturer of telecommunications transmission or switching equipment, or a provider of telecommunications support services comply with such Act.

(c) Civil penalty.—

(1) In general.—A court issuing an order under this section against a telecommunications carrier, a manufacturer of telecommunications transmission or switching equipment, or a provider of telecommunications support services may impose a civil penalty of up to $10,000 per day for each day in violation after the issuance of the order or after such future date as the court may specify.

(2) Considerations.—In determining whether to impose a civil penalty and in determining its amount, the court shall take into account—

(A) the nature, circumstances, and extent of the violation;

(B) the violator's ability to pay, the violator's good faith efforts to comply in a timely manner, any effect on the violator's ability to continue to do business, the degree of culpability, and the length of any delay in undertaking efforts to comply; and

(c) such other matters as justice may require.

(d) Definitions.—As used in this section, the terms defined in section 102 of the Communications Assistance for Law Enforcement Act have the meanings provided, respectively, in such section.

Chapter 121 ("Stored Communications Act")

18 U.S.C. 2701. Unlawful Access to Stored Communications

(a) Offense.—Except as provided in subsection (c) of this section whoever—
- (1) intentionally accesses without authorization a facility through which an electronic communication service is provided; or
- (2) intentionally exceeds an authorization to access that facility; and thereby obtains, alters, or prevents authorized access to a wire or electronic communication while it is in electronic storage in such system shall be punished as provided in subsection (b) of this section.

(b) Punishment.—The punishment for an offense under subsection (a) of this section is—
- (1) if the offense is committed for purposes of commercial advantage, malicious destruction or damage, or private commercial gain, or in furtherance of any criminal or tortious act in violation of the constitution and laws of the United States or any state—
  - (A) a fine under this title or imprisonment for not more than 5 years, or both, in the case of a first offense under this subparagraph; and
  - (B) a fine under this title or imprisonment for not more than 10 years, or both, for any subsequent offense under this subparagraph; and
- (2)
  - (A) a fine under this title or imprisonment for not more than 1 year or both, in the case of a first offense under this paragraph; and
  - (B) a fine under this title or imprisonment for not more than 5 years, or both, in the case of an offense under this subparagraph that occurs after a conviction of another offense under this section.

(c) Exceptions.—Subsection (a) of this section does not apply with respect to conduct authorized—
- (1) by the person or entity providing a wire or electronic communications service;
- (2) by a user of that service with respect to a communication of or intended for that user; or
- (3) in section 2703, 2704 or 2518 of this title.

18 U.S.C. 2702. Voluntary Disclosure of Customer Communications or Records

(a) Prohibitions.—Except as provided in subsection (b) or (c)—
- (1) a person or entity providing an electronic communication service to the public shall not knowingly divulge to any person or entity the contents of a communication while in electronic storage by that service; and
- (2) a person or entity providing remote computing service to the public shall not knowingly divulge to any person or entity the contents of any communication which is carried or maintained on that service—
  - (A) on behalf of, and received by means of electronic transmission from (or created by means of computer processing of communications received by means of electronic transmission from), a subscriber or customer of such service;

(B) solely for the purpose of providing storage or computer processing services to such subscriber or customer, if the provider is not authorized to access the contents of any such communications for purposes of providing any services other than storage or computer processing; and

(3) a provider of remote computing service or electronic communication service to the public shall not knowingly divulge a record or other information pertaining to a subscriber to or customer of such service (not including the contents of communications covered by paragraph (1) or (2)) to any governmental entity.

(b) Exceptions for disclosure of communications.—A provider described in subsection (a) may divulge the contents of a communication—

(1) to an addressee or intended recipient of such communication or an agent of such addressee or intended recipient;

(2) as otherwise authorized in section 2517, 2511(2) (a), or 2703 of this title;

(3) with the lawful consent of the originator or an addressee or intended recipient of such communication, or the subscriber in the case of remote computing service;

(4) to a person employed or authorized or whose facilities are used to forward such communication to its destination;

(5) as may be necessarily incident to the rendition of the service or to the protection of the rights or property of the provider of that service;

(6) to the National Center for Missing and Exploited Children, in connection with a report submitted thereto under section 2258A;

(7) to a law enforcement agency—

(A) if the contents—

(i) were inadvertently obtained by the service provider; and

(ii) appear to pertain to the commission of a crime; or

[(B) Repealed. P.L. 108-21, Title V, §508(b)(1) (A), April 30, 2003, 117 Stat. 684]

[(C) Repealed. P.L. 107-296, Title II, §225(d)(1)(C), November 25, 2002, 116 Stat. 2157]

(8) to a governmental entity, if the provider, in good faith, believes that an emergency involving danger of death or serious physical injury to any person requires disclosure without delay of communications relating to the emergency.

(c) Exceptions for disclosure of customer records.—A provider described in subsection (a) may divulge a record or other information pertaining to a subscriber to or customer of such service (not including the contents of communications covered by subsection (a)(1) or (a)(2))—

(1) as otherwise authorized in section 2703;

(2) with the lawful consent of the customer or subscriber;

(3) as may be necessarily incident to the rendition of the service or to the protection of the rights or property of the provider of that service;

(4) to a governmental entity, if the provider, in good faith, believes that an emergency involving danger of death or serious physical injury to any person requires disclosure without delay of information relating to the emergency;

(5) to the National Center for Missing and Exploited Children, in connection with a report submitted thereto under section 2258A7; or

(6) to any person other than a governmental entity.

(d) Reporting of emergency disclosures.—On an annual basis, the Attorney General shall submit to the Committee on the Judiciary of the House of Rcpresentatives and the Committee on the Judiciary of the Senate a report containing—
(1) the number of accounts from which the Department of Justice has received voluntary disclosures under subsection (b)(8); and
(2) a summary of the basis for disclosure in those instances where—
(A) voluntary disclosures under subsection (b)(8) were made to the Department of Justice; and
(B) the investigation pertaining to those disclosures was closed without the filing of criminal charges.

18 U.S.C. 2703. Required Disclosure of Customer Communications or Records

(a) Contents of wire or electronic communications in electronic storage.—A governmental entity may require the disclosure by a provider of electronic communication service of the contents of a wire or electronic communication, that is in electronic storage in a wire or electronic communications system for one hundred and eighty days or less, only pursuant to a warrant issued using the procedures described in the Federal Rules of Criminal Procedure (or, in the case of a State court, issued using State warrant procedures) by a court of competent jurisdiction. A governmental entity may require the disclosure by a provider of electronic communications services of the contents of a wire or electronic communication that has been in electronic storage in an electronic communications system for more than one hundred and eighty days by the means available under subsection (b) of this section.

(b)
(1) Contents of electronic communications in a remote computing service.—(1) A governmental entity may require a provider of remote computing service to disclose the contents of any wire or electronic communication to which this paragraph is made applicable by paragraph (2) of this subsection—
(A) without required notice to the subscriber or customer, if the governmental entity obtains a warrant issued using the procedures described in the Federal Rules of Criminal Procedure (or, in the case of a State court, issued using State warrant procedures) by a court of competent jurisdiction by a court with jurisdiction; or
(B) with prior notice from the governmental entity to the subscriber or customer if the governmental entity—
(i) uses an administrative subpoena authorized by a Federal or State statute or a Federal or State grand jury or trial subpoena; or
(ii) obtains a court order for such disclosure under subsection (d) of this section; except that delayed notice may be given pursuant to section 2705 of this title.
(2) Paragraph (1) is applicable with respect to any wire or electronic communication that is held or maintained on that service—
(A) on behalf of, and received by means of electronic transmission from (or created by means of computer processing of communications received by

means of electronic transmission from), a subscriber or customer of such remote computing service; and

(B) solely for the purpose of providing storage or computer processing services to such subscriber or customer, if the provider is not authorized to access the contents of any such communications for purposes of providing any services other than storage or computer processing.

(c) Records concerning electronic communication service or remote computing service.—

(1)

(A) A government entity may require a provider of electronic communication service or remote computing service to disclose a record or other information pertaining to a subscriber to or customer of such service (not including the contents of communications).

(B) A provider of electronic communication service or remote computing service shall disclose a record or other information pertaining to a subscriber to or customer of such service (not including the contents of communications covered by subsection (a) or (b) of this section) to a governmental entity only when the governmental entity—

(A) obtains a warrant issued using the procedures described in the Federal Rules of Criminal Procedure (or, in the case of a State court, issued using State warrant procedures) by a court of competent jurisdiction by a court with jurisdiction;

(B) obtains a court order for such disclosure under subsection (d) of this section;

(C) has the consent of the subscriber or customer to such disclosure; or

(D) submits a formal written request relevant to a law enforcement investigation concerning telemarketing fraud for the name, address, and place of business of a subscriber or customer of such provider, which subscriber or customer is engaged in telemarketing (as such term is defined in section 2325 of this title); or

(E) seeks information under paragraph (2).

(2) A provider of electronic communication service or remote computing service shall disclose to a governmental entity the (A) name; (B) address; (C) local and long distance telephone connection records, or records of session times and durations; (D) length of service (including start date) and types of service utilized; (E) telephone or instrument number or other subscriber number or identity, including any temporarily assigned network address; and (F) means and source of payment (including any credit car or bank account number), of a subscriber to or customer of such service, when the governmental entity uses an administrative subpoena authorized by a Federal or State statute or a Federal or State grand jury or trial subpoena or any means available under paragraph (1)

.

(3) A governmental entity receiving records or information under this subsection is not required to provide notice to a subscriber or customer.

(d) Requirements for court order.—A court order for disclosure under subsection (b) or (c) may be issued by any court that is a court of competent jurisdiction and shall issue only if the governmental entity offers specific and articulable facts showing that there are reasonable grounds to believe that the contents of a wire or electronic communication, or the records or other information sought, are relevant and material to an ongoing criminal investigation. In the case of a State governmental authority, such a court order shall not issue if prohibited by the law of such State. A court issuing an order pursuant to this section, on a motion made promptly by the service provider, may quash or modify such order, if the information or records requested are unusually voluminous in nature or compliance with such order otherwise would cause an undue burden on such provider.

(e) No cause of action against a provider disclosing information under this chapter.—No cause of action shall lie in any court against any provider of wire or electronic communication service, its officers, employees, agents, or other specified persons for providing information, facilities, or assistance in accordance with the terms of a court order, warrant, subpoena, statutory authorization, or certification under this chapter.

(f) Requirement to preserve evidence.—

(1) In general.—A provider of wire or electronic communication services or a remote computing service, upon the request of a governmental entity, shall take all necessary steps to preserve records and other evidence in its possession pending the issuance of a court order or other process.

(2) Period of retention.—Records referred to in paragraph (1) shall be retained for a period of 90 days, which shall be extended for an additional 90-day period upon a renewed request by the governmental entity.

(g) Presence of Officer not Required.—Notwithstanding section 3105 of this title, the presence of an officer shall not be required for service or execution of a search warrant issued in accordance with this chapter requiring disclosure by a provider of electronic communications service or remote computing service of the contents of communications or records or other information pertaining to a subscriber to or customer of such service.

18 U.S.C. 2704. Backup Preservation

(a) Backup preservation.—

(1) A governmental entity acting under section 2703(b)(2) may include in its subpoena or court order a requirement that the service provider to whom the request is directed create a backup copy of the contents of the electronic communications sought in order to preserve those communications. Without notifying the subscriber or customer of such subpoena or court order, such service provider shall create such backup copy as soon as practicable consistent with its regular business practices and shall confirm to the governmental entity that such backup copy has been made. Such backup copy shall be created within two business days after receipt by the service provider of the subpoena or court order.

(2) Notice to the subscriber or customer shall be made by the governmental entity within three days after receipt of such confirmation, unless such notice is delayed pursuant to section 2705(a).

(3) The service provider shall not destroy such backup copy until the later of—

(A) the delivery of the information; or

(B) the resolution of any proceedings (including appeals of any proceeding) concerning the government's subpoena or court order.

(4) The service provider shall release such backup copy to the requesting governmental entity no sooner than fourteen days after the governmental entity's notice to the subscriber or customer if such service provider—

(A) has not received notice from the subscriber or customer that the subscriber or customer has challenged the governmental entity's request; and

(B) has not initiated proceedings to challenge the request of the governmental entity.

(5) A governmental entity may seek to require the creation of a backup copy under subsection (a)(1) of this section if in its sole discretion such entity determines that there is reason to believe that notification under section 2703 of this title of the existence of the subpoena or court order may result in destruction of or tampering with evidence. This determination is not subject to challenge by the subscriber or customer or service provider.

(b) Customer challenges. —

(1) Within fourteen days after notice by the governmental entity to the subscriber or customer under subsection (a)

(2) of this section, such subscriber or customer may file a motion to quash such subpoena or vacate such court order, with copies served upon the governmental entity and with written notice of such challenge to the service provider. A motion to vacate a court order shall be filed in the court which issued such order. A motion to quash a subpoena shall be filed in the appropriate United States district court or State court. Such motion or application shall contain an affidavit or sworn statement—

(A) stating that the applicant is a customer or subscriber to the service from which the contents of electronic communications maintained for him have been sought; and

(B) stating the applicant's reasons for believing that the records sought are not relevant to a legitimate law enforcement inquiry or that there has not been substantial compliance with the provisions of this chapter in some other respect.

(2) Service shall be made under this section upon a governmental entity by delivering or mailing by registered or certified mail a copy of the papers to the person, office, or department specified in the notice which the customer has received pursuant to this chapter. For the purposes of this section, the term "delivery" has the meaning given that term in the Federal Rules of Civil Procedure.

(3) If the court finds that the customer has complied with paragraphs (1) and (2) of this subsection, the court shall order the governmental entity to file a sworn response, which may be filed in camera if the governmental entity includes in its response the reasons which make in camera review appropriate. If the court is unable to determine the motion or application on the basis of the parties' initial allegations and response, the court may conduct such additional proceedings as it deems appropriate. All such proceedings shall be completed and the motion or application decided as soon as practicable after the filing of the governmental entity's response.

(4) If the court finds that the applicant is not the subscriber or customer for whom the communications sought by the governmental entity are maintained, or that there is a reason to believe that the law enforcement inquiry is legitimate and that the communications sought are relevant to that inquiry, it shall deny the motion or application and order such process enforced. If the court finds that the applicant is the subscriber or customer for whom the communications sought by the governmental entity are maintained, and that there is not a reason to believe that the communications sought are relevant to a legitimate law enforcement inquiry, or that there has not been substantial compliance with the provisions of this chapter, it shall order the process quashed.

(5) A court order denying a motion or application under this section shall not be deemed a final order and no interlocutory appeal may be taken therefrom by the customer.

18 U.S.C. 2705. Delayed Notice

(a) Delay of notification.—

(1) A governmental entity acting under section 2703(b) of this title may—

(A) where a court order is sought, include in the application a request, which the court shall grant, for an order delaying the notification required under section 2703(b) of this title for a period not to exceed ninety days, if the court determines that there is reason to believe that notification of the existence of the court order may have an adverse result described in paragraph (2) of this subsection; or

(B) where an administrative subpoena authorized by a Federal or State statute or a Federal or State grand jury subpoena is obtained, delay the notification required under section 2703(b) of this title for a period not to exceed ninety days upon the execution of a written certification of a supervisory official that there is reason to believe that notification of the existence of the subpoena may have an adverse result described in paragraph (2) of this subsection.

(2) An adverse result for the purposes of paragraph (1) of this subsection is—

(A) endangering the life or physical safety of an individual;

(B) flight from prosecution;

(C) destruction of or tampering with evidence;

(D) intimidation of potential witnesses; or

(E) otherwise seriously jeopardizing an investigation or unduly delaying a trial.

(3) The governmental entity shall maintain a true copy of certification under paragraph (1)(B).

(4) Extensions of the delay of notification provided in section 2703 of up to ninety days each may be granted by the court upon application, or by certification by a governmental entity, but only in accordance with subsection (b) of this section.

(5) Upon expiration of the period of delay of notification under paragraph (1) or (4) of this subsection, the governmental entity shall serve upon, or deliver by registered or first-class mail to, the customer or subscriber a copy of the process or request together with notice that—

(A) states with reasonable specificity the nature of the law enforcement inquiry; and

(B) informs such customer or subscriber—
(i) that information maintained for such customer or subscriber by the service provider named in such process or request was supplied to or requested by that governmental authority and the date on which the supplying or request took place;
(ii) that notification of such customer or subscriber was delayed;
(iii) what governmental entity or court made the certification or determination pursuant to which that delay was made; and
(iv) which provision of this chapter allowed such delay.

(6) As used in this subsection, the term "supervisory official" means the investigative agent in charge or assistant investigative agent in charge or an equivalent of an investigating agency's headquarters or regional office, or the chief prosecuting attorney or the first assistant prosecuting attorney or an equivalent of a prosecuting attorney's headquarters or regional office.

(b) Preclusion of notice to subject of governmental access.—A governmental entity acting under section 2703, when it is not required to notify the subscriber or customer under section 2703(b)(1), or to the extent that it may delay such notice pursuant to subsection (a) of this section, may apply to a court for an order commanding a provider of electronic communications service or remote computing service to whom a warrant, subpoena, or court order is directed, for such period as the court deems appropriate, not to notify any other person of the existence of the warrant, subpoena, or court order. The court shall enter such an order if it determines that there is reason to believe that notification of the existence of the warrant, subpoena, or court order will result in—
(1) endangering the life or physical safety of an individual;
(2) flight from prosecution;
(3) destruction of or tampering with evidence;
(4) intimidation of potential witnesses; or
(5) otherwise seriously jeopardizing an investigation or unduly delaying a trial.

18 U.S.C. 2706. Cost Reimbursement

(a) Payment.—Except as otherwise provided in subsection (c), a governmental entity obtaining the contents of communications, records, or other information under section 2702, 2703, or 2704 of this title shall pay to the person or entity assembling or providing such information a fee for reimbursement for such costs as are reasonably necessary and which have been directly incurred in searching for, assembling, reproducing, or otherwise providing such information. Such reimbursable costs shall include any costs due to necessary disruption of normal operations of any electronic communication service or remote computing service in which such information may be stored.

(b) Amount.—The amount of the fee provided by subsection (a) shall be as mutually agreed by the governmental entity and the person or entity providing the information, or, in the absence of agreement, shall be as determined by the court which issued the order for production of such information (or the court before which a criminal prosecution relating to such information would be brought, if no court order was issued for production of the information).

(c) Exception.—The requirement of subsection (a) of this section does not apply with respect to records or other information maintained by a communications common carrier that relate to telephone toll records and telephone listings obtained under section 2703 of this title. The court may, however, order a payment as described in subsection (a) if the court determines the information required is unusually voluminous in nature or otherwise caused an undue burden on the provider.

18 U.S.C. 2707. Civil Action

(a) Cause of action.—Except as provided in section 2703(e), any provider of electronic communication service, subscriber, or other person aggrieved by any violation of this chapter in which the conduct constituting the violation is engaged in with a knowing or intentional state of mind may, in a civil action, recover from the person or entity other than the United States which engaged in that violation such relief as may be appropriate.

(b) Relief.—In a civil action under this section, appropriate relief includes—

(1) such preliminary and other equitable or declaratory relief as may be appropriate;

(2) damages under subsection (c); and

(3) a reasonable attorney's fee and other litigation costs reasonably incurred.

(c) Damages.—The court may assess as damages in a civil action under this section the sum of the actual damages suffered by the plaintiff and any profits made by the violator as a result of the violation, but in no case shall a person entitled to recover receive less than the sum of $1,000. If the violation is willful or intentional, the court may assess punitive damages. In the case of a successful action to enforce liability under this section, the court may assess the costs of the action, together with reasonable attorney fees determined by the court.

(d) Administrative Discipline.—If a court or appropriate department or agency determines that the United States or any of its departments or agencies has violated any provision of this chapter, and the court or appropriate department or agency finds that the circumstances surrounding the violation raise serious questions about whether or not an officer or employee of the United States acted willfully or intentionally with respect to the possible violation, the department or agency shall, upon receipt of a true and correct copy of the decision and findings of the court or appropriate department or agency promptly initiate a proceeding to determine whether disciplinary action against the officer or employee is warranted. If the head of the department or agency involved determines that disciplinary action is not warranted, he or she shall notify the Inspector General with jurisdiction over the department or agency concerned and shall provide the Inspector General with the reasons for such determination.

(e) Defense.—A good faith reliance on—

(1) a court warrant or order, a grand jury subpoena, a legislative authorization, or a statutory authorization (including a request of a governmental entity under section 2703(f) of this title);

(2) a request of an investigative or law enforcement officer under section 2518(7) of this title; or

(3) a good faith determination that section 2511(3) of this title permitted the conduct complained of; is a complete defense to any civil or criminal action brought under this chapter or any other law.

(f) Limitation.—A civil action under this section may not be commenced later than two years after the date upon which the claimant first discovered or had a reasonable opportunity to discover the violation.

(g) Improper Disclosure Is Violation.—Any willful disclosure of a "record", as that term is defined in section 552a(a) of title 5, United States Code, obtained by an investigative or law enforcement officer, or governmental entity, pursuant to section 2703 of this title, or from a device installed pursuant to section 3123 or 3125 of this title, that is not a disclosure made in the proper performance of the official duties of the officer or governmental entity making the disclosure, is a violation of this chapter. This provision shall not apply to information previously lawfully disclosed (prior to the commencement of any civil or administrative proceeding under this chapter) to the public by a Federal, State, or local governmental entity or by the plaintiff in a civil action under this chapter.

18 U.S.C. 2708. Exclusivity of Remedies

The remedies and sanctions described in this chapter are the only judicial remedies and sanctions for nonconstitutional violations of this chapter.

18 U.S.C. 2709. Counterintelligence Access to Telephone Toll and Transactional Records

(a) Duty to provide—A wire or electronic communication service provider shall comply with a request for subscriber information and toll billing records information, or electronic communication transactional records in its custody or possession made by the Director of the Federal Bureau of Investigation under subsection (b) of this section.

(b) Required certification—The Director of the Federal Bureau of Investigation, or his designee in a position not lower than Deputy Assistant Director at Bureau headquarters or a Special Agent in Charge in a Bureau field office designated by the Director, may—

(1) request the name, address, length of service, and local and long distance toll billing records of a person or entity if the Director (or his designee) certifies in writing to the wire or electronic communication service provider to which the request is made that the name, address, length of service, and toll billing records sought are relevant to an authorized investigation to protect against international terrorism or clandestine intelligence activities, provided that such an investigation of a United States person is not conducted solely on the basis of activities protected by the first amendment to the Constitution of the United States; and

(2) request the name, address, and length of service of a person or entity if the Director (or his designee) certifies in writing to the wire or electronic communication service provider to which the request is made that the information sought is relevant to an authorized investigation to protect against

international terrorism or clandestine intelligence activities, provided that such an investigation of a United States person is not conducted solely upon the basis of activities protected by the first amendment to the Constitution of the United States.

(c) Prohibition of certain disclosure—(1) If the Director of the Federal Bureau of Investigation, or his designee in a position not lower than Deputy Assistant Director at Bureau headquarters or a Special Agent in Charge in a Bureau field office designated by the Director, certifies that otherwise there may result a danger to the national security of the United States, interference with a criminal, counter terrorism, or counterintelligence investigation, interference with diplomatic relations, or danger to the life or physical safety of any person, no wire or electronic communications service provider, or officer, employee, or agent thereof, shall disclose to any person (other than those to whom such disclosure is necessary to comply with the request or an attorney to obtain legal advice or legal assistance with respect to the request) that the Federal Bureau of Investigation has sought or obtained access to information or records under this section.

   (2) The request shall notify the person or entity to whom the request is directed of the nondisclosure requirement under paragraph (1).

   (3) Any recipient disclosing to those persons necessary to comply with the request or to an attorney to obtain legal advice or legal assistance with respect to the request shall inform such person of any applicable nondisclosure requirement. Any person who receives a disclosure under this subsection shall be subject to the same prohibitions on disclosure under paragraph (1).

   (4) At the request of the Director of the Federal Bureau of Investigation or the designee of the Director, any person making or intending to make a disclosure under this section shall identify to the Director or such designee the person to whom such disclosure will be made or to whom such disclosure was made prior to the request, except that nothing in this section shall require a person to inform the Director or such designee of the identity of an attorney to whom disclosure was made or will be made to obtain legal advice or legal assistance with respect to the request under subsection (a).

(d) Dissemination by bureau—The Federal Bureau of Investigation may disseminate information and records obtained under this section only as provided in guidelines approved by the Attorney General for foreign intelligence collection and foreign counterintelligence investigations conducted by the Federal Bureau of Investigation, and, with respect to dissemination to an agency of the United States, only if such information is clearly relevant to the authorized responsibilities of such agency.

(e) Requirement that certain congressional bodies be informed—On a semiannual basis the Director of the Federal Bureau of Investigation shall fully inform the Permanent Select Committee on Intelligence of the House of Representatives and the Select Committee on Intelligence of the Senate, and the Committee on the Judiciary of the House of Representatives and the Committee on the Judiciary of the Senate, concerning all requests made under subsection (b) of this section.

(f) Libraries—A library (as that term is defined in section 213(1) of the Library Services and Technology Act (20 U.S.C. 9122(1)), the services of which include access to the Internet, books, journals, magazines, newspapers, or other similar forms of communication in print or digitally by patrons for their use, review, examination, or circulation, is not a wire or electronic communication service provider for purposes of this section, unless the library is providing the services defined in section 2510(15) ("electronic communication service") of this title.

18 U.S.C. 2711. Definitions for Chapter

As used in this chapter—

(1) the terms defined in section 2510 of this title have, respectively, the definitions given such terms in that section;
(2) the term "remote computing service" means the provision to the public of computer storage or processing services by means of an electronic communications system;
(3) the term "court of competent jurisdiction" includes
 (A) any district court of the United States (including a magistrate judge of such a court) or any United States court of appeals that -
  (i) has jurisdiction over the offense being investigated;
  (ii) is in or for a district in which the provider of a wire or electronic communication service is located or in which the wire or electronic communications, records, or other information are stored; or
  (iii) is acting on a request for foreign assistance pursuant to section 3512 of this title; or
 (B) a court of general criminal jurisdiction of a State authorized by the law of that State to issue search warrants; and
(4) the term "governmental entity" means a department or agency of the United States or State or political subdivision thereof.

18 U.S.C. 2712. Civil Action against the United States

(a) In General.— Any person who is aggrieved by any willful violation of this chapter or of chapter 119 of this title or of sections 106(a), 305(a), or 405(a) of the Foreign Intelligence Surveillance Act (50 U.S.C. 1801 et seq.) may commence an action in United States District Court against the United States to recover money damages. In any such action, if a person who is aggrieved successfully establishes a violation of this chapter or of chapter 119 of this title or of the above special provisions of title 50, the Court may assess as damages—
 (1) actual damages, but not less than $10,000, whichever amount is greater; and
 (2) litigation costs, reasonably incurred.
(b) Procedures.—
 (1) Any action against the United States under this section may be commenced only after a claim is presented to the appropriate department or agency under the procedures of the Federal Tort Claims Act, as set forth in title 28, United States Code.
 (2) Any action against the United States under this section shall be forever barred unless it is presented in writing to the appropriate Federal agency within 2 years after such claim accrues or unless action is begun within 6 months after the date of mailing, by certified or registered mail, of notice of final denial of the claim

by the agency to which it was presented. The claim shall accrue on the date upon which the claimant first has a reasonable opportunity to discover the violation.

(3) Any action under this section shall be tried in the court without a jury.

(4) Notwithstanding any other provision of law, the procedures set forth in section 106(f), 305(g), or 405(f) of the Foreign Intelligence Surveillance Act of 1978 (50 U.S.C. 1801 et seq.) shall be the exclusive means by which materials governed by those sections may be reviewed.

(5) An amount equal to any award against the United States under this section shall be reimbursed by the department or agency concerned to the fund described in section 1304 of title 31, United States Code, out of any appropriation, fund, or other account (excluding any part of such appropriation, fund, or account that is available for the enforcement of any Federal law) that is available for the operating expenses of the department or agency concerned.

(c) Administrative Discipline.—If a court or appropriate department or agency determines that the United States or any of the departments or agencies has violated any provision of this chapter, and the court or appropriate department or agency finds that the circumstances surrounding the violation raise serious questions about whether or not an officer or employee of the United States acted willfully or intentionally with respect to the possible violation, the department or agency shall, upon receipt of a true and correct copy of the decision and findings of the court or appropriate department or agency promptly initiate a proceeding to determine whether disciplinary action against the officer or employee is warranted. If the head of the department or agency involved determines that disciplinary action is not warranted, he or she shall notify the Inspector General with jurisdiction over the department or agency concerned and shall provide the Inspector General with the reasons for such determination.

(d) Exclusive Remedy.—Any action against the United States under this subsection shall be the exclusive remedy against the United States for any claims within the purview of this section.

(e) Stay of Proceedings.—

(1) Upon the motion of the united States, the curt shall stay any action commenced under this section f the court determines that civil discovery will adversely affect the ability of the Government to conduct a related investigation or the prosecution of a related criminal case. Such a stay shall toll the limitations periods of paragraph (2) of subsection (b).

(2) In this subsection, the terms "related criminal case" and "related investigation" means an actual prosecution or investigation in progress at the time at which the request for the stay or any subsequent motion to lift the stay is made. In determining whether any investigation or a criminal case is related to an action commenced under this section, the court shall consider the degree of similarity between the parties, witnesses, facts, and circumstances involved in the 2 proceedings, without requiring that nay one or more factors be identical.

(3) In requesting a stay under paragraph (1), the Government may, in appropriate cases submit evidence ex parte in order to avoid disclosing any matter that may adversely affect a related investigation or a related criminal case. If the Government makes such an ex parte submission, the plaintiff shall be given an

opportunity to make a submission to the court, not ex parte, and the court may, in its discretion, request further information from either party.

Chapter 206 ("Pen Register and Trap and Trace Devices")

18 U.S.C. 3121. General Prohibition on Pen Register and Tape and Trace Device Use; Exception

(a) In general—Except as provided in this section, no person may install or use a pen register or a trap and trace device without first obtaining a court order under section 3123 of this title or under the Foreign Intelligence Surveillance Act of 1978 (50 U.S.C. 1801 et seq.).

(b) Exception—The prohibition of subsection (a) does not apply with respect to the use of a pen register or a trap and trace device by a provider of electronic or wire communication service—

(1) relating to the operation, maintenance, and testing of a wire or electronic communication service or to the protection of the rights or property of such provider, or to the protection of users of that service from abuse of service or unlawful use of service; or

(2) to record the fact that a wire or electronic communication was initiated or completed in order to protect such provider, another provider furnishing service toward the completion of the wire communication, or a user of that service, from fraudulent, unlawful or abusive use of service; or

(3) where the consent of the user of that service has been obtained.

(c) Limitation—A government agency authorized to install and use a pen register or trap and trace device under this chapter or under State law shall use technology reasonably available to it that restricts the recording or decoding of electronic or other impulses to the dialing, routing, addressing, and signaling information utilized in identifying the origination or destination of wire or electronic communications.

(d) Penalty—Whoever knowingly violates subsection (a) shall be fined under this title or imprisoned not more than one year, or both.

18 U.S.C. 3122. Application for an Order for a Pen Register or a Trap and Trace Device

(a) Application.

(1) An attorney for the Government may make application for an order or an extension of an order under section 3123 of this title authorizing or approving the installation and use of a pen register or a trap and trace device under this chapter, in writing under oath or equivalent affirmation, to a court of competent jurisdiction.

(2) Unless prohibited by State law, a State investigative or law enforcement officer may make application for an order or an extension of an order under section 3123 of this title authorizing or approving the installation and use of a pen register or a trap and trace device under this chapter, in writing under oath or equivalent affirmation, to a court of competent jurisdiction of such State.

(b) Contents of application—An application under subsection (a) of this section shall include—

(1) the identity of the attorney for the Government or the State law enforcement or investigative officer making the application and the identity of the law enforcement agency conducting the investigation; and

(2) a certification by the applicant that the information likely to be obtained is relevant to an ongoing criminal investigation being conducted by that agency.

18 U.S.C. 3123. Issuance of an Order for a Pen Register or a Trap and Trace Device

(a) In general.

(1) Upon an application made under section 3122(a)(1) of this title, the court shall enter an ex parte order authorizing the installation and use of a pen register or a trap and trace device if the court finds, based on facts contained in the application, that the information likely to be obtained by such installation and use is relevant to an ongoing criminal investigation. Such order shall, upon service of such order, apply to any entity providing wire or electronic communication service in the United States whose assistance may facilitate the execution of the order.

(2) Upon an application made under section 3122(a)(2) of this title, the court shall enter an ex parte order authorizing the installation and use of a pen register or a trap and trace device within the jurisdiction of the court if the court finds, based on facts contained in the application, that the information likely to be obtained by such installation and use is relevant to an ongoing criminal investigation.

(3)

(A) Where the law enforcement agency implementing an ex part order under this subsection seeks to do so by installing and using its own pen register or trap and trace device on a packet-switched data network of a provider of electronic communication service to the public the agency shall ensure that a record will be maintained which will identify—

(i) any officer or officers who installed the device and any officer or officers who accessed the device to obtain information from the network;

(ii) the date and time the device was installed, the date and time the device was uninstalled, and the date, time, and duration of each time the device is accessed to obtain information;

(iii) the configuration of the device at the time of its installation and any subsequent modification thereof; and

(iv) any information which has been collected by the device.

To the extent that the pen register or trap and trace device can be set automatically to record this information electronically, the record shall be maintained electronically throughout the installation and use of the such device.

(B) The record maintained under subparagraph (A) shall be provided ex parte and under seal to the court which entered the ex parte order authorizing the installation and use of the device within 30 days after termination of the order (including any extensions thereof).

(b) Contents of order—An order issued under this section—
  (1) shall specify—
    (A) the identity, if known, of the person to whom is leased or in whose name is listed the telephone line or other facility to which the pen register or trap and trace device is to be attached or applied;
    (B) the identity, if known, of the person who is the subject of the criminal investigation;
    (C) the attributes of the communications to which the order applies, including the number or other identifier and, if known, the location of the telephone line or other facility to which the pen register or trap and trace device is to be attached or applied, and, in the case of an order authorizing installation and use of a trap and trace device under subsection (a)(2), the geographic limits of the order; and
    (D) a statement of the offense to which the information likely to be obtained by the pen register or trap and trace device relates; and
  (2) shall direct, upon the request of the applicant, the furnishing of information, facilities, and technical assistance necessary to accomplish the installation of the pen register or trap and trace device under section 3124 of this title.

(c) Time period and extensions—
  (1) An order issued under this section shall authorize the installation and use of a pen register or a trap and trace device for a period not to exceed sixty days.
  (2) Extensions of such an order may be granted, but only upon an application for an order under section 3122 of this title and upon the judicial finding required by subsection (a) of this section. The period of extension shall be for a period not to exceed sixty days.

(d) Nondisclosure of existence of pen register or a trap and trace device—An order authorizing or approving the installation and use of a pen register or a trap and trace device shall direct that—
  (1) the order be sealed until otherwise ordered by the court; and
  (2) the person owning or leasing the line or other facility to which the pen register or a trap and trace device is attached, or applied, or who is obligated by the order to provide assistance to the applicant, not disclose the existence of the pen register or trap and trace device or the existence of the investigation to the listed subscriber, or to any other person, unless or until otherwise ordered by the court.

18 U.S.C. 3124. Assistance in Installation and Use of a Pen Register or a Trap and Trace Device

(a) Pen registers—Upon the request of an attorney for the Government or an officer of a law enforcement agency authorized to install and use a pen register under this chapter, a provider of wire or electronic communication service, landlord, custodian, or other person shall furnish such investigative or law enforcement officer forthwith all information, facilities, and technical assistance necessary to accomplish the installation of the pen register unobtrusively and with a minimum of interference with the services that the person so ordered by the court accords the party with respect to whom the installation and use is to take place, if such assistance is directed by a court order as provided in section 3123(b)(2) of this title.

(b) Trap and trace device—Upon the request of an attorney for the Government or an officer of a law enforcement agency authorized to receive thc results of a trap and trace device under this chapter, a provider of a wire or electronic communication service, landlord, custodian, or other person shall install such device forthwith on the appropriate line or other facility and shall furnish such investigative or law enforcement officer all additional information, facilities and technical assistance including installation and operation of the device unobtrusively and with a minimum of interference with the services that the person so ordered by the court accords the party with respect to whom the installation and use is to take place, if such installation and assistance is directed by a court order as provided in section 3123(b)(2) of this title. Unless otherwise ordered by the court, the results of the trap and trace device shall be furnished, pursuant to section 3123(b) or section 3125 of this title, to the officer of a law enforcement agency, designated in the court order, at reasonable intervals during regular business hours for the duration of the order.

(c) Compensation—A provider of a wire or electronic communication service, landlord, custodian, or other person who furnishes facilities or technical assistance pursuant to this section shall be reasonably compensated for such reasonable expenses incurred in providing such facilities and assistance.

(d) No cause of action against a provider disclosing information under this chapter—No cause of action shall lie in any court against any provider of a wire or electronic communication service, its officers, employees, agents, or other specified persons for providing information, facilities, or assistance in accordance with a court order under this chapter or request pursuant to section 3125 of this title.

(e) Defense—A good faith reliance on a court order under this chapter, a request pursuant to section 3125 of this title, a legislative authorization, or a statutory authorization is a complete defense against any civil or criminal action brought under this chapter or any other law.

(f) Communications assistance enforcement orders—Pursuant to section 2522, an order may be issued to enforce the assistance capability and capacity requirements under the Communications Assistance for Law Enforcement Act.

18 U.S.C. 3125. Emergency Pen Register and Trap and Trace Device Installation

(a) Notwithstanding any other provision of this chapter, any investigative or law enforcement officer, specially designated by the Attorney General, the Deputy Attorney General, the Associate Attorney General, any Assistant Attorney General, any acting Assistant Attorney General, or any Deputy Assistant Attorney General, or by the principal prosecuting attorney of any State or subdivision thereof acting pursuant to a statute of that State, who reasonably determines that—

(1) an emergency situation exists that involves—

(A) immediate danger of death or serious bodily injury to any person; ~~or~~

(B) conspiratorial activities characteristic of organized crime;

(C) an immediate threat to a national security interest; or

(D) an ongoing attack on a protected computer (as defined in section 1030) that constitutes a crime punishable by a term of imprisonment greater than one year; that requires the installation and use of a pen register or a trap and trace device before an order authorizing such installation and use can, with due diligence, be obtained, and

(2) there are grounds upon which an order could be entered under this chapter to authorize such installation and use; may have installed and use a pen register or trap and trace device if, within forty-eight hours after the installation has occurred, or begins to occur, an order approving the installation or use is issued in accordance with section 3123 of this title.

(b) In the absence of an authorizing order, such use shall immediately terminate when the information sought is obtained, when the application for the order is denied or when forty-eight hours have lapsed since the installation of the pen register or trap and trace device, whichever is earlier.

(c) The knowing installation or use by any investigative or law enforcement officer of a pen register or trap and trace device pursuant to subsection (a) without application for the authorizing order within forty-eight hours of the installation shall constitute a violation of this chapter.

(d) A provider of a wire or electronic service, landlord, custodian, or other person who furnished facilities or technical assistance pursuant to this section shall be reasonably compensated for such reasonable expenses incurred in providing such facilities and assistance.

18 U.S.C. 3126. Reports Concerning Pen Registers and Trap and Trace Devices

The Attorney General shall annually report to Congress on the number of pen register orders and orders for trap and trace devices applied for by law enforcement agencies of the Department of Justice, which report shall include information concerning—

(1) the period of interceptions authorized by the order, and the number and duration of any extensions of the order;
(2) the offense specified in the order or application, or extension of an order;
(3) the number of investigations involved;
(4) the number and nature of the facilities affected; and
(5) the identity, including district, of the applying investigative or law enforcement agency making the application and the person authorizing the order.

18 U.S.C. 3127. Definitions for Chapter

As used in this chapter—

(1) the terms "wire communication", "electronic communication", "electronic communication service" and "contents" have the meanings set forth for such terms in section 2510 of this title;
(2) the term "court of competent jurisdiction" means—
  (A) any district court of the United States (including a magistrate judge of such a court) or any United States court of appeals that
    (i) has jurisdiction over the offense being investigated;
    (ii) is in or for a district in which the provider of a wire or electronic communication service is located;

(iii) is in or for a district in which a landlord, custodian, or other person subject to subsections (a) or (b) of section 3124 of this title is located; or
(iv) is acting on a request for foreign assistance pursuant to section 3512 of this title; or

(B) a court of general criminal jurisdiction of a State authorized by the law of that State to enter orders authorizing the use of a pen register or a trap and trace device;

(3) the term "pen register" means a device or process which records or decodes or other dialing, routing, addressing, and signaling information reasonably likely to identify the source of a wire or electronic communication, provided, however, that such information shall not include the contents of any communication, but such term does not include any device or process used by a provider or customer of a wire or electronic communication service for billing, or recording as an incident to billing, for communications services provided by such provider or any device or process used by a provider or customer of a wire communication service for cost accounting or other like purposes in the ordinary course of its business;
(4) the term "trap and trace device" means a device or process which captures the incoming electronic or other impulses which identify the originating number or other dialing, routing, addressing, and signaling information reasonably likely to identify the source of a wire or electronic communication, provided, however, that such information shall not include the contents of any communication;
(5) the term "attorney for the Government" has the meaning given such term for the purposes of the Federal Rules of Criminal Procedure; and
(6) the term "State" means a State, the District of Columbia, Puerto Rico, and any other possession or territory of the United States.

Appendix A. State Statutes Outlawing the Interception of Wire(w), Oral(o) and Electronic Communications(e)

Alabama: Ala.Code §§13A-11-30 to 13A-11-37(w/o);
Alaska: Alaska Stat. §§42.20.300 to 42.20.390 (w/o/e);
Arizona: Ariz.Rev.Stat.Ann. §§13-3001 to 13-3009 (w/o/e);
Arkansas: Ark.Code §§5-60-120, 23-17-107(w/o/e);
California: Cal.Penal Code §§631(w), 632(o), 632.7(e);
Colorado: Colo.Rev.Stat. §§18-9-301 to 18-9-305(w/o/e);
Connecticut: Conn.Gen.Stat.Ann. §§53a-187 to 53a-189, 54-41t (w/o);
Delaware: Del.Code tit.11 §§2401, 2402(w/o/e);

New Jersey: N.J.Stat.Ann. §§2A:156A-2, 2A:156A-3(w/o/e);
New Mexico: N.M.Stat.Ann. §30-12-1(w);
New York: N.Y.Penal Law §§250.00, 250.05(w/o/e);
North Carolina: N.C.Gen.Stat. §§15A-286, 15A-287(w/o/e);
North Dakota: N.D.Cent.Code §§12.1-15-02, 12.1-15-04(w/o);

Ohio: Ohio Rev.Code §§2933.51, 2933.52 (w/o/e);
Oklahoma: Okla.Stat.Ann. tit.13 §§176.2, 176.3 (w/o/e);

Florida: Fla.Stat.Ann. §§934.02, 934.03(w/o/e);
Georgia: Ga.Code §16-11-62 (w/o/e);
Hawaii: Hawaii Rev.Stat. §§711-1111, 803-41, 803-42(w/o/e);
Idaho: Idaho Code §§18-6701, 18-6702(w/o/e);

Illinois: Ill.Comp.Stat.Ann. ch.720 §§5/14-1 to 5/14-3(w/o/e);
Indiana: Ind.Code Ann. §§35-33.5-2-1, 35-33.5-5-6(w/o/e);
Iowa: Iowa Code Ann. §§272.8, 808B.2(w/o/e);
Kansas: Kan.Stat.Ann. §21-6101(w/o);
Kentucky: Ky.Rev.Stat. §§526.010, 526.020(w/o);
Louisiana: La.Rev.Stat.Ann. §§15:1302, 15:1303 (w/o/e);
Maine: Me.Rev.Stat.Ann. tit. 15 §§709, 710(w/o);

Maryland: Md.Cts. & Jud.Pro.Code Ann. §§10-401, 10-402(w/o/e);
Massachusetts: Mass.Gen.Laws Ann. ch.272 §99 (w/o);
Michigan: Mich.Comp.Laws Ann. §§750.539a, to 750.540(w/o/e);
Minnesota: Minn.Stat.Ann. §§626A.01, 626A.02 (w/o/e);
Missouri: Mo.Ann.Stat. §§542.400 to 542.402 (w/o/e);

Montana: Mont.Code Ann. §45-8-213(w/o/e);
Nebraska: Neb.Rev.Stat. §§86-271 to 86-290 (w/o/e);
Nevada: Nev.Rev.Stat. §§200.610, 200.620(w), 200.650(o);
New Hampshire: N.H.Rev.Stat.Ann. §§570-A:1, 570-A:2 (w/o);

Oregon: Ore.Rev.Stat. §§165.535 to 165.545 (w/o/e);
Pennsylvania: Pa.Stat.Ann. tit.18 §§5702, 5703 (w/o/e);
Rhode Island: R.I.Gen.Laws §§11-35-21(w/o/e);
South Carolina: S.C. Code Ann. §§16-17-470, 17-30-10 to 17-30-20 (w/o/e);
South Dakota: S.D.Cod.Laws §§23A-35A-1, 23A-35A-20 (w/o);
Tennessee: Tenn.Code Ann. §39-13-601(w/o/e);
Texas: Tex.Penal Code. §16.02; Tex. Crim. Pro. Code art. 18.20 (w/o/e);
Utah: Utah Code Ann. §§76-9-405, 77-23a-3, 77-23a-4 (w/o/e);

Virginia: Va.Code §§19.2-61, 19.2-62(w/o/e);
Washington: Wash.Rev.Code Ann.§9.73.030 (w/o);
West Virginia: W.Va.Code §§62-1D-2, 62-1D-3(w/o/e);
Wisconsin: Wis.Stat.Ann. §§968.27, 968.31(w/o/e);
Wyoming: Wyo.Stat. §§7-3-701, 7-3-702(w/o/e);
District of Columbia: D.C.Code §§23-541, 23-542(w/o).

APPENDIX B. CONSENT INTERCEPTIONS UNDER STATE LAW

Alabama: Ala.Code §13A-11-30 (one partyconsent);

New Jersey: N.J.Stat.Ann. §§2A:156A-4 (one party consent);

Alaska: Alaska Stat. §§42.20.300to 42.20.320 (one party consent);
Arizona: Ariz.Rev.Stat.Ann. §13-3005 (one party consent);
Arkansas: Ark.Code §5-60-120(one party consent);
California: Cal. Penal Code §§631, 632 (one party consent for police; all party consent otherwise), 632.7 (all partyconsent);
Colorado: Colo.Rev.Stat. §§18-9-303, 18-9-304 (one party consent);
Connecticut: Conn.Gen.Stat.Ann. §§53a-187, 53a-188 (criminal proscription: one party consent); §52-570d (civil liability: all party consent except for police);
Delaware: Del. Code tit.11 §2402 (one party consent);
Florida: Fla.Stat.Ann. §934.03 (one party consent for the police; all party consent for others);

New Mexico: N.M.Stat.Ann. §§30-12-1 (one party consent);
New York: N.Y.Penal Law §250.00 (one party consent);
North Carolina: N.C. Gen.Stat. §15A-287 (one party consent);
North Dakota: N.D.Cent.Code §§12.1-15-02 (one party consent);
Ohio: Ohio Rev.Code §2933.52 (one party consent);

Georgia: Ga.Code §16-11-66 (one party consent);
Hawaii: Hawaii Rev.Stat. §§711-1111, 803-42 (one party consent);
Idaho: Idaho Code §18-6702 (one party consent);
Illinois: Ill.Comp.Stat.Ann. ch.720 §§5/14-2,5/14-3 (all party consent with law enforcement exceptions);
Indiana: Ind.Code Ann. §35-33.5-5-5 (one party consent), *Parker v. State*, 800 N.E.2d 574 (Ind.App. 2003);
Iowa: Iowa Code Ann. §808B.2 (one party consent);
Kansas: Kan.Stat.Ann. §§21-6101 (one party consent);
Kentucky: Ky.Rev.Stat. §526.010 (one party consent);
Louisiana: La.Rev.Stat.Ann. §15:1303 (one party consent);
Maine: Me.Rev.Stat.Ann. tit. 15 §709 (one party consent);
Maryland: Md.Cts. & Jud.Pro.Code Ann. §10-402 (one party consent);
Massachusetts: Mass.Gen. Laws Ann.

Oklahoma: Okla.Stat.Ann. tit.13 §176.4 (one party consent);
Oregon: Ore.Rev.Stat. §165.540 (one party consent for wiretapping and all parties must consent for other forms of electronic eavesdropping);
Pennsylvania: Pa.Stat.Ann. tit.18 §5704 (one party consent for the police; all parties consent otherwise);
Rhode Island: R.I.Gen.Laws §§11-35-21 (oneparty consent);

South Carolina: S.C. Code Ann. §17-30-30 (one party consent);
South Dakota: S.D.Comp.Laws §§23A-35A-20 (one party consent);
Tennessee: Tenn.Code Ann. §39-13-601 (one party consent)
Texas: Tex.Penal Code §16.02 (one party consent);
Utah: Utah Code Ann. §§77-23a-4 (one party consent);
Virginia: Va.Code §19.2-62 (one party

ch.272 §99 (all parties must consent, except in some law enforcement cases);
Michigan: Mich.Comp.Laws Ann. §750.539c (proscription regarding eavesdropping on oral conversation: all party consent, except that the proscription does not apply to otherwise lawful activities of police officers);
Minnesota: Minn.Stat.Ann. §626A.02 (one party consent);
Missouri: Mo.Ann.Stat. §542.402 (one party consent);
Montana: Mont.Code Ann. §§45-8-213 (all party consent with an exception for the performance of official duties);
Nebraska: Neb.Rev.Stat. §86-290 (one party consent);
Nevada: Nev.Rev.Stat. §§200.620, 200.650 (onep arty consent);

consent);
Washington: Wash.Rev.Code Ann. §9.73.030 (all parties must consent, except that one party consent is sufficient in certain law enforcement cases);
West Virginia: W.Va. Code §62-1D-3 (one party consent);
Wisconsin: Wis.Stat.Ann. §968.31 (one party consent);
Wyoming: Wyo.Stat. §7-3-702 (one party consent);
District of Columbia: D.C.Code §23-542 (one party consent).

APPENDIX C. STATUTORY CIVIL LIABILITY FOR INTERCEPTIONS UNDER STATE LAW

Arizona: Ariz.Rev.Stat.Ann. §12-731;
California: Cal. Penal Code §§637.2;
Colorado: Colo.Rev.Stat. §18-9-309.5;
Connecticut: Conn.Gen.Stat. Ann. §§54-41r,52-570d;
Delaware: Del.Code tit.11 §2409;
Florida: Fla.Stat.Ann. §§934.10, 934.27;
Hawaii: Hawaii Rev.Stat. §803-48;
Idaho: Idaho Code §18-6709;
Illinois: Ill.Comp.Stat. Ann. ch.720 §5/14-6;
Indiana: Ind.Code Ann. §35-33.5-5-4;
Iowa: Iowa Code Ann. §808B.8;
Kansas: Kan.Stat.Ann. §22-2518
Louisiana: La.Rev.Stat.Ann. §15:1312;
Maine: Me.Rev.Stat.Ann. ch.15 §711;
Maryland: Md.Cts. & Jud.Pro.Code Ann. §§10-410, 10-4A-08;
Nevada: Nev.Rev.Stat. §200.690;
New Hampshire: N.H.Rev.Stat. Ann. §570-A:11;
New Jersey: N.J.Stat.Ann. §§2A: 156A-24;
New Mexico: N.M.Stat.Ann. §§30 -12-11;
North Carolina: N.C.Gen.Stat. §15A -296;
Ohio: Ohio Rev.Code §2933.65;
Oregon: Ore.Rev.Stat. §133.739;
Pennsylvania: Pa.Stat. Ann. tit.18 §§5725, 5747;
Rhode Island: R.I.Gen.Laws §12-5.1-13;
South Carolina: S.C. Code Ann. §17-30-135;
Tennessee: Tenn.Code Ann. §39-13-603;
Texas: Tex.Code Crim.Pro. art. 18.20;
Utah: Utah Code Ann. §§77-23a-11; 77-23b-8;
Virginia: Va.Code §19.2-69;
Washington: Wash.Rev.Code Ann. §9.73.060;

Massachusetts: Mass.Gen. LawsAnn. ch.272 §99;
Michigan: Mich.Comp. Laws Ann. §750.539h;
Minnesota: Minn.Stat.Ann. §§626A.02, 626A.13;
Nebraska: Neb.Rev.Stat. §86-297;
West Virginia: W.Va.Code §62-1D-12;
Wisconsin: Wis.Stat.Ann. §968.31;
Wyoming: Wyo.Stat. §7-3-710;
District of Columbia: D.C.Code §23-554.

APPENDIX D. COURT AUTHORIZED INTERCEPTION UNDER STATE LAW

Alaska: Alaska Stats. §§12.37.010 to 12.37.900;
Arizona: Ariz.Rev.Stat.Ann. §§13-3010 to 13-3019;
California: Cal.Penal Code §629.50 to 629.98;
Colorado: Colo.Rev.Stat. §§16-15-101 to 16-15-104;
Connecticut: Conn.Gen.Stat.Ann. §§54-41a to54-41u;
Delaware: Del.Code tit.11 §§2401 to 2412;
Florida: Fla.Stat.Ann. §§934.02 to 934.43;
Georgia: Ga.Code §16-11-64 to 16-11-69;
Hawaii: Hawaii Rev.Stat. §§803-41 to 803-49;
Idaho: Idaho Code §§18-6701 to 18-6709; 6719 to 6725;
Illinois: Ill.Stat.Ann. ch.725 §§5/108A-1 to108B-14;
Indiana:Ind.Code §§35-33.5-2-1to 35-33.5-5-6;
Iowa: Iowa Code Ann. §§808B.3to 808B.7;
Kansas: Kan.Stat.Ann. §§22-2514 to 22-2519;
Louisiana: La.Rev.Stat.Ann. §§15:1301 to 15:1316;
Maryland: Md.Cts. & Jud.Pro.Code Ann. §§10-401 to10-410;
Massachusetts: Mass.Gen.LawsAnn. ch.272 §99;
Minnesota: Minn.Stat.Ann. §§626A.01 to 626.41;
Missouri: Mo.Ann.Stat. §§542.400 to
North Carolina: N.C.Gen.Stat. §§15A-286 to 15A-298;
North Dakota: N.D.Cent.Code §§29-29.2-01 to 29-29.2-05;
Ohio: Ohio Rev.Code §§2933.51 to 2933.66;
Oklahoma: Okla.Stat.Ann. tit.13 §§176.1 to 176.14
Oregon: Ore.Rev.Stat. §§133.721 to 133.739;
Pennsylvania: Pa.Stat.Ann. tit.18 §§5701 to 5728
Rhode Island: R.I.Gen.Laws §§12-5.1-1 to12-5.1-16;
South Carolina: S.C. Code Ann. §§17-30-10 to 17-30-145;

South Dakota: S.D.Cod.Laws §§23A-35A-1 to 23A-35A-34;
Tennessee: Tenn.Code Ann. §§40-6-301 to 40-6-311;
Texas: Tex.Crim.Pro. Code. art. 18.20;
Utah: Utah Code Ann. §§77-23a-1 to 77-23a-16;
Virginia: Va.Code §§19.2-61 to19.2-70.3;

Washington: Wash.Rev.Code Ann. §§9.73.040 to 9.73.250;
West Virginia: W.Va.Code §§62-1D-1 to 62-1D-16;
Wisconsin: Wis.Stat.Ann. §§968.27 to

542.422;
Nebraska: Neb.Rev.Stat. §§86-271 to 86-2,115;
Nevada: Nev.Rev.Stat. §§179.410 to 179.515;
New Hampshire: N.H.Rev.Stat.Ann. §§570-A:1 to570-A:9;
New Jersey: N.J.Stat.Ann. §§2A:156A-8 to 2A:156A-26;
New Mexico: N.M.Stat.Ann. §§30-12-1 to 30-12-11;
New York: N.Y.Crim.Pro. Law §§700.05 to700.70;
968.33;
Wyoming: Wyo.Stat. §§7-3-701 to 7-3-712;
District of Columbia: D.C.Code §§23-541 to 23-556.

End Notes

[1] Portions of this report draw upon a series of earlier reports, no longer available, entitled: *Wiretapping and Electronic Surveillance: A Brief Discussion of Pertinent Supreme Court Cases, A Summary and Compilation of Federal State Statutes, and a Selected Legal Bibliography* (1970); *Wiretapping and Electronic Surveillance: A Brief Discussion of Pertinent Supreme Court Cases, A Summary and Compilation of Federal State Statutes, and a Selected Legal Bibliography* (1971); *Wiretapping and Electronic Surveillance: Federal and State Statutes* (1974); *Taps and Bugs: A Compilation of Federal and State Statutes Governing the Interception of Wire and Oral Communications* (1981); *The Interception of Communications: A Legal Overview of Bugs and Taps* (1988); *Wiretapping & Electronic Surveillance: The Electronic Communications Privacy Act and Related Matters* (1992); *Taps, Bugs & Telephony: An Overview of Federal Statutes Governing Wiretapping and Electronic Eavesdropping* (1998); *Privacy: An Overview of Federal Statutes Governing Wiretapping and Electronic Eavesdropping* (2001); *id.* (2003); *id.* (2006); *id.* (2009). It constitutes the ECPA portion of a separate report that includes a discussion of the Foreign Intelligence Surveillance Act (FISA), CRS Report 98-326, *Privacy: An Overview of Federal Statutes Governing Wiretapping and Electronic Eavesdropping.*
As used in this report "electronic eavesdropping" refers to the use of hidden microphones, recorders and any other mechanical or electronic means of capturing ongoing communications, other than wiretapping (tapping into telephone conversations). In previous versions of this report and other earlier writings, it was common to use a more neutral, and consequently preferred, term—electronic surveillance—at least when referring to law enforcement use. Unfortunately, continued use of the term "electronic surveillance" rather than "electronic eavesdropping" risks confusion with forms of surveillance that either have individualistic definitions (*e.g.*, "electronic surveillance" under the Foreign Intelligence Surveillance Act, 50 U.S.C. 1801(f)), involve surveillance that does not capture conversation (*e.g.*, thermal imaging or electronic tracking devices), or may or may not capture conversation (*e.g.*, the coverage of video surveillance depends upon the circumstances and the statutory provision question).
Related developments are discussed in CRS Report R42725, *Reauthorization of the FISA Amendments Act*; CRS Report R40138, *Amendments to the Foreign Intelligence Surveillance Act (FISA) Extended Until June 1, 2015*; CRS Report R40980, *Government Collection of Private Information: Background and Issues Related to the USA PATRIOT Act Reauthorization*; CRS Report 97-1025, *Cybercrime: An Overview of the Federal Computer Fraud and Abuse Statute and Related Federal Criminal Laws*, by Charles Doyle; CRS Report RL33424, *Government Access to Phone Calling Activity and Related Records: Legal Authorities*; CRS Report RL30677, *The Communications Assistance for Law Enforcement Act*, by Patricia Moloney Figliola; and CRS Report RL34693, *Online Data Collection and Disclosure to Private Entities: Selected Federal Laws and Self-Regulatory Regimes*, by Kathleen Ann Ruane.

[2] 18 U.S.C. 2510-2522. This part of ECPA was originally enacted as Title III of the Omnibus Crime Control and Safe Streets Act of 1968, 18 U.S.C. 2510-2520 (1964 ed,)(Supp. IV).

[3] *Id.*

[4] 18 U.S.C. 27-1-2712.

[5] 18 U.S.C. 3121-3127.

[6] 18 U.S.C. 3121.

[7] 4 BLACKSTONE, COMMENTARIES ON THE LAWS OF ENGLAND, 169 (1769).

[8] "Eavesdropping is indictable at the common law, not only in England but in our states. It is seldom brought to the attention of the courts, and our books contain too few decisions upon it to enable an author to define it with confidence.... It never occupied much space in the law, and it has nearly faded from the legal horizon." 1 BISHOP, COMMENTARIES ON THE CRIMINAL LAW, 670 (1882).

[9] 40 Stat.1017-18 (1918)("whoever during the period of governmental operation of the telephone and telegraph systems of the United States ... shall, without authority and without the knowledge and consent of the other users thereof, except as may be necessary for operation of the service, tap any telegraph or telephone line ... or whoever being employed in any such telephone or telegraph service shall divulge the contents of any such telephone or telegraph message to any person not duly authorized or entitled the receive the same, shall be fined not exceeding $1,000 or imprisoned for not more than one year or both"); 56 *Cong.Rec.* 10761-765 (1918).

[10] 44 Stat. 1172 (1927)(" ... no person not being authorized by the sender shall intercept any message and divulge or publish the contents, substance, purpose, effect, or meaning of such intercepted message to any person ... ").

[11] *Olmstead v. United States*, 277 U.S. 438, 479-80 n.13 (1928)(Brandeis, J., dissenting). *Olmstead* is remembered most today for the dissents of Holmes and Brandeis, but for four decades it stood for the view that the Fourth Amendment's search and seizure commands did not apply to government wiretapping accomplished without a trespass onto private property.

[12] Curtilage originally meant the land and buildings enclosed by the walls of a castle; in later usage it referred to the barns, stables, garden plots and the like immediately proximate to a dwelling; it is understood in Fourth Amendment parlance to describe that area which "harbors those intimate activities associated with domestic life and the privacies of the home," *United States v. Dunn*, 480 U.S. 294, 301 n.4 (1987).

[13] 277 U.S. at 466. Olmstead had not been compelled to use his phone and so the Court rejected his Fifth Amendment challenge. 277 U.S.C. at 462. Any violation of the Washington state wiretap statute was thought insufficient to warrant the exclusion of evidence, 277 U.S. at 466-68. Justice Holmes in his dissent tersely characterized the conduct of federal wiretappers as "dirty business," 277 U.S. at 470. The dissent of Justice Brandeis observed that the drafters of the Constitution "conferred as against the Government, the right to be let alone—the most comprehensive of rights and the right most valued by civilized men. To protect that right, every unjustifiable intrusion by the Government against privacy of the individual whatever the means employed, must be deemed in violation of the Fourth Amendment," 277 U.S. at 478-79.

[14] "Congress may of course protect the secrecy of telephone messages by making them, when intercepted inadmissible in evidence in federal criminal trials, by direct legislation," 277 U.S. at 465.

[15] 48 Stat. 1103-104 (1934), 47 U.S.C. 605 (1940 ed.). The Act neither expressly condemned law enforcement interceptions nor called for the exclusion of wiretap evidence, but it was read to encompass both, *Nardone v. United States*, 302 U.S. 379 (1937); *Nardone v. United States*, 308 U.S. 321 (1939).

[16] Section 605 did ban the interception and divulgence of radio broadcasts but it did not reach the radio transmission of conversations that were broadcast unbeknownst to all of the parties to the conversation. Late in the game, the FCC supplied a partial solution when it banned the use of licensed radio equipment to overhear or record private conversation without the consent of all the parties involved in the conversation, 31 *Fed. Reg.* 3400 (March 4, 1966), amending then 47 C.F.R. §§2.701, 15.11. The FCC excluded "operations of any law enforcement offices conducted under lawful authority," *id.*

[17] The volume of all Fourth Amendment cases calling for Supreme Court review increased dramatically after *Mapp v. Ohio*, 367 U.S. 643 (1961), acknowledged the application of the Fourth Amendment exclusionary rule to the states.

[18] *Goldman v. United States*, 316 U.S. 129 (1942).

[19] *On Lee v. United States*, 343 U.S. 747 (1952).

[20] *Silverman v. United States*, 365 U.S. 505 (1961).

[21] "The absence of a physical invasion of the petitioner's premises was also a vital factor in the Court's decision in *Olmstead v. United States*.... In holding that the wiretapping there did not violate the Fourth Amendment, the Court noted that the insertions were made without trespass upon any property of the defendants. They were made in the basement of the large office building. The taps from house lines were made in the streets near the houses. 277 U.S. at 457. There was no entry of the houses or offices of the defendants. 277 U.S. at 464. Relying upon these circumstances, the Court reasoned that the intervening wires are not part of (the defendant's) house or office any more than are the highways along which they are stretched. 277 U.S. at 465. "Here, by contrast, the officers overheard the petitioners' conversations only by usurping part of the petitioners' house or office—a heating system which was an integral part of the premises occupied by the petitioners, a usurpation that was effected without their knowledge and without their consent. In these circumstances we need not pause to consider whether or not there was a technical trespass under the local property law relating to party walls. Inherent Fourth Amendment rights are not inevitably measurable in terms of ancient niceties of tort or real property law . . . .

"The Fourth Amendment, and the personal rights which it secures, have a long history. At the very core stands the right of a man to retreat into his own home and there be free from unreasonable governmental intrusion ... This Court has never held that a federal officer may without warrant and without consent physically entrench into a man's office or home, there secretly observe or listen, and relate at the man's subsequent criminal trial what was seen or heard.

"A distinction between the dictaphone employed in Goldman and the spike mike utilized here seemed to the Court of Appeals too fine a one to draw. The court was unwilling to believe that the respective rights are to be measured in fractions of inches. But decision here does not turn upon the technicality of a trespass upon a party wall as a matter of local law. It is based upon the reality of an actual intrusion into a constitutionally protected area. What the Court said long ago bears repeating now: It may be that it is the obnoxious thing in its mildest and least repulsive form; but illegitimate and unconstitutional practices get their first footing in that way, namely, by silent approaches and slight deviations from legal modes of procedure. *Boyd v. United States*, 116 U.S. 616, 635. We find no occasion to re-examine Goldman here, but we decline to go beyond it, by even a fraction of an inch," 365 U.S. at 510-12 (internal quotation marks omitted).

[22] *Wong Sun v. United States*, 371 U.S. 471, 485 (1963).

[23] 389 U.S. 347 (1967).

[24] "We conclude that the underpinnings of *Olmstead* and *Goldman* have been so eroded by our subsequent decisions that the trespass doctrine there enunciated can no longer be regarded as controlling. The Government's activities in electronically listening to and recording the petitioner's words violated the privacy upon which he justifiably relied while using the telephone booth and thus constituted a search and seizure within the meaning of the Fourth Amendment. The fact that the electronic device employed to achieve that end did not happen to penetrate the wall of the booth can have no constitutional significance." Later courts seem to prefer the "expectation of privacy" language found in Justice Harlan's concurrence: "My understanding of the rule that has emerged from prior decisions is that there is a twofold requirement, first that a person have exhibited an actual (subjective) expectation of privacy and, second, that the expectation be one that society is prepared to recognize as reasonable," 389 U.S. at 361.

[25] 388 U.S. 41 (1967).

[26] 388 U.S. at 58-60.

[27] 87 Stat. 197, 18 U.S.C. 2510 -2520 (1970 ed.).

[28] 18 U.S.C. 2511(3)(1970 ed.)("Nothing contained in this chapter or in section 605 of the Communications Act ... shall limit the constitutional power of the President to take such measures as he deems necessary to protect the Nation against actual or potential attack or other hostile acts of a foreign power, to obtain foreign intelligence information deemed essential to the security of the United States, or to protect national security information against foreign intelligence activities ... ").

[29] *United States v. United States District Court*, 407 U.S. 297 (1972).

[30] 92 Stat. 1783, 50 U.S.C. 1801-1862.

[31] 425 U.S. 435, 441-43 (1976).

[32] *Id.* at 44-45.

[33] 442 U.S. 735, 741-46 (1979).

[34] *Id.* In *United States v. New York Telephone Co.*, the Court held that the Title III did not apply to the use of pen registers and that federal courts had the power to authorize their installation for law enforcement purposes, 434 U.S.157, 168 (1977).

[35] 100 Stat. 1848 (1986).

[36] 18 U.S.C. 2510-2522.

[37] 18 U.S.C. 2701-2712.

[38] 18 U.S.C. 3121-3126.

[39] P.L. 107-56, 115 Stat. 272 (2001).

[40] P.L. 107-108, 115 Stat. 1394 (2001).

[41] P.L. 107-273, 116 Stat. 1758 (2002).

[42] P.L. 107-296, 116 Stat. 2135 (2002).

[43] P.L. 109-177, 120 Stat. 192 (2006).

[44] P.L. 110-261, 122 Stat. 2436 (2008).

[45] 18 U.S.C. 2511. Elsewhere, federal law proscribes: unlawful access to stored communications, 18 U.S.C. 2701; unlawful use of a pen register or a trap and trace device, 18 U.S.C. 3121; and abuse of eavesdropping and search authority or unlawful disclosures under the Foreign Intelligence Surveillance Act, 50 U.S.C. 1809, 1827.

[46] 18 U.S.C. 2511(1).

[47] 18 U.S.C. 2510(6). Although the governmental entities are not subject to criminal liability, as noted *infra*, some courts believe them subject to civil liability under 18 U.S.C. 2520; *Smoot v. United Transportation Union*, 246 F.3d633, 640-41 (6th Cir. 2001).

[48] "In order to underscore that the inadvertent reception of a protected communication is not a crime, the subcommittee changed the state of mind requirement under Title III of the Omnibus Crime Control and Safe

Streets Act of 1968 from 'willful' to 'intentional,'" S.Rept. 541, at 23 (1986); "This provision makes clear that the inadvertent interception of a protected communication is not unlawful under this Act," H.Rept. 99-647, at 48-9 (1986). *See, e.g., In re Pharmatrak, Inc.*, 329 F.3d 9, 23 (1st Cir. 2003); *Sanders v. Robert Bosch Corp.*, 38 F.3d 736, 742-43 (4th Cir. 1994); *Lonegan v. Hasty*, 436 F.Supp.2d 419, 429 (E.D.N.Y. 2006); *Lewton v. Divingnzzo*, 772 F.Supp.2d 1046, 1059 (D. Nev. 2011)."But the plaintiffs need not produce direct evidence of the intentional interception; for often the only way to prove that a stealthy interception occurred is through circumstantial evidence," *McCann v. Iroquois Memorial Hospital*, 622 F.3d745, 752 (7th Cir. 2010), citing, *DirecTV v. Webb*, 545 F.3d 837, 844 (9th Cir. 2008).

[49] *Narducci v. Village of Bellwood*, 444 F. Supp. 924, 935 (N.D. Ill. 2006).

[50] "(1) Except as otherwise specifically provided in this chapter any person who—(a) intentionally intercepts, endeavors to intercept, or procures any other person to intercept or endeavor to intercept, any wire, oral, or electronic communication;

"(b) intentionally uses, endeavors to use, or procures any other person to use or endeavor to use any electronic, mechanical, or other device to intercept any oral communication when—(I) such device is affixed to, or otherwise transmits a signal through, a wire, cable, or other like connection used in wire communication; or (ii) such device transmits communications by radio, or interferes with the transmission of such communication; or (iii) such person knows, or has reason to know, that such device or any component thereof has been sent through the mail or transported in interstate or foreign commerce; or (iv) such use or endeavor to use (A) takes place on the premises of any business or other commercial establishment the operations of which affect interstate or foreign commerce; or (B) obtains or is for the purpose of obtaining information relating to the operations of any business or other commercial establishment the operations of which affect interstate or foreign commerce; or (v) such person acts in the District of Columbia, the Commonwealth of Puerto Rico, or any territory or possession of the United States," 18 U.S.C. 2511(1)(a),(b).

[51] "Subparagraph (a) establishes a blanket prohibition against the interception of wire communication. Since the facilities used to transmit wire communications form part of the interstate or foreign communications network, Congress has plenary power under the commerce clause to prohibit all interception of such communications whether by wiretapping or otherwise.

"The broad prohibition of subparagraph (a) is also applicable to the interception of oral communications. The interception of such communications, however, does not necessarily interfere with the interstate or foreign commerce network, and the extent of the constitutional power of Congress to prohibit such interception is less clear than in the case of interception of wire communications. . . .

"Therefore, in addition to the broad prohibitions of subparagraph (a), the committee has included subparagraph (b),which relies on accepted jurisdictional bases under the commerce clause, and other provisions of the Constitution toprohibit the interception of oral communications," S.Rept. 90-1097, at 91-2 (1968).

[52] DEPARTMENT OF JUSTICE CRIMINAL RESOURCE MANUAL §9-60.200 at 1050, available at http://www.justice.gov/usao/eousa/foia_reading_room/usam/title9/60mcrm.htm#9-60.400. As will be noted in a moment, the statutory definitions of wire and electronic communications contain specific commerce clause elements, but the definition of oral communications does not. Subsequent Supreme Court jurisprudence relating to the breadth of Congress's commerce clause powers indicates that the precautions may have been well advised, *United States v. Lopez*, 514 U.S. 549 (1995) and *United States v. Morrison*, 529 U.S. 598 (2000).

[53] 18 U.S.C. 2510(4). The dictionary definition of "aural" is "of or relating to the ear or to the sense of hearing," MERRIAM-WEBSTER'S COLLEGIATE DICTIONARY 76 (10th ed. 1996).

[54] *United States v. Luong*, 471 F.3d 1107, 1109 (9th Cir. 2006)("an interception occurs where the tapped phone is located and where the law enforcement officers first overheard the call ... *United States v. Rodriguez*, 968 F.2d 130, 136 (2d Cir. 1992); *accord, United States v. Ramirez*, 112 F.3d 849, 852 (7th Cir. 1997)(concluding that an interception occurs in the jurisdiction where the tapped phone is located, where the second phone in the conversation is located, and where the scanner used to overhear the call is located); *United States v. Denman*, 100 F.3d 399, 403 (5th Cir. 1996)").

[55] *Noel v. Hall*, 568 F.3d 743, 749 (9th Cir. 2009)("In reaching this conclusion, we join a number of other circuits that have held that replaying of tapes containing recorded phone conversations does not amount to a new interception in violation of the Wiretap Act"), *citing inter alia, United States v. Hammond*, 286 F.3d 189, 193 (4th Cir. 2002); *Reynolds v. Spears*, 93 F.3d 428, 432-33 (8th Cir. 1996); *United States v. Shields*, 675 F.2d 1152, 1156 (11th Cir. 1982).

[56] S.Rept. 99-541, at 13 (1986)(the "amendment clarifies that it is illegal to intercept the non-voice portion of a wire communication. For example, it is illegal to intercept the data or digitized portion of a voice communication"); *see also*, H.Rept. 99-647, at 34 (1986).

[57] *See, United States v. Szymuszkiewicz*, 622 F.3d 701, 705-706 (7th Cir. 2010)(an employee's surreptitiously programming his supervisor's computer, so that the server forwards duplicates to the employee of all emails sent to the supervisor, constitutes an interception in violation of Title III); *United States v. Councilman*, 418 F.3d 67, 79-80(1st Cir. 2005)(en banc)(service provider's access to email "during transient storage" constitutes "interception"; without deciding whether "interception is limited to acquisition contemporaneous with

transmission"); *Konop v. Hawaiian Airlines, Inc.*, 302 F.3d 868, 878 (9th Cir. 2002)(fraudulent access to stored communication does not constitute an "interception"; interception requires access contemporaneous with transmission); *United States v. Smith*, 155 F.3d 1051, 1058 (9th Cir. 1998)(unauthorized retrieval and recording of another's voice mail messages constitutes an "interception"); *United States v. Jones*, 451 F.Supp.2d 71, 75 (D.D.C. 2006)(government's acquisition from the phone company of text messages was no interception because there was no contemporaneous access); *Fraser v. National Mutual Insurance Co.*, 135 F.Supp.2d 623, 634-37 (E.D.Pa. 2001)("interception" of email occurs with its unauthorized acquisition prior to initial receipt by its addressee); *Steve Jackson Games, Inc. v. United States Secret Service*, 36 F.3d 457, 461-62 n.7 (5th Cir. 1994)(Congress did not intend for "interception" to apply to email stored on an electronic bulletin board; stored wire communications (voice mail), however, is protected from "interception"); *United States v. Meriwether*, 917 F.2d 955, 959-60 (6th Cir. 1990)(access to stored information through the use of another's pager does not constitute an "interception"); *United States v. Reyes*, 922 F. Supp. 818, 836-37 (S.D.N.Y. 1996)(same); *Wesley College v. Pitts*, 947 F. Supp. 375, 385 (D. Del. 1997)(no "interception" occurs when the contents of electronic communications are acquired unless contemporaneous with their transmission); *Cardinal Health 414, Inc. v. Adams*, 582 F.Supp.2d 967, 979-81 (M.D. Tenn. 2008)(same); *see also, Adams v. Battle Creek*, 250 F.3d 980, 982 (6th Cir. 2001)(use of a "clone" or duplicate pager to simultaneously receive the same message as a target pager is an "interception"); *Brown v. Waddell*, 50 F.3d 285, 294 (4th Cir. 1995)(same).

[58] 115 Stat. 283 (2001). Such recourse to the procedures of the Stored Communications Act must still comply with the demands of the Fourth Amendment, *see, United States v. Warshak*, 631 F.3d 266, 288 (6th Cir. 2010)("Accordingly, we hold that a subscriber enjoys a reasonable expectation of privacy in the contents of emails that are stored with, or sent or received through, a commercial ISP. The government may not compel a commercial ISP to turn over the contents of a subscriber's emails without first obtaining a warrant based on probable cause. Therefore, because they did not obtain a warrant, the government agents violated the Fourth Amendment when they obtained the contents of Warshak's emails. Moreover, to the extent that the SCA purports to permit the government to obtain such emails warrantlessly, the SCA is unconstitutional").

[59] 18 U.S.C. 2510(8). *In re iPhone Application Litigation*, 844 F.Supp.2d 1040, 1061 (2012)("In *United States v. Reed*, 575 F.3d 900 (9th Cir. 2009), the Ninth Circuit held that data automatically generated about a telephone call, such as the call's time of origination and its duration, do not constitute 'content' for purposes of the Wiretap Act's sealing provisions because such data 'contains no "information concerning the substance, purport, or meaning of [the] communication."' *Id.* at 916 (quoting 18 U.S.C. 2510[(8)]). Rather, 'content' is limited to information the user intended to communicate, such as the words spoken in a phone call. *Id.* Here, the allegedly intercepted electronic communications are simply users' geolocation data. This data is generated automatically, rather than through the intent of the user, and therefore does not constitute 'content' susceptible to interception").

[60] "'Post-cut-through dialed digits' are any numbers dialed from a telephone after the call is initially setup or 'cut-through.' Sometimes these digits are other telephone numbers, as when a party places a credit card call by first dialing the long distance carrier access number and then the phone number of the intended party. Sometimes these digits transmit real information, such as bank account numbers, Social Security numbers, prescription numbers, and the like. In the latter case, the digits represent communications content; in the former, they are non-content call processing numbers," *In re United States*, 441 F.Supp.2d 816, 818 (S.D. Tex. 2006).

[61] *In re United States for Orders (1) Authorizing Use of Pen Registers and Trap and Trace Devices*, 515 F.Supp.2d 325, 328-38 (E.D.N.Y. 2007); *In re United States*, 441 F.Supp.2d 816, 818-27 (S.D. Tex. 2006).

[62] 18 U.S.C. 2510(4). *United States v. Jones*, 451 F.Supp.2d 71, 75 (D.D.C. 2006)(government's acquisition from the phone company of text messages was not an interception because it did not involve contemporaneous access and because no electronic, mechanical, or other devices were used).

[63] *United States v. Szymuszkiewicz*, 622 F.3d 701, 707 (7th Cir. 2010)("Thus Szymuszkiewicz acquired the emails byusing at least three devices: Infusino's computer (where the rule [directing surreptitious duplication of incoming emails] was set up), the Kansas City server (where the rule caused each message to be duplicated and sent his way),and his own computer (where the messages were received, read, and sometimes stored").

[64] "'[E]lectronic, mechanical, or other device' means any device or apparatus which can be used to intercept a wire, oral, or electronic communication other than—(a) any telephone or telegraph instrument, equipment or facility, or any component thereof, (i) furnished to the subscriber or user by a provider of wire or electronic communication service in the ordinary course of its business and being used by the subscriber or user in the ordinary course of its business or furnished by such subscriber or user for connection to the facilities of such service and used in the ordinary course of its business; or (ii) being used by a provider of wire or electronic communication service in the ordinary course of its business, or by an investigative or law enforcement officer in the ordinary course of his duties; (b) a hearing aid or similar device being used to correct subnormal hearing to not better than normal," 18 U.S.C. 2510(5).

[65] See the cases cited and commentary in Barnett & Makar, *"In the Ordinary Course of Business": The Legal Limits of Workplace Wiretapping*, 10 HASTINGS JOURNAL OF COMMUNICATIONS AND ENTERTAINMENT LAW 715 (1988); *Application to Extension Telephones of Title III of the Omnibus Crime Control and Safe Streets Act of*

1968 (18 U.S.C. §§2510 et seq.), Pertaining to Interceptions of Wire Communications, 58 ALR Fed. 594; *Eavesdropping on Extension Telephone as Invasion of Privacy*, 49 ALR 4th 430.

66 *E.g., Deal v. Spears*, 780 F.Supp. 618, 623 (W.D.Ark. 1991), *aff'd*, 980 F.2d 1153 (8th Cir. 1992)(employer regularly taped employee calls by means of a device attached to an extension phone; most of the calls were personal and recording and disclosing them served no business purpose).

67 *Adams v. Battle Creek*, 250 F.3d 980, 983 (6th Cir. 2001); *Arias v. Mutual Central Alarm Service*, 202 F.3d 553, 558 (2d Cir. 2000); *Berry v. Funk*, 146 F.3d 1003, 1008 (D.C.Cir. 1998); *Sanders v. Robert Bosch Corp.*, 38 F.3d 736, 741 (4th Cir. 1994). *See also, Hall v. Earthlink Network Inc.*, 396 F.3d 500, 503-04 (2d Cir. 2005) (Internet service provider's receipt and storage of former customer's email after termination of the customer's account was done in ordinary course of business and consequently did not constitute an interception).
Some courts include surreptitious, extension phone interceptions conducted within the family home as part of the "business extension" exception, *Anonymous v. Anonymous*, 558 F.2d 677, 678-79 (2d Cir. 1977); *Scheib v. Grant*, 22 F.3d 149, 154 (7th Cir. 1994); *Newcomb v. Ingle*, 944 F.2d 1534, 1536 (10th Cir. 1991); *contra, United States v. Murdock*, 63 F.3d 1391, 1400 (6th Cir. 1995).

68 *Adams v. Battle Creek*, 250 F.3d at 984; *see also, United States v. Lewis*, 406 F.3d 11, 18 (1st Cir. 2005); *United States v. Hammond*, 286 F.3d 189, 192 (4th Cir. 2002); *Smith v. U.S. Dept. of Justice*, 251 F.3d 1047, 1049-50 (D.C.Cir. 2001); *United States v. Poyck*, 77 F.3d 285, 292 (9th Cir. 1996); *United States v. Daniels*, 902 F.2d 1238, 1245 (7th Cir. 1990); *United States v. Paul*, 614 F.2d 115, 117 (6th Cir. 1980).

69 *Amati v. Woodstock*, 176 F.3d 952, 955 (7th Cir. 1999)("Investigation is within the ordinary course of law enforcement, so if 'ordinary' were read literally warrants would rarely if ever be required for electronic eavesdropping, which was surely not Congress's intent. Since the purpose of the statute was primarily to regulate the use of wiretapping and other electronic surveillance for investigatory purposes, 'ordinary' should not be read so broadly; it is more reasonably interpreted to refer to routine non investigative recording of telephone conversations"); *accord, United States v. Lewis*, 416 F.3d at 11; *Colandrea v. Orangetown*, 411 F.Supp.2d 342, 347-48 (S.D.N.Y. 2007).

70 The exception, however, does not permit a county to record all calls in and out of the offices of county judges merely because a detention center and the judges share a common facility, *Abraham v. Greenville*, 237 F.3d 386, 390 (4th Cir. 2001), nor does it permit jailhouse telephone monitoring of an inmate's confession to a clergyman, *Mockaitis v. Harcleroad*, 104 F.3d 1522, 1530 (9th Cir. 1997). The courts are divided over whether private corrections officials are covered by the law enforcement exception. *Compare, United States v. Faulkner*, 323 F. Supp.2d 1111, 1113-17 (D. Kan. 2004), *aff'd on other grounds*, 439 F.3d 1221 (10th Cir. 2006) (not covered) *with, United States v. Rivera*, 292 F. Supp.2d 838, 842-43 (E.D.Va. 2003) (covered).

71 *United States v. Larios*, 593 F.3d 82, 90-91 (1st Cir. 2010); *United States v. Falls*, 34 F.3d 674, 679-80 (8th Cir. 1994); *United States v. Koyomejian*, 970 F.2d 536, 538 (9th Cir. 1992); *United States v. Biasucci*, 786 F.2d 505, 508-509 (2d Cir. 1986); *United States v. Torres*, 751 F.2d 875, 880-81 (7th Cir. 1984).

72 "'[O]ral communication' means any oral communication uttered by a person exhibiting an expectation that such communication is not subject to interception under circumstances justifying such expectation, but such term does not include any electronic communication," 18 U.S.C. 2510(2). *United States v. Larios*, 593 F.3d 82, 92 (1st Cir. 2010)(emphasis in the original but most internal quotation marks and citations omitted)(The "legislative history of this statutory provision shows that Congress intended this definition to parallel the 'reasonable expectation of privacy test' articulated by the Supreme Court in *Katz*. Thus, for Title III to apply, the court must conclude: (1) the defendant had an actual, subjective expectation of privacy—*i.e.*, that his communications were not subject to interception; and (2) the defendant's expectation is one society would objectively consider reasonable.... We conclude that the most reasonable reading of the statute is that the meaning of 'oral communication' was intended to parallel *evolving* Fourth Amendment jurisprudence on reasonable expectations of privacy in one's communications"); *Pattee v. Georgia Ports Authority*, 512 F.Supp.2d 1372, 1376-377 (S.D.Ga. 2007).

73 "'[W]ire communication' means any aural transfer made in whole or in part through the use of facilities for the transmission of communications by the aid of wire, cable, or other like connection between the point of origin and the point of reception (including the use of such connection in a switching station) furnished or operated by any person engaged in providing or operating such facilities for the transmission of interstate or foreign communications or communications affecting interstate or foreign commerce," 18 U.S.C. 2510(1).

74 "'[E]lectronic communication' means any transfer of signs, signals, writing, images, sounds, data, or intelligence of any nature transmitted in whole or in part by a wire, radio, electromagnetic, photoelectronic or photooptical system that affects interstate or foreign commerce, but does not include—(A) the radio portion of a cordless telephone communication that is transmitted between the cordless handset and the base unit; (B) any wire or oral communication; (C) any communication made through a tone-only paging device; or (D) any communication from a tracking device (as defined in section 3117 of this title)," 18 U.S.C. 2510(12).

75 18 U.S.C. 2511(2)(g).

76 18 U.S.C. 2511(1).

77 18 U.S.C. 2512, discussed, *infra*.

78 *E.g.*, 47 U.S.C. 605 (1940 ed.).

[79] *On Lee v. United States*, 343 U.S. 747 (1952); *Lopez v. United States*, 373 U.S. 427 (1963); *United States v. White*, 401 U.S. 745 (1971).

[80] *United States v. White*, 401 U.S. at 751 (1971)("Concededly a police agent who conceals his police connections may write down for official use his conversations with a defendant and testify concerning them, without a warrant authorizing his encounters with the defendant and without otherwise violating the latter's Fourth Amendment rights.... For constitutional purposes, no different result is required if the agent instead of immediately reporting and transcribing his conversations with defendant, either (1) simultaneously records them with electronic equipment which he is carrying on his person, *Lopez v. United States, supra*; (2) or carries radio equipment which simultaneously transmits the conversations either to recording equipment located elsewhere or to other agents monitoring the transmitting frequency. *On Lee v. United States, supra.* If the conduct and revelations of an agent operating without electronic equipment do not invade the defendant's constitutionally justifiable expectations of privacy, neither does a simultaneous recording of the same conversations made by the agent or by others from transmissions received from the agent to whom the defendant is talking and whose trustworthiness the defendant necessarily risks"); *Lopez v. United States* 373 U.S. 427, 439 (1963)("Stripped to its essentials, petitioner's argument amounts to saying that he has a constitutional right to rely on possible flaws in the agent's memory, or to challenge the agent's credibility without being beset by corroborating evidence that is not susceptible of impeachment. For no other argument can justify excluding an accurate version of a conversation that the agent could testify to from memory. We think the risk that petitioner took in offering a bribe to Davis fairly included the risk that the offer would be accurately reproduced in court, whether by faultless memory or mechanical recording").

[81] "(c) It shall not be unlawful under this chapter for a person acting under color of law to intercept a wire, oral, or electronic communication, where such person is a party to the communication or one of the parties to the communication has given prior consent to such interception.

"(d) It shall not be unlawful under this chapter for a person not acting under color of law to intercept a wire, oral, or electronic communication where such person is a party to the communication or where one of the parties to the communication has given prior consent to such interception unless such communication is intercepted for the purpose of committing any criminal or tortious act in violation of the Constitution or laws of the United States or of any State," 18 U.S.C. 2511(2)(c), (d).

[82] For citations to state law, *see*, **Appendix B.**

[83] *United States v. Verdin-Garcia*, 516 F.3d 884, 894-95 (10th Cir. 2008) (inmate use of prison phone); *United States v. Friedman*, 300 F.3d 111, 122-23 (2d Cir. 2002)(same); *United States v. Hammond*, 286 F.3d 189, 192 (4th Cir. 2002) (same); *United States v. Footman*, 215 F.3d 145, 154-55 (1st Cir. 2000) (same); *Griggs-Ryan v. Smith*, 904 F.2d 112, 116-17 (1st Cir. 1990) (use of landlady's phone); *United States v. Rivera*, 292 F. Supp.2d 838, 843-45 (E.D.Va. 2003) (inmate use of prison phone monitored by private contractors); *see also, United States v. Conley*, 531 F.3d 56, 58-9 (1st Cir. 2008)(explicit consent as a condition for phone privileges).

[84] *Anthony v. United States*, 667 F.2d 870, 876 (10th Cir. 1981).

[85] *United States v. Antoon*, 933 F.2d 200, 203-204 (3d Cir. 1991). *But see, O'Ferrell v. United States*, 968 F.Supp. 1519, 1541 (M.D.Ala. 1997) (an individual who spoke to his wife on the telephone after being told by FBI agents who were then executing a search warrant at his place of business that he could only speak to her with the agents listening in consented to the interception, even if FBI's initial search was unconstitutional).

[86] 18 U.S.C. 2511(2)(d); *United States v. Lam*, 271 F.Supp.2d 1182, 1183-184 (N.D.Cal. 2003).

[87] *Caro v. Weintraub*, 618 F.3d 94, 100 (2d Cir. 2010)("We join the courts that have considered this question, and hold that a cause of action under §2511(2)(d) requires that the interceptor intend to commit a crime or tort independent of the act of recording itself"), citing, *Desnick v. American Broadcasting Co.*, 44 F.3d 1345, 1347-48 (7th Cir. 1995); *Sussman v. American Broadcasting Co*, 186 F.3d 1200, 1201 (9th Cir. 1999).

[88] S.Rept. 99-541, at 17-8 (1986); H.Rept. 99-647, at 39-40 (1986).

[89] "(g) It shall not be unlawful under this chapter or chapter 121 of this title for any person—(i) to intercept or access an electronic communication made through an electronic communication system that is configured so that such electronic communication is readily accessible to the general public;

"(ii) to intercept any radio communication which is transmitted—(I) by any station for the use of the general public, or that relates to ships, aircraft, vehicles, or persons in distress; (II) by any governmental, law enforcement, civil defense, private land mobile, or public safety communications system, including police and fire, readily accessible to the general public; (III) by a station operating on an authorized frequency within the bands allocated to the amateur, citizens band, or general mobile radio services; or (IV) by any marine or aeronautical communications system;

"(iii) to engage in any conduct which—(I) is prohibited by section 633 of the Communications Act of 1934; or (II) is excepted from the application of section 705(a) of the Communications Act of 1934 by section 705(b) of that Act;

"(iv) to intercept any wire or electronic communication the transmission of which is causing harmful interference to any lawfully operating station or consumer electronic equipment, to the extent necessary to identify the source of such interference; or "(v) for other users of the same frequency to intercept any radio communication made through a system that utilizes frequencies monitored by individuals engaged in the provision or the use of such system, if such communication is not scrambled or encrypted," 18 U.S.C. 2511(2)(g).

[90] "*Except as otherwise specifically provided in this chapter* any person who (a) intentionally intercepts.... " 18 U.S.C. 2511(1)(emphasis added).

[91] "Notwithstanding any other provision of this chapter, any investigative or law enforcement officer, specially designated by the Attorney General, the Deputy Attorney General, the Associate Attorney General, or by the principal prosecuting attorney of any State or subdivision thereof acting pursuant to a statute of that State, who reasonably determines that—(a) an emergency situation exists that involves—(i) immediate danger of death or serious physical injury to any person, (ii) conspiratorial activities threatening the national security interest, or (iii) conspiratorial activities characteristic of organized crime, [—] that requires a wire, oral, or electronic communication to be intercepted before an order authorizing such interception can, with due diligence, be obtained, and (b) there are grounds upon which an order could be entered under this chapter to authorize such interception, may intercept such wire, oral, or electronic communication if an application for an order approving the interception is made in accordance with this section within forty-eight hours after the interception has occurred, or begins to occur. In the absence of an order, such interception shall immediately terminate when the communication sought is obtained or when the application for the order is denied, whichever is earlier. In the event such application for approval is denied, or in any other case where the interception is terminated without an order having been issued, the contents of any wire, oral, or electronic communication intercepted shall be treated as having been obtained in violation of this chapter, and an inventory shall be served as provided for in subsection (d) of this section on the person named in the application," 18 U.S.C. 2518(7).

[92] "(i) It shall not be unlawful under this chapter for a person acting under color of law to intercept the wire or electronic communications of a computer trespasser transmitted to, through, or from the protected computer, if—(I) the owner or operator of the protected computer authorizes the interception of the computer trespasser's communications on the protected computer; (II) the person acting under color of law is lawfully engaged in an investigation; (III) the person acting under color of law has reasonable grounds to believe that the contents of the computer trespasser's communications will be relevant to the investigation; and (IV) such interception does not acquire communications other than those transmitted to or from the computer trespasser," 18 U.S.C. 2511(2)(i).

[93] "(e) Notwithstanding any other provision of this title or section 705 or 706 of the Communications Act of 1934, it shall not be unlawful for an officer, employee, or agent of the United States in the normal course of his official duty to conduct electronic surveillance, as defined in section 101 of the Foreign Intelligence Surveillance Act of 1978, as authorized by that Act," 18 U.S.C. 2511(2)(e).

[94] "(h) It shall not be unlawful under this chapter—(I) to use a pen register or a trap and trace device (as those terms are defined for the purpose of chapter 206)...." 18 U.S.C. 2511(2)(h). Neither the stored communications sections in chapter 121 nor the pen register and trap and trace device in chapter 206 authorize the contemporaneous interception of the contents of a communication. For the citations to state statutes permitting judicial authorization of law enforcement interception of wire, oral, or electronic communications, for access to stored electronic communications, and for the use of pen registers and trap and trace devices, *see*, Appendix D.

[95] "(a)(i) It shall not be unlawful under this chapter for an operator of a switchboard, or an officer, employee, or agent of a provider of wire or electronic communication service, whose facilities are used in the transmission of a wire orel ectronic communication, to intercept, disclose, or use that communication in the normal course of his employment while engaged in any activity which is a necessary incident to the rendition of his service or to the protection of the rights or property of the provider of that service, except that a provider of wire communication service to the public shall not utilize service observing or random monitoring except for mechanical or service quality control checks....

"(h) It shall not be unlawful under this chapter ...

"(ii) for a provider of electronic communication service to record the fact that a wire or electronic communication was initiated or completed in order to protect such provider, another provider furnishing service toward the completion of the wire or electronic communication, or a user of that service, from fraudulent, unlawful or abusive use of such service," 18 U.S.C. 2511(2)(a)(I), (h).

[96] "(ii) Notwithstanding any other law, providers of wire or electronic communication service, their officers, employees, and agents, landlords, custodians, or other persons, are authorized to provide information, facilities, or technical assistance to persons authorized by law to intercept wire, oral, or electronic communications or to conduct electronic surveillance, as defined in section 101 of the Foreign Intelligence Surveillance Act of 1978, if such provider, its officers, employees, or agents, landlord, custodian, or other specified person, has been provided with—

(A) a court order directing such assistance signed by the authorizing judge, or

(B) a certification in writing by a person specified in section 2518(7) of this title or the Attorney General of the United States that no warrant or court order is required by law, that all statutory requirements have been met, and that the specified assistance is required,

setting forth the period of time during which the provision of the information, facilities, or technical assistance is authorized and specifying the information, facilities, or technical assistance required. No provider of wire or electronic communication service, officer, employee, or agent thereof, or landlord, custodian, or other specified person shall disclose the existence of any interception or surveillance or the device used to accomplish the interception or surveillance with respect to which the person has been furnished a court order or certification under this chapter, except as may otherwise be required by legal process and then only after prior notification to the Attorney General or to the principal prosecuting attorney of a State or any political subdivision of a State, as may be appropriate. Any such disclosure, shall render such person liable for the civil damages provided for in section 2520. No cause of action shall lie in any court against any provider of wire or electronic communication service, its officers, employees, or agents, landlord, custodian, or other specified person for providing information, facilities, or assistance in accordance with the terms of a court order, statutory authorization, or certification under this chapter," 18 U.S.C. 2511(2)(a)(ii).

[97] "(b) It shall not be unlawful under this chapter for an officer, employee, or agent of the Federal Communications Commission, in the normal course of his employment and in discharge of the monitoring responsibilities exercised by the Commission in the enforcement of chapter 5 of title 47 of the United States Code, to intercept a wire or electronic communication, or oral communication transmitted by radio, or to disclose or use the information thereby obtained," 18 U.S.C. 2511(2)(b).

[98] *Pollock v. Pollock*, 154 F.3d 601, 611 (8th Cir. 1998); *Wagner v. Wagner*, 64 F.Supp.2d 895, 889-901 (D.Minn. 1999); *Campbell v. Price*, 2 F.Supp.2d 1186, 1191-192 (E.D.Ark. 1998); *Thompson v. Dulaney*, 838 F.Supp. 1535,1544-45 (D.Utah 1993); cf., *Babb v. Eagleton*, 616 F.Supp.2d 1195, 1205-206 (N.D.Okla. 2007).

[99] *Glazner v. Glazner*, 347 F.3d 1212, 1215-16 (11th Cir. 2003); *Heggy v. Heggy*, 944 F.2d 1537, 1539 (10th Cir. 1991); *Kempf v. Kempf*, 868 F.2d 970, 972 (8th Cir. 1989); *Pritchard v. Pritchard*, 732 F.2d 372, 374 (4th Cir. 1984); *UnitedStates v. Jones*, 542 F.2d 661, 667 (6th Cir. 1976); *Kratz v. Kratz*, 477 F.Supp. 463, 467-70 (E.D.Pa. 1979); *Heyman v.Heyman*, 548 F.Supp. 1041, 1045-47 (N.D.Ill.1982); *Lombardo v. Lombardo*, 192 F.Supp.2d 885, 809 (N.D.Ill. 2002).

[100] *Simpson v. Simpson*, 490 F.2d 803, 809 (5th Cir. 1974); *Perfit v. Perfit*, 693 F.Supp. 851, 854-56 (C.D.Cal. 1988); *see generally, Applicability, in Civil Action, of Provisions of Omnibus Crime Control and Safe Streets Act of 1968 Prohibiting Interception of Communications (18 USCS §2511(1)), to Interception by Spouse, or Spouse's Agent, of Conversations of Other Spouse*, 139 ALR Fed. 517, and the cases discussed therein.

[101] *Anonymous v. Anonymous*, 558 F.2d 677, 678-79 (2d Cir. 1977); *Scheib v. Grant*, 22 F.3d 149, 154 (7th Cir. 1994); *Newcomb v. Ingle*, 944 F.2d 1534, 1536 (10th Cir. 1991); cf., *Babb v. Eagleton*, 616 F.Supp.2d 1195, 1203-205 (N.D. Okla. 2007); *contra, United States v. Murdock*, 63 F.3d 1391, 1400 (6th Cir. 1995).

[102] 18 U.S.C. 2511(1)(c).

[103] *McCann v. Iroquois Memorial Hospital*, 622 F.3d 745, 753 (7th Cir. 2010), citing, *Nix v. O'Malley*, 160 F.3d 343, 348 (6th Cir. 1998); *Williams v. Poulos*, 11 F.3d 271, 284 (1st Cir. 1993); and *Thompson v. Dulaney*, 970 F.2d 744, 749 (10th Cir. 1992).

[104] *Bartnicki v. Vopper*, 532 U.S. 514, 533-34 (2001). Bartnicki was a union negotiator whose telephone conversations with the union's president concerning teachers' contract negotiations were surreptitiously intercepted and recorded. During the conversation, the possibility of using violence against school board members was mentioned. After the teachers' contract was signed, the unknown wiretapper secretly supplied Yocum, a critic of the union's position, with a copy of the tape. Yocum in turn played it for members of the school board and turned it over to Vopper, a radio talk show host, who played it on his show. Other stations and media outlets published the contents as well. Bartnicki sued Vopper and Yocum for use and disclosure in violation of sections 2511(1)(c) and 2511(1)(d). Vopper and Yocum offered a free speech defense, which the Supreme Court accepted. *But see*, *Quigley v. Rosenthal*, 327 F.3d 1044, 1067-68 (10th Cir. 2003) (denying First Amendment protection for those knowingly involved with interceptors of private matters (not public concerns)); *Boehner v. McDermott*, 484 F.3d 573, 577-81 (D.C.Cir. 2007)(Members of Congress do not have a First Amendment right to disclose unlawful wiretap information in violation of House rules).

[105] "Subparagraphs (c) and (d) prohibit, in turn, the disclosure or use of the contents of any intercepted communication by any person knowing or having reason to know the information was obtained through an interception in violation of this subsection. The disclosure of the contents of an intercepted communication that had already become 'public information' or 'common knowledge' would not be prohibited. The scope of this knowledge required to violate either subparagraph reflects existing law (*Pereira v. United States*, 347 U.S. 1 (1954))," S.Rept. 90-1097, at 93 (1967).

[106] "Any investigative or law enforcement officer who, by any means authorized by this chapter, has obtained knowledge of the contents of any wire, oral, or electronic communication, or evidence derived therefrom, may disclose such contents to another investigative or law enforcement officer to the extent that such disclosure is appropriate to the proper performance of the official duties of the officer making or receiving the disclosure," 18 U.S.C. 2517(1).

[107] "Any person who has received, by any means authorized by this chapter, any information concerning a wire, oral, or electronic communication, or evidence derived therefrom intercepted in accordance with the provisions of this chapter may disclose the contents of that communication or such derivative evidence while giving testimony under oath or affirmation in any proceeding held under the authority of the United States or of any State or political subdivision thereof," 18 U.S.C. 2517(3). This does not entitle private litigants to disclosure in the view of at least one court, *In re Motion to Unseal Electronic Surveillance Evidence*, 990 F.2d 1015 (8th Cir. 1993).

When court-ordered interception results in evidence of a crime other than the crime with respect to which the order was issued, the evidence is admissible only upon a judicial finding that it was otherwise secured in compliance with Title III/ECPA requirements, 18 U.S.C. 2517(5).

[108] 18 U.S.C. 2511(1)(e). When acting with a similar intent, disclosure of the *fact* of authorized federal wiretap or foreign intelligence gathering is proscribed elsewhere in title 18: "Whoever, having knowledge that a Federal investigative or law enforcement officer has been authorized or has applied for authorization under chapter 119 to intercept a wire, oral, or electronic communication, in order to obstruct, impede, or prevent such interception, gives notice or attempts to give notice of the possible interception to any person shall be fined under this title or imprisoned not more than five years, or both," 18 U.S.C. 2232(d).

"Whoever, having knowledge that a Federal officer has been authorized or has applied for authorization to conduct electronic surveillance under the Foreign Intelligence Surveillance Act of 1978 (50 U.S.C. 1801, et seq.), in order to obstruct, impede, or prevent such activity, gives notice or attempts to give notice of the possible activity to any person shall be fined under this title or imprisoned not more than five years, or both," 18 U.S.C. 2232(e).

[109] 18 U.S.C. 2511(1)(e), (4)(a), 2520(a), (g).

[110] 18 U.S.C. 2516(2).

[111] *Id.*

[112] 18 U.S.C. 2511(3)(a) ("Except as provided in paragraph (b) of this subsection, a person or entity providing an electronic communication service to the public shall not intentionally divulge the contents of any communication (other than one to such person or entity, or an agent thereof) while in transmission on that service to any person or entity other than an addressee or intended recipient of such communication or an agent of such addressee or intended recipient").

[113] 18 U.S.C. 2511(3)(b) ("A person or entity providing electronic communication service to the public may divulge the contents of any such communication—(i) as otherwise authorized in section 2511(2)(a) or 2517 of this title; (ii) with the lawful consent of the originator or any addressee or intended recipient of such communication; (iii) to a person employed or authorized, or whose facilities are used, to forward such communication to its destination; or (iv) which were inadvertently obtained by the service provider and which appear to pertain to the commission of a crime, if such divulgence is made to a law enforcement agency").

[114] Note that subsection 2520(d) establishes a good faith defense that specifically references the prohibition: "A good faith reliance on ... (3) a good faith determination that section 2511(3) ... of this title permitted the conduct complained of; is a complete defense against any civil or criminal action brought under this chapter.... "

[115] 18 U.S.C. 2511(1)(d).

[116] *See e.g., McCann v. Iroquois Memorial Hospital*, 622 F.3d 745, 753-54 (7th Cir. 2010).

[117] "Subparagraphs (c) and (d) prohibit, in turn, the disclosure or use of the contents of any intercepted communication by any person knowing or having reason to know the information was obtained through an interception in violation of this subsection," S.Rept. 90-1097, at 93 (1967).

[118] *Compare*, 18 U.S.C. 2517(1)("Any investigative or law enforcement officer who, by any means authorized by this chapter, has obtained knowledge of the contents of any wire, oral, or electronic communication, or evidence derived therefrom, may disclose such contents to another investigative or law enforcement officer to the extent that such disclosure is appropriate to the proper performance of the official duties of the officer making or receiving the disclosure"), *with* 18 U.S.C. 2517(2)("Any investigative or law enforcement officer who, by any means authorized by this chapter, has obtained knowledge of the contents of any wire, oral, or electronic communication or evidence derived therefrom may use such contents to the extent such use is appropriate to the proper performance of his official duties").

On the other hand, the Supreme Court in *Bartnicki* seemed to parse the constitutionally suspect ban on disclosure from the constitutionally permissible ban on use. *Bartnicki v. Vopper*, 532 U.S. 514, 526-27 (2001)("[T]he naked prohibition against disclosures is fairly characterized as a regulation of pure speech. Unlike the prohibition against the ‘use' of the contents of an illegal interception in §2511(1)(d), subsection (c) is not a regulation of conduct").

[119] *Forsyth v. Barr*, 19 F.3d 1527, 1541-545 (5th Cir. 1994); *United States v. Murdock*, 63 F.3d 1391, 1400-403 (6th Cir. 1995); *contra, United States v. Crabtree*, 565 F.3d 887, 889 (4th Cir. 2009); *Berry v. Funk*, 146 F.3d 1003, 1011-13 (D.C.Cir. 1998); *Chandler v. United States Army*, 125 F.3d 1296, 1300-302 (9th Cir. 1997); *In re Grand Jury*, 111 F.3d 1066, 1077 (3d Cir. 1997); *United States v. Vest*, 813 F.2d 477, 481 (1st Cir. 1987).

[120] 18 U.S.C. 2511(4), 2520(a), (g).

[121] "It shall not be unlawful under this section for—(a) a provider of wire or electronic communication service or an officer, agent, or employee of, or a person under contract with, such a provider, in the normal course of the business of providing that wire or electronic communication service ... to send through the mail, send or carry in interstate or foreign commerce, or manufacture, assemble, possess, or sell any electronic, mechanical, or other device knowing or having reason to know that the design of such device renders it primarily useful for the purpose of the surreptitious interception of wire, oral, or electronic communications," 18 U.S.C. 2512(2)(a).

[122] "(2) It shall not be unlawful under this section for ... (b) an officer, agent, or employee of, or a person under contract with, the United States, a State, or a political subdivision thereof, in the normal course of the activities of the United States, a State, or a political subdivision thereof, to send through the mail, send or carry in interstate or foreign commerce, or manufacture, assemble, possess, or sell any electronic, mechanical, or other device knowing or having reason to know that the design of such device renders it primarily useful for the purpose of the surreptitious interception of wire, oral, or electronic communications.

"(3) It shall not be unlawful under this section to advertise for sale a device described in subsection (1) of this section if the advertisement is mailed, sent, or carried in interstate or foreign commerce solely to a domestic provider of wire or electronic communication service or to an agency of the United States, a State, or a political subdivision thereof whichis duly authorized to use such device," 18 U.S.C. 2512(2)(b),(3).

[123] *United States v. Spy Factory, Inc.*, 951 F.Supp. 450, 473-75 (S.D.N.Y. 1997); *United States v. Bast*, 495 F.2d 138, 141 (D.C.Cir. 1974).

[124] *United States v. Simels*, 654 F.3d 161, 171 (2d Cir. 2011).

[125] 18 U.S.C. 2512.

[126] S.Rept. 90-1097, at 95 (1968).

[127] The two appellate panel decisions that found the devices beyond the bounds of section 2512, *United States v. Herring*, 933 F.2d 932 (11th Cir. 1991) and *United States v. Hux*, 940 F.2d 314 (8th Cir. 1991) were overturned en banc, *United States v. Herring*, 993 F.2d 784, 786 (11th Cir. 1993); *United States v. Davis*, 978 F.2d 415, 416 (8th Cir. 1992).

[128] *United States v. Harrell*, 983 F.2d 36, 37-39 (5th Cir. 1993); *United States v. One Macom Video Cipher II*, 985 F.2d 258, 259-61 (6th Cir. 1993); *United States v. Shriver*, 989 F.2d. 898, 901-06 (7th Cir. 1992); *United States v. Davis*, 978 F.2d 415, 417-20 (8th Cir. 1992); *United States v. Lande*, 968 F.2d 907, 910-11 (9th Cir. 1992); *United States v. McNutt*, 908 F.2d 561, 564-65 (10th Cir. 1990); *United States v. Herring*, 993 F.2d 784, 786-89 (11th Cir. 1991).

[129] *DirecTV, Inc. v. Treworgy*, 373 F.3d 1124, 1129 (11th Cir. 2004); *DirecTV, Inc. v. Robson*, 420 F.3d 532, 538-39 (5th Cir. 2005)(citing several district court cases that have reached the same conclusion). Proof that the possessor used the device to intercept satellite transmission evidences a violation of section 2511 and exposure to civil liability under section 2520, *DirecTV, Inc. v. Nicholas*, 403 F.3d 223, 227-28 (4th Cir. 2005); *DirecTV, Inc. v. Pepe*, 431 F.3d 162, 169 (3d Cir. 2005).

[130] 18 U.S.C. 2516-2518.

[131] 18 U.S.C. 2511(2)(c).

[132] 18 U.S.C. 2511(2)(i)("It shall not be unlawful under this chapter for a person acting under color of law to intercept the wire or electronic communications of a computer trespasser transmitted to, through, or from the protected computer, if—(I) the owner or operator of the protected computer authorizes the interception of the computer trespasser's communications on the protected computer; (II) the person acting under color of law is lawfully engaged in an investigation; (III) the person acting under color of law has reasonable grounds to believe that the contents of the computer trespasser's communications will be relevant to the investigation; and (IV) such interception does not acquire communications other than those transmitted to or from the computer trespasser").

A computer trespasser is a person who: (A) "accesses a protected computer without authorization and thus has no reasonable expectation of privacy in any communication transmitted to, through, or from the protected computer; and

(B) does not include a person known by the owner or operator of the protected computer to have an existing contractual relationship with the owner or operator of the protected computer for access to all or part of the protected computer," 18 U.S.C. 2510(21).

[133] "The Attorney General, Deputy Attorney General, Associate Attorney General, or any Assistant Attorney General, any acting Assistant Attorney General, or any Deputy Assistant Attorney General or acting Deputy Assistant Attorney General in the Criminal Division specially designated by the Attorney General, may authorize an application to a Federal judge of competent jurisdiction for, and such judge may grant in conformity with section 2518 of this chapter an order authorizing or approving the interception of wire or oral communications by the Federal Bureau of Investigation, or a Federal agency having responsibility for the investigation of the offense as to which the application is made, when such interception may provide or has provided evidence of [the predicate offenses]...." 18 U.S.C. 2516(1).

Subsection 2516(1) "plainly calls for the prior, informed judgment of enforcement officers desiring court approval for intercept authority, and investigative personnel may not themselves ask a judge for authority to wiretap or eavesdrop. The mature judgment of a particular, responsible Department of Justice official is interposed as a critical precondition of any judicial order," *United States v. Giordano*, 416 U.S. 505, 515-16 (1974). Evidence generated without such senior approval must be suppressed, *id.* at 23. However, "suppression is not warranted ... when a wiretap application or order either misidentifies a DOJ official who could not legally authorize the wiretap or, ... identifies no official at all, so long as the record shows that a statutorily designated official actually gave the authorization," *United States v. Gray*, 521 F.3d 514, 526-27 (6th Cir. 2008), *citing in accord, United States v. Callum*, 410 F.3d 571, 576 (9th Cir. 2005); *United States v. Radcliff*, 331 F.3d 1153, 1160-163 (10th Cir. 2003); *United States v. Fudge*, 325 F.3d 910, 918 (7th Cir. 2003).

[134] The list appears in 18 U.S.C. 2516(1).

[135] 18 U.S.C. 2516(1)(*l*).

[136] "Any attorney for the Government (as such term is defined for the purposes of the Federal Rules of Criminal Procedure) may authorize an application to a Federal judge of competent jurisdiction for, and such judge may grant, inconformity with section 2518 of this title, an order authorizing or approving the interception of electronic communications by an investigative or law enforcement officer having responsibility for the investigation of the offense as to which the application is made, when such interception may provide or has provided evidence of any Federal felony," 18 U.S.C. 2516(3); *e.g., United States v. Benjamin*, 72 F.Supp.2d 161, 189 (W.D.N.Y. 1999).

[137] 18 U.S.C. 2516(2).

[138] Identification of the place where, or facilities over which, the targeted communications are to occur may be excused where the court finds that the suspect has or will take steps to thwart interception, 18 U.S.C. 2518(11), (12); *United States v. Oliva*, 686 F.3d 1106, 1109-110 (9th Cir. 2012).

[139] 18 U.S.C. 2518(1), (2).

[140] 18 U.S.C. 2518(3). Paragraphs 2518(3)(a) and (b) mirror the probable demands of the Fourth Amendment, *i.e.*, that the court find probable cause to believe that the interception will capture evidence of a specific offense, *United States v.Abu-Jihaad*, 630 F.3d 102, 122 (2d Cir. 2010), *citing, Dalia v. United States*, 441 U.S. 238, 255 (1979). Title III,however, provides its own particularity requirements relating to targets, facilities, locations, and crimes, *United States v. Gaines*, 639 F.3d 423, 430 (8th Cir. 2011), *citing inter alia, United States v. Donovan*, 429 U.S. 413, 427 n.15 (1977).

[141] 18 U.S.C. 2518(3). As for the necessity requirement of paragraph 2518(3)(c), the Supreme Court explained in the infancy of Title III that: "[I]t is at once apparent that [Title III] not only limits the crimes for which intercept authority may be obtained but also imposes important preconditions to obtaining any intercept authority at all. Congress legislated in considerable detail in providing for applications and orders authorizing wiretapping and evinced the clear intent to make doubly sure that the statutory authority be used with restraint and only where the circumstances warrant the surreptitious interception of wire and oral communications. These procedures were not to be routinely employed as the initial step in criminal investigation. Rather, the applicant must state and the court must find that normal investigative procedures have been tried and failed or reasonably appear to be unlikely to succeed if tried or to be too dangerous. §§2518(1)(c) and (3)(c)," *United States v. Giordano*, 416 U.S. 505, 515 (1974).

Thus, "[t]he necessity requirement was intended to ensure that wiretaps are not used as the initial step in a criminal investigation. However, officials need not exhaust every conceivable investigative technique before obtaining a wiretap." *United States v. Forrester*, 616 F.3d 929, 944 (9th Cir. 2010)(internal citations omitted); *see also*, United States v. Long, 639 F.3d 293, 301 (7th Cir. 2011)(internal citations omitted)("While this necessity requirement discourages the use of wiretaps as a first-line investigative tool in the mine run of cases, it was not intended to ensure that wiretaps are used only as a last resort in an investigation. Hence, the government's burden of establishing necessity is not high, and whether it met the burden is reviewed in a practical, common-sense fashion"); *United States v. Glover*, 681 F.3d 411, 420 (D.C.Cir. 2012)("That [necessity] requirement is satisfied when traditional investigative techniques have proved inadequate to reveal the operation's full nature and scope"); *United States v. Perez*, 661 F.3d 568, 581 (1st Cir. 2011); *United States v. Foy*, 641 F.3d 455, 464 (10th Cir. 2011); *United States v. Wilson*, 484 F.3d 267, 281 (4th Cir. 2007).

[142] Under subsection 2518(5), officers executing an interception order must make efforts to minimize the capture of communications that are outside the scope of the orders; *United States v. De La Cruz Suarez*, 601 F.3d 1202, 1215 (11th Cir. 2010). Whether their efforts are sufficient is matter governed by the circumstances surrounding the interception, *Scott v. United States*, 436 U.S. 128, 135-37 (1978); *United States v. Glover*, 681 F.3d 411, 420-21 (D.C. Cir. 2012);*United States v. West*, 589 F.3d 936, 939-40 (8th Cir. 2009); *United States v. Yarbrough*, 527 F.3d 1092, 1098 (10th Cir.2008)("In *United States v. Willis*, this court articulated the proper procedure for determining the reasonableness of governmental efforts to avoid monitoring non-pertinent calls. 890 F.2d 1099, 1102 (10th Cir. 1989). The government must make an initial prima facie showing of reasonable minimization. *Id.* 'Once the government has made a prima facie showing of reasonable minimization, the burden then shifts to the defendant to show more effective minimization couldhave taken place." *Id.* In determining whether the government has made a prima facie showing of reasonable efforts to minimize the interception of non-pertinent calls, we consider the factors identified by the Supreme Court in *Scott*: (1)whether a large number of the calls are very short, one-time only, or in guarded or coded language; (2) the

breadth ofthe investigation underlying the need for the wiretap; (3) whether the phone is public or private; and (4) whether thenon-minimized calls occurred early in the surveillance. 436 U.S. at 140-41. It is also appropriate to consider (5) theextent to which the authorizing judge supervised the ongoing wiretap. *United States v. Lopez*, 300 F.3d 46, 57 (1st Cir.2002); *United States v. Daly*, 535 F.2d 434, 442 (8th Cir. 1976); *United States v. Vento*, 533 F.2d 838, 853 (3d Cir.1976)").

[143] 18 U.S.C. 2518(4).

[144] 18 U.S.C. 2518(7). An observation made a quarter of a century ago remains true: "very little case-law inter pretation of the emergency requirement exists," *United States v. Crouch*, 666 F.Supp. 1414, 1416 (N.D. Cal. 1987)(holding that twenty-day-old information indicating the defendants would commit a bank robbery within the next sixty days did not constitute a sufficient emergency to justify invocation of subsection 2518(7)); *but see*, *Nabozny v. Marshall*, 781 F.2d 83, 84-5 (6th Cir. 1986)(holding with respect to a hostage situation "an emergency situation existed within the terms ofthe statute").

[145] 18 U.S.C. 2518(5).

[146] 18 U.S.C. 2518(6).

[147] 18 U.S.C. 2518(8)(a),(b). Paragraph 2518(8)(a) requires that court ordered interceptions be recorded and that the recording immediately be sealed by the court, upon expiration of the interception authority. The seal or a satisfactory explanation for its absence is a prerequisite to the admissibility of the contents or anything derived from the contents as evidence.

"The 'absence' the Government must satisfactorily explain encompasses not only the total absence of a seal but also the absence of a timely applied seal," *United States v. Ojeda Rios,* 495 U.S. 257, 263 (1990). "[T]he 'satisfactory explanation' language in §2518(8)(a) must be understood to require that the Government explain not only why a delay occurred but also why it is excusable," *Id.* at 265; *United States v. Martin*, 618 F.3d 705, 716, 718 (7th Cir. 2010)(some internal citations omitted)("[W]hat should be deemed 'satisfactory' in the context of a statute aimed at preventing government tampering with electronic evidence must depend largely on the statutory objective. A satisfactory explanation must dispel any reasonable suspicion of tampering, and also must be both accurate and believable. Whether the explanation is satisfactory also may depend on the delay in sealing, unique pressure on the Government to obtain a conviction due to particularly notorious charges or defendants, the importance of the recordings to the Government's case and whether the Government has established a procedure for complying with its sealing obligations.... *Cf. United States v. Quintero*, 38 F.3d 1317, 1328-330 (3d Cir. 1994) (rejecting the prosecutor's heavy workload as a satisfactory explanation for a sealing delay because to do so 'would be rendering extraordinary that which is ordinary'); *United States v. Carson*, 969 F.2d 1480, 1498 (3d Cir. 1992) (rejecting the need to enhance the audibility of tapes as a satisfactory explanation for a sealing delay because that need was "readily foreseeable and could just as readily become routine"); *but see, United States v. Bansal*, 663 F.3d 634, 651-53 (3d Cir. 2011)(finding the government's reasonable mistake of fact a satisfactory explanation for its failure to seal in a timely manner).

The section does not preclude use or disclosure other than admissibility of the intercepted contents in judicial proceedings, *United States v. A manuel*, 615 F.3d 117, 125-28 (2d Cir. 2010)(uphold the admissibility of evidence secured under a warrant based on interceptions that were recorded in violation of section 2518(8)(a)).

[148] 18 U.S.C. 2518(8)(d), (9).

[149] 18 U.S.C. 2517(1), (2), (5), (7). This includes the disclosures to a criminal defendant required in 18 U.S.C. 2518(9), cf., *SEC v. Rajaratnam*, 622 F.3d 159, 172-87 (2d Cir. 2010)(holding that a government attorney may disclose wiretap communications to a criminal defendant under 18 U.S.C. 2517(2) and that under some circumstances the defendant may be compelled to disclose them in the context of a governmental civil enforcement action).

[150] 18 U.S.C. 2517(6). "'[F]oreign intelligence information,' for purposes of section 2517(6) of this title, means—(A) information, whether or not concerning a United States person, that relates to the ability of the United States to protect against—(i) actual or potential attack or other grave hostile acts of a foreign power or an agent of a foreign power; (ii) sabotage or intentional terrorism by a foreign power or an agent of a foreign power; or (iii) clandestine intelligence activities by and intelligence service or network of a foreign power or by an agent of a foreign power; or (B) information, whether or not concerning a United States person, with respect to a foreign power or foreign territory that relates to—(i) the national defense or the security of the United States; or (ii) the conduct of the foreign affairs of the United States," 18 U.S.C. 2510(19).

[151] 18 U.S.C. 2518(8).

[152] 18 U.S.C. 2517(3), (5).

[153] 18 U.S.C. 2517(4).

[154] 18 U.S.C. 2511(2)(c).

[155] *United States v. Verdin-Garcia*, 516 F.3d 884, 894-95 (10th Cir. 2008) (inmate use of prison phone); *United States v. Friedman*, 300 F.3d 111, 122-23 (2d Cir. 2002)(same); *United States v. Hammond*, 286 F.3d 189, 192 (4th Cir. 2002) (same); *United States v. Footman*, 215 F.3d 145, 154-55 (1st Cir. 2000) (same); *Griggs-Ryan v. Smith*, 904 F.2d 112, 116-17 (1st Cir. 1990) (use of landlady's phone); *United States v. Rivera*, 292 F. Supp.2d 838, 843-45 (E.D.Va. 2003) (inmate use of prison phone monitored by private contractors); *see also*, *United States v. Conley*, 531 F.3d 56, 58-9 (1st Cir. 2008)(explicit consent as a condition for phone privileges).

[156] *Anthony v. United States*, 667 F.2d 870, 876 (10th Cir. 1981).

[157] *United States v. Antoon*, 933 F.2d 200, 203-204 (3d Cir. 1991). *But see, O'Ferrell v. United States*, 968 F.Supp. 1519, 1541 (M.D.Ala. 1997) (an individual who spoke to his wife on the telephone after being told by FBI agents who were then executing a search warrant at his place of business that he could only speak to her with the agents listening in consented to the interception, even if FBI's initial search was unconstitutional).

[158] *See, Clemnts-Jeffrey v. Springfield*, 810 F.Supp.2d 857, 871-72 (S.D.Ohio 2011)("As Plaintiffs correctly point out, §2511(2)(i) is completely inapposite because the Absolute Defendants, who intercepted Plaintiffs' electronic communications, were not 'acting under color of law'").

[159] Section 217, P.L. 107-56, 115 Stat. 291 (2001).

[160] *Implementation of the USA PATRIOT Act: Crime, Terrorism and the Age of Technology: Hearing Before the Subcomm. on Crime, Terrorism, and Homeland Security of the House Comm. on the Judiciary*, 109th Cong., 2d sess. 30-1 (2005)(prepared statement of FBI Dep. Ass't Director Steven M. Martinez).

[161] "Except as provided in (b) of this subsection or in subsection (5), whoever violates subsection (1) of this section shall be fined under this title* or imprisoned not more than five years, or both." 18 U.S.C. 2511(4)(a).
* Section 3559 of title 18 classifies as a felony any offense with a maximum penalty of imprisonment of more than one year; and as a Class A misdemeanor any offense with a maximum penalty of imprisonment set at between six months and one year. Unless Congress clearly rejects the general fine ceilings it provides, section 3571 of title 18 sets the fines for felonies at not more than $250,000 for individuals and not more than $500,000 for organizations, and for class A misdemeanors at not more than $100,000 for individuals and not more than $200,000 for organizations. If there is monetary loss or gain associated with the offense, the offender may alternatively be fined not more than twice the amount of the loss or gain, 18 U.S.C. 3571.

[162] 116 Stat. 2158 (2002).

[163] 18 U.S.C. 2511(4)(b)(2000 ed.).

[164] "(b) Conduct otherwise an offense under this subsection that consists of or relates to the interception of a satellite transmission that is not encrypted or scrambled and that is transmitted—(i) to a broadcasting station for purposes of retrains mission to the general public; or (ii) as an audio subcarrier intended for redistribution to facilities open to the public, but not including data transmissions or telephone calls, is not an offense under this subsection unless the conduct is for the purpose of direct or indirect commercial advantage or private financial gain," 18 U.S.C. 2511(4)(b).

[165] "(5)(a)(I) If the communication is—(A) a private satellite video communication that is not scrambled or encrypted and the conduct in violation of this chapter is the private viewing of that communication and is not for a tortious orillegal purpose or for purposes of direct or indirect commercial advantage or private commercial gain; or (B) a radio communication that is transmitted on frequencies allocated under subpart D of part 74 of the rules of the Federal Communications Commission that is not scrambled or encrypted and the conduct in violation of this chapter is not fortortious or illegal purpose or for purposes of direct or indirect commercial advantage or private commercial gain, then the person who engages in such conduct shall be subject to suit by the Federal Government in a court of competent jurisdiction. (ii) In an action under this subsection—(A) if the violation of this chapter is a first offense for the personunder paragraph (a) of subsection (4) and such person has not been found liable in a civil action under section 2520 of this title, the Federal Government shall be entitled to appropriate injunctive relief; and (B) if the violation of this chapter is a second or subsequent offense under paragraph (a) of subsection (4) or such person has been found liable in any prior civil action under section 2520, the person shall be subject to a mandatory $500 civil fine.
"(b) The court may use any means within its authority to enforce an injunction issued under paragraph (ii)(A), and shall impose a civil fine of not less than $500 for each violation of such an injunction." 18 U.S.C. 2511(5). Under 18 U.S.C. 2520, victims may recover the greater of actual damages or statutory damages of not less than $50 and not more than $500 for the first offense; those amounts are increased to $100 and $1000 for subsequent offenses.

[166] 18 U.S.C. 2513 ("Any electronic, mechanical, or other device used, sent, carried, manufactured, assembled, possessed, sold, or advertised in violation of section 2511 or section 2512 of this chapter may be seized and forfeited to the United States ... "); 18 U.S.C. 983(a)(3)(C)("In lieu of, or in addition to, filing a civil forfeiture complaint, the Government may include a forfeiture allegation in a criminal indictment ... ").

[167] "A good faith reliance on—(1) a court warrant or order, a grand jury subpoena, a legislative authorization, or a statutory authorization; (2) a request of an investigative or law enforcement officer under section 2518(7) of this title; or (3) a good faith determination that section 2511(3) [electronic communications provider authority to disclose content of an electronic communication "(i) as otherwise authorized in section 2511(2)(a) or 2517 of this title; (ii) with the lawful consent of the originator or any addressee or intended recipient of such communication; (iii) to a person employed or authorized, or whose facilities are used, to forward such communication to its destination; or (iv) which were inadvertently obtained by the service provider and which appear to pertain to the commission of a crime, if such divulgence is made to a law enforcement agency] or 2511(2)(I) [interception of communications of a trespasser in a computer system] of this title permitted the conduct complained of; is a complete defense against any civil or criminal action brought under this chapter or any other law," 18 U.S.C. 2520(d).

[168] The $10,000 lump sum for liquidated damages is limited to a single award per victim rather than permitting $10,000 multiples based on the number of violations or the number of types of violations, as long as the violations are "interrelated and time compacted," *Smoot v. United Transportation Union*, 246 F.3d 633, 642-645 (6th Cir. 2001); *Desilets v. Wal-Mart Stores, Inc.*, 171 F.3d 711, 713 (1st Cir. 1999); *see also, Dish Nework v. Delvecchio*, 831F.Supp.2d 595, 601 (W.D.N.Y. 2011)(""Although a range is given for violations under 2520(c)(1), Congress provided no such range under 2520(c)(2). Therefore, in the Court's view, the discretion provided to it allows it only to decide between no damages and $10,000").

[169] 18 U.S.C. 2520(b), (c).

[170] *Compare, e.g., DirecTV, Inc. v. Barczewski*, 604 F.3d 1004, 1006-1008 (7th Cir. 2010); *DirecTV, Inc. v. Brown*, 371 F.3d 814, 818 (11th Cir. 2004); *Dorris v. Absher*, 179 F.3d, 420, 429-30 (6th Cir. 1999); *Nalley v. Nalley*, 53 F.3d 649, 651-53 (4th Cir. 1995), *Reynolds v. Spears*, 93 F.3d 428, 433 (8th Cir. 1996); *DirecTV, Inc. v. Neznak*, 371 F.Supp.2d 130, 133-34 (D.Conn. 2005) (each concluding that courts have discretion), *with, Rodgers v. Wood*, 910 F.2d 444, 447-49 (7th Cir. 1990) and *Menda Biton v. Menda*, 812 F.Supp. 283, 284 (D. Puerto Rico 1993) (courts have no such discretion) (note that after *Menda*, the First Circuit in *Desilets v. Wal-Mart Stores, Inc.*, 171 F.3d at 716-17 treated as a matter for the trial court's discretion the question of whether the award of plaintiff's attorneys' fees should be reduced when punitive damages have been denied).
Section 2520(c) has a second statutory damage provision, available for violations involving private satellite videos or radio communications, 18 U.S.C. 2520(c)(1). This provision is more clearly mandatory (18 U.S.C. 2520(c)(1): "the court *shall* access damages" versus 18 U.S.C. 2520(c)(2): "the court *may* assess as damages")(emphasis added in both instances).

[171] *Adams v. Battle Creek*, 250 F.3d 980, 984 (6th Cir. 2001); *Organizacion JD Ltda. v. United States Department of Justice*, 18 F.3d 91, 94-5 (2d Cir. 1994); *Garza v. Bexar Metropolitan Water District*, 639 F.Supp.2d 770, 773-74 (W.D.Tex. 2009); *Connor v. Tate*, 130 F.Supp.2d 1370, 1374 (N.D.Ga. 2001); *Dorris v. Absher*, 959 F.Supp. 813, 820 (M.D.Tenn. 1997), *aff'd/rev'd in part on other grounds*, 179 F.3d 420 (6th Cir. 1999); *PBA Local No. 38 v. Woodbridge Police Department*, 832 F.Supp. 808, 822-23 (D.N.J. 1993) (each concluding that governmental entities may be held liable); *contra, Abbott v. Winthrop Harbor*, 205 F.3d 976, 980 (7th Cir. 2000); *Amati v. Woodstock*, 176 F.3d 952, 956 (7th Cir. 1999).

[172] *Narducci v. Moore*, 572 F.3d 313, 323 (7th Cir. 2009); *Tapley v. Collins*, 211 F.3d 1210, 1216 (11th Cir. 2000); *Blake v. Wright*, 179 F.3d 1003, 1011-13(6th Cir. 1999); *Babb v. Eagleton*, 614 F.Supp.2d 1232, 1237-238 (N.D.Okla. 2008); *contra, Berry v. Funk*, 146 F.3d 1003, 1013 (D.C.Cir. 1998); *see generally*, *Qualified Immunity as Defense in Suit Under Federal Wiretap Act (18 U.S.C.A. §§2510 et seq.)*, 178 ALR FED. 1.

[173] 18 U.S.C. 2520(d) ("A good faith reliance on—(1) a court warrant or order, a grand jury subpoena, a legislative authorization, or a statutory authorization; (2) a request of an investigative or law enforcement officer under section 2518(7) of this title; or (3) a good faith determination that section 2511(3) or 2511(2)(i) of this title permitted the conduct complained of; [—] is a complete defense against any civil or criminal action brought under this chapter or any other law"); *SEC v. Rajaratnam*, 622 F.3d 159, 175 (2d Cir. 2010); *Clements-Jeffrey v. Springfield*, 810 F.Supp.2d 857, 872 (S.D. Ohio 2011).

[174] *Williams v. Poulos*, 11 F.3d 271, 285 (1st Cir. 1993); *United States v. Wuliger*, 981 F.2d 1497, 1507 (6th Cir. 1992); *Rice v. Rice*, 951 F.2d 942, 944-45 (8th Cir. 1991); *but see, McCready v. eBay*, 453 F.3d 882, 892 (7th Cir. 2006).

[175] 50 U.S.C. 1885a("Notwithstanding any other provision of law, a civil action may not lie or be maintained in a Federal or State court against any person for providing assistance to an element of the intelligence community, and shall be promptly dismissed, if the Attorney General certifies to the district court of the United States in which such action is pending that - (1) any assistance by that person was provided pursuant to an order of the court established under section 1803(a) of this title [relating to electronic surveillance under FISA] directing such assistance; (2) any assistance by that person was provided pursuant to a certification in writing under section 2511(2)(a)(ii)(B)[relating to the Attorney General's assurance that no court approval is required] or 2709(b)[relating to a national security letter] of title 18; (3) any assistance by that person was provided pursuant to a directive under section 1802(a)(4)[relating to electronic surveillance without a court order under FISA] ... or 1881a(h)[relating to communications of overseas targets under FISA] of this title directing such assistance; [or] (4) in the case of a covered civil action, the assistance alleged to have been provided by the electronic communication service provider was—(A) in connection with an intelligence activity involving communications that was - (i) authorized by the President during the period beginning on September 11, 2001, and ending on January 17, 2007 ... ").

[176] 18 U.S.C. 2712.

[177] 18 U.S.C. 2712(a).

[178] "If a court or appropriate department or agency determines that the United States or any of its departments or agencies has violated any provision of this chapter, and the court or appropriate department or agency finds that the circumstances surrounding the violation raise serious questions about whether or not an officer or employee of the United States acted willfully or intentionally with respect to the violation, the department or agency shall, upon receipt of a true and correct copy of the decision and findings of the court or appropriate department or agency promptly initiate a proceeding to determine whether disciplinary action against the

officer or employee is warranted. If the head of the department or agency involved determines that disciplinary action is not warranted, he or she shall notify the Inspector General with jurisdiction over the department or agency concerned and shall provide the Inspector General with the reasons for such determination," 18 U.S.C. 2520(f).

[179] *Ala. Opinion 84-22* (1984); *People v. Smith*, 778 P.2d 685, 686, 687 (Colo. 1989); *Haw. Formal Opinion No. 30* (1988); *Ind.State Bar Ass'n Op.No.1* (2000); *Iowa State Bar Ass'n v. Mollman*, 488 N.W.2d 168, 169-70, 171-72 (Iowa 1992); *Mo.Advisory Comm. Op. Misc. 30* (1978); *Tex.Stat.Bar Op. 514* (1996); *Va. LEO #1635* (1995), *Va. LEO #1324*; *Gunter v. Virginia State Bar*, 238 Va. 617, 621-22, 385 S.E.2d 597, 600 (1989). The federal courts seem to have been in accord, *Parrott v. Wilson*, 707 F.2d 1262 (11th Cir. 1983); *Moody v. IRS*, 654 F.2d 795 (D.C.Cir. 1981); *Ward v. Maritz, Inc.*, 156 F.R.D. 592 (D.N.J. 1994); *Wilson v. Lamb*, 125 F.R.D. 142 (E.D.Ky. 1989); *Haigh V. Matsushita Electric Corp.*, 676 F.Supp. 1332 (E.D.Va. 1987).

[180] *Ariz. Opinion No. 95-03* (1995); *Alaska Bar Ass'n Eth.Comm. Ethics Opinions No. 95-5 (1995) and No. 91-4* (1991); *Idaho Formal Opinion 130* (1989); *Kan.Bar.Ass'n Opinion 96-9* (1997); *Ky.Opinion E-279* (1984); *Minn.Law.Prof. Resp.Bd. Opinion No. 18* (1996); *Ohio Bd.Com.Griev.Disp. Opinion No. 97-3* (1997); *S.C. Ethics Advisory Opinion 92-17* (1992); *Tenn.Bd.Prof.Resp. Formal Ethics Opinion No. 86-F-14(a)* (1986).

[181] *D.C. Opinion No. 229* (1992) (recording was not unethical because it occurred under circumstances in which the uninformed party should have anticipated that the conversation would be recorded or otherwise memorialized); *Mississippi Bar v. Attorney ST.*, 621 So.2d 229 (Miss. 1993)(context of the circumstances test); *Conn.Bar Ass''n Op. 98-9* (1998)(same); *Mich.State Bar Op. RI-309* (1998)(same); *Me.State Bar Op.No. 168* (1999)(same); *N.M.Opinion 1996-2* (1996)(members of the bar are advised that there are no clear guidelines and that the prudent attorney avoids surreptitious recording); *N.C. RPC 171* (1994)(lawyers are encouraged to disclose to the other lawyer that a conversation is being tape recorded); *Okla.Bar Ass'n Opinion* 307 (1994)(a lawyer may secretly recording his or her conversations without the knowledge or consent of other parties to the conversation unless the recording is unlawful or in violation of some ethical standard involving more than simply recording); *Ore.State Bar Ass'n Formal Opinion No. 1991-74* (1991) (an attorney with one party consent he or she may record a telephone conversation "in absence of conduct which would reasonably lead an individual to believe that no recording would be made"); *Utah State Bar Ethics Advisory Opinion No. 96-04* (1996) ("recording conversations to which an attorney is a party without prior disclosure to the other parties is not unethical when the act, considered within the context of the circumstances, does not involve dishonesty, fraud, deceit or misrepresentation"); *Wis.Opinion E-94-5* ("whether the secret recording of a telephone conversation by a lawyer involves 'dishonesty, fraud, deceit or misrepresentation' under SCR 20:8.4(c) depends upon all the circumstances operating at the time"). In New York, the question of whether an attorney's surreptitiously recording conversations is ethically suspect is determined by locality, compare, *Ass'n of the Bar of City of N.Y. Formal Opinion No. 1995-10* (1995)(secret recording is per se unethical), with, *N.Y.County Lawyer's Ass'n Opinion No. 696* (1993)(secret recording is not per se unethical).

[182] *Cf., Nissan Motor Co., Ltd. v. Nissan Computer Corp.*, 180 F.Supp.2d 1089, 1095-97 (C.D. Cal. 2002).

[183] *E.g., State v. Murtagh*, 169 P.3d 602, 617-18 (Alaska 2007)("undisclosed recording is not unethical"); *In re Crossen*, 450 Mass. 533, 558, 880 N.E.2d 352, 372 (2008) (undisclosed recording was unethical where it was part of scheme to coerce or manufacture testimony against the judge presiding over pending litigation); *Midwest Motor Sports v. Arctic Cat Sales, Inc.*, 347 F.3d 693, 699 (8th Cir. 2003) (citing *ABA Comm. on Ethics and Prof'l Responsibility*, Formal Op. 01-422, which states that recording without consent should be prohibited when circumstances make it unethical); *United States v. Smallwood*, 365 F. Supp.2d 689, 697-98 (E.D. Va. 2005) (holding that a lawyer cannot ethically record a conversation without the consent of all parties, even though doing so is not illegal under Virginia law). Declaring the new ABA opinion to be an "overcorrection," one bar association explained that secret taping should not be routine practice, but that it should be permitted if it advances a "societal good." *Ass'n of the Bar of the City of New York Formal Opinion No. 2003-02* (2003). For a New York state bar opinion employing a similar line of reasoning, *see, Mena v. Key Food Stores Co-operative, Inc.*, 758 N.Y.S.2d 246, 247-50 (N.Y. Sup. Ct. 2003) (conduct of attorney who obtained a private investigator's services for a client and instructed the client on the use of recording equipment held *not* to warrant severe sanctions, because there was a compelling public interest in exposing the racial discrimination that was the subject of the secret recordings); *see also, S.C. Bar Ethics Advisory Op. 08-13* (November 14, 2008)(noting that the S.C. ethical prohibition on undisclosed recording by attorneys, based on the earlier ABA opinion, had not been withdrawn); *Tex. Ethics Op.* 575 (November 2006)(undisclosed recording by an attorney is not a per se violation of the Texas Disciplinary Rules of Professional Conduct); *Mo. Formal Advisory Op. 123* (March 8, 2006)(agreeing with ABA Formal Opinion 01-422); see generally, CRS Report R42650, *Wiretapping, Tape Recorders, and Legal Ethics: An Overview of Questions Posed by Attorney Involvement in Secretly Recording Conversation.*

[184] "Whenever any *wire or oral communication* has been intercepted, no part of the contents of such communication and no evidence derived therefrom may be received in evidence in any trial, hearing, or other proceeding in or before any court, grand jury, department, officer, agency, regulatory body, legislative committee, or other authority of the United States, a State, or a political subdivision thereof if the disclosure of that information would be in violation of this chapter," 18 U.S.C. 2515 (emphasis added); *United States v. Chavez*, 416 U.S.

562, 570 (1974); *United States v. Lnu*, 575 F.3d 298, 301 (3d Cir. 2009); *United States v. Lam*, 271 F.Supp.2d 1182, 1183-184 (N.D.Cal. 2003). Note that suppression does not extend to unlawfully intercepted *electronic* communications, *United States v. Amanuel*, 615 F.3d 117, 125 (2d Cir. 2010); *United States v. Steiger*, 318 F.3d 1039, 1050-52 (11th Cir. 2003); *United States v. Jones*, 364 F. Supp.2d 1303, 1308-09 (D.Utah 2005); nor does it extend to evidence secured in violation the pen register/trap and trace provisions, *United States v. German*, 486 F.3d 849, 852-53 (5th Cir. 2007).

185 18 U.S.C. 2510(11)("'aggrieved person' means a person who was a party to any an intercepted wire, oral, or electronic communication or a person against whom the interception was directed"); *United States v. Oliva*, 686 F.3d 1106, 1108-109 (9th Cir. 2012).

186 *United States v. Lomeli*, 676 F.3d 734, 739 (8th Cir. 2012)(internal citations omitted)("Suppression is not justified if the facial insufficiency of the wiretap order is not more than a technical defect. According to *Moore*, our analysis is two tiered, first identifying the omission or defect at issue ... and second, determining whether that defect violates a core statutory requirement or whether it is a mere technical defect not warranting suppression"); *see also*, *United States v. Lopez*, 300 F.3d 46, 55-6 (1st Cir. 2002); *United States v. Staffeldt*, 451 F.3d 578, 582-85 (9th Cir. 2006); *United States v. Gray*, 521 F.3d 514, 522 (6th Cir. 2008); *United States v. Foy*, 641 F.3d 455, 463 (10th Cir. 2011). This is the case even where the court is clearly troubled by the government's failure to comply with the requirements of Title III, *United States v. Callum*, 410 F.3d 571, 579 (9th Cir. 2005)("Under the force of precedent, we uphold the challenged wiretap applications and orders. Still, we note that the Department of Justice and its officers did not cover themselves with glory in obtaining the wiretap orders at issue in this case. Title III is an exacting statute obviously meant to be followed punctiliously, yet the officers repeatedly ignored its clear requirements").

187 *Gelbard v. United States*, 408 U.S. 41, 52 (1972).

188 *United States v. Moore*, 41 F.3d 370, 376 (8th Cir. 1994); *United States v. Ambrosio*, 898 F.Supp. 177, 187 (S.D.N.Y. 1995); *United States v. Malelzadeh*, 855 F.2d 1492, 1497 (11th Cir. 1988); *United States v. Mullen*, 451 F.Supp.2d 509, 530-31 (W.D.N.Y. 2006); *contra, United States v. Rice*, 478 F.3d 704, 711-14 (6th Cir. 2007).

Gelbard held that a grand jury witness might claim the protection of section 2515 through a refusal to answer questions based upon an unlawful wiretap notwithstanding the fact that the Fourth Amendment exclusionary rule does not apply in grand jury proceedings. *Gelbard*, 408 U.S. at 51-52. The good faith exception to the Fourth Amendment exclusionary rule permits the admission of evidence secured in violation of the Fourth Amendment, if the officers responsible for the breach were acting in good faith reliance upon the apparent authority of a search warrant or somelike condition negating the remedial force of the rule, *United States v. Leon*, 468 U.S. 897, 909 (1984).

189 *United States v. Simels*, 654 F.3d 161, 169-70 (2d Cir. 2011)(citing cases in accord); *Culbertson v. Culbertson*, 143 F.3d 825, 827-28 (4th Cir. 1998); *United States v. Echavarria-Olarte*, 904 F.2d 1391 (9th Cir. 1990); *United States v.Vest*, 813 F.2d 477, 484 (1st Cir. 1987); cf., *United States v. Crabtree*, 565 F.3d 887, 891-92 (4th Cir. 2009)(noting thatthe Circuit's recognition of admissibility for impeachment purposes does not require recognition of a clean hands exception under which the government may admit introduce illegal wiretap evidence as long as it was not involved in the illegal interception).

190 *United States v. Thompson*, 130 F.3d 676, 683 (5th Cir. 1997); *United States v. Panaro*, 241 F.3d 1104, 1111 (9th Cir. 2001); *United States v. Smith*, 242 F.3d 737, 741 (7th Cir. 2001).

191 *United States v. Webster*, 84 F.3d 1056, 1064 (8th Cir. 1996); *United States v. Green*, 175 F.3d 822, 830 n.3 (10th Cir. 1999); *United States v. Green*, 324 F.3d 375, 379 (5th Cir. 2003)(citing 4 of the 7 factors); cf., *United States v.Calderin-Rodriguez*, 244 F.3d 977, 986-87 (8th Cir. 2001). These seven factors have been fairly widely cited since they were first announced in *United States v. McKeever*, 169 F.Supp. 426, 430 (S.D.N.Y. 1958), *rev'd on other grounds*,271 F.2d 669 (2d Cir. 1959). They are a bit formalistic for some courts who endorse a more ad hoc approach to the assessment of whether the admission of what purports to be a taped conversation will introduce fraud or confusion into the court, *e.g., Stringel v. Methodist Hosp. of Indiana, Inc.*, 89 F.3d 415, 420 (7th Cir. 1996)(McKeever "sets out arather formal, seven step checklist for the authentication of tape recordings, and we have looked to some of the features[in the past]"); *United States v. White*, 116 F.3d 903, 921 (D.C.Cir. 1997)("tapes may be authenticated by testimony describing the process or system that created the tape or by testimony from parties to the conversation affirming that the tapes contained an accurate record of what was said"); *United States v. Tropeano*, 252 F.3d 653, 661 (2d Cir.2001)("[T]his Circuit has never expressly adopted a rigid standard for determining the admissibility of tape recordings"); *United States v. Westmoreland*, 312 F.3d 302, 310-11 (7th Cir. 2002); *United States v. Dawson*, 425 F.3d389, 393 (7th Cir. 2005)("But there are no rigid rules, such as chain of custody, for authentication; all that is required is adequate evidence of genuineness. (There are such rules for electronic surveillance governed by Title III, but Title III is in applicable to conversations that, as here, are recorded with the consent of one of the participants)").

192 *E.g., State Analysis, Inc. v. American Financial Services Ass'n*, 621 F.Supp.2d 309, 317-18 (E.D.Va. 2009); *Pure Power Boot Camp v. Warrior Fitness Boot Camp*, 587 F.Supp.2d 548, 555 (S.D.N.Y. 2008).

193 *KLA-Tencor Corp. v. Murphy*, 717 F.Supp.2d 895, 905 (N.D.Cal. 2010); *Cardinal Health 414, Inc. v. Adams*, 582 F.Supp.2d 967, 976 (M.D.Tenn. 2008).

[194] *Penrose Computer Marketgroup, Inc. v. Camin*, 682 F.Supp.2d 202, 210-12 (N.D.N.Y. 2010) citing cases on each side of the debate including cases under the Computer Fraud and Abuse Act (18 U.S.C. 1030) where the "access" terms are used, *e.g., Shurgard Storage Ctrs., Inc. v. Safeguard Self Storage, Inc.*, 119 F.Supp.2d 1121, 1125 (W.D.Wash. 2000)("[T]he authority of the plaintiff's ... employees ended when they allegedly became agents of the defendant [although still employed by the plaintiff] ... [T]hey lost their authorization and were without authorization when they allegedly obtained and sent the proprietary information to the defendant via email"); *Ass'n of Machinists and Aerospace Workers v. Werner*, 390 F.Supp.2d 479, 496 (D.Md. 2005)("Because section 2701 prohibits only unauthorized access and not the misappropriation or disclosure of information, there is no violation of section 2701 for a person with authorized access to the database no matter how malicious or larcenous his intended use of that access").

[195] *KLA-Tencor Corp. v. Murphy*, 717 F.Supp.2d 895, 905-906 (N.D.Cal. 2010)("Finally, plaintiff has not established that Chen's conduct [of deleting her e-mails in her employer's system] was unauthorized. Plaintiff asserts that Chen was 'without authorization or exceeded authorization to access these e-mails on KT's e-mail server in [her] last days at KT because [she] did not have any legitimate business reasons for doing so and [is] prohibited, as a condition of their employment, from unauthorized use of KT information.' However, this claim is not supported by the evidence. As an initial matter, it appears that employees were generally authorized to use their own e-mail account.... The agreements cited by plaintiff in its motion only restrict use of *confidential* information, and plaintiff has provided no evidence that the contents of the deleted e-mails were confidential or that deleting e-mails would constitute 'use.' Inaddition, Chen states that there was no company policy prohibiting her from deleting her own e-mail").In a case under the Computer Fraud and Abuse Act, that might as easily have been brought under the SCA, however, the court held that "if any conscious breach of a website's terms of service is held to be sufficient by itself to constitute intentionally accessing a computer without authorization or in excess of authorization, the result will be that section1030(a)(2)(C) becomes a law 'that affords too much discretion to the police and too little notice to citizens who wish to use the [Internet]' [and consequently is unconstitutionally vague]," *United States v. Drew*, 259 F.R.D. 449, 467(C.D. Cal. 2009).

[196] *Cardinal Health 414, Inc. v. Adams*, 582 F.Supp. 967, 977 (M.D. Tenn. 2008)("Adams used the log-in information for another person, a former co-worker, to spy on the activities of his former company. On these facts, to argue that continued access was 'authorized' is absurd"); *see also, State Analysis, Inc. v. American Financial Services Assoc.*, 621F.Supp.2d 309, 318 (E.D.Va. 2009).

[197] *Devine v. Kapasi*, 729 F.Supp.2d 1024, 1027-28 (N.D.Ill. 2010), *citing, Fraser v. Nationwide Mutual Ins. Co*, 352F.3d 107, 115 (3d Cir. 2003); *In re iPhone Application Litigation*, 844 F.Supp.2d 1040, 1057 (N.D.Cal. 2012)("To state a claim under the SCA, Plaintiffs must allege that Defendants accessed without authorization 'a facility through which an electronic communication service is provided.' 18 U.S.C. 2701(a)(1). An 'electronic communication service' ('ECS') is 'any service which provides to users thereof the ability to send and receive wire or electronic communications.' 18 U.S.C. 2510(15). While the computer systems of an e-mail provider, a bulletin board system, or an ISP are uncontroversial examples of facilities that provide electronic communications services to multiple users, less consensus surrounds the question presented here: whether an individual's computer, laptop, or mobile device fits the statutory definition of a 'facility through which an electronic communication service is provided.' The Court agrees with Defendants that it does not").

[198] 18 U.S.C. 2711(1)("As used in this chapter [18 U.S.C. 2701-2712]—(1) the terms defined in section 2510 of this title have, respectively, the definitions given such terms in that section"); 18 U.S.C. 2510(17)("'electronic storage' means—(A) any temporary, intermediate storage of a wire or electronic communication incidental to the electronic transmission thereof; and (B) any storage of such communication by an electronic communication service for purposes of backup protection of such communication").

[199] *See e.g., KLA-Tencor Corp. v. Murphy*, 717 F.Supp.2d 895, 904-905 (N.D.Cal. 2010)("As an initial matter, it is not clear to the court that e-mails on KT's server were in 'electronic storage' within the meaning of the SCA. In *Theofel v.Farey-Jones*, 359 F.3d 1066, 1075 (9th Cir. 2004), the Ninth Circuit held that messages remaining on an ISP's server after delivery could fall within the SCA. The court found that '[a]n obvious purpose for storing a message on an ISP's server after delivery is to provide a second copy of the message in the event that the user needs to download it again-if, for example, the message is accidentally erased from the user's own computer.' *Id.* However, 'the mere fact that a copy *could* serve as a backup does not mean it is stored for that purpose' *Id.* at 1076. The court noted that there would be instances where an ISP could hold messages not in electronic storage, such as 'messages a user has flagged for deletion from the server.' *Id.* In an apparent attempt to mirror *Theofel* language, plaintiff suggests that its server's storage of e-mail has a backup purpose because a user could 'download them again when, for instance, his or her e-mails areaccidentally deleted from the computer while working in an offline mode.' Gurule SJ Decl. ¶ 7. However, plaintiff also explains that the server's software 'is configured to synchronize a user's e-mail account so that the account contains the same set of e-mails regardless of where it is accessed.' *Id.* ¶ 10. It seems to the court that these two purposes cannot coexist. Either the server is linked to the computer and flags for deletion a message that is deleted on the computer, or it acts as a backup and would not automatically delete messages that are deleted on a computer. Under either theory, plaintiff's SCA claim fails. Even if the system's operation is as plaintiff describes, the

fact that automatic deletion does not occur in the specific situation of a message being deleted while the computer is offline does not establish that the server stores e-mails for the purposes of backup protection rather than only for purpose of synchronization").

In re iPhone Application Litigation, 844 F.Supp.2d 1040, 1059 (N.D.Cal. 2012) ("The Court finds persuasive the reasoning in *In re Doubleclick, Inc. Privacy Litigation*, 154 F.Supp.2d 497 (S.D.N.Y. 2001). There, the court dismissed an SCA claim upon finding that the identification numbers for browser cookies the defendants installed on the plaintiffs' computers were not in 'electronic storage' because they resided on the plaintiff's hard drives and thus were not in temporary electronic storage, as is required by the Act. In *In re Double Click*, the district court, after considering the plain language of the statute, concluded that '[the SCA] only protects electronic communications stored for a limited time in the middle of a transmission, i.e. when an electronic communication service temporarily stores a communication while waiting to deliver it.' 154 F.Supp.2d at 512 (quoting dictionary definitions of 'temporary' and 'intermediate'). The district court concluded that '[t]he cookies' long-term residence on plaintiffs' hard drives places them outside of §2510(17)'s definition of 'electronic storage' and, hence, Title II [of the ECPA's] protection.' *Id.* at 511").

[200] 18 U.S.C. 2701(c). Here, the word "user" means "any person or entity who—(A) uses an electronic communication service; and (B) is duly authorized by the provider of such service to engage in such use," 18 U.S.C. 2510(13), 2711(1); *Webapps v. Accelerize New Media, Inc.*, 847 F.Supp. 912, 917 (E.D.La. 2012).

[201] "(a) Except as provided in paragraph (b) of this subsection, a person or entity providing an electronic communication service to the public shall not intentionally divulge the contents of any communication (other than one to such person or entity, or an agent thereof) while in transmission on that service to any person or entity other than an addressee or intended recipient of such communication or an agent of such addressee or intended recipient.

"(b) A person or entity providing electronic communication service to the public may divulge the contents of any such communication—(i) as otherwise authorized in section 2511(2)(a) or 2517 of this title; (ii) with the lawful consent of the originator or any addressee or intended recipient of such communication; (iii) to a person employed or authorized, or whose facilities are used, to forward such communication to its destination; or (iv) which were inadvertently obtained by the service provider and which appear to pertain to the commission of a crime, if such divulgence is made to a law enforcement agency," 18 U.S.C. 2511(3).

[202] 18 U.S.C. 2702(a)(1), (2).

[203] 18 U.S.C. 2702(a)(3).

[204] 18 U.S.C. 2702(a)(1).

[205] 18 U.S.C. 2702(a)(2).

[206] 18 U.S.C. 2702(a)(3).

[207] 18 U.S.C. 2702(b)(emphasis added).

[208] "A provider described in subsection (a) may divulge a record or other information pertaining to a subscriber to or customer of such service (not including the contents of communications covered by subsection (a)(1) or (a)(2))—(1) asotherwise authorized in section 2703; (2) with the lawful consent of the customer or subscriber; (3) as may be necessarily incident to the rendition of the service or to the protection of the rights or property of the provider of that service; (4) to a governmental entity, if the provider, in good faith, believes that an emergency involving danger of death or serious physical injury to any person requires disclosure without delay of information relating to the emergency; (5) to the National Center for Missing and Exploited Children, in connection with a report submitted there to under section 227 of the Victims of Child Abuse Act of 1990 (42 U.S.C. 13032); or (6) to any person other than a governmental entity," 18 U.S.C. 2702(c).[209] *Quon v. Arch Wireless Operating Co., Inc.*, 529 F.3d 892, 900-903 (9th Cir. 2008), *rev'd on other grounds sub nom.,City of Ontario v. Quon*, 130 S.Ct. 2619 (2010).

[210] *Id.* (ECS provider that supplied the city police department with pager service for some of its officers violated section2702 when it provided the department with the content of the officers' pager messages).

[211] 18 U.S.C. 2701-2712.

[212] The SCA also authorizes the issuance of national security letters for foreign intelligence gathering rather than law enforcement purposes, 18 U.S.C. 2709, *see generally*, CRS Report RL33320, *National Security Letters in ForeignIntelligence Investigations: Legal Background and Recent Amendments*, by Charles Doyle.

[213] 18 U.S.C. 2702(b)("A provider described in subsection (a) may divulge the contents of a communication ... (7) to a law enforcement agency—(A) if the contents—(i) were inadvertently obtained by the service provider; and (ii) appear to pertain to the commission of a crime").

[214] 18 U.S.C. 2702(b)("A provider described in subsection (a) may divulge the contents of a communication ... (8) to a governmental entity, if the provider, in good faith, believes that an emergency involving danger of death or serious physical injury to any person requires disclosure without delay of communications relating to the emergency").

[215] 18 U.S.C. 2702(c)("A provider described in subsection (a) may divulge the contents of a communication ... (4) to a governmental entity, if the provider, in good faith, believes that an emergency involving danger of death or serious physical injury to any person requires disclosure without delay of information relating to the emergency").

[216] 18 U.S.C. 2711("As used in this chapter ... (4) the term 'governmental entity' means a department or agency of the United States or State or political subdivision thereof"); *but see, United States v. Amawi*, 552 F.Supp.2d 679, 680 (N.D.Ohio 2008)(the Office of the Federal Public Defender is not a "governmental entity").

[217] Recall that "'electronic storage' means—(A) any temporary, intermediate storage of a wire or electronic communication incidental to the electronic transmission thereof; and (B) any storage of such communication by an electronic communication service for purposes of backup protection of such communication," 18 U.S.C. 2510(17).

[218] 18 U.S.C. 2703(a). At least one court has held that opened web-based e-mail stored on a service provider's server is no longer is "electronic storage," because the service provider storage is not necessary for backup purposes once the e-mail has been opened (i.e., after storage is not only incidental to transmission). The original remains on the web server and the service provider is simply supplying remote storage. Consequently, a governmental entity may secure access using a subpoena, *United States v. Weaver*, 636 F.Supp.2d 769, 770-72 (C.D.Ill. 2009)(distinguishing and finding unpersuasive *Theofel v. Farey-Jones*, 359 F.3d 1066 (9th Cir. 2004), thought to support a contrary view).

[219] 18 U.S.C. 2703(a)(" ... A governmental entity may require the disclosure by a provider of electronic communications services of the contents of a wire or electronic communication that has been in electronic storage in an electronic communications system for more than one hundred and eighty days by the means available under subsection (b) of this section").
18 U.S.C. 2703(b)("(1) A governmental entity may require a provider of remote computing service to disclose the contents of any wire or electronic communication to which this paragraph is made applicable by paragraph (2) of this subsection—(A) without required notice to the subscriber or customer, if the governmental entity obtains a warrant issued using the procedures described in the Federal Rules of Criminal Procedure by a court with jurisdiction over the offense under investigation or equivalent State warrant; or (B) with prior notice from the governmental entity to the subscriber or customer if the governmental entity—(i) uses an administrative subpoena authorized by a Federal or State statute or a Federal or State grand jury or trial subpoena; or (ii) obtains a court order for such disclosure under subsection (d) of this section; except that delayed notice may be given pursuant to section 2705 of this title").

[220] *Compare*, 18 U.S.C. 2703(d)("A court order for disclosure under subsection (b) or (c) may be issued by any court that is a court of competent jurisdiction...."); 18 U.S.C. 2711(3)("As used in this chapter ... (3) the term 'court of competent jurisdiction' has the meaning assigned by section 3127, and includes any Federal court within that definition, without geographic limitation"); 18 U.S.C. 3127(2)(emphasis added) ("As used in this chapter ... (2) the term "court of competent jurisdiction" means—(A) any district court of the United States (*including a magistrate of such a court*) or a United States Court of Appeals having jurisdiction over the offense being investigated ..."), *with*, 18 U.S.C. 2516(3)("Any attorney for the Government ... may authorize an application to a Federal judge of competent jurisdiction for, and such judge may grant ... an order authorizing or approving the interception of electronic communications ..."); 18 U.S.C. 2510(9)(" As used in this chapter ... 'Judge of competent jurisdiction' means—(a) a judge of a United States district court or a United States court of appeals").

[221] *United States v. Berkos*, 543 F.3d 392, 397 (7th Cir. 2008), *quoting* 18 U.S.C. 2703(a), ("[W]hen 'a court with jurisdiction over the offense' issues an out-of-district warrant for the seizure of electronic communications, it must do so 'using the procedures described in the Federal Rules of Criminal Procedure'"); *see also*, 18 U.S.C. 2711(3)(above).

[222] 18 U.S.C. 2705(a)(1)(A), (4).

[223] 18 U.S.C. 2705(a)(1)(B), (4).

[224] 18 U.S.C. 2705(a)(2), (b).

[225] 18 U.S.C. 2703(d)("A court order for disclosure under subsection (b) or (c) may be issued by any court that is a court of competent jurisdiction and shall issue only if the governmental entity offers specific and articulable facts showing that there are reasonable grounds to believe that the contents of a wire or electronic communication, or the records or other information sought, are relevant and material to an ongoing criminal investigation. In the case of a State governmental authority, such a court order shall not issue if prohibited by the law of such State. A court issuing an order pursuant to this section, on a motion made promptly by the service provider, may quash or modify such order, if the information or records requested are unusually voluminous in nature or compliance with such order otherwise would cause an undue burden on such provider").

[226] *United States v. Warshak*, 631 F.3d 266, 288 (6th Cir. 2010)(internal quotation marks and citations omitted) ("Accordingly, we hold that a subscriber enjoys a reasonable expectation of privacy in the contents of emails that are stored with, or sent or received through, a commercial ISP. The government may not compel a commercial ISP to turn over the contents of a subscriber's emails without first obtaining a warrant based on probable cause. Therefore, because they did not obtain a warrant, the government agents violated the Fourth Amendment when they obtained the contents of Warshak's emails. Moreover, to the extent that the SCA purports to permit the government to obtain such emails warrant lessly, the SCA is unconstitutional"); *see*

also, In re Application of the United States, 620 F.3d 304, 313 (3d Cir.2010)("We also conclude that this [§2703(d)] standard is a lesser one than probable cause").

[227] *United States v. Warshak*, 631 F.3d at 283-88.

[228] *Id.* at 288-92 (exception for good faith reliance on the SCA); *see also, United States v. Ferguson*, 508 F.Supp.2d 7, 8-10 D.D.C. 2007)(even if a Fourth Amendment violation occurred, officers could rely in good faith on the magistrate's order issued before any court had raised the specter of constitutional suspicion which surfaced later in *Warshak*).

[229] 18 U.S.C. 2703(f)(1)("A provider of wire or electronic communication services or a remote computing service, upon the request of a governmental entity, shall take all necessary steps to preserve records and other evidence in its possession pending the issuance of a court order or other process").

[230] *United States v. Warshak*, 631 F.3d 266, 283, 290 n.21 (6th Cir. 2010)(internal citations omitted)("Warshak had a number of email accounts with various ISPs, including an account with NuVox Communications. In October 2004, the government formally requested that NuVox prospectively preserve the contents of any emails to or from Warshak's email account. The request was made pursuant to 18 U.S.C. §2703(f) and it instructed NuVox to preserve all future messages. NuVox acceded to the government's request and began preserving copies of Warshak's incoming and outgoing emails—copies that would not have existed absent the prospective preservation request. Per the government's instructions, Warshak was not informed that his messages were being archived. In January 2005, the government obtained a subpoena under §2703(d) and compelled NuVox to turn over the emails that it had begun preserving the previous year. In May 2005, the government served NuVox with an *ex parte* court order under §2703(d) that required NuVox to surrender any additional email messages in Warshak's account. In all, the government compelled NuVox to reveal the contents of approximately 27,000 emails. Warshak did not receive notice of either the subpoena or the order until May 2006.... Some courts and commentators have suggested that §2703(f) applies only retroactively. However, the language of the statute, on its face, does not compel this reading").

[231] 18 U.S.C. 2704(b)(4)("If the court finds that the applicant is not the subscriber or customer for whom the communications sought by the governmental entity are maintained, or that there is a reason to believe that the law enforcement inquiry is legitimate and that the communications sought are relevant to that inquiry, it shall deny the motion or application and order such process enforced. If the court finds that the applicant is the subscriber or customer for whom the communications sought by the governmental entity are maintained, and that there is not a reason to believe that the communications sought are relevant to a legitimate law enforcement inquiry, or that there has not been substantial compliance with the provisions of this chapter, it shall order the process quashed").

[232] 18 U.S.C. 2704(a)(1), (2)(emphasis added)("A governmental entity acting under section 2703(b)(2) may include in its subpoena or court order a requirement that the service provider to whom the request is directed create a backup copy of the contents of the electronic communications sought in order to preserve those communications. Without notifying the subscriber or customer of such subpoena or court order, such service provider shall create such backup copy as soon as practicable consistent with its regular business practices and shall confirm to the governmental entity that such backup copy has been made. *Such backup copy shall be created within two business days after receipt by the service provider of the subpoena or court order.* (2) Notice to the subscriber or customer shall be made by the governmental entity within three days after receipt of such confirmation, unless such notice is delayed pursuant to section 2705(a)").

[233] 18 U.S.C. 2703(c)(1).

[234] 18 U.S.C. 2703(c)(2)("A provider of electronic communication service or remote computing service shall disclose to a governmental entity the (A) name; (B) address; (C) local and long distance telephone connection records, or records of session times and durations; (D) length of service (including start date) and types of service utilized; (E) telephone or instrument number or other subscriber number or identity, including any temporarily assigned network address; and (F) means and source of payment (including any credit car or bank account number), of a subscriber to or customer of such service, when the governmental entity uses an administrative subpoena authorized by a Federal or State statute or a Federal or State grand jury or trial subpoena or any means available under paragraph (1)"); *United States v. Cray*, 673 F.Supp.2d 1368, 1378-379 (S.D.Ga. 2009).

[235] 18 U.S.C. 2703(c)(3); *In re Application of the United States*, 830 F.Supp.2d 114, 127-28 (E.D.Va. 2011).

[236] *See, In re Application of the United States*, 733 F.Supp.2d 939, 940 n.1 (N.D.Ill. 2009)(listed cases decided up to that point).

[237] *In re Application of the United States*, 620 F.3d 304, 313-19 (3d Cir. 2010); *see also, In re Application of the United States*, 747 F.Supp.2d 827, 838-40 (S.D.Tex. 2010)(access to provider records relating to cell phone location over the course of an earlier two month period requires a warrant); *In re Application of the United States*, 727 F.Supp.2d 571,583-84 (W.D.Tex. 2010)(access to provider records relating to cell phone location either historically or prospectively should be only be available under a warrant, at least until a circuit court rules otherwise).

[238] *United States v. Jones*, 132 S.Ct. 945 (2012).

[239] *Id.* at 949; *id.* at 957 (Alito, J., with Ginsburg, Breyer, and Kagan)(concurring in the judgment).

[240] *United States v. Jones*, 132 S.Ct. at 949.

[241] *Id.* at 964 (Alito, J., with Ginsburg, Breyer, and Kagan)(concurring in the judgment)("[T]he longer term GPS monitoring in investigations of most offenses impinges on expectations of piracy").

[242] *Id.* at 945-55 (Sotomayor, J.)(concurring).

[243] *See, United States v. Skinner*, ___ F.3d ___, ___ (6th Cir. August 14, 2012)("Justice Alito's concurrence and the majority in *Jones* both recognize that there is little precedent for what constitutes a level of comprehensive tracking that would violate the Fourth Amendment. Skinner's case, however, comes nowhere near that line"); *In re Application of the United States*, 849 F.Supp.2d 177, 179 (D.Mass. 2012)(declining to undo district precedent concerning the collection of "cumulative historical cell site location records ... [u]ntil either the First Circuit Court of Appeals or the Supreme Court rule otherwise, or Congress enacts legislation dealing with the problem").

[244] "The punishment for an offense under subsection (a) of this section is—(1) if the offense is committed for purposes of commercial advantage, malicious destruction or damage, or private commercial gain, or in furtherance of any criminal or tortious act in violation of the constitution and laws of the United States or any state—(A) a fine under this title or imprisonment for not more than 5 years, or both, in the case of a first offense under this subparagraph; and (B) a fine under this title or imprisonment for not more than 10 years, or both, for any subsequent offense under this subparagraph; and (2)(A) a fine under this title or imprisonment for not more than 1 year or both, in the case of a first offense under this paragraph; and (B) a fine under this title or imprisonment for not more than 5 years, or both, in the case of an offense under this subparagraph that occurs after a conviction of another offense under this section," 18 U.S.C. 2701(b).

[245] "(a) Cause of action—Except as provided in section 2703(e)[relating to immunity for compliance with judicial process], any provider of electronic communication service, subscriber, or customer aggrieved by any violation of this chapter in which the conduct constituting the violation is engaged in with a knowing or intentional state of mind may, in a civil action, recover from the person or entity other than the United States which engaged in that violation such relief as may be appropriate.

"(b) Relief—In a civil action under this section, appropriate relief includes—(1) such preliminary and other equitable or declaratory relief as may be appropriate; (2) damages under subsection(c); and (3) a reasonable attorney's fee and other litigation costs reasonably incurred;

"(c) Damages—The court may assess as damages in a civil action under this section the sum of the actual damages suffered by the plaintiff and any profits made by the violator as a result of the violation, but in no case shall a person entitled to recover receive less than the sum of $1,000...." 18 U.S.C. 2707.

To be eligible for statutory damages, a plaintiff must show actual damage, but attorneys' fees and punitive damages may be award without proof of actual damages, *VanAlystyne v. Electronic Scriptorium, Ltd.*, 560 F.3d 199, 202 (4th Cir. 2009).

[246] "Any person who is aggrieved by any willful violation this chapter or of chapter 119 of this title [18 U.S.C. 2510-2520] ... may commence an action in United States District Court.... If ... any of the departments or agencies has violated any provision of this chapter ... the department or agency shall ... promptly initiate a proceeding to determine whether disciplinary action ... is warranted...."18 U.S.C. 2712(a),(c).

[247] *Cardinal Health 414, Inc. v. Adams*, 582 F.Supp.2d 967, 976 (M.D.Tenn. 2008).

[248] *United States v. Perrine*, 518 F.3d 1196, 1202 (10th Cir. 2008); *United States v. Clenney*, 631 F.3d 658, 667 (11th Cir. 2011); *United States v. Navas*, 640 F.Supp.2d 256, 262 (S.D.N.Y. 2009), rev'd on other grounds, 597 F.3d 492 (2d Cir. 2010).

[249] *See e.g., United States v. Warshak*, 631 F.3d 266, 282-89 (6th Cir. 2010).

[250] No liability under section 2707 accrues, however, as a consequence of aiding or abetting a provider's violation of section 2702, *Freeman v. DirecTV*, 457 F.3d 1001, 1009 (9th Cir. 2006).

[251] "(3) [T]he term 'pen register' means a device which records or decodes electronic or other impulses which identify the numbers dialed or otherwise transmitted on the telephone line to which such device is attached, but such term does not include any device used by a provider or customer of a wire or electronic communication service for billing, or recording as an incident to billing, for communications services provided by such provider or any device used by a provider or customer of a wire communication service for cost accounting or other like purposes in the ordinary course of its business; (4) the term 'trap and trace device' means a device which captures the incoming electronic or other impulses which identify the originating number of an instrument or device from which a wire or electronic communication was transmitted," 18 U.S.C. 3127(3),(4). Although clone pagers are not considered pen registers, *Brown v. Waddell*, 50 F.3d 285, 290-91 (4th Cir. 1995), "caller id" services have been found to constitute trap and trace devices by some courts, *United States v. Fregoso*, 60 F.3d 1314, 1320 (8th Cir. 1995), but not others, *Sparshott v. Feld Entertainment, Inc.*, 311 F.3d 425, 432-33 (D.C. Cir. 2003).

[252] *United States v. New York Telephone Co.*, 434 U.S. 159 (1977).

[253] 18 U.S.C. 3121-3127.

[254] "'Post-cut-through dialed digits' are any numbers dialed from a telephone after the call is initially setup or 'cut through.' Sometimes these digits are other telephone numbers, as when a party places a credit card call by first dialing the long distance carrier access number and then the phone number of the intended party. Sometimes

these digits transmit real information, such as bank account numbers, Social Security numbers, prescription numbers, and the like. In the latter case, the digits represent communications content; in the former, they are non-content call processing numbers," *In re United States*, 441 F.Supp.2d 816, 818 (S.D. Tex. 2006); *see also*, *In re United States for Orders (1)Authorizing Use of Pen Registers and Trap and Trace Devices*, 515 F.Supp.2d 325, 328-38 (E.D.N.Y. 2007); *In re United States*, 622 F.Supp.2d 411, 419-22 (S.D. Tex. 2007); *In re Application of the United States*, 632 F.Supp.2d 202,203-204 (E.D.N.Y. 2008)(granting a pen register/trap and trace application that would capture post-cut-through numbers after the government assured the court that its computers would be configured to delete them upon receipt).

255 115 Stat. 288-91 (2001).

256 18 U.S.C. 3121 ("Except as provided in this section, no person may install or use a pen register or a trap and trace device without first obtaining a court order under section 3123 of this title or under the Foreign Intelligence Surveillance Act of 1978 (50 U.S.C. 1801 et seq.)").

257 18 U.S.C. 3121(b)("The prohibition of subsection (a) does not apply with respect to the use of a pen register or a trap and trace device by a provider of electronic or wire communication service—(1) relating to the operation, maintenance, and testing of a wire or electronic communication service or to the protection of the rights or property of such provider, or to the protection of users of that service from abuse of service or unlawful use of service; or (2) to record the fact that a wire or electronic communication was initiated or completed in order to protect such provider, another provider furnishing service toward the completion of the wire communication, or a user of that service, from fraudulent, unlawful or abusive use of service; or (3) where the consent of the user of that service has been obtained").

258 18 U.S.C. 3125(a)("Notwithstanding any other provision of this chapter, any investigative or law enforcement officer, specially designated by the Attorney General, the Deputy Attorney General, the Associate Attorney General, any Assistant Attorney General, any acting Assistant Attorney General, or any Deputy Assistant Attorney General, or by the principal prosecuting attorney of any State or subdivision thereof acting pursuant to a statute of that State, who reasonably determines that—(1) an emergency situation exists that involves—(A) immediate danger of death or serious bodily injury to any person; (B) conspiratorial activities characteristic of organized crime; (C) an immediate threat to a national security interest; or (D) an ongoing attack on a protected computer (as defined in section 1030) that constitutes a crime punishable by a term of imprisonment greater than one year [—] that requires the installation and use of a pen register or a trap and trace device before an order authorizing such installation and use can, with due diligence, be obtained, and (2) there are grounds upon which an order could be entered under this chapter to authorize such installation and use [—] may have installed and use a pen register or trap and trace device if, within forty-eight hours after the installation has occurred, or begins to occur, an order approving the installation or use is issued in accordance with section 3123 of this title").

259 18 U.S.C. 3122.

260 18 U.S.C. 3123.

261 18 U.S.C. 3122(a), 3127(2); *In re United States*, 10 F.3d 931, 935-36 (2d Cir. 1993).

262 18 U.S.C. 3125(a).

263 18 U.S.C. 3121(b).

264 *E.g., In re Application of the United States*, 849 F.Supp.2d 526 (D.Md. 2011); *In re Application of the United States*, 733 F.Supp.2d 939 (N.D.Ill. 2009); *In re Application of the United States*, 534 F.Supp.2d 585 (W.D.Pa. 2008); In *re Application of the United States*, 497 F.Supp.2d 301 (D. P.R. 2007); *In re United States*, 441 F.Supp.2d 816 (S.D. Tex. 2006); *In re Application of the United States*, 416 F.Supp. 390 (D.Md. 2006); *In re Application of the United States*, 415 F.Supp.2d 211 (W.D.N.Y. 2006); *In re Application of the United States*, 412 F.Supp.2d 947 (E.D.Wis. 2006); *In re Application of the United States*, 407 F.Supp.2d 134 (D.D.C. 2006) (each denying the application); *but see*, *In re Application of the United States*, 632 F.Supp.2d 202 (E.D.N.Y. 2008); *In re Application of the United States*, 509 F.Supp.2d 76 (D.Mass. 2007); *In re Application of the United States*, 460 F.Supp.2d 448 (S.D.N.Y. 2006); *In re Application of the United States*, 433 F.Supp.2d 804 (S.D. Tex. 2006); *In re Application of the United States*, 411 F.Supp.2d 678 (W.D.La. 2006)(each granting the application).

265 18 U.S.C. 3121(d), 3571.

266 18 U.S.C. 3124(e).

267 *United States v. Forrester*, 512 F.3d 500, 512-13 (9th Cir. 2008); *United States v. German*, 486 F.3d 849, 852-53 (5th Cir. 2007); *United States v. Fregoso*, 60 F.3d 1314, 1320 (8th Cir. 1995); *United States v. Thompson*, 936 F.2d 1249, 1249-250 (11th Cir. 1991). To the extent that the unlawful use captures content, the Fourth Amendment exclusionary rule may apply, *cf., In re United States for Orders (1) Authorizing Use of Pen Registers and Trap and Trace Devices*, 515 F.Supp.2d 325, 328-38 (E.D.N.Y. 2007).

268 Subsection 3124(d) makes the denial of a cause of action explicit for service providers and others assisting in execution of an order or emergency request. Subsection 3124(e) provides a good faith defense to civil liability on other grounds.

269 *In re Sealing and Non-Disclosure of Pen/Trap/2703(d) Orders*, 562 F.Supp.2d 876, 879, 886-87 (S.D.Tex. 2008) ("Section 3123(d)(2) provides that the 'the person owning or leasing the line or other facility to which the pen

register or a trap and trace device is attached, or applied, or who is obligated by the order to provide assistance to the applicant' shall be directed not to disclose to any other person the existence of the pen/trap or the investigation 'unless or until otherwise ordered by the court.' Again, no particular showing by the government is required to justify non-disclosure, and no minimum time period is imposed or even suggested. In fact, the 'unless' clause implies that the court may refuse to enjoin disclosure even in the first instance. In the end, the duration of any gag order remains subject to the court's discretion.
An indefinite non-disclosure order is tantamount to a permanent injunction of prior restraint. To the extent such an order enjoins speech beyond the life of the underlying investigation, it must be narrowly tailored to serve a compelling governmental interest in order to pass muster under the First Amendment. The governmental interests considered here—the integrity of an ongoing criminal investigation, the reputational interests of targets, and the sensitivity of investigative techniques—are not sufficiently compelling to justify a permanent gag order. And because the statutes authorizing these non-disclosure orders must be construed whenever possible in a manner that avoids constitutional infirmity, it follows that neither 18 U.S.C. §2705(b) nor §3123 may be interpreted to permit a gag order of indefinite duration").

[270] *E.g.*, ARIZ.REV.STAT.ANN. §13-3005; FLA.STAT.ANN. §934.31; IOWA CODE ANN. §808B.10; N.H. RV.STAT.ANN. §570-B:2; UTAH CODE ANN. §77-23-13.

[271] *But see*, MINN.STAT.ANN. §626A.391. **Appendix E** contains the citations of state statutes that authorized court ordered installation and use of pen registers and trap and trace devices. **Appendix C** lists the citations of state statutes that create a separate cause of action for unlawful interception.

INDEX

#

A

B

C

D

E

G

H

I

J

K

L

M

N

Q

R

S

T